DISCARD

DATE DUE

DEC 1 2 2010	
APR 0 9 2012	
DEC 1 6 2012	
APR 2 8 2015	

BRODART, CO.

Cat. No. 23-221

Who Chooses?

UNIVERSITY PRESS OF FLORIDA

Florida A&M University, Tallahassee
Florida Atlantic University, Boca Raton
Florida Gulf Coast University, Ft. Myers
Florida International University, Miami
Florida State University, Tallahassee
New College of Florida, Sarasota
University of Central Florida, Orlando
University of Florida, Gainesville
University of North Florida, Jacksonville
University of South Florida, Tampa
University of West Florida, Pensacola

Who Chooses?

American Reproductive History since 1830

Simone M. Caron

University Press of Florida
Gainesville/Tallahassee/Tampa/Boca Raton
Pensacola/Orlando/Miami/Jacksonville/Ft. Myers/Sarasota

13   12   11   10   09   08   6   5   4   3   2

Library of Congress Cataloging-in-Publication Data
Caron, Simone M.
Who chooses? : American reproductive history since 1830 / Simone M. Caron.
p. cm.
Includes bibliographical references and index.
ISBN 978–0–8130–3199–6 (alk. paper)
1. Contraception—United States—History—19th century. 2. Contraception—Government policy—United States—History—19th century. 3. Birth control—United
States—History—19th century. 4. Birth control—Government policy—United
States—History—19th century. 5. Abortion—United States—History—19th century. 6. Abortion—Government policy—United States—History—19th century.
7. Human reproduction—Government policy—United States—History—19th
century. I. Title.
HQ766.5.U5C37 2008
363.4609739–dc22   2007038091

The University Press of Florida is the scholarly publishing agency for the State
University System of Florida, comprising Florida A&M University, Florida Atlantic
University, Florida Gulf Coast University, Florida International University, Florida
State University, New College of Florida, University of Central Florida, University
of Florida, University of North Florida, University of South Florida, and University
of West Florida.

University Press of Florida
15 Northwest 15th Street
Gainesville, FL 32611-2079
www.upf.com

To my children, Quaid and Alden, for bringing joy and purpose to my life.

In memory of my father
Leo O. Caron Jr.
1936–2007

Contents

List of Tables ix

Abbreviations xi

Preface xiii

Acknowledgments xv

1. A Brief Overview of American Reproductive History 1

2. Abortion and Contraception in the Nineteenth Century 14

3. Race Suicide, Eugenics, and Contraception, 1900–1930 44

4. Population Control and the Great Depression, 1930–1939 81

5. World War II, the Baby Boom, and the Population Explosion, 1939–1963 119

6. Who Pays? Contraceptive Services and the Welfare State, 1963–1975 149

7. Who Pays for What? Abortion and Sterilization, 1960–1975 187

8. Backlash, 1973–2000 221

9. Conclusion 251

Appendix A. Henry Miller, "Letter to the President and Councilors of the State Medical Society," 1860 257

Appendix B. Henry Miller, "Memorial to the Governor and Legislature of the State of Rhode Island," 1860 259

Appendix C. Recommended State Statute by Horatio R. Storer 261

Appendix D. 1861 Rhode Island Abortion Statute 263

Appendix E. 1867 Rhode Island Abortion Statute 265

Notes 267

Bibliography 323

Index 357

Tables

Table 4.1.   Ethnicity of RIBCL Clients and State Residents 102

Table 4.2.   Referral of Women to RIBCL, 1935–1939 104

Table 6.1.   Estimated Number of Illegitimate Births and Illegitimacy Ratios, United States, 1920–1968 159

Table 6.2.   Percent Pregnant, 1968, by Age and Race 161

Table 6.3.   Legitimate, Illegitimate, and Total Out-of-Wedlock Conceived Birthrates per 1,000 Unmarried Women by Color and Age, U.S. 1964–1966 Annual Average 162

Table 7.1.   Percent of Wives Who Approve Different Reasons for Abortion, 1965–1970 191

Table 7.2.   Characteristics of Women Having Abortions, New York City, 1970–1971 196

Abbreviations

ABA	American Breeders Association
ABCL	American Birth Control League
ACLU	American Civil Liberties Union
ACOG	American College of Obstetricians and Gynecologists
ADC	Aid to Dependent Children
AFDC	Aid for Families with Dependent Children
AID	Agency for International Development
ALI	American Law Institute
AMA	American Medical Association
ANA	American Neurological Association
ARAL	Association for the Repeal of Abortion Laws
ASCA	Anglo Saxon Clubs of America
AVS	Association for Voluntary Sterilization
BAL	Black Americans for Life
BCCRB	Birth Control Clinical Research Bureau
BCFA	Birth Control Federation of America
BSH	Bureau of Social Hygiene
BVCAP	Blackstone Valley Community Action Program
CAP	Community Action Pittsburgh
CMH	Committee on Maternal Health
CMJ&R	*Charleston Medical Journal & Review*
CORE	Congress of Racial Equality
DHEW	Department of Health, Education and Welfare
DNS	Division of Negro Service
DP	Depo Provera
FDA	United States Food and Drug Administration
FSA	Farm Security Administration
HBF	Human Betterment Foundation
ICMCA	Illinois Citizens for the Medical Control of Abortion
IHS	Indian Health Service
MBL	Massachusetts Blacks for Life
MSRB	Margaret Sanger Research Bureau
NAAC	National Abortion Action Committee
NAACP	National Association for the Advancement of Colored People

NARAL   National Abortion Rights Action League
NBWHP   National Black Women's Health Project
NCFL   National Committee on Federal Legislation
NIH   National Institutes of Health
NOW   National Organization for Women
NWHN   National Women's Health Network
NWPC   National Women's Political Caucus
NWSA   National Women's Suffrage Association
NYCCSA   New York Clergy Consultation Service on Abortion
OEO   Office of Economic Opportunity
PPCP   Planned Parenthood Center of Pittsburgh
PPFA   Planned Parenthood Federation of America
PPRI   Planned Parenthood of Rhode Island
RIBCL   Rhode Island Birth Control League
RIMHA   Rhode Island Maternal Health Association
RIMS   Rhode Island Medical Society
SCMS   South Carolina Medical Society
TFR   total fertility rate
ULRI   Urban League of Rhode Island
VPL   Voluntary Parenthood League
WAC   Women's Army Corps
WHO   World Health Organization

Preface

The intent of this book is to analyze national policies on reproductive issues and their connection to population concerns since the nineteenth century. An inherent conflict has existed between a population-control agenda that permeated the national discourse on sexual politics and individuals' desires to be in command of their reproduction. Elite white officials, influenced by genetic and eugenic theories as well as by race, class, and gender biases, used abortion, birth control, and sterilization to control the fertility of the indigent, many of whom were women of color. In sum, political, moral, and economic forces shaped reproductive policies that impacted women's ability to choose how to control their bodies.

This book contributes to understanding reproductive history by synthesizing secondary material that treats abortion, birth control, and sterilization as separate entities and placing these three areas of reproductive control into a cohesive framework. As such, this work is intended to suit the needs of undergraduate and graduate students while also being accessible to the public. Over the past two centuries, restrictive reproductive policies have served as barriers to women's equality. The impact of these policies has been felt most poignantly at the local level by women endeavoring to control their daily lives. This work examines the national context while simultaneously analyzing developments at the state and local level, with particular attention to Rhode Island. This microanalysis demonstrates that the national consensus on sexual politics had variants at the state level. Rhode Island restricted abortion yet was one of only two states to exempt women from prosecution. When most states adopted laws modeled on Comstock and eugenic sterilization legislation, Rhode Island did not. It allowed the only birth control clinic in New England to operate from 1931 to 1965. While immigrant or female doctors worked at many freestanding clinics, "respectable" white male physicians staffed the Rhode Island clinic. The clinic prioritized clients' health and choices rather than following population control advocates, including Planned Parenthood Federation of America.

Acknowledgments

This book would not have been possible without the help of many people along the way. David Culver mesmerized me during my undergraduate years with his ability to bring history to life in his classroom. I strive to emulate his example in my own classes today. David also supported my dream of attending graduate school; I will always be grateful for his friendship and support over the years. In graduate school Ballard Campbell insisted that I write in concise, jargon-free prose; appreciative of the results, I now insist on the same for my own students. Paul Ropp helped me negotiate the politics of academia. Ronald Formisano has been a mentor and a friend. I am grateful to Allan Brandt for his insights and willingness to read drafts of this work. I thank Sarah Bradford Campbell and David Epperson for sharing their insights in interviews with me.

This book has been read by many people. Sections of it have been commented on at conferences and seminars. I appreciate the thoughtful contributions from Gail Bederman, MariJo Buhle, Janet Golden, Ellen Goodman, Michael Hughes, Ester Katz, Carol McCann, James Patterson, Johanna Schoen, and Lauri Umansky. For medical advice I thank Dr. Gregory Cherr. Julie Edelson read the entire manuscript and helped me cut it to a more manageable size. Michael Sinclair's assistance with computer technology was indispensable; I owe him enormous gratitude for helping me whenever I called upon him. I have also benefited from comments by participants in the Social Science Research Seminar at Wake Forest University, in particular Michael Lawlor and Ian Taplin. I thank them not only for their critiques but also for the intellectual atmosphere they help perpetuate on campus.

Funding and librarians make research possible. I thank the Griffin Fund in the History Department of Wake Forest University for financing research trips to the archives. The librarians at the Z. Smith Reynolds Library at WFU are the most supportive colleagues one could hope to encounter. Rick Statler at the Rhode Island Historical Society has been a great asset to my research projects, and I thank him for his sense of professionalism and his great efficiency. I must also thank Planned Parenthood of Rhode Island for allowing me to conduct research on-site at their facility, where the records of the organization have been kept since its opening in the 1930s. Spending countless days there made me realize the stress the staff must experience, from crossing picket lines to listening for ticking bombs. To these staff members and others similar to them women across the country owe a debt of gratitude that can never be repaid.

Personally, I have many people to thank. My parents, Leo and Eva Caron, taught me the value of hard work. My sister, Therese Caron, and brother, Robert Caron, have supported my academic pursuits from day one. Mike, Jan, Emma, and Moria Lawlor have been our substitute family in Winston-Salem, North Carolina. My son, Quaid, and daughter, Alden, have been the pride and joy of my life. Their laughter and tears have kept me going, and their soccer games and swim meets have given me needed time away from the manuscript. Finally, my husband, Christopher O'Neill, has provided editorial comments, love and emotional support, and gourmet meals these many years.

A Brief Overview of American Reproductive History

Americans have struggled to define the government's relationship to their private lives, and few contests have been more rancorous than government attempts to control sexuality. The public realm passes reproductive legislation, but these laws affect the most intimate and private aspects of citizens' lives.[1] In *Buck v. Bell* 274 U.S. 200 (1927), for example, Supreme Court Justice Oliver Wendell Holmes upheld a 1924 Virginia state law that allowed state officials to sterilize the "unfit"; the law was primarily a cost-saving measure in the face of rapid congestion at state institutions for the "feebleminded." Carrie Buck, the daughter of a supposed "feebleminded" single mother, gave birth out of wedlock to a daughter deemed an "imbecile." Dr. Albert Priddy, superintendent of the Virginia Colony for the Epileptic and Feebleminded, characterized the Bucks as belonging "to the shiftless, ignorant, and worthless class of anti-social whites of the South." Holmes agreed, arguing that the precedent set in compulsory vaccination was "broad enough to cover cutting the Fallopian tubes." In his now infamous conclusion Holmes declared that "three generations of imbeciles are enough." What the state and the Court failed to uncover was that Carrie Buck's mother was not "feebleminded"; her adoptive family had institutionalized her against her will after the family's nephew raped her. Carrie also was not an "imbecile"; she had earned a spot on her school's honor roll. This tragedy, for which Virginia governor Mark Wagner apologized in 2003, happened as a result of the state's power to enforce legally eugenic desires to, as Holmes stated, "prevent our being swamped with incompetence."[2]

This book examines policy changes concerning reproductive rights. Policy transformations have resulted in part from anxieties over high birthrates among women deemed undesirable by the white elite establishment, including, during the nineteenth century, certain groups of immigrants (namely, the Irish, southeastern Europeans, and Asians) and, during the twentieth century, nonnorthwestern European immigrants as well as the poor, the uneducated, racial minorities, the "unfit" (a term used to denote the mentally or physically handicapped), and sexual "deviants," such as Carrie Buck and her mother. Statements deeming the high fertility among these groups a "threat" to the "racial purity" and intelligence level of the country dominated the national discourse on the "problem of population." By the 1960s population controllers—advocates of policies to control the socioeconomic and/or racial composition of the population—and fiscal conservatives blamed these groups for burgeoning welfare expenditures. Population concerns, therefore, governed national discussions of reproductive policy. In local communities many women ignored or were unaware of the invidious arguments employed by population controllers to shape policy. Whether reproductive policies became more restrictive or more lenient, many women consistently sought means—legal or illegal—to control their fertility and therefore their lives, and they received help in their endeavors from some sympathetic health officials, clergy, and feminists.[3]

This book examines the reproductive choices available to individuals since the mid-nineteenth century. It seeks to determine who chooses for whom and on what grounds. It traces the emergence of contraception and abortion as social, medical, and legal issues in the nineteenth century to the contemporary policy of publicly supported fertility control. The driving force for legislation dealing with abortion, contraception, and sterilization was the high fertility rate among the "wrong" type of people, but the agenda of population controllers did not represent reality for most Americans. The history of reproductive control is a complex tale reflecting the interests of two distinct factions: those pushing to control the reproductive capacity of others and those determined to control their own reproductive choices. The former have attempted to control the choices available to women, presuming the latter cannot intelligently and rationally choose for themselves.

This book is unique in that it examines the three main fields of reproduction over a period of nearly two hundred years. Many historians analyze either abortion, contraception, or sterilization in a focused study of one aspect of fertility control. This book synthesizes these topically and temporally focused secondary works to provide a broad overview of national trends in policy developments and the impact they have had on people's private choices. While variations in federal and state laws existed in the nineteenth century, a national consensus did emerge to control women's abilities to procreate. The twentieth century witnessed a liberalization of policies, but these changes were not a reaction or response to organized feminist demands for reproductive control. Legislators did not care at all what women wanted—that is, control over their bodies. Instead, public expenditures dominated the discourse that shaped policies in a way that wrested control of reproductive matters from indigent women and placed it in the hands of white elites concerned with the composition of the population.

Historical Overview

From the colonial period through the early nineteenth century control of reproduction, similar to other family matters, remained a private concern. Legislators did not obstruct the use or dispersal of contraceptives.[4] The majority of Americans did not consider abortion legally or morally wrong as long as it occurred before quickening, the mother's first perception of fetal movement. In 1873, however, the Comstock Law forbade the importation, mailing, and interstate transportation of articles and literature concerning both contraception and abortion. By the end of the century every state in the Union except Kentucky had outlawed abortion.[5]

What brought about this change in policy? While many factors played a role, nativism constituted the most publicly employed justification for the repressive changes in reproductive policies during the nineteenth century. Earlier, Thomas Jefferson had expressed such fears: "The circumstances of superior beauty is thought worthy of attention in the propagation of our horses, dogs, and other domestic animals; why not in that of man?" He contended that children born of mixed-race unions produced "a degradation to which no lover of this country, no lover of excellence in the human character can innocently consent." The fate of the white race in his home state of Virginia weighed heavily on his mind: "Under the mild treatment our slaves experience, and their wholesome, though coarse, food, this blot in our country increases as fast, or faster, than whites."[6]

Racial concerns mounted as the fertility rate of white American women steadily declined in the late eighteenth century and plummeted between 1830 and 1870, the same period during which immigrants began to flood the United States. These anxieties continued in the early twentieth century as many population controllers agonized over the disparity between the fertility of the "best"—defined as wealthy, educated, white Protestants—and the "inferior"—variously defined as poor, uneducated, immigrant, Catholic, Jewish, mentally or physically impaired, sexually deviant, or criminal. Race suicide theorists espoused racial doom propaganda to convince the "best" that their incessant use of contraceptives would eventually lead to their extinction. When these arguments failed to alter the reproductive patterns of the elite, tactics changed during the 1910s and 1920s. Rather than ban birth control (a term first used in 1914 by Otto Bobsein) to coerce the "best," these theorists attempted to liberalize legislation to make contraceptives available to the "inferior."[7]

By this point, birth control and abortion became two distinct issues. While few called for the relegalization of abortion, a vocal movement for the liberalization of contraceptive restrictions was well under way. The notion of population control gained increased public support during the economic devastation of the Great Depression. Reports concerning the high fertility rates of families on government relief helped ignite widespread indignation against "dole babies." Such propaganda fueled a push for contraceptive dispersal among the poor through welfare organizations.

During World War II the national discourse shifted to view contraception as a means to utilize most effectively man- and womanpower. The military's campaign to rid its ranks of debilitating venereal diseases promoted the use of condoms. The war years saw contraceptives touted for their contribution to soldiers' fitness, national health, and women's ability to undertake war work. The conclusion of the war brought a baby boom that affected women of all races and socioeconomic classes. The first significant increase in white middle-class fertility rates during the late 1940s and 1950s allayed the anxieties of many population controllers on the domestic scene, but they soon turned their attention to the "population explosion" in the Third World. Not until the 1960s did the issue of reproductive policy again become significant in domestic policy discussions.

Liberalizing Contraception

By the 1960s the judicial system had handed down a number of decisions that had gradually loosened restrictions on contraceptives. Two cases in the appellate courts abrogated many federal limitations. *Bours v. United States*, 229 F. 950 (7th Cir. 1915) and *United States v. One Package*, 85 F. 2d 737 (2d Cir. 1935) exempted physicians from the contraceptive restrictions of the Comstock Law. The first successful challenge to a state statute came with *Griswold v. Connecticut*, 381 U.S. 471 (1965). The Supreme Court declared unconstitutional a Connecticut statute that made the use of contraceptives by both married and single persons a criminal offense. For the first time the Court identified a "zone of privacy" guaranteed by the Constitution: the First Amendment ensures the right of association, while the Fourth Amendment affirms citizens' immunity from unreasonable search and seizure in their homes. Since this case the Court has interpreted the "zone of privacy" as a Fourteenth Amendment right under the equal protection clause. Although *Griswold* invalidated an outdated law that regulated sexual morality, the Supreme Court supported contraceptive aids for married women only. Seven years later *Eisenstadt v. Baird*, 405 U.S. 440 (1972), declared unconstitutional a statute that imposed a five-year jail term for distributing contraceptives. Invoking the equal protection clause of the Fourteenth Amendment, the Court found no reason to restrict contraceptive privileges to married women: "If the right of privacy means anything, it is the right of the individual, married or single, to be free from unwarranted governmental intrusion into matters so fundamentally affecting a person as the decision whether to bear or beget a child." This decision finally removed the institutionalization of punitive sex standards regarding premarital intercourse.

Several factors led to this transformation in contraceptive policy. In the late nineteenth and early twentieth centuries many social activists, religious groups, and physicians actively opposed birth control because they believed it threatened the values and morals of society. Of these three groups, doctors exerted the most influence.[8] Descriptions of available contraceptives appeared in medical journals after 1865, yet many doctors opposed dispersal for a number of reasons: the lack of government regulation led to defective and ineffective products in many instances, and many doctors rejected contraceptives for their moral implications because they allowed intercourse without consequences. By the 1930s the American Medical Association (AMA, established in 1847) held a more conservative view of contraception than most middle-class Americans. As lay groups pressured for change, the medical profession cautiously endorsed contraceptives but insisted on a monopoly over delivery. Many poor and working-class women could not afford a private doctor's fees; these women found contraceptive care on the black market or at freestanding clinics generally staffed by outcast physicians such as foreigners and women. These doctors tended to apply stricter standards for dispersal than private physicians because the former feared their colleagues' disapproval. Because clinics provided the largest percent of legal contraceptive care, women, especially single women, continued to face barriers in their attempts to procure contraceptives.[9]

Even after the AMA endorsed contraceptives in the 1930s, according to Elizabeth Siegel Watkins, some doctors maintained their opposition, and others experienced "lingering ambivalence" regarding the medical role of contraception. Most doctors, according to Watkins, "gained little by offering birth control services to their patients: the work was not financially rewarding, medically challenging, or professionally acknowledged." With the marketing in 1960 of Enovid-10, commonly known as the pill, doctors began to see contraception as a legitimate medical service because of its place in prescriptive pharmacology. The pill, unlike earlier forms of contraception, was lucrative for physicians: women had to return for regular checkups and prescription renewals.[10] The development of the pill along with the 1965 *Griswold* decision helped bring the issue of reproductive rights to the public eye.

During the 1960s the federal government finally positioned itself behind the liberalization of reproductive legislation. Donald T. Critchlow asserts that much of this change was the result of the "population lobby" that emerged in the 1950s to argue that contraceptives could help ameliorate "an array of social problems, including poverty, welfare, crime, urban decay, and pollution." This lobby shared racial, religious, and socioeconomic characteristics and had access to policy makers not only in Congress and the White House but at social clubs and private dinners. Interest groups were able to influence policy developments by the 1960s because most Americans accepted the notion of family planning. The Catholic Church was another matter. No matter how much the church supported the social welfare programs of the Great Society and the War on Poverty, desired to be accepted in American society, endeavored to be seen as progressive rather than regressive, and realized that Protestant and Jewish leaders supported birth control, church leaders could not in good faith participate in federal programs that involved family planning because church policy deemed birth control immoral. American church leaders agreed not to oppose federal funding of birth control as long as all programs were voluntary and offered instruction in the rhythm method.[11] The population lobby's advocacy of subsidized family-planning services for the medically indigent gained support at the same time as national concern over poverty intensified. Many political and social critics favored the removal of contraceptive restrictions as a means to decrease the cost of Aid to Families with Dependent Children and to curb the high fertility of the poor.

Some promoted sterilization as a permanent solution to large families among welfare recipients. This proposal was not new to the 1960s. It had entered the public debate during the depressed 1930s. Many eugenicists promoted the sterilization of genetically "defective" dependents in publicly funded institutions. Periodicals reported mounting resentment against taxes spent on the mentally impaired, imbeciles, idiots, the insane, epileptics, and, in some states, criminals, drug addicts, and prostitutes and argued that only sterilization could save American society from the continued breeding of these "unfit." The connection between sterilization and economics slackened but did not disappear when the Great Depression ended and when during World War II it was associated with Nazi Germany. By the 1960s the national debate over increasing government expenditures influenced federal and state decisions not only to legalize sterilization but also to fund it. This method of birth control became increasingly popular during the 1970s and constituted the single most used form of contraception by the end of the century. While sterilization was liberating for people who chose it on their own initiative, officials and physicians sometimes used it to control the reproduction of poor and minority women without their consent.

Abortion

Such manipulation occurred with abortion as well. The antiabortion crusade in the nineteenth century resulted in part from publicized vexation over the perceived imbalance in fertility rates between the "best" and "inferior" stock. Abortion among the middle and upper classes was supposedly to blame for the imminent downfall of the race. Banning abortion, crusaders argued, was one way to force the "best" women to fulfill their duty to the nation in bringing forth "proper" children, that is, white, Protestant, and financially secure citizens.

Other factors influenced this antiabortion campaign. By the mid-nineteenth century, doctors were attempting to monopolize the medical profession. As Faye D. Ginsburg argues, in order for this campaign to succeed, doctors had to redefine abortion from a common practice women learned from their mothers, other relatives, or midwives to a practice that undermined family stability.[12] New state laws that permitted physicians to perform abortions only to preserve the health and/or life of the mother effectively allowed male doctors rather than women to control procreation. Because almost all medical schools excluded women, access to a legal abortion rested in the hands of male physicians who took the Hippocratic oath, which enjoins against abortion. Moreover, state license requirements usually excluded quacks and "irregulars," a term used to denote practitioners without formal training from a recognized medical school, from the lucrative abortion market. Safety may have also influenced some antiabortion crusaders' attitudes. Abortion, similar to other surgeries at that time, often endangered the health of the mother. Some irregulars and quacks performed abortions badly, often killing or seriously injuring patients.[13] Scientific advancements by midcentury undermined earlier notions of quickening, beginning a concern for fetal life that began at the moment of conception. Despite the organized movement by physicians to regulate abortion, doctors were not a monolithic bloc. Some remained sympathetic to the plight of women facing unwanted pregnancies; some were more concerned with the life and health of the mother; and some were more interested in the life and health of the fetus. Physicians opposed to abortion carried the day.

Doctors gained allies in their cause. Nicola Beisel argues that advocates of social purity supported banning abortion as part of a larger antivice movement that "endangered elite children because moral corruption threatened to topple them from the peak of the social hierarchy, rendering them unfit for respectable society." The shared resentment of immigrants by many doctors and Social Purity advocates helped cement their alliance.[14] Feminists also joined the effort to ban abortions. Doctors and feminists, according to

Ginsburg, "each held the opposite sex responsible for what they saw as the decay of the culture and especially, in their view, the pernicious increase in abortion."[15] Together these groups succeeded in banning abortion and, in most states, the dispersal of birth control.

Abortion, similar to gambling, prostitution, and drinking, did not disappear when the state decreed it illegal. Women continued to resort to abortion in steady numbers. Leslie J. Reagan argues that while many historians have viewed illegal abortion as "static," it was in fact "dynamic." State laws allowed an abortion if it saved the life of the mother. The definition of lifesaving varied over time and among individual physicians; this leeway made the doctor's role "complex." While doctors gained control over women's reproductive choices through antiabortion legislation, the state increased its control over doctors by forcing them to "police the practices of . . . members."[16] Nevertheless, numerous doctors continued to provide abortions, as did midwives and irregulars in states across the nation through the 1950s.

Historians generally agree on the reasons for the reemergence of the abortion controversy in the mid-twentieth century. Some of the incentives included the concern about population growth and environmental issues; openness about sex, marital problems, and contraception; and the introduction of relatively simple and safe abortion procedures.[17] Many doctors realized that one hundred years of criminalization had not put an end to the practice: illegal abortions continued at a steady rate throughout the twentieth century.[18] New restrictive policies passed in the 1940s and 1950s that tightened the loopholes allowing for lifesaving abortions coincided with increased demand for the procedure, resulting in an increased death rate and health risk from illegal abortions.[19]

The horrible aftermath of incompetent and untrained abortionists finally led some professionals to argue for a reconstruction of abortion policies. The first group to question restrictive abortion laws in the early 1950s was psychiatrists who had close contact with individual women facing unwanted pregnancies. Some medical doctors joined because they resented laws that interfered with their best medical judgment. They signed a statement in 1955 advocating statutes that would allow doctors to decide conditions for abortion. In 1958 Planned Parenthood Federation of America (PPFA) requested that the American Law Institute (ALI) draft a new, model abortion law. The ALI complied because lawyers could sympathize with physicians constrained in their practice by law. The resulting ALI recommendation allowed for legal abortions in three instances: if the pregnancy would likely cause serious physical or mental damage to the mother; if the birth would result in a physically or mentally handicapped baby; and if the pregnancy resulted from rape or incest.[20]

Shortly after the ALI proposal two events helped trigger support for revisions in abortion policies. First, researchers found that the new tranquilizer Thalidomide caused birth defects. Second, an epidemic of German measles swept the United States between 1962 and 1965. Because infected mothers face a 50 percent risk of bearing a deformed child, many women sought abortions. After substantial lobbying the California legislature passed a bill that legalized abortion in the case of a severely deformed fetus and to protect the mental health of the woman; ironically, then-governor Ronald Reagan, later a zealous abortion opponent, signed the measure in 1967.[21] That same year Colorado became the first state to adopt a new abortion law modeled on the example proposed by the ALI. Between 1967 and 1970 twelve states enacted new bills that extended the grounds for the legal termination of pregnancy. While still specifying certain conditions under which women could obtain abortions, these statutes were substantially less restrictive than laws they replaced. In 1970 four states adopted legislation that placed no conditions on the termination of pregnancy: Alaska, Hawaii, New York, and Washington in effect legalized abortion on request.[22] By 1973 sixteen states had passed legislation that liberalized abortion policies.

Although feminist actions for abortion reform were important, they were not pivotal. Some feminists attempted to expand the right of marital privacy secured in *Griswold* to include the right to safe, legal abortions for all women, married or single. Many women and some sympathetic men picketed meetings of the AMA, demanding support for change. They also staged protests to influence state legislators and to raise public awareness of the issue. Notions of women's rights in this arena, however, had little impact on decisions to reform abortion legislation. Feminists acknowledged that they downplayed this angle because it often alienated powerful groups willing to support changes in abortion laws for nonfeminist reasons, such as population control, welfare savings, environmental concerns, and freedom to practice medicine without government interference. Because legal abortions did not emerge based on feminist reasoning, the right to abortion in the twenty-first century is on precarious ground.

Judicial Review

The volume of cases brought before state courts in the late 1960s and early 1970s influenced the decision of the Supreme Court to consider the abortion issue. In *United States v. Vuitch*, 402 U.S. 62 (1971), the Court decided that abortion was a surgical procedure; physicians should determine if it was necessary to protect the mother's health. Two years later *Roe v. Wade*, 410 U.S. 113 (1973), confirmed this medical jurisdiction: the Court struck down

xas statute that considered an attempt "to procure an abortion" a crimi-
act unless "procured or attempted by medical advice for the purpose of
iving the life of the mother." This statute interfered with a doctor's medical
judgment to pursue the optimum medical care for individual patients. As
Justice Harry Blackmun argued, the exception for the mother's life was "in-
sufficiently informative to the physician to whom it purports to afford a measure of professional protection but who must measure its indefinite meaning
at the risk of his liberty," a liberty denied only to the doctor, not the woman,
involved.[23] While medical autonomy was paramount, Blackmun added an
important privacy protection in *Roe*, drawing on precedents in *Griswold*,
Loving v. Virginia, and *Eisenstadt*: "This right of privacy, whether it be found
in the Fourteenth Amendment's concept of personal liberty and restrictions
upon state action, as we feel it is, or, as the District Courts determined, in the
Ninth Amendment's reservation of rights to the people, is broad enough to
encompass a woman's decision whether or not to terminate her pregnancy."[24]
Blackmun stated that the availability of abortion in the early nineteenth century confirmed the Supreme Court's conclusion that a fetus is not a person
under the Constitution. Although *Roe* legalized abortion, it did not remove
all restrictions. After the first trimester a state may regulate abortions to
preserve the mother's health. Because the end of the second trimester usually constitutes the point of viability (the fetus's capacity to live outside the
womb), the state may prohibit abortions at that time unless the mother's
health or life is endangered.

Blackmun introduced this trimester approach—an "arbitrary" one, as
Blackmun himself admitted. His rationale was "to leave the states free to
draw their own medical conclusions with respect to the period after three
months and until viability."[25] Neither side arguing the case to the Court had
developed a rationale based on a division of pregnancy. This approach has
placed restrictions on the right to an abortion and has led to state efforts to
limit access through mandated testing of fetal viability before performing the
procedure.

Doe v. Bolton, 410 U.S. 179 (1973), the companion case to *Roe*, declared
Georgia's abortion statute unconstitutional. The Court struck down requirements for prior approval by a hospital staff committee and two consulting
physicians. The justices concluded that the judgment of the attending physician was sufficient. *Doe* also removed the residency requirement to prevent
patients from entering states solely for the medical assistance available there.
No other medical procedure had residency requirements for patients seeking
medical care. Together, *Roe* and *Doe* invalidated the state's traditional power
to criminalize abortion.

Prochoice or Prolife?

Abortion has galvanized activists on both sides of the issue since *Roe*. Prior to *Roe* prochoice activists worked almost exclusively to legalize abortion; since *Roe* they have been fighting to keep abortion legal and, more recently, have responded to pressure from women of color to ensure full access to all reproductive choices, including contraceptives, birthing healthy babies, and raising children in households above the poverty line.[26] This expanded agenda can be seen in the transformation of the National Abortion Rights Action League to the National Abortion and Reproductive Rights Action League in 1994.

While the issues of birth and adult access to contraception may serve as a bridge between prochoice and prolife camps, major differences exist. Prochoicers endorse government programs that empower women to make the reproductive choice that is right for them, be it abortion, contraception, or childbirth. Prolifers insist that the government ban abortion, sex education in schools, and access to contraceptives for teens. The largest divide is over abortion. Ginsburg argues that prolifers consider abortion a "condensed symbol for the devaluation of motherhood." Women in both camps recognize existing sexual inequality but disagree over its basis. Prochoice activists, according to Ginsburg, "criticize those structures that confine women to nurturance in the domestic domain and suggest it be expanded to become a more collective responsibility. Prolife advocates critique a cultural and social system that assigns nurturance to women yet degrades it as a vocation."[27] Some prolifers, such as the Southern Baptist Convention, believe women are inferior and are destined to fulfill their natural role as mothers.

The prolife camp has remained very visible, well organized, and well funded. A coalition of forces, it includes the Catholic Church, the New Right, and the Republican Party along with a host of nationwide and local organizations. This coalition has been joined by a radical fringe that has become increasingly violent and often uses "shock tactics," such as bombings, murders, shootings, obstructing entrances to clinics, threats and harassment, and broadcasting graphic depictions of fetuses, including the highly sensationalized and fraudulent film *The Silent Scream*.[28]

Although their combined efforts have not resulted in the recriminalization of abortion, their propaganda and their political and economic power have influenced state legislators to pass laws restricting access to this procedure. In the immediate wake of *Roe*, for example, a cost-savings rationale influenced the decision of federal and state governments to fund abortions. Fiscal conservatives argued that an abortion was much more cost-effective than paying the expenses of childbearing and childrearing for welfare recipients.

This argument fell out of favor quickly due to the politically charged nature of the abortion debate by the late 1970s. The prolife coalition campaigned to eliminate funding for virtually all abortions with the Hyde Amendment. With abortion no longer a feasible option for most indigent women, population controllers sought permanent means to control these women's ability to procreate. Their answer was sterilization. Medicaid funds 90 percent of the cost of sterilization, a fail-safe procedure from the perspective of population controllers. This discrimination in funding sends a message to indigent women that the government prefers to sever their reproductive capacities rather than allow them to control their fertility. These regulations act coercively and detrimentally in the lives of many women, especially the young and the indigent.

The Case of Rhode Island

A microanalysis of Rhode Island demonstrates that the national consensus on sexual politics had variants at the state level. Rhode Island followed the national debate and policy developments but in many ways pursued a divergent path, especially from other New England states. In the nineteenth century the state legislature restricted abortion, apparently persuaded by nativist arguments employed by the Rhode Island Medical Society (RIMS, founded in 1821), yet the law was one of only two in the nation to exempt women from prosecution. When most states adopted a version of the Comstock Law in the late nineteenth century, Rhode Island did not. It was the only state in New England that did not ban the distribution of contraceptives, and it allowed the first and only fully operating birth control clinic in New England from 1931 to 1965, alternatively called the Rhode Island Birth Control Clinic, the Rhode Island Maternal Health Association, and finally Planned Parenthood of Rhode Island (PPRI), a name under which it continues to operate in the twenty-first century. Unlike most clinics, which did not record personal characteristics of clients, the Rhode Island clinic offers insights into the racial, ethnic, and religious aspects of patrons. While immigrant or female doctors worked at many freestanding birth control clinics, "respectable" white male physicians staffed the Rhode Island clinic. During the 1920s and 1930s most states passed eugenic sterilization legislation. Rhode Island legislators twice debated the issue but defeated the proposals. The legislators deemed sterilization a private medical issue to be decided between physician and patient, a stance later vocalized by Blackmun with regard to abortion in *Roe*. This privacy stand allowed PPRI to open the first vasectomy clinic in New England in 1970. Throughout its history the clinic has prioritized the health and individual choices of clients rather than following the agenda of population control advocates, including PPFA. Women and men of different races, ethnicities, religions, and classes were bound by the shared desire to allow individual choice in reproduction.

This book focuses on the conflict inherent between a population control agenda that permeated the national discourse on sexual politics for well over a century and a half and a desire by individuals to be in command of their reproduction. It synthesizes secondary material that treats abortion, birth control, and sterilization as separate entities and places these three areas of reproductive control into a cohesive framework. While various factors influenced policy in each of these three areas, the thread that ties them together is population control. Elite white officials, influenced by genetic and eugenic theories as well as by race, class, and gender biases, used all three—abortion, birth control, and sterilization—to control the fertility of the indigent, many of whom were women of color. In sum, political, moral, and economic forces together shaped reproductive policies that impacted women's ability to choose how to control their bodies. Doctors, nurses, and social workers also influenced this choice: not a monolithic bloc, some supported women's right to choose; some employed the rhetoric of the population control agenda to secure services for their clients; and some endorsed the notion of population control. The conflict between population controllers and individual choice in reproductive matters continues today, albeit with less overtly racist and classist rhetoric than that used in the nineteenth and twentieth centuries. The covert nature of the campaign, however, does not diminish its impact on policy development that controls who chooses for whom in reproductive matters.

2

Abortion and Contraception in the Nineteenth Century

In the 1840s a flood of predominantly Irish immigrants joined the amalgam that was American society and released a nativist backlash. Not only were these immigrants generally poor, uneducated, and Catholic, but their fertility rate was much higher than that of Protestant citizens, whose total fertility rate (TFR, the predicted number of children a woman will have between the ages of fifteen and forty-four) had steadily declined since the late eighteenth century and plunged between 1830 and 1870. Many physicians attributed this slump to a rapid rise in the number of abortions among white middle- and upper-class married Protestant women. Dr. Horatio R. Storer, a Boston gynecologist, a surgeon at the New England Hospital for Women, as well as an assistant in obstetrics at Harvard University and a professor of obstetrics at Berkshire Medical College, persuaded the AMA in 1860 to launch a campaign to convince state legislators to prohibit abortions. The main argument driving the campaign was nativism; leaders of the antiabortion movement harped on escalating xenophobic fears among the white Protestant bourgeoisie. The campaign also played on male indignation at the growing empowerment of women.[1] The assumption of women as the sole power broker with regard to abortion decisions discounted the role of husbands and lovers, as seen in the Cornell/Avery case in Rhode Island. While not all physicians condoned the antiabortion campaign, the AMA crusade was legislatively successful, especially among states such as Rhode Island where nativism was strong. This chapter summarizes the national discourse on contraception and then examines the changing context for abortion and birth control in Rhode Island from the 1830s to the turn of the twentieth century. Nativism influenced the abortion statutes passed in that state, but legislators pursued their own course with regard to contraception.

The State of Knowledge in the Mid-Nineteenth Century

The decline in TFR signaled individual steps to limit progeny. Some women prolonged breast-feeding and refrained from sex while nursing, but this method was short-term.[2] As one physician warned, "The influence of lactation in averting menstruation or conception, cannot for the most part be kept up longer than twelve months."[3] Some "very poor" urbanites continued to practice infanticide, while others tried folk remedies to prevent conception. The vulcanization of rubber in 1844 brought mass production of condoms, although this development did not translate into an instant market, as condoms continued to be connected to prostitution and venereal disease. Still, many couples did use them. Three other contraceptive methods were far more common: coitus interruptus, or withdrawal; douching syringes, made of rubber by the 1850s; and the rhythm method, introduced in the 1840s as a nonintrusive means of contraception.[4] By midcentury intrauterine devices (IUDs) could be made by those with knowledge about and access to substances such as wood, rubber, and metal; and pharmaceutical products such as sponges, suppositories, and chemically coated tampons were available.[5]

Public lectures and tracts on sexuality increased the circulation of knowledge regarding contraception. *Moral Physiology* (1831) by the utopian socialist Robert Dale Owen recommended withdrawal, the vaginal sponge, and the condom (made from animal skin or membrane or from oiled silk before 1844). His work influenced Charles Knowlton, author of *Fruits of Philosophy* (1832).[6] Health guru Sylvester Graham and Presbyterian minister and reformer Henry C. Wright argued for male self-control, while the tract *Reproductive Control* rejected various drugs, condoms, exercise, coitus interruptus, and the sponge as either ineffective or too inhibiting of sexual pleasure; it advocated douching with a syringe, available at any local drugstore for "twenty five cents," filled with cold water.[7]

The justification for employing contraceptives varied. Wright and others employed early feminist arguments: women had a right to decide when and if to bear children. Some used Enlightenment rationalism, attributing the "silly prejudice" against birth control "to religious education . . . and not to any dictate of reason." Contraceptives would allow people to control their destiny, permit the poor to advance economically, make marriages happier and sexually fulfilling, and stop prostitutes from bearing children doomed to "vices." The sexual double standard, especially men's ability to avoid "any just retribution" for intercourse, and superficial prudery were also attacked: the "pretended squeamishness of the American people on this subject" contradicted the fact that "no class of books finds a readier sale, or is more eagerly sought after in private."[8] While mostly middle-class readers had access to such books, newspaper advertisements reached a large audience.[9]

After 1840 abortion came into public view as a free-market service. Midwives, druggists, and some physicians competed for clients with advertisements in newspapers, magazines, and religious journals. Observers claimed that the overall incidence of abortion began to rise sharply after 1840 and remained high through the 1870s. Madame Restell (Ann Lohman) operated a lucrative abortion service during this period that catered primarily to white elite women attempting to control their bodies.[10]

Various abortion methods were available. Many women used home remedies passed on from previous generations composed of ordinary botanical ingredients. Many abortifacients included "aloes or black hellebore"; although effective, they posed considerable health hazards. Some black women relied on a blend of mercurous chloride and turpentine or on indigo plants.[11] The *Charleston Medical Journal and Review (CMJ&R)* claimed that the "Negro" population discovered the benefits of "Black Root" and "mistletoe . . . to induce abortion," while one physician informed the South Carolina Medical Society (SCMS) that "a negress had procured abortion by the use of Tobacco. Leaves of the plant were found adherent to the placenta."[12] The root of the cotton plant was "one of the best emmenagogues . . . superior to . . . ergot," "handy to all, and free of expense." Some hailed the Japanese remedy "Keytse-Sing," "Indian hemp," "Uva Ursi," or "extract of belladonna" over ergot. Chloroform ointment was useful; others swore by the "Purgative Properties of the Argemone Mexicana." Quinine was effective and accessible because "it constituted the *base* of . . . prescriptions of physicians practising in the South and West." Physicians also touted douching. The "Tepid douche" from Vienna required that water be placed twelve feet above a seated woman with a vaginal tube so that the water was "projected against the os uteri" twice daily for one week. The "Kiwisch Plan" involved "keeping up a continuous stream of water against the os uteri by means of a syphon tube." "Dry cupping" was also successful: "Applied to the lowest part of the sacrum, dilation of the *os uteri* is produced; and applied higher up, contraction of the uterus follows." Some believed that "measures which act directly and primarily upon the breast, such as warm clothing to the bust, and the application of stimulant," including the "cupping glass" and especially "suckling," brought about abortions. Carbonic acid gas "conducted into the vagina by means of an elastic tube" was also effective.[13] Finally, the use of a probe by a doctor, midwife, or the woman herself usually aborted the fetus.

There were few legal restrictions on abortions. Although Lord Ellenborough's Act of 1803 expanded British common law by prohibiting abortion prior to quickening, the legal codes of the United States did not adopt this interpretation, and abortion remained unregulated prior to quickening.[14] During this period "abortion" denoted miscarriage, or the body's "natural expulsion of the fetus."[15] Physicians and the public alike generally did not believe pregnancy could be confirmed during the first trimester. Many women and their doctors assumed the abeyance of the menstrual cycle could result from a blockage as much as from pregnancy. As Dr. J. Gaston of Columbia,

South Carolina, argued, "We may emphatically pronounce that the health of woman depends on the secretion of the womb, and it is consequently of great importance that this should be corrected whenever any derangement as to quantity or quality may occur."[16] Thus, the use of drugs and potions to resume menses was common. "Criminal abortion," on the other hand, signified actions taken to end an unwanted pregnancy after quickening. In 1839 Hugh L. Hodge of the University of Pennsylvania Medical School alerted his students to the frequent demands for abortion they would encounter in their practice.[17] Historian Cornelia Hughes Dayton argues that "abortion attempts were far from rare" and that "outrage over the destruction of the fetus or denunciations of those who would arrest 'nature's proper course'" were "strikingly absent."[18]

Yet some authors did express moral outrage regarding abortion. In a tract published in the United States in 1796 British physician Hugh Smith criticized couples who resorted to the "dreaded evil" as "selfish and unsocial . . . ; those persons, who think and act thus narrowly, can neither be accounted good characters in themselves, nor worthy members with respect to society."[19] In 1810 Dr. Joseph Brevitt attacked the "horrid depravity of human weakness, in wretches lost to every sense of religion, morality, and that mutual attachment from a mother to her offspring, and every tender tie in nature, [that] seek the means to procure abortion." Although men were guilty of such depraved behavior, Brevitt saw women as more degenerate because they eschewed their natural role as mothers. Men were culpable, but only as accomplices to independent women.[20] Conversely, William Buchan, a British writer whose works were popular in the United States, considered a woman seeking an abortion a "victim of seduction" trying to avoid "public shame or private scorn," but even this reason was "no excuse for murder."[21] While the *CMJ&R* touted the new and safer means to procure abortions in the 1850s, they were only acceptable to save the life or health of the mother.[22]

Nativism and the Decline in TFR

The increasing visibility of abortion combined with demographic trends to stimulate concern. The emphasis on abortion resulted in part from perceived changes in who sought this procedure by the mid-nineteenth century. Prior to 1840, according to physicians, abortion was the recourse of desperate single women. By midcentury numerous physicians accused a growing number of married white middle- and upper-class women of resorting to abortion.[23] This perception may have been false. Married bourgeois women may have sought abortions all along but from midwives, not physicians. With the professionalization of medicine by midcentury, doctors defined themselves as experts in all fields, including gynecology, and wealthy married women may have forgone midwives in favor of physicians. Intentional abortion, according to these doctors, explained the dramatic decrease in the TFR among whites from 7.04 in 1800 to 3.56 in 1900, with the most significant decline between 1830 and 1870 (from 6.55 to 4.55).[24]

While the TFR among white citizens declined, more than three million immigrants settled in the United States between 1846 and 1855 alone. The great majority were Catholic, and, according to many physicians, they did not abort their pregnancies. Their large families not only symbolized a lack of sexual self-control but also threatened Protestant hegemony. Midcentury books and tracts as well as accounts of foreign travelers attest to the increasing vexation over white middle- and upper-class Protestant women seeking abortions and the resultant decrease in the TFR in the face of waves of Catholic immigrants.[25]

Numerous factors influenced the fertility decline. It began in the industrialized North among the middle class and gradually affected other groups and regions, although fertility rates remained higher in frontier areas and in the South, where agriculture continued to dominate. Economic factors in the decline included the transformation from an agricultural to an industrial society. Children who had previously contributed to financial stability on the farm now drained urban factory workers' budgets, especially with the introduction of compulsory education to the age of 16. Land also had an impact: the less land a middle- or upper-class family had to pass on, the more likely the parents were to limit their offspring. Fewer children meant economic solvency for the middle class and possibly even upward mobility for heirs. Culturally, the decrease can be seen as an attempt by white middle-class families to sustain their standing in the community. The diminishing belief that all events were the will of God influenced some couples: reproductive control reflected their desire to control their future, including the size of their family.[26]

The decline in the TFR also reflected increased autonomy for women. Women used abortion to decrease their chances of dying in childbirth and to free themselves from the constant burden of children. Fewer children coincided with the modern emphasis on childrearing over childbearing. With smaller families, white middle- and upper-class mothers could intensify their maternal "duties" to raise pious children. Fewer children also allowed these women to become active in social and moral causes such as abolitionism, temperance, health and fashion reform, and the woman's rights movement. Although relatively few women were activists, many elite white men considered them threatening because of the example they set.[27] Moreover, these reforms called for changes in male behavior.

The fertility decline among these women raised nativist concerns. The Know-Nothing Party, an antiforeign and anti-Catholic organization, burst into the political arena during the 1850s and in 1854 carried Massachusetts, Delaware, and, with a Whig coalition, Pennsylvania. The party also sent seventy-five members to Congress. The following year it swept Rhode Island, Massachusetts, Connecticut, Maryland, and Kentucky, and most state officers in New York, Pennsylvania, and California described themselves as party affiliates. In the South the Know-Nothings nearly carried Virginia, Georgia, Alabama, Mississippi, and Louisiana.[28]

Nativist commentary attracted many doctors. Most physicians in the AMA were white American-born Protestants, and xenophobic sentiment ran high among them. This group insisted that the majority of women seeking abortions were white, married, American-born, Protestant, "educated and refined ladies." Medical journals and physicians' speeches warned that the "ignorant, the low lived and the alien" would control the nation by outbreeding "our own population." Dr. Martin Luther Holbrook claimed that American women were "addicted" to the "wicked" practice. Dr. Nathan Allen, an obstetrician in Lowell, Massachusetts, found that in Lowell white Protestant family size had declined by about one-half since the end of the eighteenth century due to increased abortion and contraception. Immigrants, he warned, were quickly outmultiplying Americans.[29] Writing on the approaching U.S. centennial celebration, one Michigan doctor claimed that "the annual destruction of fetuses" had become so "truly appalling" that "the Puritanic blood of '76 [would] be but sparingly represented in the approaching centenary."[30]

The Antiabortion Campaign

The connection between abortion, the declining white TFR, and growing female autonomy attracted the attention of doctors. While not speaking in a united voice, many physicians cited abortion as a key factor in the discrepancy between immigrant and white Protestant middle- and upper-class birthrates. The legal status of abortion became a central concern of the AMA, which in 1860 initiated a state-by-state campaign to outlaw the practice.

As James Mohr argues, campaign leaders pointed to advances in science.[31] By midcentury most "regulars" or allopaths were aware that quickening was not a magic moment at which the fetus came to life; it developed gradually. As early as 1808 Dr. John Burns stated that "many people at least pretend to view attempts to excite abortion as different from murder, upon the principle that the embryo is not possessed of life. . . . It undoubtedly can neither think nor act; but, upon the same reasoning, we should conclude it to be innocent to kill the child in birth." Dr. Hodge informed students that the "embryo" was "endowed, at once, with the principles of vitality," and thus abortion was "murder." Dr. Storer wrote that physicians had "arrived at the unanimous opinion, that the foetus in utero is alive from the moment of conception." Thus, criminal abortions were "a crime against life, the child being always alive." A number of physicians referred to the fetus as "the little being." A physician and the anonymous author of *Satan in Society* criticized "modern sophists" who used Plato and Aristotle to justify abortion. While the latter "advocated" abortion to prevent "excessive population," they "taught that the child only acquires a soul at the moment of mature birth." Modern medical science had disproved them: life began at conception, not quickening.[32]

Circumstances within the medical profession also impacted the campaign. Many young men apprenticed only one or two years before hanging out a shingle. Middle- and upper-class doctors trained in the traditional European fashion faced competition from them and from homeopaths, hydropaths, botanical physicians, and eclectics, who often offered reliable alternatives to treatments by "regulars." These reformers encouraged men and women to cure themselves and made medical information available to the public through pamphlets, thereby undermining the social, gender, and intellectual order. Regulars also competed with abortionists, whom many women consulted on other medical matters, thus draining regulars' economic and professional security. Because regulars had taken the Hippocratic oath opposing contraceptives and abortion, they could not benefit from this growing, lucrative trade. If nothing else, laws restricting abortion to licensed physicians to save a woman's life would strip irregulars of patients.[33]

Regulars often couched this economic concern in rhetoric accusing irregulars of botching abortions, leading to death or serious injury. Dr. Storer, for example, claimed that "a very large proportion of women become confirmed invalids, perhaps for life," or died following an abortion. Dr. J. R. McFadden claimed that the "violent producing cause" of abortion posed a serious danger; "the most serious of all is an abortion brought on by medicines administered internally or by manipulations." The fatalities due to abortions reported in the *New York Times* verify such assertions.[34] These deaths and injuries most likely resulted from improper training, ignorance of improved methods of abortion, or lack of sanitary care: the drive to outlaw abortion occurred when medical knowledge increased its safety. In 1856 the *CMJ&R*, for example, concluded that "our knowledge of the nature of the condition of pregnancy has vastly increased within a few years; and the means by which its progress may be interrupted, without endangering life, have been more correctly and definitely ascertained."[35] Nevertheless, safety arguments probably influenced some states to regulate abortion.

Social purists, white middle- and upper-class Protestant men and women, joined physicians' efforts. Abortion and other means of fertility control allowed sexual gratification without accepting parental responsibility. Some crusaders argued that abortion increased divorce and ruined the American family. Such arguments influenced legislators, who designed laws to inhibit sexual conduct and to protect prenatal life.[36] Anthony Comstock, a leader in the New York Society for the Suppression of Vice, latched onto abortion in his antiobscenity campaign because he believed abortion reflected sexual promiscuity among the young influenced by "lascivious reading." Comstock's main concern was not to control women as much as to protect children.[37] He and other crusaders also shared physicians' concerns over immigrant influence in society. Immigrants threatened not only the racial stock but also the political and professional dominance of elite white men in some urban areas. Historian Nicola Beisel argues that the legislative campaign was successful in part because its leaders appealed to the insecurities of men in power at the state and federal levels.[38]

Part of these insecurities stemmed from gendered expectations. Two primary roles for upper- and middle-class women were to serve as a "Republican Mother," raising virtuous citizens to lead the nation, and to fulfill the cult of domesticity. Aborting women shirked their republican duties. Pious, submissive, dependent, and domestic women would not take independent action to abort the next generation. Yet the very women whom leaders most expected to fulfill these two roles seemed most prone to abortion, thereby undermining the cultural and social gendered order. Instead of serving as the civilizing agent to protect the nation from chaos and immorality, these women were traveling a path of debauchery. Criminalizing abortion could reinstitute a gendered order.

Dr. Storer mounted this antiabortion crusade in the 1850s. His father, Dr. D. Humphreys Storer, a professor of midwifery at Harvard University, had earlier "appreciated the frequency of criminal abortions, pointed out their true character, and denounced them." In 1857 the younger Storer persuaded the AMA to let him chair a committee, "On Criminal Abortion, with a View to Its General Suppression," to investigate the annual number of abortions in the United States.[39] Why was Storer so intent on leading this campaign? In his home state the Massachusetts Supreme Court had twice upheld the right of women to obtain an abortion prior to quickening. Guaranteeing the right to abortion was not tantamount to approval. Chief Justice Lemuel Shaw concluded the court's ruling with a damning statement: "The court are all of the opinion that, although the acts set forth are, in a high degree, offensive to good morals and injurious to society, yet they are not punishable at common law."[40] Storer rejected this legal right to abortion, especially because the wrong women were taking advantage of this prerogative: "In the state of Massachusetts at large," he wrote, " . . . the increase of the population . . . has been wholly of those of recent foreign origin; this in 1850. In 1853," he continued, " . . . births within the Commonwealth . . . resulted in favor of foreign parents in an increased ratio." Storer argued that the imbalance between birthrates resulted from differences in abortion practices.[41]

Between 1857 and 1859 Storer wrote to doctors, warning them of increasing numbers of women seeking abortions. The worst offenders were middle- and upper-class married women: they preferred "to devastate with poison and with steel their wombs rather than . . . forego the gaieties of a winter's ball, parties or plays, or the pleasures of a summer's trips and amusements." Storer resented forthright women who aborted, commenting that "ladies boast to each other of the impunity with which they have aborted, as they do of their expenditures, of their dress, of their success in society. There is a fashion in this." By portraying aborting women as hedonists, Storer ignored the anguish many women faced when deciding to abort. His flippant depiction made others willing to condemn these women and helped silence aborting women and their supporters. In another publication he claimed that "these wretched women, these married lawful mothers . . . are thus murdering their children by thousands."[42] Storer believed that married women above all had no right to terminate pregnancies because a "marriage where conception or the birth of children is intentionally prevented" is nothing "but legalized prostitution, a sensual rather than a spiritual union."[43]

By 1859 Storer had won support from some physicians and a strong ally in Dr. Henry Miller, newly appointed AMA president and professor of obstetric medicine at the University of Louisville. At the AMA's national convention that year the Storer committee presented a "mass of evidence" on the frequency of abortion and proposed measures, "chiefly of a legislative character," to suppress it. The AMA "unanimously indorsed" these suggestions, requested that committee members "continue their labors," and adopted an antiabortion resolution that allowed the procedure only to save the mother's life.[44]

While in agreement with the antiabortion resolution, the SCMS took issue with Storer's findings. Members criticized his mere "three pages" of "generalizations" with little substantive argument. The SCMS concluded that "the committee appear to have treated the Association with a discourtesy scarcely short of contempt." They rejected Storer's assertion that criminal abortion was prevalent among "all classes of society," at least "as regards our section." Dr. McFadden argued that in South Carolina abortion occurred in two scenarios: by "the physician, for a laudable purpose, or by the patient or her *friends* for the purpose of concealing an illicit intercourse." While the SCMS considered abortion a sign of "social demoralization," the evidence pointed to its practice primarily in "our Northern States," not in the South. Growing sectional tensions were implicit in the records: married middle- and upper-class Southern white women would not shirk their duty to bear children; only Northern women would behave so immorally. The SCMS believed that "every intelligent or honest physician" should perform abortion "only" under "really desperate circumstances" to save the mother's life.[45]

Not only did Southern physicians refuse to admit that abortion was common among proper married women, but some argued that even slave women did not stoop to this practice. This defense conflicted with planters' assertions. Dr. E. M. Pendleton of Sparta, Georgia, challenged the belief, common among slave owners, that slaves practiced abortion more than whites. "Every practitioner of medicine in the South," he contended, "is aware that an opinion generally prevails among the planters, that the blacks have a secret unknown to the whites, by which they either produce an incapacity to bear children, or destroy the foetus in embryo." The first question asked of a physician tending a slave woman was, "Don't you think the woman has been taking something to keep her from having children?" and "very often his reply is in the affirmative, without any just data upon which to found any opinion, but just to please the prejudices of the inquirer." The planters desired "to obtain a more rapid increase" among slaves. Pendleton argued that physicians should no longer "maintain the hypothesis that our negro females are forever drenching themselves with nostrums, injurious to their health, and fatal to their offspring." Miscarriage, not criminal abortion, as planters assumed, was more prevalent among slaves due to "over-exertion at the wash-tub, scouring mop and plough." If planters wanted to breed slaves, they should "pay more attention" to the workload they imposed upon women. Pendleton argued that slaves were women first: "It would require a considerable stretch of one's credulity to believe that the negress is an exception to those general laws of nature . . . which lead them to desire offspring, and to protect them from harm."[46] Certainly, some slave women did resort to abortion.[47] Yet perhaps slave owners exaggerated its extent because blaming slaves for self-induced abortions was easier than admitting that overwork foiled the masters' breeding plans. Storer and his followers gave no attention to this Southern controversy.

Following the AMA convention, Miller contacted each state medical society requesting its "zealous cooperation . . . in pressing this subject upon the legislatures of their respective States" (see appendixes A and B).[48] The decisions reached at this convention formally launched an antiabortion crusade that has lasted intermittently for nearly 150 years.

Even prior to the physician campaign some states had regulated abortion. Connecticut passed the first antiabortion bill in 1821, followed by Missouri in 1825, Illinois in 1827, and New York in 1828. Ten more states had incorporated similar laws by 1840. Most regulations made abortion a crime only after quickening and punished only those performing the abortion, not those seeking it. The immunity of women suggests that laws were intended to regulate incompetent practitioners, not proscribe abortion. Indeed, most laws banned only abortions injurious to the mother, usually those employing noxious drugs and poisons.[49]

Storer and the AMA considered these laws "a dead letter" and demanded a unified approach to the "problem." As of 1860, for example, only New York, New Hampshire, and Wisconsin had eliminated women's immunity from prosecution. Maine, New Hampshire, Massachusetts, New York, Ohio, Indiana, Michigan, Missouri, Alabama, Mississippi, Arkansas, Texas, Minnesota, California, Oregon, and the territories of Kansas and Washington allowed abortions to save the woman's life. Connecticut, Mississippi, Arkansas, Minnesota, and Oregon recognized abortion as a crime only if it occurred after quickening. Maine, New Hampshire, New York, Ohio, Michigan, and Washington Territory acknowledged abortion as a crime throughout pregnancy, but the penalty varied with the stage of the pregnancy. Vermont, Illinois, Wisconsin, Virginia, Missouri, Alabama, Louisiana, Texas, California, and Kansas Territory considered abortion a crime throughout the pregnancy but required proof of pregnancy to prosecute—proof virtually impossible to obtain after the fact. Only Indiana required no proof of pregnancy and punished an attempted abortion even if pregnancy did not exist. Rhode Island, New Jersey, Pennsylvania, Delaware, Maryland, North Carolina, Georgia, Florida, Kentucky, Tennessee, Iowa, the District of Columbia, and South Carolina had no antiabortion statutes.[50]

Although South Carolina had no law, doctors there did not heed Storer's call. Physicians differentiated nonetheless between "abortion" (miscarriage) and "criminal abortion."[51] Dr. Myddleton Michel of Charleston wrote an article for the *CMJ&R* entitled "Poisoning by Ergot in Attempting Criminal Abortion," admitting that information on how to procure such an abortion was widespread.[52] Still, the SCMS did not petition the state legislature to ban abortion. Several factors may explain this inaction. First, a dispute between Storer and the editors of the *CMJ&R* in the early 1850s may have made many SCMS members reluctant to support him. The controversy centered on Storer's address to the Massachusetts Medical Society in which he argued that physicians must divulge any illegal or immoral actions taken by patients. The *CMJ&R* regretted being "forced to take exception to, and enter a protest against, the views expressed by Dr. Storer, in reference to the alleged obligation of the physician to reveal secrets that are entrusted to his professional safeguard." Patient confidentiality must remain paramount.[53] Second, SCMS members remained unconvinced by his argument that middle- and upper-class white married women resorted to abortion. Third, the nativist rhetoric Storer employed was not particularly applicable to the South. Last and more salient to SCMS abeyance was the outbreak of the Civil War and Reconstruction during the height of Storer's campaign. Because the war and its aftermath brought less disruption to the North, Storer and other physicians were able to continue their legal campaign.[54]

To further this campaign Storer, with AMA support, drafted an "ideal" law for states to adopt. In *Criminal Abortion in America* (1860) he recommended that laws eliminate women's immunity: "The part played by the mother, herself so often a victim, is almost always that of a principal, yet as the law now stands, she can scarcely ever be reached. . . . If the mother does not herself induce the abortion, she seeks it, or aids it, or counsels to it, and is therefore . . . fully accountable." Abortion to save the woman's life should occur only if two physicians concurred on its urgency; this stipulation would deter women from convincing a friendly doctor to perform an unnecessary abortion. Storer's law removed quickening, established equal guilt for abortions performed at any time and by any means, and imposed stiff sentences.[55] Storer hoped physicians would convince states to enact his measure (see appendix C).

In 1864 he convinced the AMA to offer a prize for the best essay by a physician to educate American women on the evils of abortion.[56] Not surprisingly, *Why Not? A Book for Every Woman* by Storer won in 1865. The AMA circulated copies of this tract to the public.[57] Nativist anxieties pervade *Why Not*. Referring to the loss of American lives from the Civil War, Storer asked, "Shall they be filled by our own children or by those of aliens?" "This is a question that our own women must answer; upon their loins depends the future destiny of the nation."[58] The perceived threat to Protestant hegemony weighed heavily on the minds of crusaders, especially in light of the differential fertility rates between immigrants, most of whom were Catholic, and white Protestants.[59]

Most contemporary observers claimed that the vast majority of women who sought abortions were Protestant.[60] Perhaps these critics overestimated the incidence of this practice, especially because many physicians at this time designed their reports to influence state legislatures and public opinion. Moreover, because the majority of Catholic immigrants were probably too poor to consult allopaths, these doctors would have had little knowledge of Catholic abortion practices. Physicians' fears of Protestant reproductive rates falling behind those of Catholics undoubtedly fueled the campaign, which included a vested interest in the continued Protestant domination of society.

Despite the religious dimension of abortion, religious leaders generally remained silent. One anonymous minister who was also a physician criticized abortion in an 1855 tract: "ABORTION: the writer regards that practice as essentially immoral."[61] Few others joined his condemnation. In 1860 Storer declared: "We are compelled to admit that Christianity itself, or at least Protestantism, has failed to check the increase of criminal abortion."[62] Several factors may explain this silence: some religious leaders avoided addressing sexuality, some adhered to the quickening doctrine, some refused to believe their followers terminated pregnancies, and others realized the existence of the practice among their members and avoided adopting an unpopular position. Organized religion offered limited support to the antiabortion movement, especially compared to the active role assumed by some religious leaders in the twentieth century.

Ironically, the first religious endorsement came from a Catholic leader. Until the mid-nineteenth century the Catholic Church accepted abortion prior to quickening, the point at which church leaders believed "ensoulment" occurred. The church also accepted abortion to save the mother's life. Some individual church leaders permitted abortion in rape cases or other "extenuating circumstances," but this stand was not official policy. A change began in 1854, when Pope Pius IX affirmed the immaculate conception of Mary and emphasized the sacredness of motherhood.[63] Bishop John B. Fitzpatrick of Boston sent a letter to Storer in 1858 praising the crusade: "It affords me great pleasure to learn that the American Medical Association has turned its attention to the prevention of criminal abortion." Storer printed the letter in his antiabortion tract *Criminal Abortion in America*.[64] In view of Storer's anti-Catholic sentiment, his decision to duplicate the letter is interesting. It could represent his desire to demonstrate Catholic aversion to abortion versus Protestant practices and thus confirm his allegations to his audience. Alternatively, it could suggest his need for legitimacy among religious leaders. No further backing followed for almost a decade.

The Congregationalists broke through Protestant reticence. The Reverend John Todd of Massachusetts denounced abortion in "Fashionable Murder," which appeared in the journal *Congregationalist and Boston Recorder* in 1867. Todd, who knew Storer from the Berkshire Medical Institution, shared Storer's nativist sentiments. In response to increasing immigration he wrote that "God has given this continent to the strongest race on earth, and to the freest and best educated part of that race, and I do not believe he is going to let it drop out of hands that can handle the globe, and put it into hands that are hands without educated brains."[65] Several other Congregationalists crusaded at the state level. The Reverend E. Frank Howe addressed his church in Terre Haute, Indiana: "It is with extreme reluctance that I touch the subject, not simply because of its delicate nature, but because I cannot doubt that an evil so wide-spread, has invaded my own church and congregation. . . . The sacred gift of human life is taken . . . and this constitutes . . . murder." He called for the "preacher [to] join hands with the honest physician" to end this horrible "crime."[66] *Satan in Society* called on religious leaders to add their "powerful voice" to the campaign.[67] In 1869 Presbyterians pledged to help eradicate abortion. The same year the Old School Presbyterian Assembly, a splinter group, rejected a similar resolution. Thus, by no means were Protestants united in opposition. In fact, one doctor was astonished to receive a letter from a "clergyman of great influence in the community" who was seeking advice on how to obtain an abortion for his wife, demonstrating that abortion was not solely a woman's concern.[68] Catholic archbishop Martin John Spalding of Baltimore, on the other hand, confirmed Catholic unity, denouncing abortion in the wake of a bishops' meeting. In 1869 church doctrine stated that anyone performing an abortion would be excommunicated from the church.[69]

The antiabortion crusade influenced some states, especially those with large immigrant populations, to modify statutes. In 1845–46 New York became the first state to abolish the mother's immunity; the law also deemed the abortion of a quick child as manslaughter in the second degree. This law passed at the same time that large numbers of Irish landed in New York and on the heels of the much-publicized death of Mary Rogers from an "abortion gone awry." New York removed the quickening doctrine in 1869.[70] Massachusetts passed its first antiabortion statute in 1845. Two years later it enacted the first law in the nation that prohibited the advertisement or distribution of abortion-related materials. In 1869 legislators conformed to Storer's recommendation to eliminate proof of pregnancy to prosecute. Virginia proscribed abortion in 1848 and enforced a five-year jail term if it occurred after quickening but only one to twelve months if before. The state abolished this distinction in 1873. California outlawed all methods of abortion at any stage of the pregnancy in 1849–50 and eliminated the mother's immunity in 1872. Louisiana regulated abortions produced by drugs and potions in 1856; in 1870 it prohibited all methods.[71] Connecticut followed AMA guidelines in 1860, removing the quickening distinction, banning advertisements, deeming the practice a felony, and eliminating women's immunity. Pennsylvania's 1860 statute also adhered to AMA guidelines: requiring no proof of pregnancy, it outlawed abortion by any means at any stage of gestation and held mothers liable for prosecution. Ten years later Pennsylvania prohibited the advertisement or distribution of all materials related to this "crime." In 1868 Maryland banned abortion at any period of the pregnancy and sentenced offenders to three-year jail terms.[72] South Carolina banned the procedure in 1883, apparently without the assistance of the state medical society. The

Medical Society Minutes of the SCMS from 1880 to 1884 make no mention at all of abortion.[73] Delaware in 1883 deemed the operation a felony, considered the attempt grounds to prosecute, and prohibited the advertisement and distribution of materials.[74]

Other states, primarily in the South, adopted less stringent measures. Alabama's first abortion statute (1840) made it illegal only if performed after quickening. In 1866 the legislature stiffened the penalty from three to six months to three to twelve months, hardly a drastic alteration. Mississippi's 1848 law deemed abortion of an "unborn quick child" manslaughter in the first degree and attempted abortion of a quick child manslaughter in the second degree. This law remained unaltered into the twentieth century. While Georgia proscribed abortion in 1876, it distinguished between punishments assigned for quick and unquick operations. The state considered the former a felony punishable by death or life imprisonment and the latter an assault with intent to murder.[75] North Carolina's 1881 law differentiated between quick and unquick as well, with the former a felony punishable by one to ten years' imprisonment and the latter a misdemeanor with a sentence of one to five years.[76] Kentucky remained the only state with no abortion law in the nineteenth century and did not adopt one until 1910.[77]

Although the physicians' crusade did not succeed in all states, in general it influenced the actions of many legislatures that had also experienced Know-Nothing success in the 1850s. Both campaigns drew on nativist fears of immigrants destroying Protestant hegemony, an anxiety not as relevant to Southern as to Northern states. Between 1860 and 1880 forty antiabortion statutes passed legislatures: thirteen states or territories outlawed it for the first time, while twenty-seven broadened existing measures. By the end of the century the United States had evolved from a society that placed few restrictions on abortion to one that strictly regulated the procedure.

Feminist Reaction

Most feminists did not oppose new regulations that restricted women's ability to control reproduction. Feminists did not view abortion as a symbol of autonomy. In fact, they denounced it as vehemently as Storer and his followers but considered men, not women, the threat to the social order because male demands for sex led to undesired reproduction for women. Feminist protests were less concerned with abortion per se than with the circumstances that compelled some women to resort to abortion.[78]

Henry C. Wright in *The Unwelcomed Child* (1858) enunciated the earliest feminist position. He believed women resorted to abortion because of the overbearing selfish sexual demands of husbands. Because women refused "to bear the cross and endure the crucifixion," abortion was an undesirable necessity. To avoid abortion women must have full access to contraceptives because "woman, alone, has a right to say when, and under what circumstances, she shall assume the office of maternity." He contended that husbands kept information from wives about how they became pregnant as a way to keep them in slavery.[79] Feminists in the National Women's Suffrage Association (NWSA) agreed. In the NWSA newspaper, *Revolution*, Elizabeth Cady Stanton argued that the growing incidence of abortion did not reflect the increasing independence of women but the "degradation of woman" at the hands of tyrannical husbands. Although she and other feminists could understand a woman who resorted to abortion under certain circumstances, they did not condone it. They hoped the practice would disappear if marriage reform brought egalitarian respect and sexual discretion among couples. Women were not the culprits, Mathilda E. J. Gage argued; rather, "this crime of 'child-murder,' 'abortion,' 'infanticide,' lies at the door of the male sex."[80] Even free-love advocates refused to endorse abortion. Free-love philosophy demanded the right of both men and women to choose sexual partners based on mutual love without church or state interference. They considered abortion a repulsive end to which women resorted because of the repressive nature of the marriage institution.[81]

Free lovers and feminists rejected not only abortion but also contraceptives. Contraception was artificial and allowed men the privilege of sex on demand both inside and outside marriage. Instead, they advocated abstinence and "Voluntary Motherhood," a late-nineteenth-century feminist slogan that emphasized reproductive autonomy for women while at the same time exalted their role as mothers. Darwin's ideas permeated Voluntarism: pregnancies resulting from mutually willing intercourse would produce healthy, stable children and thus advance the race; those conceived during involuntary sex were at risk of becoming criminals, idiots, or paupers. The reality of abortion was problematic for women reformers who assumed the high moral ground in condemning male sexual transgressions through the Voluntary Motherhood campaign, which accepted the notion that women engaged in sex primarily for childbearing purposes.[82]

Family limitation—either by voluntary motherhood, contraceptives, or abortion—did affect fertility by the end of the century, with the white TFR dropping from 7.04 in 1800 to 3.56 in 1900. In 1900 50 percent of educated black wives and 25 percent of all black women were childless, despite restrictions on abortion and contraceptives.[83] The lack of organized feminist opposition to state restrictions on abortion eased the task of doctors in pressuring legislatures to criminalize this practice and in keeping these laws on the books, although even a vocal feminist outcry would have had little influence on male legislators in the political culture of the time.

What impact did this change in policy have on women? It banned abortion and attempted to reinforce traditional marital relations and obligations. It also reflected progressive philosophy by enacting legislation to "solve" perceived societal problems, including issues previously considered private. Yet the campaign did not eliminate abortion. Instead, it restricted access to women with money and connections or to women desperate enough to chance back-alley procedures. While legislative exemptions to save a woman's life allowed private doctors of middle- and upper-class women to provide safer abortions, lower-income women lacked this recourse. Laws also brought the possibility of incrimination, imprisonment, and social ostracism for both women and physicians who breached newly accepted codes of conduct. The popular press avoided any overt material on abortion, although veiled advertising continued in magazines and newspapers. Ultimately, the late nineteenth century witnessed a decline in the caliber of accessible contraceptive information, but a competitive black market in devices continued to thrive.[84]

The Case of Rhode Island

Many of the changes that occurred on the national level from the 1830s to the end of the century can be seen in a microanalysis of Rhode Island. In the early period abortion and contraceptives were relatively commonplace. By midcentury the Know-Nothing Party dominated the state and heeded the RIMS's call to ban abortion. Contraceptives, on the other hand, remained legal into the twentieth century. The geopolitical situation of Rhode Island helps explain the path legislators chose regarding reproductive legislation.

The Cornell/Avery case in the 1830s was one of the first in the state to deal with abortion. Sarah Cornell first encountered the Reverend Ephraim K. Avery when he was pastor of a Methodist church in Lowell, Massachusetts, where Sarah was a mill operative. Avery charged her with lying and fornication; she wrote letters of confession to Avery, which he kept, and he excommunicated her in 1830. He later assumed the pastorship of the Methodist Church in Bristol, Rhode Island; she relocated to Fall River. Cornell and Avery, a married man with children, met again at a camp meeting in Thompson, Connecticut, in August 1832. When she asked him to recommend her for membership in the Methodist church of Fall River under the pastorship of the Reverend Ira Biddle, Avery informed her that there was "one condition on which" he would "burn" the letters of confession and "settle the difficulty." He proceeded to place his hand on her bosom and "then had a connexion with her." In other words, he would not alert Biddle to her previous excommunication if she had sex with him. Seduced "under the mask of religion," Cornell "finally surrendered herself" and became a member of Biddle's church.[85]

In October Cornell visited Dr. Thomas Wilbur of Fall River, who told her she was pregnant. She informed Wilbur that Avery was the father but that she would not publicize her pregnancy because she did not want to ruin his reputation or embarrass his family. Cornell sought the aid of a lawyer to compel Avery to support her and the child in a clandestine fashion. Avery attempted to convince Cornell to take a "medicine" called "oil of tansy" that would "at once obliterate the effects of their connexion." Before ingesting the potion Cornell returned to Wilbur's office, where he alerted her to its life-threatening potential. While tansy water, tansy tea, and essence of tansy were used for abortion, he indicated that oil of tansy should "never" be used because it caused death or serious lifelong health problems. She responded, "Then I won't take it; for I would rather have my child and do the best I can with it than endanger my life" (7, 44, 45).[86] She was not opposed to abortion per se, just to a life-threatening procedure.

Her resolve led Avery to meet her in December, at which time he beat her about the belly and lower back, hoping to induce a miscarriage but instead killing her. Although counsel for the state did not believe that Avery arranged the meeting with the express intent of murder, he "might have been suddenly induced to take her life by the dreadful state in which his cruel attempts at producing abortion by violence may have left her." He tried to conceal the murder by hanging her from the rafters, implying that she had committed suicide (50). His plan failed: a note in her trunk said, "If I am missing inquire of Rev. Mr. Avery of Bristol, he will know where I am gone" (16). Apparently, Cornell met Avery under the assumption that he had made arrangements for her seclusion for the remainder of her pregnancy.[87] Police arrested Avery but released him until trial. He fled to New Hampshire and disguised himself, but he was found and brought back to Rhode Island.[88]

The resulting trial in May 1833 received national attention and "created excitement unprecedented in the history of our State." Three million members of Methodist churches awaited "anxiously to know whether a minister who stood high among them be guilty of the crime of murder" (4).[89] The community was outraged that Avery might have used his influential religious position to seduce a woman, force her to abort her fetus, and ultimately murder her. The transcripts of the trial do not ask whether Cornell agreed to this last abortion attempt. The consensus was that Avery forced it upon her to save his marriage and his reputation. The state portrayed her as a poor factory girl, blackmailed into a sexual liaison by a powerful man willing to take any action, including abortion and murder, to save himself. One state witness remembered that shortly before Cornell's death she asked if "a girl innocently" could "be led away by a man in whom she puts much confidence, and rather looks up to; . . . what can a poor innocent girl do in the hands of a strong man, and he, too, using all kinds of arguments?"[90]

The main tactic of the defense, one still commonly employed, was to defame Cornell's character and portray her as a vengeful woman. The defense also endeavored to depict Cornell as a disreputable woman, and an undeserving victim. Avery's lawyers contended that she was suicidal and hanged herself, which the state proved was impossible. As W. M. R. Staples, counsel for the state, surmised, Avery's lawyers asked that their client be dismissed because of "his good character. Bad character of deceased."[91] Their opening statement claimed that from "her strange conduct and conversation, the appearance of her eyes, and from other circumstances, she was generally considered to be deranged. We will lay before you the history of this girl's lewdness and misconduct for fourteen years." Doctors testified to treating Cornell for the "most loathsome disorder" of "venerial disease" (17). One witness claimed that Cornell had blackmailed a man into believing that she was pregnant and buying her silence. Others testified that Cornell had been "to a tavern with a gentleman on [the] Sabbath" (23), that she had stolen a "piece of cambric" (24), that she had engaged in "improper conduct" when she "patted" a young man on the shoulder (25), and that she had displayed "very unbecoming" behavior when she once "put her arms round" the neck of a "respectable man" (27). Still others testified that she was a "loose woman" and that "her character was generally bad" (31). As counsel for the state concluded,

> I cannot forbear remarking on that large portion of the testimony and argument for the defense which has been directed against the character of the unfortunate deceased. The efforts made for this purpose are I believe unexampled in the records of any capital trial. For the last ten years of her life every lewd or improper act which she either did or confessed to have done; and every passionate, remorseful or indiscreet expression which she uttered, have been collected, collated and brought forward for the purpose of endowing her with motives for suicide and revenge. (49)

The defense depicted Cornell as unworthy of sympathy and credence.

Avery participated in this smear campaign. Following Cornell's death, he instructed a man named Stephen Bartlett to go to Lowell and "obtain information respecting the bad character of the girl." Bartlett testified that Avery desperately needed "evidence to rebut the charges which might be brought against him. He said she had a revenge against him for expelling her from the church at Lowell, and had laid this trap for him" (12). As soon as Avery realized that his staged suicide had been exposed, he defended himself by defaming Cornell's character and undermining her credibility.

The defense also argued that Cornell was already pregnant by the time of the camp meeting, implying that Avery could not have been the father. Much of the trial was devoted to determining the age of the fetus, an eight-inch, five-ounce female. Had Cornell become pregnant at the camp meeting, the fetus would have been three months and twenty days old. The defense introduced doctors to testify that a fetus this size must be at least five months old. Cross-examination, however, led the doctors to admit uncertainty and that the pregnancy could have occurred at the camp meeting, as Cornell said (6, 19). The defense asserted that Cornell's "lewdness" affected fetal growth: "I think we shall satisfy you that the children of women of bad fame, of diseased women, and of those who indulge in promiscuous intercourse are smaller than the children of other women; that the deceased at the period of her death must have been pregnant five months or more" (17). This strategy failed when Cornell's sister and roommate testified that Cornell had had her period one week prior to the meeting (13). The defense responded with doctors claiming that some women did have periods after pregnancy and with witnesses claiming Cornell was visibly pregnant at the meeting. The Reverend Henry Mayo swore she was pregnant even though he "did not see her front" (19). Several women agreed: Cornell's "countenance was pale and sickly," and her "bosom was rather full" (20). The state discredited them. At four to six weeks pregnant "her pregnancy could not . . . have been perceived or suspected . . . from external appearances" (30). Mayo's wife testified that "I saw nothing in the appearance of Miss Cornell at Thompson, that warranted the remark by my husband" (50). Although the defense undermined its own case, the jury found Avery not guilty.

The Cornell/Avery case is interesting for several reasons. First, the records attest to the rigorous pressures that forced women to conform to accepted codes of conduct. Numerous people who had encountered Cornell over the years took steps to shape her behavior and punish her for her transgressions. Brooks Shaddock, manager of a Lowell factory, fired Cornell because he "was satisfied she was not a good character." He told her she must confess to Avery about her "intercourse with different individuals," but when "she did not go . . . I went and told him myself" (23). Nathan Howard of Northwich, Massachusetts, believed Cornell's character to be good until he heard rumors "of her having illicit intercourse with different men" (23). He informed Avery and pushed for charges against her in the Methodist church. Dr. William Graves of Lowell treated Cornell for venereal disease in 1830 and, disregarding patient confidentiality, informed Avery (22). This betrayal dismayed Cornell: Dr. Noah Martin of Great Falls testified that when Cornell came to him (Graves had not cured her), she bemoaned the fact that Graves had broken her confidentiality. Another witness testified that Cornell had "complained of [Graves] having violated his professional confidence in speaking as he had of her disease." Graves may have taken this step to force Cornell to leave the community to save his own reputation. Cornell told one person that Graves "had attempted to take improper liberties with her." She told another that Graves "had closed the door, and insulted her, threatening to report that she had the foul disease, unless she complied with his importunities." A third witness said Graves "locked the door, put his hand round her waist, and told her she was a pretty girl." When Cornell rejected his advances, he "threatened if she did not comply with his wishes to inform Mr. Avery that she had the bad disorder" (22, 26, 27). This information led Avery to charge her with fornication and expel her from the church.[92] He then wrote to the Reverend John Dow of Somersworth, Great Falls, where Cornell had moved, conveying the information about her "fornication and lying" charges and her venereal disease and calling her a "common strumpet." Her actions so offended Dow that he ignored traditional church rules of readmittance following proof of "contrition and repentance" and refused to accept Cornell in his church even on a trial basis (26). At the camp meeting Avery and others "agreed that it was our duty to inform the people at the tent where she boarded of her character" (29). These men controlled women's behavior and acceptance in a given community through economic reprisals, sexual exploitation, and religious ostracism.

Second, the case exemplifies some of the dangers single young women faced in nineteenth-century American cities. Rhode Island cities were in a sea of change brought by industrialization and urban growth, which stimulated economic transformations, cultural diversity, and tensions over accepted gender roles. Cornell's life and death in many ways were similar to those of Mary Rogers and Helen Jewett, two young women who died violent deaths in New York City. All three were single, sexually active women who enjoyed the excitement and peril of antebellum urban culture. As such, they were a threat to the gendered social norms of the period: engaging in sex as a single man was a rite of passage; the same behavior for a single woman defined her as an immoral tramp and ruined her and her family's reputation. Both Rogers and Cornell died from an "abortion gone awry." Jewett and Cornell had both left family behind in rural areas as they set off for the city; both were seduced and abandoned, Jewett by a businessman rather than a minister. Both men wielded power and influence over single unprotected young women. Jewett, who turned to prostitution, was brutally murdered.

Jewett and Cornell shared enough similarities that their wax figures appeared together in a traveling East Coast exhibit of famous murder cases. In all three cases no man was held legally responsible for the deaths.[93]

Third, the case demonstrates how the Methodist Church closed ranks in support of Avery (not unlike the Catholic Church prior to the sex scandals of 2002). Members of the New England Conference of the Methodist Episcopal Church found Avery not guilty. They concluded that he was not the father of Cornell's child because they accepted the concerted smear campaign against Cornell. Because he was not the father, he could not have been involved in the abortion attempts. They ignored the evidence against Avery, accepted the testimony of defense doctors, and resolved that Avery should continue in his ecclesiastical privileges and ministerial office.[94]

Fourth, this case sheds light on doctors' knowledge about pregnancy and birth control in the 1830s. Based on the testimony, no medical consensus on pregnancy existed. Dr. Usher Parsons, lecturer on obstetrics in Providence and Philadelphia, argued that women could suspect their condition in six to eight weeks, but there was no definitive proof until quickening, which occurred at three to four months. Misogyny was rampant in his testimony. "The foetuses of women of very lewd characters are generally supposed to be smaller than those of virtuous women." He concluded that "promiscuous intercourse is certainly a well known preventive of impregnation" (20). Only virtuous women could be blessed with motherhood. His colleagues did not agree: promiscuity had no bearing on conception. Dr. Nathaniel Miller of Franklin, Massachusetts, displayed knowledge of the rhythm method: women were most likely to get pregnant within the "first week or fortnight after menstruation than at a later period in the month." The first sign of pregnancy was the "cessation of the menstrual discharge," which could then be used to judge the time of impregnation. He did not mention quickening. Dr. William Turner of Newport argued that the early sign of pregnancy was "equivocal quickening, which generally takes place at the middle of the fifth month," much later than Parsons believed (19–21). Despite an active medical society in Rhode Island, these doctors did not agree on the basic facts.

Finally, reports of the trial paid little attention to abortion. Abortion was not illegal in Rhode Island at the time, and Wilbur's testimony confirmed that knowledge about certain abortifacients was common. Cornell did not mention to Wilbur any objection to abortion, nor did he try to convince her that she must carry the pregnancy to term. He simply warned her about the dangers of Avery's proposed method. The records do not disclose whether they discussed safer methods. The state, however, concluded that Avery, not Cornell, decided to abort the fetus to avoid accepting responsibility for his actions. This belief in male power over decisions to abort foreshadowed later policy developments in Rhode Island. While historian Carroll Smith-Rosenberg concludes that doctors, ministers, and others pointed to aborting women as independent, strong-willed, selfish, "unnatural and monstrous . . . , lethal to men and babies alike," women in Rhode Island were generally considered victims of male manipulations.[95] Men, not women, were held responsible for abortion.

Such attitudes were prevalent in the 1830s records of the Ladies Moral Reform Association of Rhode Island. They condemned abortion because it allowed men to "cloak their sins" and because it "invaded the sanctuary of the home." The high incidence of abortion in Rhode Island appalled these women: "Aware, as we all must be," they wrote, of the "increasing facilities for beguiling the wary and the unprotected," these women committed themselves "to stay this rising and swelling tide of abomination."[96] This theme of women as victims of male seducers pervaded popular tracts and works of fiction in the 1840s. As historian Amy Gilman Srebnick argues, for some of these authors abortion symbolized "the end of innocence for the virtuous republic."[97] But such works as well as the endeavors of the Ladies Moral Reform Association had no impact on state policy.

One reason for the lack of legislative change may have been the state tradition of not regulating medical matters. During the colonial period Massachusetts, Connecticut, and New York, among others, enacted numerous laws suppressing quacks, regulating inoculations, and quarantining ships. Rhode Island, however, passed only a 1743 law to prevent the spread of infectious diseases.[98] Legislators therefore grew up in an atmosphere where medical decisions, presumably including abortion, remained a matter considered outside legislative jurisdiction.

Through the 1840s and early 1850s few people in Rhode Island openly opposed abortion. Advertisements for abortion remedies appeared regularly in newspapers and journals. The *Rhode Island Medical Reformer: A Family Journal for the Promotion of Health and Longevity* advertised "female restoratives" (a common nineteenth-century term for abortifacients) among the list of medications a family might need. The Davol Manufacturing Company of Providence competed nationally in the field of autoabortive instruments. The bylaws of the Providence Medical Association for 1855 listed abortion as a common procedure done for twenty dollars.[99] Yet after receiving the letter from AMA President Miller as well as a copy of Storer's *Criminal Abortion in America* in 1860, the RIMS pressured the state legislature to adopt an antiabortion statute in 1861.

Why did most Rhode Island physicians modify their attitude toward abortion? Although pressured to conform to new AMA guidelines, nativist assertions seem to be key. Rhode Island experienced rapid economic growth between 1830 and 1860. Industrial expansion required cheap labor, a demand satisfied primarily by immigrants. Many communities resented their intrusion. The 1850 census provides evidence of a significant change in the state's ethnic composition. In 1828 only 237 foreigners lived in Rhode Island. Over the next fifteen years the influx remained very low. By 1850, however, the alien population had reached 23,902, or 16 percent of the total residents. During the next decade immigration accounted for half of the total population increase. The state census of 1865 reported that foreigners according to nativity numbered 39,703 (21.46 percent of the total population) but according to parentage numbered 67,649 (36.57 percent). The great majority were Irish Catholics. Fewer than one thousand Catholics, both native and foreign, lived in Rhode Island in 1835. By 1854 nearly ten thousand lived in Providence alone, and Catholicism had emerged as a major denomination in urban areas.[100] These circumstances contributed to the popularity of the Know-Nothing Party in the mid-1850s. Making its first showing in the 1854 election, it swept state elections in 1855 and 1856. From 1857 to 1861 a coalition of Know-Nothings and the newly formed Republican Party dominated the General Assembly and state offices.[101]

The presence of the Know-Nothing Party in the General Assembly in 1860–61 influenced the first antiabortion law. Storer's nativist arguments prompted the RIMS to draft a bill and lobby for its passage. Dr. Edwin Snow of the RIMS underlined every passage in Storer's gift copy of *Criminal Abortion in America* dealing with declining white Protestant fertility rates due to abortion and all statements discussing foreign inundation. When Storer's book went into print, Rhode Island had no statute on abortion, a fact mentioned in his essay. Snow noted on its back cover: "R.I. has good Statute now. Law in R.I. obtained through influence and action of State Medical Society."[102] The consensus among doctors by the 1850s that the fetus was alive from conception versus quickening may have also influenced its passage, although Snow made no mention of this aspect in his notes. Nativism was the deciding factor for him.

Yet relative to AMA guidelines, the 1861 statute set fairly liberal standards (see appendix D). Although it excluded references to quickening and banned all methods of abortion, it imposed only one year in jail or a one-thousand-dollar fine. While adhering to Storer's recommendation to allow abortions to preserve the mother's life, the measure failed to ban advertisements for abortions or for abortifacients, probably a result of lobbying by the Davol Manufacturing Company. The law also rejected Storer's wish to eliminate women's immunity.[103] This exemption could be the result of two factors. First, legislators may have believed eradicating abortion would be easier if women could be compelled to testify against abortionists. Immunity denied women the right to invoke the Fifth Amendment privilege against self-incrimination. Second, male legislators may have disagreed with Storer's conclusion that women were to blame for abortion. Most men in the legislature in the 1860s would have been teenagers or young men during the Cornell/Avery scandal. That case could have biased them to believe that men were the more responsible party.[104]

On 14 March 1867 the legislature revised the 1861 statute in line with AMA guidelines (see appendix E). It increased the penalty to five to twenty years if the woman died and one to seven years if she did not. It also prohibited advertisements and publications as well as any verbal communication regarding abortion methods or locating abortionists. Yet it maintained women's immunity from prosecution—an immunity they retained into the twentieth century.[105] Storer was unable to persuade legislators that women were the culprits in the ethnic and religious fertility imbalance. In light of the AMA's desire to eliminate this "unnecessary" and "invalid" protection Rhode Island was exceptional, one of only two states that retained this clause. The wording of the act seems to confirm male legislators' belief that women did not willingly undergo abortion but were coerced by men. The law convicted anyone "advising or prescribing for such woman or causing to be taken by her . . . or [of] counselling and procuring" an abortion. It also stated that "the woman whose miscarriage shall have been caused or attempted shall not be liable to the penalties" of the act.[106] The important emphasis here is *causing* and *caused*, again implying that some outside force was responsible.

This stand conflicts with what Smith-Rosenberg and others conclude regarding the physicians' antiabortion campaign. Smith-Rosenberg argues that physicians persuaded the white male power structure that abortion undermined patriarchal control. They portrayed white middle-class females who sought abortions as unnaturally independent and argued that, through abortion, women repudiated the role of motherhood that men expected of them. Physicians participated in the antiabortion movement in part to return women to the home, reversing their growing tendency to enroll in college or participate in reform movements. White bourgeois doctors correlated abortion and contraception with female promiscuity and recalcitrance.[107]

Rhode Island legislators, however, appeared unconvinced by such rhetoric, if, in fact, it was employed in the state campaign. Unfortunately, Rhode Island has never kept records of legislative sessions; the only evidence regarding the doctors' crusade are tracts at the RIMS that confirm the national crusade's nativism but do not reflect the misogynistic tone that Smith-Rosenberg finds.[108] The wording of the 1867 law also does not reflect such misogyny, although the law could be interpreted as paternalistic: legislators did not seem to believe that women would reject motherhood without being forced to do so by men. Women were unempowered victims in need of legislative protection.

The 1867 act was also significant because of a unique section dealing with the murder of pregnant women and infant children. Any person charged with the murder of a pregnant woman could also be charged with abortion. If a jury acquitted on murder, the state could still prosecute for abortion.[109] Perhaps this stipulation was a result of the Cornell/Avery case. Under the new law the state could have gone after Avery for abortion despite the not-guilty verdict on the murder charge. The stipulation dealing with the "murder of any infant child" allowed the state to charge for murder *and* abortion. If the jury found a defendant not guilty of murder, they could still convict "him" of abortion. This stipulation confirmed legislators' adherence to the woman-centered notion of pregnancy versus the fetal rights obsession of the late twentieth century. Even after birth an infant was not always entitled to the full rights of citizenship. The act implied that an infant was as dependent on its mother for survival outside as inside the womb.

Again, such attitudes conflict with those uncovered by other historians analyzing bourgeois notions of pregnancy. They find that a desire to control female behavior dominated antiabortion tracts. Misogynistic writings asserted that the uterus was there to serve the fetus, the mother becoming a vehicle. She had no more control over her fetus than the father. In fact, some tracts claimed that because the male's sperm was more powerful than the egg, he had a more pronounced impact on the fetus than the mother. Moreover, physicians contended that the womb caused women to make illogical decisions; Storer and others believed that hysterectomies solved all women's mental disorders. The antifeminist rhetoric used by crusaders demonstrated their hostility toward women's reproductive powers.[110] Yet in Rhode Island legislators do not appear to have been swayed by such propaganda.

Thus, the misogyny stressed by other historians is not as universal as some might suppose. Similar to trends in Rhode Island, the records and minutes of the SCMS do not reflect misogyny. Physicians in South Carolina seemed genuinely concerned with women's health. Some physicians contended that the fetus should be considered the "enemy of the mother" if it endangered her life: "Placed in the cruel alternative of choosing between the life of her infant and her own preservation, the woman has, by the law of nature, the right to decide upon the mutilation of the foetus." Dr. Michel criticized practitioners who "ignorantly . . . administered" substances to procure an abortion that "too often . . . destroyed" the mother when her "only desire was to shelter her[self] from harm and secure her[self] from shame." His statement clearly sympathizes with women facing tough choices. Other members of the SCMS advocated abortion to preserve women's health: it was their "duty to resort to the measures under consideration" to ensure the "rapid and complete" recovery of their female patients. The editors of the *CMJ&R* lambasted doctors who allowed a pregnant Charlotte Brontë to suffer "morbidly severe" symptoms and eventually die in 1855 rather than perform an abortion: "It was the duty of the physician to remove the cause, viz: *to remove the fetus from the womb*." The *CMJ&R* subsequently argued that abortion should be used more frequently to preserve the mother's health and criticized doctors who regarded the child's life above that of the mother, especially when "the life of the child is so much regarded" that "women are exposed to more risk for its preservation."[111] Thus, the misogynistic antiabortion tracts did not lead to a medical consensus on this issue. Many doctors prioritized their patients' health, not fetal protection at all costs.

The alliance among bourgeois men to which Smith-Rosenberg refers must have been on shaky ground.[112] While confirmation of misogyny does exist, it is countered by evidence of men—doctors, ministers, and others—who were sympathetic to women, willing to attack male colleagues, and concerned with women's health and rights. This latter recognition can be seen in Rhode Island legislation regarding reproduction as well as in other progressive laws in that state. Married women had rights to divorce, to establish life insurance for their own benefit, and to sign contracts as early as the 1840s.

Rhode Island was also one of only a few states that did not prohibit contraceptives. When the federal government passed the Comstock Act in 1873, banning the distribution and mailing of any information concerning birth control or abortion, most states followed suit with laws passed within the context of antiobscenity and social purity crusades. Rhode Island passed an antiobscenity law on 14 May 1897, but it did not mention contraceptives.[113] The state never restricted access to or information on birth control. This liberal stance remained in force throughout the twentieth century, despite the state's large Catholic presence. The passage of the abortion bills in Rhode Island cannot be attributed to Catholic pressure, because the church could have exerted its influence to prohibit all birth control. Its failure to do so could reflect ethnic divisions among state Catholics that prevented the church from speaking in one voice and/or the Protestant domination of the state legislature.[114] The passage of these bills represented larger forces at work in state politics.

An explanation for both the immunity of women and the lack of contraceptive restrictions may be the unique location and size of Rhode Island. Not only was it the smallest state, but large ports dominated Providence, Newport, Bristol, and Narragansett Bay.[115] Rhode Island had a concentrated naval presence: the United States Naval Academy moved from Baltimore to Newport during the Civil War because of security concerns, and the Naval

College located there in the 1880s. Legislators may have been apprehensive that the loose sexuality among sailors as well as foreign traders could lead to liaisons with local women. The lack of contraceptive regulation could have been an effort to halt the spread of venereal disease—a growing anxiety when Rhode Island passed its obscenity law absent any ban on birth control—and to prevent pregnancy among seduced and abandoned women. Immunity from prosecution for abortion could have been a result of legislators' concern that transient men would coerce women to undergo abortion.

How Successful Was the Antiabortion Campaign?

Despite attempts to eliminate abortion, the practice remained prevalent and continued to draw attention from critics concerned with the constitution of the American population.[116] Doctors surmised that two million procedures occurred annually.[117] Admitting to these statistics must have been discomforting: they implied that the AMA campaign was not as successful as they had hoped.

This sense of failure led some doctors to launch a second antiabortion campaign in 1895. Leslie Reagan argues that they implemented a three-pronged approach: convincing women of their wrongdoing, revoking the licenses of physicians who performed illegal abortions, and working with officials to enforce existing statutes and use "dying declarations" to root out abortionists. Some doctors refused treatment until the woman divulged the abortionist's name. The censuring of physicians' behavior took place behind the closed doors of medical societies, while criticism of midwives' abortion practices took public stage. Despite efforts, abortion continued. Between 1876 and 1920 the Providence County Coroner's Office investigated nineteen deaths caused by abortions; 8 were married and 11 were single women.[118] Presumably, many more were done safely. Although this campaign failed, the Catholic Church endorsed it. In 1895 church policy no longer accepted abortions to save the mother's life, elevating the fetus over the woman. Protestants and Jews, on the other hand, continued to condone life-saving abortions, in line with AMA guidelines and mainstream sentiment.[119]

The turn of the century saw abortion debated in medical journals. As with earlier discourses, no consensus existed. Similar to Rhode Island legislators, Dr. Denslow Lewis of Cook County Hospital in Chicago blamed men, not women, for abortion. Women resorted to this procedure because capitalists exploited them with such meager wages that they had to seek supplemental food, clothing, and entertainment from male companions, leading to unintended pregnancy. Subsequent male desertion caused women to transform their "usual sentiment of affection and of joy" regarding motherhood into a "feeling of aversion." He criticized Christian hypocrisy for shunning these women rather than assisting them with "emotional support." Such sympathy was not present among the editors of the *Medical Age: A Semi-Monthly Journal of Medicine and Surgery*: abortion was murder because life began at conception; aborting women were criminals deserving punishment. Dr. Thomas G. Atkinson disputed this conclusion as well as the notion that legal protection should be extended to the fetus in utero from conception: the fetus had no independent life until it left the mother's body; thus, the mother's, not the fetus's, interest was paramount. Others disagreed, asserting that "the child must be saved at almost all costs," in part due to "the sharpening of the moral sense" but also to race suicide: "The instinct for self-preservation—in a society with a declining birth rate . . . is at the root of this new tenderness for the lives of our children."[120] In other words, while a growing appreciation for infant and even fetal life influenced some antiabortionists, population concerns continued to play a role in shaping attitudes on abortion among white elites. Physicians, as part of this elite, did not speak in one voice.

Major tracts, the *New York Times*, and Rhode Island cases point to abortion as a continuing problem in the North.[121] The South drew little attention. Abortion laws in many Southern states were generally more lenient and continued their adherence to quickening. As such, Southern women ostensibly could obtain legal, safe abortions early in their pregnancy. Data from Winston-Salem, North Carolina, demonstrate that abortion remained a resort of many white married women.[122] SCMS physicians, however, rarely mentioned abortion in the post-Reconstruction era. When they did, they discussed it as a practice to which some black women resorted. But even here there was no consensus. Dr. Prioleau informed the SCMS of his belief "as to the greater tendency of mulattos to abort than shown by whites." Dr. Kinloch, however, responded that in his opinion "blacks seldom abort."[123] Centering discussion of this "immoral" business on race fit well within the late-nineteenth-century Southern context. Southern elites attempted to separate the races physically and morally. By pointing to blacks as the main culprits in abortion, they further distanced white women from their black counterparts.

Conclusion

The physicians' campaign succeeded in altering abortion laws, but it failed to suppress the practice for several reasons. Many state laws retained proof of pregnancy. Procuring such proof in the nineteenth century made indictments for abortion virtually impossible. According to Dr. Whitehead, "the only positive proofs . . . of pregnancy [were] those afforded by the movements of the foetus in utero, being communicated to the sense of touch."

Reliance on such a nonscientific method caused problems for prosecutors. The latter also rarely found anyone willing to testify that an abortion had occurred. Those performing the operation often swore that they did not realize the woman was pregnant and had treated her for irregularity or blockage. Women usually admitted that an abortion had been performed only if they found themselves in an emergency situation and believed they were near death.[124] Both abortion-seeking women and abortion providers had a stake in foiling prosecutors' attempts to enforce the law. Although the physicians' campaign transformed abortion statutes, loopholes allowed most people to escape prosecution.

Regardless of the legislative success of the campaign, abortion continued as a means of birth control. Women across the nation, both married and single, resorted to this form of fertility control. Although the AMA was the driving force behind the crusade, doctors did not speak in one voice: some believed abortion to be murder under any circumstances; others argued for abortion to save the mother's life and protect her health; and a minority expressed sympathy for women seeking abortions due to economic exploitation, seduction, or abandonment. While misogyny influenced both doctors' and legislators' attitudes, this sentiment may not be quite as prevalent as some historians have noted. A growing interest late in the century to protect children extended to the fetus in some minds, and medical advances that suggested life began at conception rather than quickening also entered the discourse on abortion.

By the turn of the century the debate over abortion and interest in pursuing abortionists died down. The *Reader's Guide to Periodical Literature* from 1890 to 1930 lists only four articles dealing with abortion, while the *New York Times* index for 1897 to 1917 lists two. Yet the preoccupation with fertility imbalance between "best" and "inferior" stock did not disappear. The early twentieth century witnessed a strong, vocal movement to convince WASP women to abandon fertility control to preserve American Anglo-Saxon culture. Race suicide theorists shifted attention from abortion to birth control as a primary cause of racial decay.

Race Suicide, Eugenics, and Contraception, 1900–1930

The rhetoric of racial suicide emerged in the mid-nineteenth century in re-action to differential birthrates between white Protestant Americans and Catholic immigrant women. It expanded by the turn of the century to differ-entiate between the "fit" or "best" and the "unfit" or "undesirable." The former included white, wealthy, educated Protestants, while the latter referred to the poor, uneducated, criminals, diseased, mental and physical "defectives," and ethnic, racial, and religious minorities. Arthur W. Calhoun, an early-twenti-eth-century historian, claimed that the "desire to prevent conception [was] general among the people of the aspiring middle class," but the condition was "most extreme among native Americans of the upper classes." Historian Arthur Schlesinger Sr., noted that the use of contraceptive devices produced "a reversal of the principle of natural selection, for the progeny of poor and undernourished parents multiplied while the better-nurtured classes barely held their own."[1]

This naive understanding of natural selection and social Darwinism was common among twentieth-century advocates of population control—a term not synonymous with birth control. Groups associated with the former were concerned mostly with the class, ethnic, and racial implications of popu-lation growth, especially the possibility that the lower classes would over-populate and destroy the American "race." Birth control, on the other hand, denotes individual control over reproduction. The continued decline in fer-tility among middle- and upper-class white women persisted despite doctors' success in criminalizing abortion, the federal government's ban on circulat-ing birth control information through the mails, and censorship eliminating contraceptive discussion from marital guides. Race suicide theorists, there-fore, launched a campaign to reduce the fertility of the "unfit" and "undesir-able" and to increase the number of children born to the educated white Protestant middle and upper classes. With the exception of new legislation to sterilize "defectives," however, the laws remained unchanged. Women per-sisted in their quest to control their own fertility with both birth control and abortion, while population controllers influenced by race, class, and gender biases persisted in their quest to shape the population along lines suitable to the white elite establishment.

Race Suicide Arguments

The specter of race degeneration haunted the writings of many prominent officials and social critics across the political spectrum. The term *race* as employed by nineteenth- and early-twentieth-century scientists and race suicide theorists was vague. It could pertain to the color, class, religion, or geographic origin of certain groups.[2] When race suicide theorists referred to the American race, they usually meant white, educated, financially secure, Protestant citizens. In the 1880s Samuel W. Dike, a Protestant minister, re-former, and sociologist, expressed fear over the declining birthrate among the "native stock." He found that in Massachusetts foreign women averaged 50 percent more children than native women. In an 1891 article in the *Nation* William Potts, a liberal and cofounder of the Free Religious Association with Ralph Waldo Emerson, wrote that in financially secure families "the numbers become stationary, then decline, and finally the families themselves . . . be-come extinct."[3] Census director Francis A. Walker, who considered himself a "social scientist" intent on controlling demographic trends through con-certed planning, found immigration partially responsible for the annihilation of native stock. The "excess of foreign arrivals" in the nineteenth century "constituted a shock" to the native element.[4]

Some radicals took up the banner. In a 1905 investigation of New Eng-land, Robert Hunter, a member of the Socialist Party, found that the annual increase of children to foreign parents was ten times greater than that to native parents; the annual death rate of natives exceeded the birthrate by 1.5 per 1,000, while the annual birthrate of immigrants exceeded the death rate by 44.5 per 1,000. He deduced that "the annihilation of the native ele-ment is only a matter of time" and warned that "the direct descendants of the people who fought for and founded the Republic [were] being displaced by the Slavic, Balkan, and Mediterranean peoples." The high fertility of groups with "alien" religions directly threatened Anglo-Saxon heritage in the United States.[5]

Hunter exemplified the new twentieth-century race suicide theorist in that he added a class perspective to a formerly cultural concern. In addition to high immigrant fertility, race suicide theorists feared the extraordinary birthrate among the poor and uneducated classes. Hunter predicted that the "poorest classes" were the "greatest population-producing classes" and would eventually cause the "annihilation" of the "wealthiest class."[6]

Such arguments influenced prominent figures, including Theodore Roosevelt. He believed that the Yankee upper class should provide the economic and political leadership of the country and was distressed that wealthy white Protestants had the lowest birthrate in the nation. Roosevelt set out to convince the upper classes of their duty to increase childbirth. In an early statement (1895) he argued that Yankee women who refused to proliferate were "cold and selfish." The only way to preserve the race was to "subordinate the interests of the individual to the interests of the community," an interesting comment in light of its socialist implications. Two years later he commented on his abhorrence of the "pronounced tendency among . . . the most highly civilized portions of all races, to lose the power of multiplying."[7] As president, Roosevelt used his position to sway public opinion. Addressing the National Congress of Mothers in 1905, he condemned the "viciousness, coldness, [and] shallow-heartedness" of women who sought to avoid their "duty." He denounced these women as decadent and branded them "criminal against the race."[8]

While the tendency toward small families prevailed among the wealthy, journalist Lydia Kingsmill Commander found in 1907 that only "the most ignorant and irresponsible," particularly immigrants, made no effort to limit their children. One doctor she interviewed stated, "The Irish, the Germans, and the Italians go ahead and have children. We are depending on our poor foreign element for our population." Poverty-stricken German and Irish immigrants, dependent upon public and private assistance, had the largest families. Commenting on "distressingly prolific" foreign patients, a doctor argued that American leaders should have barred immigrants because they constituted the "poorest imaginable material for making Americans" but would soon constitute the majority.[9] By 1900 more than ten million foreign-born lived in the United States, and one or both parents of more than fifteen million were born outside the country. Between 1900 and 1907 approximately four million foreigners, many of them poor Jews, Catholics, or Eastern Orthodox, came to the United States, prompting William Z. Ripley to ask, "Is it any wonder that serious students contemplate the racial future of Anglo-Saxon America with some concern? They have seen the passing of the American Indian and buffalo, and now they query as to how long the Anglo Saxon may be able to survive."[10]

Publication of the 1910 census added fuel to the fire. It showed that immigrant women's fertility was significantly higher than that of native-born women. Within the immigrant population, the birthrate of southern and eastern European immigrants, the least "desirable" of that continent, exceeded that of northern and western Europeans.[11] In Rhode Island a 1912 headline claimed: "Providence Approaching Race Suicide Condition: DECREASE CAUSES CONCERN." Of 5,662 births in Providence the previous year, only 1,521 (26.8 percent) had two "American" parents; 145 (2.5 percent) had two black parents; 2,944 (51.9 percent) had two "foreign" parents; the remainder had mixed "American" and foreign parentage. Italians alone accounted for 1,520, just one shy of "American" births. The article lamented the decline in native American births, including those to black parents, in the face of foreign inundation.[12] No racism toward blacks was apparent; such hostility was reserved for immigrants.

This attitude was apparent in Roosevelt's speech at the Pacific Theological Seminary in the spring of 1911. He asserted that "two-thirds of our increase now comes from the immigrants . . . not from young Americans who are to perpetuate the blood and traditions of the old stock." By 1911 Roosevelt no longer attributed race suicide to immigrants alone. Rather, he blamed the "wrong type" of people (aliens, the poor, the uneducated, criminals), who reproduced at alarming speeds, while the "proper" stock sustained an artificially low birthrate. In an article in *Outlook* the same year he wrote:

Criminals should not have children. Shiftless and worthless people should not marry and have families which they are unable to bring up properly. . . . In our civilization today, the great danger is that there will be failure to have enough children of the marriages that ought to take place. What we most need is insistence upon the duty of decent people to have enough children, and the sternest condemnation of the practices commonly resorted to in order to secure sterility.[13]

Whereas before he had urged native-born women in general to increase their family size, now he encouraged only the "proper" natives to "save" the race.

Roosevelt was not alone in his anxiety. Robert Reed Rentoul, a British eugenicist who supported infanticide for defectives and controlled fertility among the indigent, gained an audience among some Americans.[14] In *Race Culture or Race Suicide?* (1906) he asked, "If . . . a nation has its population recruited, not from those who are physically, mentally, financially able to have and to bring up the best stock, but from the poorer classes, what can be expected of the coming race?" He answered, "Nothing but evil. . . . No nation can survive if its population be recruited from slumdom." The Reverend John Scudder of Jersey City advocated the forced limitation of poor families and other "undesirables" in society: "Inveterate paupers, hopeless drunkards, incorrigible criminals, insane and idiotic people . . . should be denied the privilege of reproducing their kind. A birth forbidden by law should be considered as a criminal offense and the parents should be punished by fine or imprisonment."[15] Advocacy of such harsh penalties was unusual, but many urged serious measures be taken to slow the growth of the poor and "undesirable" and to increase the "fit."

Yet many upper-class whites, the "fit," did not consider their small families a national menace. Commander found they restricted family size because they believed the "secret of success" was "education and training." With fewer dependents, parents could guarantee financial security for children. Wealthy and highly educated parents generally had the increasingly common two-child norm among this class.[16] College women married later and less often, and they had fewer children than non-college-educated women, a trend developing since Reconstruction. The Boston Association of Collegiate Alumnae indicated that just 25 percent of students from twenty-three area colleges had married. Only 16.5 percent of Radcliffe's 1900 class had married by 1909.[17] Many of these women presumably chose a career over marriage and children—a choice race suicide theorists condemned.

That declining birthrates among the educated and wealthy resulted from voluntary restriction was of little doubt. Charles F. Emerick, a professor of biology, concluded that the "diminishing birth-rate [was] primarily volitional." Dr. Charles Harrington, an American sanitarian, also found that the decline was due to "artificial and purposeful and not natural causes." Octavius Charles Beale, author of *Racial Decay* (1911), compared the situation in the United States to that of the Greek and Roman empires, which fell not by conquest but "from an intentional decline in their fertility" that reduced their populations. In the *Journal of the American Medical Association* (1907) Dr. J. Newton Hunsberger agreed and, similar to Roosevelt, believed women's "curse of selfishness" would destroy the national character.[18]

The distress over race suicide was a reaction to social transformations in family size and gender relations. Economically, children in urban areas no longer fulfilled the role they had played in an agricultural society. In fact, they constituted an economic drain in light of growing expectations for higher education. Feminism played a role as well: the Victorian woman gave way to the Gibson girl and the "Modern Woman," many of whom were more interested in pursuing higher education, careers, and reform activities than in marriage and families. Race suicide theorists viewed this shirking of motherhood as "unnatural" and detrimental to the race.[19] Many men felt threatened by rapid changes affecting their daily lives. Temperance and antiprostitution campaigns criticized male behavior. Suffrage and women in the workforce undermined the male culture of politics and office work. Business consolidations forced the closing of many small firms, leaving middle-class men dependent on large firms for employment.[20] Pushing white middle- and upper-class women into the home as mothers preserved male hegemony over higher educational and professional opportunities. Women with young children could not realistically compete with men for respected career openings.

Eugenics in the United States

Race suicide arguments captured adherents of eugenics, a social philosophy that became popularized after the works of Gregor Mendel, an Austrian monk and botanist, and August Weismann, a German biologist, on genetic mutation and germinal continuity. Their hypotheses asserted that germinal plasma transmitted hereditary but not acquired characteristics. Francis Galton, a British statistician, leader of the eugenics movement in his country, and cousin of Charles Darwin, originated the term *eugenics* from the Greek word "eugenes," meaning "good in birth," and defined it as the "science of improving stock." Galton also influenced eugenics' incorporation of social Darwinist theories, which held that people were locked in a sociocultural struggle in which those who had wealth and power possessed the biological superiority to survive. Eugenicists proposed a solution to the problems of race degeneration: encourage breeding among those with "desirable" and discourage it among those with "undesirable" traits.[21]

Recent historians have dispelled the notion that geneticists frowned upon eugenics. Labeling eugenics a pseudoscience supported by naive followers and genetics a true science supported by respected scientists, according to Marouf Arif Hasian, Jr., treats eugenics "as a temporary aberration, an irrational political appropriation of genetics." But as Diane B. Paul has found, "every member" of the editorial board of *Genetics* (founded in 1916 in the United States) supported eugenics. Charles Davenport, a champion of eugenics influenced by Galton and others, founded the Eugenics Record Office in Cold Spring Harbor, Long Island. At the same time, he produced significant genetic work on Huntington's chorea and on traits such as skin and eye color. Hasian argues that genetics did not move "unilinearly out of the dark ages of ignorance and toward the light of scientific progress." It remained intertwined with eugenics well into the post–World War II period. It was not a belief held only by a few elites but one in which a "substantial percentage of the Anglo-American public believed."[22]

In the early twentieth century eugenics gained a diverse audience, in part due to its ambiguous nature. Eugenicists agreed on heredity but not on which traits were inheritable. They agreed on the need to improve the race but not on the methods to achieve this goal or who should choose them. Hard-line eugenicists, heavily influenced by Weismann's theory that germ plasma is unmalleable, called for controlled reproduction or coerced sterilization as

a "final solution." As biological determinists, hard-liners rejected environmental, educational, or parental influence on children's development. They
inundated the public with claims that the good of society superseded any individual right to reproduce. Some endorsed infanticide for defective babies,
while others advocated the killing of older "imbeciles." Moderate or reform
eugenicists and millions of Americans believed in the need to improve the
race but not necessarily through the coerced sterilization of those deemed
unfit. Reform eugenics accepted the influence of education and other social
programs as well as parental behavior. As Hasian argues, the "very lack of
univocality meant that its goals could be construed in many ways. . . . Eugenics was part of dozens of local projects, including better-baby contests,
improved parenthood programs, control of race poisons, conservation of
resources, women's temperance movements, and even military preparation
for war." Children learned of reform eugenics in school, church, and scouts.
Adults and children encountered it at state fairs and exhibits throughout the
early decades of the twentieth century.[23]

While physical traits were important, eugenicists were primarily concerned
with nonphysical traits: intelligence, character, and morality. In the mid- to
late nineteenth century the degenerative theory stated that the feebleminded
and mentally ill posed no significant threat to the race because they generally
disappeared within four generations. By the turn of the century hard-line
eugenicists had rejected this theory: inherited defective genes presented a
menace to the race. Both hard-line and reform eugenicists believed the problem could be handled because experts could discern mental defects through
physical attributes such as a low brow, a small head, or grossly protruding
ears. Psychologists had dispelled such notions by the 1910s, when they determined that attractive, "normal"-looking humans could also be mentally
deficient, a condition defined by the new term *moron*. Morons were more
threatening to the race than "groveling idiots" because the former were quite
liable to procreate.[24]

The eugenics movement received a boost from family studies. Richard
Dugdale, an executive committee member of the Prison Association of New
York, assessed the inmates of the state prison system. He traced the Juke
family through five generations, concluding in his 1877 report that they had a
startling inclination for poverty and crime and that the public had spent $1.3
million to support them. Dugdale was a reform eugenicist: while criminality
could be inherited, the environment also shaped behavior. Thus, he advocated
public health programs and increased education for children. Early-twenti-
eth-century hard-line reevaluations of the Juke family, however, concluded
that this family demonstrated the need for sterilization or sexual segregation,

not social programs.[25] Similar reports of family depravity among poor "white trash" advocated their sterilization.[26]

The eugenic notion of racial improvement through population control gained an audience among professionals, particularly intellectuals, scientists, and physicians. These mostly elite white men believed, according to historian Mark Haller, that "college-educated, native, white Protestants (like themselves) were the bearers of the valuable genes of society."[27] Wendy Kline argues that eugenics attracted professionals because it could halt the "moral and racial decay" they decried. It also implied a new twist on motherhood: only wealthy white women had an inherent right to procreate. "Womanhood was double-edged," argues Kline, because women could be the "mother of tomorrow" or the "moron" who "symbolized the danger of female sexuality unleashed." As such, women could be "responsible not only for racial progress but also for racial destruction."[28] In 1903 university biologists cooperated with agricultural breeders to form the American Breeders Association Committee to Study and to Report on the Best Practical Means of Cutting off the Defective Germ Plasm in the American Population (ABA). Three years later the ABA established a committee on eugenics "to investigate and report on heredity in the human race [and] to emphasize the value of superior blood and the menace to society of inferior blood." Davenport's Eugenics Record Office became the ABA's main propaganda agency, and human breeding was its main focus. In 1913 the ABA became the American Genetics Association and concentrated on the study of genetics and eugenics. Many eugenicists received financial backing from foundations, and they affected state and federal policy concerning a host of issues, from immigration to sterilization.[29]

Several reasons account for the acceptance of eugenics by some Americans. First, its emphasis on the permanence of human inequalities sustained assertions of Anglo-Saxon superiority. Second, eugenics supported a two-part program: positive eugenics encouraged the "best stock" to reproduce; negative eugenics discouraged reproduction among undesirables. Contraceptives should be distributed to the latter but avoided by the former. Eugenics warned that excessive breeding of the "unfit" and avoidance of conception by the "best stock" would lead to race degeneration. Eugenics, therefore, converged with popular notions of race suicide. Third, it suited progressive reformers' belief in scientific principles and government intervention to correct the worst abuses in the social, economic, and political realms. Eugenicists advocated government intervention based on scientific philosophy either to sterilize or segregate "undesirables." Eugenicists offered simple answers to some of the problems with which progressives were struggling, including poverty, crime, and the mentally or physically handicapped. Eugenic attempts to raise robust, intelligent offspring meshed well with progressive attempts to eliminate tuberculosis, diphtheria, and venereal disease and to reduce maternal and infant mortality. Eugenicists and progressives alike believed the race would benefit from the propagation of the "fit" and decreased fertility among undesirables.[30]

Eugenics attracted other groups as well. White middle-class educated women believed in state intervention to protect the family from prostitution, pollution, ignorance, poor nutrition, and "morons." Thousands of women served as field workers collecting data for family studies that hard-liners used to justify segregation and sterilization. Other women hailed eugenics for its emphasis on improving the race and its importance in choosing mates and becoming good parents. Yet some feminists, while enticed by reform-eugenic emphasis on the health and fitness of mothers and children, bristled at talk of saving the race at the expense of women's individual liberty. Catholic leaders opposed sterilization and birth control but supported sexual segregation and "race betterment" programs: because the environment shaped heredity, programs should help the poor and working class. Hard-liners disagreed, believing such programs wasted time and money. For blacks eugenics was "a sword that cut two ways": through education and other social programs blacks could improve themselves and their children; but hard-line eugenics provided ammunition for racists to deny blacks access to educational and political power. Psychiatrists supported eugenics for "professional reasons," not race prejudice. With most psychiatrists working in asylums, eugenics offered them comfort: their patients failed to improve because of defective genes, not inadequate treatment. Eugenics also extended psychiatrists' role outside the asylum, allowing them to be part of progressive and scientific reforms and therefore gain legitimacy for their specialty within the medical profession. Many working in asylums became hard-liners until World War I.[31]

Eugenics attracted followers across the political spectrum. It appealed to conservatives interested in class and race. Many Marxists, according to Diane Paul, supported "the improvement of the genetic stock of the human race through selective breeding." Eugenics rejected laissez-faire and called for state intervention in reproduction. The right of every man and woman to bear children was too individualistic; the good of society, including race preservation, must be protected. Marxists supported eugenics as long as it stressed heredity, not class or race biases.[32] Yet such biases remained, evidenced by calls for restricted immigration. Foreigners flooded northern urban almshouses. This problem paled in comparison to the animosity among native-born workers who faced job competition from immigrants willing to work for subsistence wages. The Knights of Labor called for immigration restrictions in 1892, as did the American Federation of Labor in 1894. Xenophobic groups backed these demands. Eugenicists joined the campaign, arguing that immigrants disproportionately came from "defective" stock. These combined efforts brought restrictive legislation before Congress between 1890 and 1924.[33]

Increasing state marriage restrictions also reflected racial purity. Although miscegenation had taken place throughout American history, many believed it was rising dangerously in the post–Civil War period. Numerous states prohibited whites from marrying anyone with "one-sixteenth or more of Negro blood." Some western states prohibited marriage between whites and Asians. Eugenicists expanded restrictions to include epileptics, imbeciles, and the feebleminded unless the woman was forty-five or older. Connecticut passed the first such law in 1895; by 1913 twenty-four states, the District of Columbia, and Puerto Rico had followed. Many eugenicists, however, considered the laws ineffective because they believed the feebleminded lacked the morality to wait for marriage to procreate.[34] The International Congress for Eugenics, held in London in 1912, discussed solutions to the "dilemma." More than three hundred people, mostly Europeans and Americans, attended. Americans included Davenport; Alexander Graham Bell; Charles Eliot, president emeritus of Harvard; and David Starr-Jordan, president of Stanford. The final session of the conference dealt with means to advocate the multiplication of the "fit" through eugenic education and to obviate "unfit" propagation through sterilization and sex segregation.[35]

Numerous works in the 1910s called for lifetime segregation of "defectives." Some argued that their high prolificity posed a financial, institutional, and societal strain. Building on antebellum state mental hospitals, eugenicists called for "custodial colonies" to segregate the "village idiot." Eugenic demands transformed state institutions' rationale from safeguarding the afflicted to shielding society from "defectives," especially their potential offspring. This new goal generated funds for the construction or expansion of institutions. H. H. Goddard's 1908 "intelligence quotient," or IQ, test made specifying inmates easier. The use of this test in schools, prisons, the military, and poorhouses as well as on Ellis Island led society to perceive feeblemindedness as a burgeoning problem that segregation alone could not handle. The difficulty with segregation was twofold: many parents spurned it, due either to devotion or to the desire to employ mildly retarded children; and eugenicists identified far more people who should not breed than institutions could accommodate. By the 1910s they estimated that 10 percent of the population carried the recessive trait for feeblemindedness. These "normal"-looking people were a real danger if they married another person with the recessive trait and then conceived a feebleminded child. The expense to detain individuals solely to prevent their propagation became prohibitive. A cheaper, permanent solution was to eliminate their ability to reproduce.[36]

Sterilization

While both geneticists and eugenicists believed in sterilizing the feeble-minded, the former resented the latter's claims that this procedure would solve the population problem. At best, it could reduce feeblemindedness by 10 percent. But it did demonstrate the ability to restrict parenthood. The earliest recorded cases in the United States date to the late 1890s. In 1898 the trustees at the Kansas State Institution for Feeble-Minded Children approved the work of Dr. F. Hoyt Pilcher, who castrated forty-four boys and sterilized fourteen girls because the board considered them "unfit." When local newspapers carried the story, public outrage over castration forced Pilcher to resign. Castration, however, laid the basis for more acceptable methods of sterilization.[37]

During the late nineteenth century European doctors developed new sterilization techniques. The vasectomy eliminated male reproductive powers while preserving pleasure, just as the salpingectomy did for women, although the latter procedure was more risky. Dr. A. J. Ochsner, chief surgeon at St. Mary's Hospital in Chicago, performed the first vasectomy in 1897. He believed the vasectomy provided a civil means by which to eliminate "hereditary criminals," alcoholics, "imbeciles, perverts, and paupers." Despite the lack of scientific proof that these traits were genetically controlled, Ochsner's logic took hold among eugenicists.[38]

Between 1899 and 1912, for example, Dr. Harry Sharp of the Purity Society of Indiana and medical officer at Jefferson Reformatory carried out on his own initiative at least 236 compulsory vasectomies. Writing to the *Eugenics Review* in 1912, he stated that he had "operated on many against their will and over their vigorous protest" and "without administering an anesthetic either general or local." He acted without legal sanction. Sharp encouraged his colleagues to petition legislatures to allow male sterilization in prisons, reformatories, and institutions for the feebleminded, resulting in many pros-terilization medical tracts.[39]

Not all doctors supported sterilization for eugenic purposes. In a study of Stockton State Hospital in California, Joel T. Braslow found that doctors sterilized patients because they "saw sterilization, not as an instrument of the state to prevent the procreation of the insane, but as a therapeutic intervention to alleviate individual suffering." Doctors believed the procedure had great "psychological benefits" in protecting mentally impaired women from the strain of childbearing and childrearing, "a goal women often shared with their physicians." Doctors maintained that sterilization had "a direct and positive biological effect" on men: it diminished manifestations of manic-depressive psychosis and dementia praecox. These doctors consulted patients and acted in their interests; eugenicists ignored individual will.[40]

Individual will was easier to ignore once states passed sterilization laws. In 1897 Michigan proposed but failed to pass the first such law.[41] In 1907 Indiana enacted the first statute, which allowed a board of experts to order the sterilization of state-institutionalized idiots, imbeciles, convicts, and rapists.[42] Between 1907 and 1913 sixteen states passed laws: governors vetoed four, and twelve became law. The responsibility for these laws lay with some zealous doctors who informed state legislators about vasectomy. Legislators hoping to diminish criminal activity and costs embraced these experts' advocacy of a method less brutal than castration. Eugenic sterilization never became a grassroots movement but remained an elitist answer to perceived social and economic problems. Even some eugenicists rejected sterilization except as a last resort. In the 1910s Davenport and Paul Popenoe, author of *Applied Eugenics* (1918), believed sterilization was un-Christian because it allowed officials to sterilize the feebleminded and then discharge them to fend for themselves, which many could not do. They believed segregation was more humane.[43] Family members' reaction varied. Some spouses sanctioned it as a means of permanent contraception. Other family members accepted it because they believed in the therapeutic impact. Some supported it because institutionalized patients could be discharged and rejoin their families. Others refused to consent because they were unwilling to accept the responsibility. Some repudiated sterilization because it implied a genetic defect in their family line.[44]

Many sterilization laws faced legal challenges. While eugenic theories influenced many state legislators, far fewer judges and scientists were convinced. Between 1913 and 1918 state courts declared seven of the twelve laws invalid because they instituted cruel and unusual punishment, violated due process, or constituted punishment without a trial. Judges required evidence that the procedure would benefit the individual, not society. Some scientists also challenged the laws, attacking the naive view of inheritance promulgated by eugenicists, especially the notion of inherited criminality. These objections were only a minor setback for eugenic proponents. A second wave of legislation passed in the 1920s. Eugenicists benefited from rising xenophobia in the face of increasing southeastern European immigration and mounting anxieties regarding the migration of blacks to northern cities.[45]

Perhaps the most significant impetus for new state laws came from the Supreme Court's endorsement of sterilizing the "unfit" with *Buck v. Bell* (1927). Writing for the majority, Justice Holmes accepted the basic tenets of the eugenicists: mental defects and criminality were inherited; the fertility of mental defectives could overrun society with incompetence. Carrie Buck, he argued, was a potential parent of *"socially* inadequate offspring," and, as such, she could be "sexually sterilized without detriment to her general health and . . . her welfare and that of society [would] be promoted by her sterilization." Holmes believed that society had the right to "call upon those who already sap the strength of the State . . . in order to prevent our being swamped with incompetence." He argued that society should "prevent those who are manifestly unfit from continuing their kind."[46] Any concern over whether the procedure benefited the individual rather than society was noticeably absent from this decision.

Buck v. Bell increased sterilizations. Numerous judges based their interpretation of state laws on Holmes's findings. With this decision, Harry H. Laughlin, a former high school biology teacher from Missouri and now director of the Cold Spring Harbor Laboratories, gained the legitimacy he lacked in the early 1920s when he drafted a sterilization law that drew opposition from prominent physicians. He had approached the Mental Hygiene Association, the American Social Hygiene Association, and the Bureau of Social Hygiene requesting support for the publication of his work *Eugenical Sterilization in the United States*. While Dr. Thomas W. Salmon, Dr. William F. Snow, and Dr. Katherine Davis of the three organizations, respectively, found valuable material on state laws and court decisions on sterilization, none would help fund the book's publication because none wanted to be "responsible for that part of the book which had to do with direct propaganda favoring sterilization legislation." Salmon believed that Laughlin's law represented "the view point of only a relatively small group of persons in the United States." Following *Buck v. Bell*, Laughlin's model bill captured increased attention. Laughlin defined "a socially inadequate person" as someone who "fails chronically . . . as a useful member of the organized social life of the state." The "socially inadequate classes," which encompassed the feebleminded, delinquent, epileptic, blind or deaf, deformed, and "dependent (including orphans, ne'er-do-wells, the homeless, tramps and paupers)," certainly a broadly defined category, were subjects for state sterilization. This procedure, according to Laughlin, would save society from overbreeding the wrong people.[47] By the late 1920s twenty-three states had laws.[48]

Rhode Island did not jump on the bandwagon. Daniel F. McLaughlin (R) unsuccessfully introduced H 1050 in 1925. The bill defined a "mentally defective person" as "either an idiot, an imbecile, a feebleminded person, an epileptic, an insane person, or a person convicted of the crime of rape," procreation by whom would not be desirable or beneficial to the community. The bill would have empowered the secretary of the State Public Welfare Commission to recommend to the court for sterilization anyone "mentally defective." Three physicians would examine the candidate and testify to their findings. If the court determined the candidate defective, the state would pay for "such person to be eugenically sterilized."[49] While many state bills dealt with both eugenic and economic implications of sterilization (i.e., saving state money by reducing dependent offspring or by discharging sterilized inmates from institutions), McLaughlin's bill pertained only to eugenics. His interest was to save the community from the breeding of the unfit.

The failure of this bill cannot be attributed to the influence of the Catholic Church. Although church officials rejected sterilization, they more strongly opposed birth control and yet were not able to make that practice illegal in Rhode Island despite their strong presence. Other factors played a role. McLaughlin's law would have applied to anyone deemed unfit, institutionalized or not. This aspect may have been too harsh for many legislators. It would have applied to affluent patients in private homes or sanitariums rather than only to inmates of public institutions, as in some other states. Some legislators may have been leery of supporting a bill to benefit society at the expense of individual rights, a hallmark of Rhode Island legislation.[50]

Rhode Island was in the minority of states rejecting sterilization. Such repudiation did not distress most eugenicists; sterilization was only part of the solution. Race suicide theorists and negative eugenicists concluded that contraceptive knowledge must be made available to the "unfit." The problem with this strategy was the continued existence of the Comstock Law.

The Contraceptive Campaign

The federal government placed no restrictions on contraceptive devices and literature until 1873, when the lobbying efforts of Anthony Comstock culminated in the Comstock Act. Comstock jammed through at the end of a busy congressional session legislation that dealt with obscenity, vice, and crime. Congress passed the bill, and President Ulysses Grant signed it on 4 March 1873. The act's language was vague and rambling, yet Congress passed it swiftly, without discussion and without a roll-call vote. Many representatives did not realize that the act banned the distribution and mailing of any information concerning birth control or abortion. In 1876 the National Liberal League organized between forty and seventy thousand citizens to protest the Comstock Law as un-American, unjust, unwise, and unconstitutional because it enforced particular moral, religious, and medical opinions. Congress failed to repeal the law.[51]

The law forbade the distribution of information about, not the actual practice of, birth control. Moreover, it was rarely enforced, with few arrests and even fewer convictions. Many women continued to obtain borax, carbolic acid, and other substances with which to make homemade suppositories. A bootleg trade flourished among small entrepreneurs and large corporations that employed advertising language the public understood but that still shielded businesses from prosecution. While numerous contraceptive options were available, no government agency regulated or inspected these products, leaving the buyer to beware. Wealthy women obtained contraceptives from this black market but also from physicians who trusted them. Catalogs advertised IUDs and other forms of birth control within a medical context to avoid the ban. IUDs, for example, were to correct prolapsed uteri.[52] Poor women, who could rarely afford to see doctors, could not avail themselves of these options and relied on bootleggers and their often unreliable contraceptives. Those who needed contraceptives most in the eyes of race suicide theorists and proponents of negative eugenics had little access to affordable, effective methods.

The solution, according to these two groups, was to modify restrictive legislation. In 1916 Maurice Parmelee published *Poverty and Social Progress*. Claiming that the cries of racial suicide had gone unheeded by the upper classes, Parmelee recommended a campaign whereby the poor, "ordinarily too ignorant and too careless," would be taught how to regulate family size. Laws would have to be repealed: "While the abolition of this restriction will not increase the birth rate of the upper classes, it will doubtless lower the birth rate of the lower classes somewhat. The result will then be to increase the proportion of those who are alleged to be eugenically more desirable."[53] Similar arguments permeated magazines during the 1910s.[54]

Theodore Roosevelt claimed that the survival of the nation depended upon "encouraging the fit and discouraging the unfit" to breed. These eugenic terms were missing in his early writings on race suicide. In an article in *Outlook* (1914) he contended: "I wish very much that the wrong people could be prevented entirely from breeding," yet he refused to endorse contraception. He believed that if contraceptives were more easily available, the "best stock" would reduce their birthrate even more, while the "poor stock" would continue on their present path.[55] Roosevelt, however, was in the minority among race suicide theorists, who pressed for liberalized laws to balance birthrates between "fit" and "unfit."

Ironically, national feminist organizations avoided involvement in the movement to ease restrictions. Feminists were cognizant of the popular connection between contraception and sexual lewdness. Moreover, many feminists bought into the racist and classist doctrines of race suicide theorists.[56] The National American Woman Suffrage Association, the National Woman's Party, and the Women's Trade Union League assumed no role in the controversy and especially distanced themselves from any discussion of abortion.[57]

While no movement emerged to loosen abortion restrictions, two main groups lobbied for contraceptive liberalization in the 1910s. Eugenicists promoted it to protect the Anglo-Saxon character of the nation, while some leftists supported it as part of the class struggle.[58] The primary proponents on the left were Emma Goldman and Margaret Sanger. Goldman, an anarchist, saw contraception in economic rather than feminist terms; she wanted to help raise working-class wages and expand workers' political power. Unlike the male-dominated Socialist Party, which remained silent because it accepted woman's role as housewife and mother, Goldman actively supported contraceptives. Her writings display concern for the plight of workers. Fewer children would ameliorate their living conditions and allow parents to devote more time to the class struggle. In the inaugural issue of the *Woman Rebel* Goldman argued that "the defenders of authority dread the advent of a freed motherhood lest it rob them of their prey. Who would fight wars? Who would create wealth? Who would make the policeman, the jailer, if women were to refuse the indiscriminate breeding of children?" Goldman contended that "woman no longer wants to be a party to the production of a race of sickly, feeble, decrepit, wretched human beings. . . . Instead she desires fewer and better children, begotten and reared in love and through free choice."[59] Despite her advocacy of contraception, Goldman had little impact due to her reputation as a leftist agitator.

Sanger, on the other hand, had become an influential leader for contraceptive dispersal by the late 1910s. Sanger resented her role as a rank-and-file organizer within the Socialist Party. Her biographers as well as a number of historians have noted her strong ego and desire for attention. Her son Grant agreed: "There's no question about mother's ego. She always thought that her work was the greatest work in the world, and any other work was purely secondary."[60] This hankering for the limelight led Sanger to branch off from the Socialist Party in the mid-1910s and pursue full time the reform of laws.[61] Early on she employed feminist ideology: every woman had the right to decide without government interference whether to have a child. Her concern was for women who could not afford large families but had no access to contraceptives. Traditional historical accounts asserted that her concern for the poor made her hostile to the eugenics movement and that she maintained contact with its leaders only to gain their support for the reform of federal contraceptive legislation.[62]

Recent historiography suggests, however, that Sanger did accept eugenic ideas by the 1920s. Havelock Ellis, British psychologist, social radical, and proponent of free love, influenced her; according to Grant Sanger, she "was terribly in love with Havelock Ellis," and he served as her tutor for the year she spent in England.[63] Sanger's biographer, Ellen Chesler, concludes that Sanger "deliberately courted the power of eugenically inclined academics and scientists to blunt the attacks of religious conservatives against her . . . ; there is no denying that she allowed herself to become caught up in the eugenic zeal of the day."[64] Similarly, Angela Franks argues that Sanger "had a genuine commitment to the eugenic ideology . . . ; at no time did her belief in eugenics lag."[65] Many advocates of contraceptive liberalization, including Sanger, accepted eugenic tenets and wanted to join forces.

Sanger centered attention on legislation by deliberately defying the Comstock Law. In 1915 her distribution of contraceptive information to working-class women earned her an official warning. The following year she agitated nationwide to amend the federal law. She and her sister Ethel Byrne, both nurses, opened the first educational center in the Brownsville section of Brooklyn that distributed contraceptive information, not devices, to working-class women.[66] Ten days later the police arrested Sanger and Byrne for violating New York's version of Comstock. Sanger used her trial and imprisonment to capture attention for reform. While in prison she garnered sympathy from the public as a martyr severed from her children.[67]

By 1917 a variety of local and national organizations run almost entirely by women had fought for the legalization of contraceptives. Mary Ware Dennett established the National Birth Control League in 1915, but it did not reach beyond New York City and had disintegrated by 1919. Many other reform groups were affiliated with the Socialist Party or with local socialist societies, despite the party's opposition to contraception. In addition, the New York Woman's Publishing Company began to distribute the *Birth Control Review* in 1917, with Margaret Sanger as editor. Sanger published this periodical, which had over eight thousand subscribers, throughout World War I.[68]

Several events and trends show the growing acceptance of contraceptives in the 1910s. First, in 1916 two judges, one in New York City and one in Cleveland, released women accused of theft because they stole to feed their children; both judges spoke of the need to disperse contraceptives to the poor to prevent such situations. Second, the more liberal sexual climate eased the discomfort of requesting contraceptive advice. By the early twentieth century a growing number of women considered premarital intercourse acceptable in some situations, and a middle-class norm began to emerge whereby couples spent their early married years attaining financial and emotional stability prior to having children. An underground contraceptive network continued, circumventing both state and federal laws.[69] Third, the antiprostitution crusade prior to and during World War I increased the pressure for contraceptive liberalization. As sex gradually evolved from a danger to be controlled to a natural outlet for male and female passion, sexually active single women needed safeguards. Fourth, the prevalence of venereal disease increased the acceptance of condoms because of their dual role in preventing pregnancy and disease. Venereal disease affected not only men engaging in unprotected sex but also "innocent women," who contracted it through their husbands.[70] In July 1918 Congress created the Division of Venereal Disease in the U.S. Public Health Service with a four-million-dollar budget. That same year Judge Frederick Crane of the New York Court of Appeals ruled contraceptives legal as a public health measure if prescribed by a doctor. Drugstores ignored the latter aspect, and the condom business boomed under the guise of preventive health and medical necessity. Crane's decision opened the way for clinics to prescribe female contraceptives.[71]

These developments did not lead to wholesale approval of birth control. The growing acceptance of a female sex drive undermined some men's sense of marital security, and contraceptives were a convenient target for this anxiety.[72] Opposition also derived from contraception's unorthodox antecedents. Recognizing that the movement's early ties with leftist and socialist groups impaired its chance of success, Sanger severed them and altered tactics.[73] She abandoned feminism and adopted eugenics in her drive for reform.

During the 1920s Sanger's objectives included lobbying the federal government to amend Comstock and forming educational bodies that did not defy it. In November 1921 she organized the First National Conference on Birth Control in New York City at which activists laid plans for the establishment of the American Birth Control League (ABCL). The ABCL was to organize state leagues and local committees to make contraceptives accessible and to educate the public on their social and "eugenic" importance.[74] The average ABCL supporter was a white, Protestant, native-born, upper-middle-class, thirty-five-year-old housewife. More than half the members were Republicans; 17 percent were professional men.[75] Sanger incorporated the ABCL as an educational body under New York State law in April 1922 with the *Birth Control Review* as its official organ. In its first twenty months the ABCL received 11,525 calls and 132,000 letters requesting contraceptive information, drew 175,000 attendees to lectures across the country, and published 600,000 copies of the *Birth Control Review*. Because the ABCL could not distribute contraceptive information, it answered inquiries by explaining federal and state restrictions and encouraging people to write their legislators to insist on repeal.[76] The ABCL launched its own campaign with a letter strong in nativist and eugenic rhetoric to the federal government. It demanded the creation of a federal birthrate commission composed of scientists to study the problems "menacing the racial health" of the nation: "The stock which has made America a great nation (the sturdy old native stock with its vision, courage and high ideals) is being swamped by a different order of humanity, of which a huge proportion is biologically undesirable and will inevitably, through unrestrained breeding, work a vast change in the character of the population."[77] The immigration restriction of 1917 would not eliminate the threat to the race.[78] Only contraceptive distribution to undesirables would solve the problem.

Anxieties concerning immigration increased in the early 1920s. Although World War I temporarily halted the flow, after the war the numbers surged: 111,000 in 1919, 430,000 in 1920, and 805,000 in 1921. Many were of the "inferior" and "darker" populations of southeastern European countries. The Ku Klux Klan reemerged, and Congress passed immigration restrictions in 1921 and 1924.[79] Many Americans joined nativist groups. Two slogans spoke for millions—"America for Americans" and "One Hundred Percent Americanism."[80] The underlying factor, according to demographer Louis Dublin, was distrust of the newcomer, especially "the fear engendered by his greater fertility and rapid increase in numbers after his arrival." The 1920 census confirmed the continuing disparity between white native-born and immigrant fertility rates, a fact bemoaned by William S. Rossiter, statistician and chief clerk of the census.[81]

The 1920s also witnessed a recapitulation of statements concerning the birth differential between the "ignorant" poor and the educated rich. William L. Poteat, president of the North Carolina Society for Mental Hygiene, of the Southern Baptist Education Association, and of Wake Forest College, argued that "the alarming thing is that the upper grades of intelligence are not reproducing themselves, while the lower grades show an amazing fertility. . . . Now the enemies of society are recruited from this rapidly increasing lower section of the population, and it is not unreasonable that it will accomplish the overthrow of civilized society."[82] Others argued similarly. These doomsayers advocated population control—a concerted effort to manipulate population growth by distributing contraceptives among the "undesirable," which necessitated a repeal of the Comstock Law.[83]

Yet the federal government failed to amend the law. Why? For some, prudery prevailed. Attempting to uphold the outdated Victorian sex code, moralists believed that liberalized legislation would lead to increased pre- and extramarital sex. Some scholars contend that a liberalized law would have loosened the traditional bonds men had on women.[84] Without constant childbearing and childrearing burdens, women could compete with men in the public realm. Perhaps pronatalist attitudes played a role. In 1921 the Sheppard-Towner Act became the first federal legislative foray into welfare as well as pregnancy and childbirth, encouraging states to develop programs to benefit infants and mothers through grants-in-aid.[85] Population control advocates expressed concern over legislation that underwrote childbirth but did nothing to discourage it: the clinics established under this act did not provide contraceptive information. The Bureau of Social Hygiene (BSH), in particular, called for linking contraceptive clinics with prenatal, natal, and postnatal clinics, but the federal government refused.[86] The greatest barrier came from the Catholic Church, the AMA's failure to endorse a new bill, and the public's fear that easy access to contraceptives would worsen the difference in birthrates between the desirable and undesirable.

The Catholic Church's opposition to birth control remained firm.[87] In 1902 the church banned abortions even for ectopic pregnancies, and in 1917 a new policy excommunicated women who sought abortions. American cardinal James Gibbons reiterated the doctrine on birth control: "To defeat Nature in marriage is as criminal as to commit murder," he stated. "No excuse is possible—neither financial reasons nor any other. The question of economics has no place, should have none, in regulating the size of families. That Catholics are taught this explains why, as a rule, they have large families."[88] Father Ward, executive director of Organized Work Against Birth Control, stated that although "Birth Control has every appearance of being a real remedy for much poverty and disease, [it] is too material and sinful a remedy to be adopted by the Church." In an interview with Anne Kennedy, executive secretary of the ABCL, Ward asserted:

> The opposition of the Roman Catholic Church against Birth Control is based on the fact that there is only one true Church recognized by God. This is the Roman Catholic Church. . . . They are responsible for the morals of the entire human race; therefore it is their duty to interfere and block all legislation that will affect the morals of Catholics and non Catholics. . . . The Roman Catholic Church never loses the hope that non Catholics will be some day counted in the fold. Therefore, it is necessary to supervise all social and moral legislation.[89]

To enforce Catholic morality on American society, Ward and other priests not only used the pulpit but also developed a powerful lobby to defeat liberal bills that came before Congress.

Unlike the Catholic Church, the AMA did not attempt to block legislative reforms, yet its failure to endorse bills hindered the liberalization campaigns. Why did it hesitate to ratify a new bill? When nativist fears of the high immigrant fertility rate peaked in the 1850s and 1860s, the AMA responded with a campaign to outlaw abortion among wealthy Anglo-Saxon women; most state laws also banned the sale and distribution of contraceptive devices. Once the AMA had helped condemn these means of limitation, it was slow to reverse its position.[90] At Yale Medical School, for example, faculty taught that doctors should not disperse contraceptive information, even if a pregnancy would kill their patient. A report by the Committee on Maternal Health, organized by Robert L. Dickinson in March 1923 in New York City, observed that the conservative stand of the medical profession on contraception was not unique; it paralleled the profession's initial attitude toward tuberculosis, venereal disease, industrial hygiene, and health examinations. Physicians' reticence into the 1920s, according to Dr. Alice C. Boughton, executive secretary of the Committee on Maternal Health of the Academy of Medicine, resulted from several factors: inertia, an interest in disease rather than health, the potential loss of lucrative returns from obstetric services, and a lack of relevant training in medical schools.[91] The AMA's failure to endorse contraception wielded considerable influence because doctors increasingly dominated reproductive matters.[92] This failure left some doctors in a Catch-22: they opposed lay marketing of contraceptives, but the AMA's refusal to alter its position left women reliant on this bootleg trade.[93]

The final major opposition to liberalization concerned race suicide. Dr. John Fulton, secretary of the Maryland State Health Department, objected because he believed liberalization would quicken the "race suicide of . . . the intellectual and leisure classes." Caroline Hadley Robinson from Columbia University found that many people opposed it because they believed it would have a "tremendous effect in lowering the quality or quantity of the population." As one person told Robinson: "The fear haunts many that the contraceptive teachings will be practiced principally by the well endowed, so that the percentage of well endowed children will fall in subsequent generations." The presumption that relaxed restrictions would "decrease the children of the cautious, 'well-endowed' man . . . while those of the wild, 'ill-endowed' men would still flourish" led many to oppose reform.[94]

Those in favor of change set out to counter adversaries' arguments. Realizing they had little chance of altering the Catholic position, they concentrated on physicians. Sanger and the ABCL attempted to secure the support of the profession by offering a medical monopoly over services.[95] In the early 1920s the ABCL released a publicity packet confirming the "common knowledge" that the "well to do and educated people of America" practiced birth control. Because many methods were "injurious and unsafe," contraception must be placed on a "higher plane of scientific knowledge." Anne Kennedy declared: "We feel that the medical profession is the natural channel through which contraceptive information should be given, and in changing the United States laws, we emphasize this point as the distinct principle of the ABCL."[96] The ABCL commissioned Dr. James F. Cooper in 1924 to lecture medical societies. Cooper, a clinical obstetric instructor at Boston University Medical School, became convinced of the need for regulated fertility during his visits to the Boston slums. During his two-year lecture tour doctors showed "great interest," and he gained their attention as no female activist could. Although some physicians feared that contraceptives would lower women's morals, most doctors supported the idea.[97] The major obstacle Cooper encountered was the reluctance of societies to endorse ABCL actions until the AMA took a stand. In 1925 the AMA considered but split over the issue. The scientific section on obstetrics and gynecology called for a law to allow physicians to give contraceptive information. But the political committee rejected it, Sanger claimed, because most members were general practitioners who did not face women's problems on a daily basis. One board member concluded that the AMA was "composed of a heterogeneous group of men and we have to go conservatively, but it does not mean that the physicians in the organization are not for it."[98] As a body, the AMA remained silent on the issue in the mid-1920s.

The AMA was not the only respectable element that the ABCL courted. By the 1920s the eugenics movement had gained strength, and a number of university science departments studied eugenics. With some of these white male professionals on board, the national movement in the 1920s sought to shape the populace in the likeness of the elite.[99]

Some eugenicists applied this attitude specifically to white-black relations, especially in the South. Earnest Sevier Cox, a racial purity zealot and advocate of eugenics, and John Powell, a composer and musician from an aristocratic southern family, founded the Anglo-Saxon Clubs of America (ASCA) in 1922. Their primary goal was to preserve Anglo-Saxon civilization in the United States by strengthening the "original American stock"; selecting and excluding immigrants; and discovering the solution for "our racial problems," defined as the intermingling of blacks with whites. Cox expanded on his ideology in *White America* (1923): blacks "insanely" obsessed with coupling with white women to birth "whiter" offspring would ruin the white race. To avoid race mixing the ASCA supported a twofold plan. First, it drafted a model bill that would require states to institute a registration system using birth certificates to show individuals' racial composition. No marriage could take place without presenting this certificate, and whites could only marry others with pure Caucasian blood. Historian Lisa Lindquist Dorr argues that an ancillary motive behind such marriage laws was to prevent independent white women from engaging in sexual liaisons with black men. Second, these groups supported Marcus Garvey, who advocated black separatism and a "Back to Africa" movement in the 1920s. Garvey argued that the key to race progress was strong women, virtuous mothers, stable homes, and racial purity. Cox, Powell, and the KKK believed Garvey's movement was the best safeguard against the contamination of the white race.[100]

The influence of the ASCA was apparent in Virginia, where a marriage law based on the ASCA model passed in 1924. The following year the Virginia State Board of Health distributed a pamphlet to place "before the better class of young people in Virginia knowledge as to the two great dangers threatening the integrity and supremacy of the native white American race." The first was the "decrease in the birthrate of the upper and middle classes of whites as a result of the 'Race Suicide' movement," and the second was the "ultimate complete intermixture of the white and colored races if they continue to live together." The "remedies" to these dangers were "self-evident": the "better class of whites" must stop the "interference with the normal increase in the growth of the family," while the lower classes must stop the "mixture of the blood with that of another race." These racial concerns were particularly relevant to Virginia and North Carolina because "forty per cent of our choicest young manhood" left their homes during the Civil War "never to return." This situation forced "splendid young women" to secure mates from the "lower circle" or from those who, "because of their very unfitness, escaped the dangers of the battle line." The pamphlet condemned white affluent couples who interfered with "the laws of nature, established by our Maker," to be "fruitful and multiply."[101]

Similar anxieties over racial purity were obvious in the American Eugenics Society, founded in 1921 at the Second International Conference on Eugenics in New York. George Eastman, Irving Fisher, and other prominent eugenicists joined. Racist attitudes prevailed, especially under the leadership of Frederick Osborn, secretary from 1928 to 1972, and Executive Director Leon Whitney. Its Committee on Selective Immigration urged white-only immigration. Similar to the ASCA, the American Eugenics Society sanctioned antimiscegenation laws. White supremacists exploited the popularity of eugenics to perpetuate racial discrimination.[102] The Second International Congress also led to the establishment of the Eugenics Committee of the United States. Irving Fisher chaired, and other members included Charles Davenport and Henry Fairfield Osborn, president of the American Museum of Natural History and a zoology professor at Columbia University. The congress appointed this committee because the time was "ripe for a strong public movement to stem the tide of threatened racial degeneracy." The United States in particular, according to Fisher, must be protected against "indiscriminate immigration, criminal degenerates and the race suicide deplored by President Roosevelt." The committee elected Dr. Katherine Davis to serve on the advisory council;

she accepted this post as an individual, not as representative of the BSH, because its board of trustees did not authorize involvement in eugenics.[103]

The BSH did provide financial backing to two other organizations established in 1923. The Committee on Maternal Health (CMH), a voluntary organization of doctors, laymen, social workers, and nurses, planned to produce a scientific evaluation of contraceptive effectiveness and safety. While Dr. Samuel W. Lambert chaired and Mrs. Gertrude Minturn Pinchot, former president of the National Birth Control League, provided the organizational strength, Dickinson, as secretary of the executive committee, set the conservative tone and direction of the CMH.[104] He disassociated contraception from abortion in the same way Sanger later did to gain the backing of professionals. He believed contraceptives should be distributed only to married women who had already had all the children "called upon [them] to bear" or "where progeny would be reasonably certain to constitute a social menace."[105] The BSH then provided Dr. F. A. E. Crew, a physician and director of the Animal Breeding Research Department, with a ten-thousand-dollar grant to undertake the Crew study, which the CMH hoped would find "a contraceptive simple enough to be practicable for the most ignorant and dull person and cheap enough to be within reach of the poorest."[106] The study's five-year report stressed that "attempts to improve racial stock depend upon control of fertility, negative and positive."[107]

The same year Dickinson established the CMH, Sanger founded the Birth Control Clinical Research Bureau (BCCRB) in New York City as a department of the ABCL. Its purpose was to give contraceptives to married women who met legal provisions that permitted physicians to offer contraceptive advice for the cure or prevention of disease and to study "some of the medical, eugenic, economic, and social implications of birth control." The BCCRB also served as an education center in contraceptive techniques for physicians, a service to which the BSH contributed financially to fill the void in medical school curriculum. In its first two years Dr. Dorothy Bocker served as medical director, replaced by Dr. Hannah Stone in 1925. By the end of the decade the BCCRB had received more than fifteen thousand patients.[108]

Sanger, the ABCL, and the BCCRB sought the support of eugenicists and the medical profession to amend the New York statute in 1923. Sanger advocated a bill that would allow "doctors only" to disperse contraceptives for fertility limitation as well as disease prevention, a tactic to attract physicians who could benefit economically from such control. To garner the sanction of eugenicists, she wrote to Harry H. Laughlin, director of the Eugenics Record Office in Long Island. He encouraged her to integrate eugenicists into her movement and suggested further steps to gain their full endorsement:

Let me take this opportunity to say that in order to attract to the present birth control movement . . . the support of persons whose primary
interest is eugenics, it would be necessary to make it much clearer in
future policy and propaganda that the purpose of birth control is eugenical—that is to say, its activities must be directed toward a differential birth rate in reference not only to maternal health and economic
condition, but also should demand a higher birth rate among persons
best endowed by nature with fine mental, physical, and moral qualities,
and, at the same time, to forbid and positively prevent reproduction by
the defective and degenerate family stocks. Would it not be possible in
the future to emphasize more strongly this possible eugenical feature
of birth control?[109]

Sanger and the ABCL willingly obliged, evidenced by the strong eugenic tone
of their propaganda in the wake of Laughlin's letter.[110]

The ABCL publicity packet in 1923 first petitioned the medical profession
for recognition of the movement and then courted eugenicists. "The main
objective in conducting [this] campaign is that the knowledge now confined
to 'the best families' should be extended to the poor, the ignorant, the immigrant, and the crowds of slum dwellers who are populating the United
States." The ABCL launched a lecture tour of women's clubs to gather financial support but often could address them only if the ABCL agreed to present
eugenic or economic, not feminist, sides of contraception.[111] Club members
were most concerned with high fertility among "inferiors" and the tax money
spent on them.

In late October 1923 the ABCL sponsored a conference in Chicago with
four goals: to decrease delinquents; to reduce the burden on charities and
taxation from the dependent and "defective" classes; to awaken social workers, physicians, and the public to the notion of "racial responsibility"; and to
secure the cooperation of social welfare groups, which had the most contact
with the poor and "unfit." Progress could be achieved if social workers sorted
out the "least fit" and pursued them with "persistent contraceptive instruction."[112] Absent from these goals was any mention of feminist rights to reproductive control, an argument that would have alienated the very eugenicists
to whom Sanger appealed for support and legitimacy. Instead, the ABCL
exhibited data to demonstrate the cost to the state of one marriage between a
"feeble-minded man and woman" and their five children, who should "never
have been born." New York State statistics for 1921 showed that the Department of Public Welfare had spent $20,676,624.40, while private charities had
dispensed $7,483,754.35, totaling $28,160,378.75 by one state in one year to
support people defined as diseased, defective, delinquent, or dependent.[113]

The sessions held at the conference substantiate its eugenic agenda. Professor E. M. East spoke of the "perils facing civilization" if the "reckless breeding of the unfit" continued. The luncheon discussion delved into "Super Race and the Genius." One session reviewed the social cost of the "wrong" people multiplying; the "Deterioration of the Race"; and state cost of providing for the "unfit," delinquent, and feebleminded. The final discourse concluded that the "evils" discussed during the conference could only be ameliorated by a "practical application of birth control."[114]

The ABCL's correspondence following this conference illustrates its continuing drift toward eugenics. Writing to Professor Thomas D. Eliot of Northwestern University, Sanger asserted that the people whom the ABCL had the "most desire to help" were those "whose multiplication [was] causing dysgenic effect to the race." Dr. W. J. Hickson, head of the psychopathic laboratory of the municipal court of Chicago, wrote that his work among certain "unfit" groups provided "conclusive and convincing evidence of the need of the application of the principles of Birth Control among certain definite types of people." At a meeting of the Tioga County Medical Society in Pennsylvania Dr. James Cooper reported that "practically all of these men were very favorable to the . . . sterilization of the unfit and Birth Control for the undesirable elements of society." According to his statistics, the "unfit" were increasing three times faster than the "best stock" and two times faster than the "average stock." These data, according to Cooper, provided the biological justification for contraceptive dispersal among the "undesirable."[115]

Sanger sponsored another conference, the Sixth International Neo-Malthusian Conference in New York City, in 1925. In the opening address Sanger attacked the federal government for its ineffective population control policies. Although laws allowed the country to "shut its gates" to "undesirable foreigners," no attempt had been made to "discourage the rapid multiplication of undesirable aliens" within the nation. On the contrary, Sanger claimed the U.S. government "deliberately encourage[d] and even [made] necessary by its laws the breeding—with a breakneck rapidity—of idiots, defectives, diseased, feeble minded and criminal classes." Governments as well as private charities squandered money for "the care, the maintenance, and the perpetuation of these classes." As a result, the American public was "heavily taxed . . . to maintain an increasing race of morons which threaten[ed] the very foundations of our civilization." She called on Congress to "decrease or to restrict the incessant and uninterrupted advent of the hordes of the unfit."[116] Missing from this speech is any of her earlier feminist notions of birth control. When feminist arguments failed, Sanger grasped eugenics.[117]

The most persistent arguments offered at the conference were race suicide and race improvement. Owen R. Lovejoy, executive secretary of the National

Child Labor Committee, claimed that the "ignorant, self-indulgent, [and] vicious" as well as the "mentally inferior and the physically unfit" continued "to propagate their kind and thus more and more tip the balance in favor of the victory of inferiority and race depreciation." Others maintained that as long as the "cultured classes" limited fertility while the "poor in our slums" did not, future generations would spring predominantly from the "poorest stocks." Professor Raymond Pearl, head of the Department of Biometry at Johns Hopkins University, summed up: "The wrong kind of people have too many children, and the right kind too few. . . . [I]f it is not possible to make desirable people have more babies, why not try teaching other people how to have fewer?"[118] Oswald Garrison Villard, editor of the *Nation*, supported contraception aimed at the "gradual improvement of the race." Hudson Maxim, noted inventor and antipacifist, believed that society had a duty "to improve and protect . . . the human blood stream." Protection included the separation of black and white blood, not only in conception but also in transfusions. The blood of "undesirables" should be "in some way led to sewers and not allowed to flow into the stream of life." Maj. Haldane MacFall wrote that "the only way to breed a fine race is by Birth Control." Author M. P. Willcocks regarded "scientific birth control" as the "foundation-stone" upon which the new social order must be built. No utopian ideals could be achieved unless society allowed only those births that contributed to the populace as a whole.[119]

By the end of the conference Sanger had concluded that attendees approved her goal to increase "persons of superior stock" and to check the "poor and ignorant."[120] Yet historian James Reed asserts that Sanger only reluctantly tolerated eugenicists. Although she desired the "respectability" and organizational backing they offered, Reed argues that she repudiated any plans for "positive" eugenics. In regard to launching a campaign to foster large families among college-educated women, Reed claims that Sanger was "unequivocal in her rejection of that strange argument." Yet the papers of the ABCL as well as publications by Sanger document the eugenic tone of both Sanger and the ABCL in general during the 1920s.[121]

The Struggle for Legislative Change

The ABCL launched a crusade to convince federal legislators to manipulate population growth to preserve the race. It was not the first such endeavor. Mary Ware Dennett and the Voluntary Parenthood League (VPL) in 1923 had introduced the Cummine-Vaile Bill, which called for the repeal of the Comstock Law.[122] This "open bill" sought to remove restrictions on contraceptive dispersal. The ABCL refused to support it because it would allow mail distribution of contraceptive information without regard to safety standards.

Dennett saw contraception as a free-speech and free-press issue well into the 1920s and rejected the need for a "medical monopoly." Sanger, on the other hand, believed only professionals could predict the consequences of some devices.[123] While concern for safety and effectiveness was legitimate, federal regulation of devices could have addressed this problem without a medical monopoly. Sanger's insistence on such a monopoly was a ploy to gain AMA support and therefore legitimacy for her cause, which by this point had little to do with Dennett's free-speech approach. Coercion, not freedom, was necessary to save the race.

Reaction to the Cummine-Vaile Bill was mixed. In Rhode Island Mrs. Isabelle Ahearn O'Neill introduced H 665 in 1923 to beseech Rhode Island representatives in Congress to oppose Cummine-Vaile "and any other legislation which permits the practice of birth control." The General Assembly failed to pass it.[124] At this time the state had no restrictions on contraceptives. Legislators believed either that birth control was a matter outside government jurisdiction or that couples had the right to limit their families. The state could have passed a law limiting contraceptives to disease prevention, as other states had. No one introduced such a measure on the state level. At the national level Cummine-Vaile failed by a large margin. Because most politicians criticized the lack of regulation, Dennett reintroduced the bill a year later, stipulating that all contraceptive literature must be certified by five physicians as "not injurious to life or health." This impractical specification led to the bill's death in committee. Dennett retired from the VPL the following year, and it disbanded in 1925. Sanger and the ABCL then began a push for their own bill.[125]

In January 1926 Sanger and Anne Kennedy traveled to Washington, D.C., to open campaign headquarters. Their measure proposed the mailing of contraceptive information only to the medical profession and scientists and thereby placed contraception in the field of preventive medicine and scientific research.[126] As Grant Sanger recalled, his mother saw the value in introducing science and medicine to her movement: she wanted "big names" to help legitimize contraceptives among the public.[127] This measure received mixed reactions in Rhode Island. O'Neill again opposed it because it was "prejudicial to the morals of the American people," but again, the state failed to pass her bill. In fact, U.S. Senator Jesse H. Metcalf (RI) favored the ABCL measure "as a protection to future generations." He told Kennedy he would have endorsed a stronger measure providing for the sterilization of the "unfit," an attitude not reflective of that of his state peers.[128]

The ABCL received similar endorsements from politicians who felt strongly about eugenics or race degeneration. Senator Ellison D. Smith (SC) favored contraception and sterilization of the "unfit," as did Congressman

Charles A. Eaton (NJ), who told ABCL Executive Secretary Mrs. R. Huse that the "production of morons and unfit in this country must cease, if we are to maintain ourselves as a nation." Representative Theodore E. Burton (OH) admitted that he was "much impressed with the idea of eliminating the unfit" and that he believed in "selection." Comparing animal and human breeding, Senator Lawrence D. Tyson (TN) argued that because Congress regulated the breeding of livestock by compelling the extermination of all diseased stock, the time had come for the "government to consider and apply the same principles to the human race." Congressman Sol Bloom (NY) not only endorsed the "sterilization of [the] unfit and feeble-minded and insane" but also believed that Congress should pass laws "making it a crime for undesirables to marry."[129] Some senators approved the proposed amendment as a means to correct the fertility imbalance between the classes. Senator C. C. Dill of Washington, for example, believed "every effort should be made to get the knowledge to the poor women" but that it was a "great wrong . . . to have this information used by more wealthy women." Maryland Senator William C. Bruce concluded that nothing could be done to force wealthy women to relinquish their methods of fertility limitation. Rather, reformers should spread the custom of the upper class to the lower and less educated classes.[130] Politicians supportive of the bill, however, were in the minority.

Most congressional members opposed altering the federal statute. Some believed easy access to contraceptives would only augment the class difference in TFR. Senator James A. Reed (MO) "violently opposed" contraception on the grounds that it was "chipping away the very foundation of our civilization." Likewise, Senator W. H. McMaster (SD) opined that once such knowledge was readily available, white upper-class women would reduce their already artificially low births. Espousing a traditional nativist viewpoint, Senator Ralph H. Cameron (AZ) would only support the bill if the ABCL vowed to do its "propaganda work among the poor foreigners." Claiming himself "100% Nordic," he deplored the fact that "our native stock" used family limitation "to such an alarming degree." The KKK lobbyist opposed contraception because the younger white generation refused to accept its responsibility to bear children; the fiber of the country had weakened to the point where danger existed of the "race dying out." The KKK also favored the sterilization of undesirables as a measure to maintain good racial stock.[131]

Many politicians opposed contraceptives for other reasons. Some thought easier access would "lead to immorality." Others believed that the federal government had no right to intervene in or even discuss childbirth or child prevention.[132] Still others objected to the "doctors-only" limitation. Senator Clause A. Swanson (VA) condemned physicians as "an irresponsible class of men who would profit by this amendment." There already existed a "sufficient number of charlatans and crooks in the profession"; the new law would only give them "one more method of preying on the public." Numerous politicians made similar attacks on the economic motivation of the medical profession.[133] Others refused to endorse the bill due to Catholic influence. Sanger did not meet with church leaders, perhaps because of her strong antipathy toward Catholics.[134] Instead, Kennedy unsuccessfully attempted to convince leaders of the Catholic Welfare Conference that the doctors-only bill would safeguard the public from the misuse of contraceptives. They informed Kennedy they would do all they could to defeat the ABCL measure, including writing the AMA protesting its passage.[135]

Sanger too sought out the AMA and appeared willing to do whatever was necessary to gain its support. In 1914, for example, Sanger had written an article in the *Woman Rebel* criticizing the restrictions placed on both contraception and abortion.[136] In the 1920s she recanted her earlier support of abortion and purposely separated contraceptives from abortion.[137] By delegitimizing abortion Sanger hoped to win legitimacy for contraception. She offered to word her 1926 bill in any way suitable to the AMA, but the AMA board recommended the House of Delegates allow the issue to die in committee.[138] The AMA adopted a neutral stance, allowing neither the Catholic Church nor the ABCL a victory. This position worked to the advantage of the church.

Although the Catholic Welfare Conference failed to gain AMA support, it met with success among politicians. Letters dispatched to all senators expressed church hostility to the ABCL bill—a tactic that Kennedy concluded "created an atmosphere of fear toward this legislation, especially where that particular Senator had many Catholic constituents." Even though the Sixty-ninth Congress was overwhelmingly Protestant, Catholic influence seemed to hold sway over the voting behavior of its members.[139] Some politicians who personally supported the legislation would not endorse it for fear of political repercussions.[140] Congressman Albert R. Hall (IN) affirmed that his Catholic constituents, especially the "conservative element," objected to liberalization. According to Huse, he was "scared to death to even discuss the subject." Senator Edwin S. Broussard (LA) refused to meet with the ABCL because he was a Catholic from a predominantly Catholic state. The second senator from Louisiana concurred; John R. Ransdall postulated that God knew how many children a woman should bear, and, therefore, no one had need of contraceptives.[141]

Despite heavy Catholic opposition, the ABCL continued its fight. Between January and May ABCL members interviewed 86 senators but only 52 of 422 members of Congress. Of the senators, 11 supported, 22 favored, 14 opposed, 39 were noncommittal, and 6 refused to be interviewed. Of the representa-

tives, 9 supported, 5 opposed, and 38 were noncommittal. The number of actual supporters, however, may have been smaller than the figures recorded by
the ABCL. Congressman E. C. Michener (MI) claimed that many members
of Congress lied to ABCL representatives because "it was easier to permit the
ladies to leave their office believing they were sympathetic." He predicted that
once these politicians were behind closed doors they would veto the ABCL
bill.[142] His prediction was accurate: Congress defeated it by a large margin.

Following this failure, Sanger renewed her efforts with the medical profession. In 1927 she severed the connection between the BCCRB and the
ABCL, hoping that the clinic would receive a favorable reception from the
medical profession if it were disassociated from the nonmedical activities
of the ABCL. The following year she resigned as president of the ABCL and
became director of the BCCRB, a position that drew criticism from some
doctors.[143] Dr. Boughton did not consider Sanger, a layperson, qualified to
lead the movement for a medical monopoly over contraceptives.[144]

Sanger encountered opposition from other professionals. In 1927 she
organized the first World Population Conference in Geneva. She invited
internationally renowned scientists, including statisticians, biologists, and
economists. Many of them were leery of her role as organizer and did not
formally acknowledge her. Moreover, they refused to allow any discussion of
contraception at the conference.[145] Ironically, the very professionals Sanger
actively sought to bring into her cause often rebuffed her because of her lack
of acceptable credentials and her gender. These white male elites did not
believe they needed the direction or input of a female nurse to decide the
proper course for population growth.

Doctors' efforts were generally more effective than those of lay workers.
Dickinson and his CMH received an invitation in 1927 to house CMH headquarters in the New York Academy of Medicine building. This invitation, according to Dr. Katherine Davis, offered "proof of the growing recognition of
the importance of the work of this committee." Two organizations concerned
with women's reproductive health—the American Gynecological Society and
the New York Obstetrical Society—also endorsed the CMH.[146]

Female physicians and lay workers on the local level had more success
than Sanger and other national leaders in tapping into a grassroots movement to disperse contraceptives to women who desired them. The Baltimore
Bureau for Contraceptive Advice opened in 1927, headed by Dr. Bessie Moses with an all-female staff. It soon changed its name to the Baltimore Birth
Control Clinic. Moses established this clinic as a medical service, consciously
divorced from the lay-directed ABCL. Initially, Moses lobbied to incorporate
the clinic as one of the services provided by Johns Hopkins Hospital, where
she worked, but the board did not want to face repercussions for breaking the

federal statute.[147] The Comstock Act continued to intimidate conservative institutions and physicians, but it did not retard the establishment of clinics, either in hospitals or in extramural centers.

Most activists involved in establishing clinics were women, primarily white, educated, middle- and upper-class volunteers or paid staff. Missing from their agenda was any blatant eugenic rhetoric. These women sought to help others gain access to supplies necessary to control their fertility as they saw fit rather than to fulfill a population control agenda. Dr. Sarah Marcus practiced in a south-side Cleveland neighborhood of predominantly eastern European immigrants. In 1928 she began working in Cleveland's birth control clinic, established that year by the Maternal Health League. The founders of the clinic, "society women [and] . . . Shaker Heights women," sought out Marcus because as a woman she could ease clients' discomfort discussing sexual matters. These volunteers smuggled in supplies from Canada to provide for their mostly white working-class clientele. In 1927 Dr. Emily Mudd set up the state's first clinic in West Philadelphia, an area under the jurisdiction of Judge Allen Olmstead. He and his wife, Mildred, were "great liberals" supporting the cause. East Philadelphia, on the other hand, fell under the jurisdiction of hostile Catholic judges. Mudd eliminated "birth control" from the clinic title and instead decided upon the Maternal Health Clinic because she was "trying to straddle between the acceptable health care and the not yet acceptable spacing of children." She expected the clinic to be closed by officials, but the influential sponsors listed in her brochure protected the clinic. Moreover, little religious opposition emerged: "Apparently other religious groups either didn't think we were doing enough to bother about, or they were not organized at that time . . . to protest and fight." Almost all her clientele came from "rather underprivileged groups," referred by "friends" on the boards of social agencies.[148] Women came despite possible legal repercussions.

These doctors and volunteers risked a great deal in their actions. The state could have revoked medical licenses to practice and/or jailed staff members for illegal distribution of contraceptives. They assumed these risks because they believed in women's rights to bear healthy children, to space their children according to growing middle-class norms, and to avoid pregnancy if health or socioeconomic conditions contraindicated it. Promoting free and open sexuality did not enter the formula, nor did eugenic notions of population control.

Illegal Abortions: North Carolina and Rhode Island

The lack of legal sanction also did not stop women from seeking or doctors and others from performing abortion from the turn of the century through the 1920s. The records of one North Carolina hospital attest to the continued prevalence of abortion. Data from Rhode Island during the 1920s confirm that both doctors and midwives performed abortions. Both examples disprove the notion that only single, desperate women resorted to this procedure. The majority of women were married and financially secure.

The admittance log of the Twin City Hospital in Winston-Salem, North Carolina, from 1896 to 1914 disclosed that 190 white women sought medical assistance as a result of abortion complications.[149] The term *abortion* in the records did not imply miscarriage; "pregnancy with nonviable fetus," "pregnancy with early dead fetus," "incomplete miscarriage," or "premature miscarriage" denoted the natural expulsion of the fetus. Two instances of therapeutic abortion, both for cases of typhoid fever, were not counted in the sample.[150]

These records provide characteristics of women seeking abortions. Of 190 patients, 133 (70 percent) were married, while 36 (18.9 percent) were single. The remaining 21 women were listed as "Mrs." but were checked off as single; they could have been recently widowed during one of the numerous epidemics that swept the region, or their husbands might have deserted them. With these 21 women added to the married category, the numbers are startling: 154 (81.1 percent) were married. The women's ages, recorded in 179 cases, averaged 29.7 years. Occupations appeared for 164 of the women: 135 (82.3 percent) were homemakers; 7 (4.26 percent) were factory hands; 3 each (1.82 percent each) were mill hands, nurses, seamstresses, domestic workers, and teachers; 2 (1.21 percent) were stenographers; and 1 each (0.6 percent each) was a college student, student, milliner, cook, and vaudeville actress. Only 25 of the 190 women (13.15 percent) were "poor/nonpaying." Of them, 19 were married and 6 were single; 11 worked outside the home. Religion was registered in 30 cases: 12 (40 percent) Baptists; 10 (33.33 percent) Moravians; 4 (13.33 percent) Catholics; 2 (6.66 percent) Methodists; 1 (3.33 percent) Presbyterian; and 1 (3.33 percent) listed as "Chinese." All were from North Carolina except seven: two from South Carolina, two from Illinois, and one each from Virginia, Alabama, and Maryland. All but one survived the complications after an average hospital stay of 14.24 days.[151]

These records contribute insights into the abortion controversy during the Progressive Era. They do not confirm the assertion by some historians that abortion disappeared from the national discourse during this period because the women seeking the procedure were mainly single and poor.[152] In this sample the overwhelming percentage of women were older, married, and able to pay for a prolonged hospital stay. The log is also important because it attests to the continued prevalence of abortion. The women recorded here experienced complications from the procedure; many more presumably underwent safe and uncomplicated abortions. Of the seven outsiders, two cases are straightforward: a married vaudeville actress from Chicago performing in Winston-Salem and a seventeen-year-old college student from Rock Hill, South Carolina, presumably attending Salem College.[153] The other five were married, paying housewives. Perhaps they traveled to the area to seek the assistance of a sister or friend in procuring an abortion without the knowledge of their husbands. Their spouses, on the other hand, could have been part of the decision and either traveled with their wives or remained at home to work while their wives set off to obtain and recuperate from the procedure among family or friends.

A case in Rhode Island also confirms the continuation of this practice. The state charged Walter L. Johnson with "aiding, assisting, and counseling an abortion upon the body of Dorothy V. Hughes," with death resulting. The Superior Court found Johnson guilty, but he won an appeal based on a technicality. The transcripts reveal telling attitudes and trends. First, the case substantiates the prevalence of abortion: the justices discussed numerous cases in which women "survived the operation." Second, the justices held men, not women, responsible for abortion, just as legislators had in the previous century. "We are aware," they argued, "that there is substantial authority for the introduction of testimony, in cases of abortion, to the effect that the defendant was responsible for the pregnancy in order to show a motive for the procurement of the operation."[154] The defendants in these cases were male. Once evidence pointed clearly to the defendant as the father, he, not the mother, was held responsible for coercing and arranging the abortion.

If abortion continued to be relatively prevalent, why did the national discourse abate by the turn of the century? Compared to the nineteenth century, physicians were noticeably quiet on abortion and race suicide in general. Eugenicists in academic settings were the main purveyors of racial doom. Perhaps the successful legal campaign to ban abortion unless performed by a licensed physician to save the mother's life fulfilled the AMA's agenda. This legal loophole also allowed physicians great latitude in deciding who should obtain an abortion. Other doctors who faced the "cleanup" of abortionists could take no further legal action against women without violating doctor-patient confidentiality. With continued professionalization and regulation of medicine, many doctors no longer faced a significant financial threat from irregulars or midwives.

The characteristics of women seeking abortions may have also played a role in the relative silence surrounding the issue. According to the Twin City Hospital database, most women were older, full-time wives and mothers. They most likely already had children, and doctors did not see them "shirking" their motherly duties. In fact, physicians may have considered that these women were endeavoring to fulfill new notions of childrearing by limiting their progeny to benefit their existing family economically and socially. Doctors' silence was not tantamount to acceptance of abortion as a means of birth control. They made no attempt to ease access to the procedure.

Abortion remained illegal during the 1920s, yet women continued to seek it. In a case study of Chicago Leslie Reagan found that 16 percent of women who went to birth control clinics in 1927 were seeking an abortion. While the public perceived midwives as the primary practitioners of this trade, doctors and midwives performed abortions at equal rates.[155]

Evidence shows the same to be true in Rhode Island. In 1921 the state found Dr. Arthur O'Leary guilty of performing an abortion but asked for a deferred sentence because he was a "user of drugs and had lost his means of obtaining a livelihood." Moreover, the woman had recovered from the procedure. The court agreed, but eight months later a Boston woman traveled to Providence to seek out O'Leary; she also recovered. The prosecutor asked for a three-year jail term. The court agreed.[156] O'Leary demonstrates the relative safety of abortion if done properly. Moreover, that a Boston woman sought him out specifically confirms an underground information network through which women could obtain the services they desired. Lastly, O'Leary was from a respectable Providence family and had enjoyed a reputable medical practice until his foray into drugs. Once he had fallen from grace, he could rely on the lucrative abortion market to sustain his drug habit.

Only two other male abortionists faced charges in Rhode Island in the 1920s. Fred Carrington Brooks of Providence pleaded nolo contendere to abortion in 1924; the court deferred his sentence because no injury resulted. Dr. Benjamin J. Butler of East Providence was arrested when Rhode Island Hospital notified police of a woman in critical condition who identified Butler as the abortionist.[157] The use of dying declarations and cooperation between medical and police officials that Reagan found in Chicago holds for Rhode Island as well.

Female abortionists also continued to compete in this profitable venture. Alice Stone, a single woman, died in 1921 following a procedure performed by a Providence female abortionist. The state was unable to prosecute her because Stone refused to identify the woman. Even though she was dying, Stone was grateful to and thus protected her abortionist. Two years later the state arrested Elizabeth Rodier, a married woman in Kent County, for performing an abortion on Florence Bacon, a mill operative, but asked for a deferred sentence because "no serious results had followed the operation," an indication that officials, as with the Brooks case, may have been more concerned with women's safety than with eradicating abortion per se. That same year Mrs. Josephine Moretti of Cranston was arrested after she performed an abortion on Mable E. Hourtal, who died subsequently at Rhode Island Hospital. Mertys Patterson, a divorced twenty-eight-year-old woman from Seekonk, died at Pawtucket Memorial Hospital in 1924 from abortion complications. Despite state pressure, Patterson, similar to Stone, refused to identify the abortionist. Dr. Charlotta N. Goline, thirty-six years old, was not so lucky. A woman critically ill at Rhode Island Hospital identified Dr. Goline as the abortionist after repeated questions by police and social workers. Two weeks later Eva Roberts of West Warwick was arrested for performing abortions. Three cases in 1926 also involved female abortionists. Anastazia Mostecki of Woonsocket faced two charges of criminal abortion. Raffaela Napolillo, a thirty-year-old Providence midwife, had performed several abortions of which officials were aware. The case of Emelda Bourqui, a seventeen-year-old from Mossup, Connecticut, confirms the underground network. She traveled to Rhode Island with a friend to see an unnamed female abortionist. At home she became violently ill and later died of septic peritonitis. The same fate awaited Lodier B. Leveille, twenty-one years old, of Providence following an abortion performed in her home. Police arrested a young man, presumed to be her lover, and a woman, apparently the abortionist, seen leaving the domicile.[158]

Either Rhode Island had a remarkable number of incompetent abortionists or the number of abortions performed was quite high. The only cases to reach the newspaper involved death or serious injury. Presumably, the majority of abortions took place secretly and brought positive results. For cases in the public eye, the gender implications are significant. Many more women than men were arrested, at least according to available newspaper evidence. This imbalance could signify that women dominated the abortion trade and therefore were more likely to face a higher number (but not percentage) of injuries or fatalities among their clients. It could also indicate that male doctors were better trained and more competent. Alternatively, it could reflect reluctance on the part of male police officers and state officials to interfere with the medical practice of physicians but not with female abortionists or midwives. Lastly, the skewed gender arrests could reflect the ability of male doctors to convince officials that they performed only life-saving and thus legal abortions, a justification female abortionists could not employ.

Conclusion

Race suicide theorists blended well with eugenic doomsayers concerned with the constitution of the population. Both groups attracted significant followers among influential elites. Sanger attempted to gain legitimacy for contraceptive changes by appealing to these eugenicists and to the AMA with her medical monopoly for dispersal. Permanent means of fertility control in the form of sterilization gained a mantle of respectability with the *Buck v. Bell* decision, but sterilization was impractical for the "unfit" at large. Only legislative changes to allow access to these groups could save the nation from the propagation of inferior peoples. This contraceptive campaign failed for numerous reasons: the lack of AMA endorsement; fears that easy access to cheap products would exacerbate, not alleviate, fertility differentials between the "fit" and "unfit"; and anxieties among legislators about the political fallout from the Catholic Church's opposition. Legal obstacles in the 1920s did not discourage grassroots activists from providing or women from seeking means to control fertility to suit individual women's needs. Abortion remained a recourse for women, many of whom were married. The establishment of birth control clinics spread in many areas. By 1932 there were 118 clinics; by 1934, 144 clinics; and by 1935, 240 clinics in the United States and its territories.[159] Many existed through legal loopholes that allowed contraceptives as a preventive health measure. The Great Depression revitalized the national movement to liberalize contraceptives with economic arguments concerning the continuing high fertility of the poor on public relief.

Population Control and the Great Depression, 1930–1939

The economic severity of the Depression increased attention to reproductive policies. While concern over the fertility of "defectives" continued, a new public commentary focused on the high fertility of families on relief. In this context the distribution of contraceptives could save not only the race but also taxpayers' money. Similarly, sterilization would save state money in institutional care for the socially, physically, and mentally "unfit" or "undesirable" and their potentially defective offspring. While the federal courts lent a mantle of respectability to contraceptives and sterilization, no similar push occurred for abortion. Women continued to obtain this procedure, but no groundswell of activism to change its illegal status occurred. Many state officials, however, looked the other way as women sought abortions to control their fertility in the midst of economic devastation. Proponents of selective growth did not tout abortion as a solution to the nation's problems, relying instead on birth control and sterilization to shape the population along lines suitable to the white elite power structure. Many women took advantage of the newly eased restrictions on birth control to suit their own purposes, namely, to limit their family size. This climate of growing acceptance spurred the establishment of birth control clinics. Activists in Rhode Island opened the first such clinic in New England. They ignored the classist and racist arguments dominating the national discourse and instead concentrated on the connection between contraception and women's improved health and life choices. Unlike the sense of doom prevailing in the national debate, Rhode Island activists quietly served the contraceptive needs of thousands of clients.

Limiting Families on Relief

Population control advocates continued their racial doom rhetoric. Reducing the birthrate among people of "inferior hereditary" was the only way to improve society. The quality of the race would be regenerated, they contended, if the "masses of stupid people" with their "unrestrained fecundity" produced fewer children. Unless society checked the births of "feebleminded" parents, the continual "weakening of the race" would lead to "another Roman ruin."[1] White middle- and upper-class educated groups, on the other hand, had a "duty" to procreate. Louise Gilman Hutchins, a physician and reformer, avowed that "this was the word that we were given at Wellesley." Loraine Leeson Campbell, Vassar graduate and birth control activist, claimed that during the Depression there was a "good deal of talk of so-called 'race suicide.' A lot of people were collecting figures about how the college-educated man or woman weren't [sic] replacing themselves, and the growth of the population was all lopsided and it all came from the poor, or the uneducated." Emily Hartshorne Mudd, a physician and founder of the first birth control clinic in Pennsylvania, recounted a similar story:

> I do remember tremendous pressures that if you were what they used to consider . . . superior in terms of your education and background that you should have children, that this was essential for the future of the country[,] . . . that people who were more privileged should not be completely outnumbered by the so-called underprivileged. And there was tremendous pressure and many young women gained both status and stature in the eyes of their community, of their families, and their husbands by having another healthy, pink-cheeked baby. . . . [T]his was the most important contribution you could make to the future of the country.[2]

Educated women such as Hutchins, Campbell, and Mudd became the target of positive eugenicists—those concerned with promoting childbearing among the "fit."

ABCL resolutions adopted in January 1933 reflect this desire to reduce the "unfit" and increase the "fit." ABCL propaganda placated race suicide theorists by emphasizing "birth selection." While favoring sterilization laws for people with serious hereditary defects, the ABCL encouraged births in families with "good hereditary and environmental endowment." The "gifted, capable and socially minded" members of society had a duty to multiply. As Eleanor Jones, president of the ABCL, stated: "We want families that should have children to have them . . . ; we are just as much interested in helping the right sort of persons to have more children when they want them as in helping others to have fewer."[3] Such rhetoric allowed the ABCL to continue to curry favor with eugenicists.

Who should have fewer children? The Milbank Memorial Foundation worked with the United States Public Health Service on an economic health survey in 1932. Investigating eight thousand families in the "wage-earning class" in eight cities, the foundation found that family size increased as economic means decreased: white-collar workers had a birthrate of 134 per 1,000, skilled laborers 150, and unskilled laborers 182. Families with no employed workers had a 48 percent higher birthrate than those with one or more full-time workers. Relief families had a birthrate 54 percent higher than nonrelief families. People who were poor in 1929 and remained so in 1932 had the highest birthrate of all. The authors concluded that "a high birth rate during the depression prevailed in families which could least afford, from any point of view, to assume this added responsibility."[4] In another investigation the Federal Unemployment Relief Census ascertained that the 3,134,678 families on relief between October 1932 and October 1933 produced 233,822 infants. These same families already had 1,589,480 children between the ages of one and five. Additional surveys provided the same evidence: relief families had the highest birthrates.[5]

The publication of these surveys in the press led to a demand for the dispersal of contraceptives among the poor and unemployed. As Dr. Mudd recalled, "Almost everybody saw this as a means of avoiding the tremendous impact on community monies from the welfare sources . . . where more and more pregnancies . . . were piling up the expenses." A *New Republic* editorial promoted government distribution to those on relief: "It could be done, easily, as a common-sense relief measure, supported by a tide of public opinion even more powerful than that which overwhelmed the Eighteenth Amendment." *Harper's Magazine* concurred: "With the individual need so great and the relief problem so acute, it might be expected that birth control would have become during the past few years a recognized phase of public health." Such a program would decrease the economic strain on public health and hospital facilities while simultaneously bettering maternal health.[6]

Why was the fertility rate among relief and poor women so high? A Milbank Memorial Foundation study under the direction of Dr. Raymond Pearl investigated birth control practices among 30,949 urban women of all classes in thirteen states east of or on the Mississippi River. Among whites, 51.6 percent of married and 88 percent of unwed mothers and, among blacks, 79.2 percent of married and 93.3 percent of unwed mothers had never used contraception. These statistics may not have reflected national norms: many single women using birth control effectively would not have come to Pearl's attention, as he only looked at women giving birth in hospitals; moreover, only one-third of deliveries occurred in hospitals. Nevertheless, his study provides insights into racist and classist notions. "Only about a third as many Negro as white women resort to contraception," he argued, confirming the lack of access historian Johanna Schoen demonstrates for many African American women. Among many poor black and white women, their "obviously stupid practice of contraception" led to their high fertility; practices among some blacks were "far less effective than even the relatively poor ones the white women are able to achieve." He continued his racist assertions in an article in *Science*: "Negroes do not practice contraception effectively, even after they have been instructed." In the 1933 Milbank study he asserted that blacks "exercise less prudence and foresight than white people do in all sexual matters" and, in the 1936 report, that they lacked the "self-control" to practice birth control. Pearl concluded that the poor's inability to exercise birth limitation, not their desire to have a large family, appeared "alone to be responsible for their too rapid propagation." Only the "prompt removal of all legal restriction to the free dissemination of contraceptive information, and barriers to the unrestricted distribution of contraceptive devices, would tend to have the effect of bringing the differential fertility of social classes more nearly into balance again."[7]

For women who did use birth control, a number of options were available. Many Catholics relied on the rhythm method, but while improved medical information more accurately pinpointed the fertile period, this method remained unreliable. Women encountered other problems. Although the 1930s witnessed a "revolution" with the debut of the latex condom, many men refused to use them.[8] Women bought female-oriented devices at a rate of "five to one" compared to condom sales. Douching (primarily with Lysol), despite its ineffectiveness, was their first choice and remained so through the 1950s. Such feminine hygiene products were available at local five-and-dime stores, through catalogs, and through door-to-door sales.[9] Diaphragms, one of the more reliable methods, were not an option for many indigent and working-class women: they could not afford to visit doctors, who legally monopolized the distribution of diaphragms, and they either had no knowledge of existing clinics or lived in areas with no clinics.[10] By 1932 eighty-six birth control clinics were distributed among only eighteen states. Twenty-seven states had no such facilities for low- or no-income women.[11]

In the early 1930s some organizations pushed for social and welfare workers to incorporate contraceptive information into their regular duties. The ABCL cooperated with welfare organizations to inform the poor about clinics. In a speech in Providence ABCL President Jones stated: "The poor will use birth control after they have learned the methods and the poor are the people who need it the most." The only way to reach these women, she continued, was through the help of social workers, who developed personal relationships with relief women and could talk candidly about family limitation.[12] The American Conference on Birth Control and National Recovery held in Washington, D.C., in January 1934 advocated birth limitation as a necessary component of social work.[13] Dr. Sidney E. Goldstein, a rabbi at the Free Synagogue in New York, summed up the conference's attitude: "Every social worker knows that it is not only cruel and heartless but socially unwise to allow families to increase during periods of distress and dependency. . . . The government must give not only food and clothing and shelter to these families, it must give in addition that information and instruction that is necessary to keep the family within reasonable limits." Directors of Temporary Emergency Relief Administrations across the country supported adding contraceptive services to welfare and social agencies.[14]

The association of social work with contraception was new. Before the Depression few social workers discussed such private issues with clients. Economic distress altered this trend. In most instances, contraceptives were recommended on the initiative of individual social workers concerned either with maternal and infant health or with population concerns; welfare organizations generally had no set policy. Only two large welfare agencies in New York, the Jewish Social Service and the Association for Improving the Condition of the Poor, instructed field workers to send clients to clinics when the situation seemed to require family limitation. Some believed this "wise policy" should be modeled by other "overly cautious organizations."[15]

Why were other agencies reluctant to adopt such a stand? Some dreaded accusations of coercion. Allegations that relief recipients were compelled to use contraceptives plagued some leaders. In Providence the Reverend William Appleton Lawrence of the Grace Episcopal Church guaranteed at a fund drive that contraceptives were not a prerequisite for public assistance. Yet Public Safety Director James J. McMahon of New Jersey received reports from clergymen in Montclair that Emergency Relief Administration caseworkers compelled relief families to practice contraception or forfeit public assistance. Caseworkers denied the allegations; McMahon threatened to fire anyone who spread contraceptive information to clients.[16] Although most social workers did not force clients to use contraception, the evidence suggests that many recommended fertility limitation to large families on relief. Any recommendation from a government official could be construed as coercive on the part of the recipient.

Other agencies forbade workers to discuss contraception because they feared charges of interference in private family matters. *Commonweal* agreed that relief families should limit offspring, but the decision should be theirs alone; the state should not initiate conversations to safeguard the separation between public and private lives.[17] That a Catholic periodical advocated family limitation demonstrates the growing acceptance of fertility control, although this periodical's view did not reflect church policy.

Legislative Campaigns

Most government agencies refused to adopt contraception as part of their programs because of the Comstock Law. Clinics operated mostly through legal loopholes that allowed contraceptives to prevent disease and/or to protect maternal health.[18] Still working to remove the Comstock Law, Sanger founded the National Committee on Federal Legislation (NCFL) in Chicago in 1929, with Katherine Houghton Hepburn, mother of the rising film star, serving as legislative chair. The NCFL's goal was to amend the law to allow physicians, hospitals, and clinics to receive contraceptive information and supplies through the mail. Sanger was determined to change the statute because "big money" would not be invested in an enterprise that was against the law. Three years later the NCFL moved its headquarters to Washington, D.C., and surpassed the lobbying efforts of the ABCL.[19]

Finding sponsors to introduce a bill in 1931 proved difficult. Retiring Senator Frederick Huntington Gillet (R-MA) agreed because he had no reelection concerns. The bill reached a judiciary committee comprised of William E. Borah (R-ID), Sam G. Bratton (D-NM), and Gillet. Although opponents were predominantly Catholic, many employed anti-Communist propaganda rather than church doctrine to defeat the bill. Arguing that contraception was a Russian innovation, they claimed it ruined motherhood and the family. Representative Mary T. Norton (D-NJ), a Catholic, testified that the happiest families had many children. The majority of Americans were born poor, she argued, but poverty was a "blessing" because it made people ambitious.[20] Cloaking their moral opposition in Red Scare rhetoric was effective; the committee killed the bill. Sanger concluded that it failed because foreign and domestic problems dominated politicians' minds: "To the frantic, worried, harassed, driven Congressmen of 1931 the announcement of a birth control bill was like a message from Mars, only less interesting and more remote." Refusing to admit Catholic influence, she instead blamed congressional preoccupation with the war in Manchuria, foreign debt, peace conferences, disarmament, tariffs, Prohibition, sales taxes, budgets and bonuses, and unemployment relief.[21]

The NCFL launched another campaign the following year. Senator Henry D. Hatfield of West Virginia introduced S 4436, while Representative Frank Hancock of North Carolina introduced HR 11082, both bills to exempt licensed doctors, chartered medical colleges, legitimate druggists, and licensed hospitals or clinics from federal provisions on contraception. This careful wording intended to exclude medical sects outside the purview of the AMA. Advocates of the bills employed various arguments, but the glaring absence was a feminist defense. In hundreds of pages of testimony only the Reverend Charles Francis Potter of the First Humanist Society of New York claimed that women had "an inalienable right to all information which affected their health and their economic condition, and no masculine supervision of their morals . . . can possibly in the long run succeed."[22] Other advocates steered clear of feminist terminology. Some argued that restrictions interfered with states' rights, while others employed public and maternal health justifications. Sanger appealed to conservatives by guaranteeing that the bills would "place the responsibility of giving contraceptive instruction in the hands of the medical profession, where it rightly belongs."[23] Doctors testified that the bills would ensure the "freedom for physicians . . . to use their judgment with . . . their patients in this matter" and help decrease abortions. As in the 1920s, Sanger distanced abortion from the bills, contending that the "colossal" number of annual abortions was "extremely detrimental to the health and happiness of women."[24]

Far more frequently, reproductive policy was associated with unemployment, child labor, crime, low living standards, and, especially, eugenic reform. Senator Hatfield agreed to introduce the 1932 bill because, as a physician and former governor, he had witnessed the "imbecilic conditions" in state institutions and the rapid propagation of the "unfit"; the bill would improve the quality of the race. Writer Charlotte Perkins Gilman argued that the "intellectual level of our country is that of the 12-year-old," and the population suffered from an "enormous proportion of handicapped children, inferior, delinquent, degenerate, a weight upon us to bring up."[25] Sanger claimed that 40 percent of the population was "generally classed as unfit, mentally and physically," and included "morons and mental defectives who usually come upon our social vista as permanent unemployables and dependents." Others argued that "the least intelligent sixth" was "begetting half of the next generation," calling for a greatly "needed intelligent birth control procedure." Dr. Henry Pratt Fairchild of New York University, who was also president of the Population Reference Bureau, testified that population increase must come "from the better elements of society."[26]

Advocates also endeavored to place the bill within the economic context of the 1930s. Amos W. Butler of the Indiana Society for Mental Hygiene maintained that the public could be "saved great expense" if "public charges supported by the taxpayer" were decreased through "proper legislation." James S. Bossard of Philadelphia found that 20–40 percent of state expenditures during the 1920s went for the care of dependent and "defective classes" and that this percentage had "increased greatly" during the Depression. Although not all expenditures could be eliminated by "intelligent birth control," he concluded that "it could contribute appreciably toward that end." L. Foster Wood of Colgate-Rochester Divinity School claimed that "this bill . . . would end the depression." Rabbi Sidney Goldstein maintained that "the unemployment problem will not be permanently solved until we adopt the birth-control procedure." The Utah State Federation of Labor stressed that the lack of contraceptives among the working classes "contributed to our present unemployment situation."[27]

The economic and eugenic rhetoric of advocates did not convince Congress, and the bills died in committee again.[28] Several factors explain this failure. First, the Catholic Church, with Norton as its mouthpiece, continued well-organized opposition. The American Federation of Labor opposed the bill because its president, William Green, could not support any measure that "leaders of the church denounce as conducive to bad morals." As Rabbi Edward L. Israel of the Central Conference of American Rabbis stated: "Religious fanaticism of a sincere but a misguided sort alone prevents this wise legislation."[29] Second, Congress remained unconvinced of the social and economic necessity for fertility control. The Reverend John A. Ryan of the National Catholic Welfare Conference ignored moral condemnations and appealed instead to social welfare liberals: the "advocacy of birth prevention as a remedy for poverty diverts attention from measures of economic and social justice." He criticized population control proponents because "they look upon themselves as a superior stock, unmindful of the obvious mathematical fact that they and their kind are not reproducing themselves." Stricter, not more lenient, legislation would correct the fertility imbalance. Third, many Southern senators were unwilling to discuss the issue. Because child labor substituted for agricultural and industrial mechanization in the South, many parents considered large families an economic asset. In fact, when the Protestant Federal Council of Churches endorsed contraception in mid-1931, the Southern Presbyterian General Assembly withdrew from the federation.[30] Fourth, several witnesses employed Red-baiting tactics, claiming that contraceptives were synonymous with Communism and "superpacifism." Fifth, opponents contended that the bill would encourage promiscuity, free love, and abortions as well as destroy "the normal God-given function of womanhood," that is, childbearing. Last, some opponents adopted racist arguments, claiming that only whites used contraception; legitimizing it would lead to a further decrease among the "best" group, while the "blacks, yellows, browns, and the mongrels" would "multiply their rate of increase."[31] With so much opposition, legislators believed the status quo was the best option.

Following defeat, reformers placed hope in Franklin D. Roosevelt's ascent to the presidency. Eleanor Roosevelt had been active in the movement during the 1920s, serving as a board member of the ABCL. Moreover, Franklin Roosevelt appointed some contraceptive supporters to his inner circle. Expectations for a shift in federal policy disappeared when the press reacted adversely to Eleanor's support of contraception; she kept her opinions private after 1932. The president refused to meet with Sanger. Perhaps he feared alienating Catholics, who voted in large numbers for Democrats. Gradually, his inner circle disassociated themselves from the movement and remained silent on the issue.[32] Not surprisingly, bills before the House and Senate the following year met with defeat.

At the same time, the Senate Committee on Interoceanic Canals considered amending the penal code in the Panama Canal Zone to allow physicians to distribute contraceptives and receive them in the mail. Racism toward blacks dominated. Charles F. Wahl of the Canal Zone Central Labor Union testified that there were thirteen thousand employees in the zone: three thousand "American citizens" and ten thousand "aliens" from Jamaica, Barbados, and the West Indies. The "aliens" were raising eighteen thousand children, and "just by that one statement you can visualize what chance a white man in Panama has, if it keeps up." One senator asked Wahl if the target of the code was "aliens," to which Wahl responded: "If they could get that advice and use it, they would be better off, and so would we, down there." Although receptive, the senators decided that a uniform policy must be maintained; when the House and Senate defeated the contraception bills for the mainland, the penal code in Panama remained unchanged.[33]

Undaunted by defeat, advocates for change used the rest of 1933 to regroup for a push in 1934. By that time more than one thousand organizations had endorsed contraceptive reform, including the Federal Council of Churches, with twenty-three million members; the National Council of Jewish Women; the Central Conference of American Rabbis; the General Federation of Women's Clubs; the Young Women's Christian Association; the National Committee on Maternal Health; the National Women's Trade Union League of America; the American Civil Liberties Union; and local Junior Leagues, representing twelve to thirteen million members.[34] With this support Sanger kicked off the 1934 campaign with an American Conference on Birth Control and National Recovery rally in Washington, D.C. The rally's banner depicted the National Recovery Act's blue eagle using lightning bolts to fight off multitudes of storks and carried the slogan: "Six millions [*sic*] children in the United States on public relief. Two birth control bills pending in Congress." The NCFL succeeded in getting two bills introduced, in the House by Walter M. Pierce (D-OR) and in the Senate by Daniel O. Hastings (R-DE). The NCFL gained the support of a few celebrities, including Amelia Earhart, and *Newsweek* endorsed the bills.[35]

The Catholic Church led the resistance, using nativist and race suicide notions rather than church doctrine to defeat the bills. Father Charles E. Coughlin, the Detroit radio priest, argued that if the government repealed the law, alien races would drive the Anglo-Saxon stock out of existence, resulting in Washington, D.C., being renamed "Washingtonski" and "prolific" blacks overrunning the country. Mary Norton applauded Coughlin: "Instead of spreading information on how to prevent child birth, we should endeavor to instruct women how to bring happy, healthy children into the world, for the time is fast approaching when we shall be obliged to depend upon the countries of the old world for future generations."[36] Coughlin and Norton ignored the fact that the groups they denigrated, Poles and Old World populations, were primarily Catholic. Rather than base their resistance to change on moral grounds, they chose the politically expedient path of aligning themselves with nativists who believed that liberalized reproductive policies would lead to the downfall of the "American race."

Advocates of a new population policy fought back. Hepburn testified that the "theory that [the bill] is going to bring about race suicide is absolute nonsense, because of the strong maternal instinct in women." Here again, reformers were quick to affirm white upper- and middle-class woman's true role as mother: birth control would allow her to choose when to have children, not to avoid having them altogether. Pierce argued, "No one need worry about race suicide. What we seek is protection of the race from the suicidal effects of the present conditions of things." Both Guy Irving Burch of the Population Reference Bureau and Professor Ellsworth Huntington of Yale University argued that in countries where contraception was accessible to all, "the more fortunate classes" and the "most successful people" had more children than the "less fortunate." Such a trend would improve the American population and lead to economic recovery because these families would have more disposable income to spend on their children.[37] These arguments failed to convince politicians.

The NCFL launched one last attempt in 1935. Again, it emphasized the economic and social need for a liberalized policy. The Federation of Women's Clubs, an upper-class Protestant organization, endorsed the campaign and passed resolutions stating that "because of the over 4,000,000 families depending on Federal relief and the 250,000 babies born to these families, the federation is in favor of the relief administration taking steps as to prevent the recurrence of such situations."[38] The government refused to comply. A sarcastic exposé on the congressional defeat of the 1935 bill appeared in the *New Republic*. "I judge from what I read in the newspapers that officialdom is very pleased with the high birth rate among our millions . . . on the relief rolls. . . . Congress was importuned to pass a law permitting the spread of information about birth control . . . and declined." Advocates of the bill argued that "people on relief ought not to have so many babies. Congress evidently disagreed with this view."[39] Public opinion did not support congressional actions. A *Farm and Fireside* poll showed a two-to-one margin in favor of contraceptive distribution by physicians, while a Protestant *Churchman* poll found almost unanimous approval in 1935. A *Fortune* survey in 1936 found that 63 percent endorsed the transportation of contraceptive devices through the mails, 23 percent were opposed, and 14 percent were undecided. Among Catholics, 42.8 percent supported a liberalized policy, while 45 percent objected. Although the samples in these surveys are suspect, a Gallup poll the same year found that 70 percent approved and 30 percent disapproved.[40]

Why was Congress so reluctant to modify its stance? Social and economic dislocation from the Depression heightened anxieties regarding sexual behavior. The marriage rate fell, while the divorce rate increased. These statistics prompted opposition to birth control among sexual conservatives who feared an increase in illicit sex.[41] Perhaps growing wariness of German, Italian, and Japanese aggression motivated politicians' concern about maintaining a source of able bodies for a draft, if needed.

More important, many politicians feared a loss of votes if they opposed the church's will. A 1930 papal encyclical reiterated the church's antipathy to all "artificial" contraception and now condemned all abortions without exception.[42] This latter aspect devalued the mother's life in favor of the fetus. The National Catholic Welfare Council lobbied successfully: "I ask you, gentlemen, in the name of the twenty million Catholic citizens of the country, to whose deep religious convictions these vices are abhorrent . . . to report unfavorably on this diabolical and damnable bill!" The church also used the pulpit to keep its flock in line. Sanger told her son Grant that she had "wasted five years" because much of Congress was "full of fears . . . mainly fear of Catholic opposition."[43] Politicians realized that reformers were not one united powerful bloc. Catholics, on the other hand, could exact political reprisal if Congress liberalized the statute. The safest route was to avoid political responsibility and let the proposals die in committee.

Judicial Reform

With legislative change unlikely, Sanger and her associates shifted tactics and sought a judicial resolution. They arranged to have a case of vaginal pessaries shipped from Japan to Dr. Hannah Stone, a gynecologist and longtime ABCL ally, and informed the customs office of its arrival. When the government seized the products, the ABCL had a respectable doctor as a claimant.[44] *United States v. One Package* came before Judge Grover Moscowitz of the U.S. District Court of Southern New York in January 1936. Moscowitz decided in favor of Stone: while the statute seemed to forbid the importation of articles to prevent conception, he believed it should be construed more reasonably with regard to physicians. The government appealed the case, but judges Augustus N. Hand, Learned Hand, and Thomas Swan in the Circuit Court of Appeals upheld Moscowitz in December 1936. They added that doctors had the right to bring such articles into the country, to send them through the mails, and to use them for the well-being of their patients. The judges contended that the legislative intent was to prevent contraceptives' "immoral," not proper medical, use, especially disease prevention.[45] These judgments confirmed judicial interpretation offered by Crane almost twenty years earlier. *One Package* obviated the NCFL because its goals had finally been achieved, although many state restrictions remained intact.

Several court decisions in the early 1930s had laid the basis for loosening medical restrictions on contraception. In three cases concerning imported books that mentioned birth control the courts ruled that the material did not constitute obscenity. In another case involving a trademark infringement on contraceptive devices Swan recommended a reevaluation of the legislative intent of the Comstock Law.[46] These four cases established the favorable judicial climate that culminated in *One Package*.

What impact did these court cases have? Physicians gained the legal right to distribute contraceptives. Most Americans, however, purchased birth control through bootleg trade. Only one percent of an annual $250 million in contraceptive sales came from diaphragms; the majority obtained diaphragms from pharmacists without a doctor's prescription. The sale of condoms boomed under the guise of disease prevention. The surge in manufacturing as well as easier access did not symbolize a rejection of motherhood. The initiative for contraceptive use came from women who wanted to improve their domestic situation.[47] They were generally not avoiding childbirth but controlling the timing of births either to achieve economic stability or to attain the growing norm of a smaller family size.

The 1936 decision was a turning point. In its wake the AMA endorsed contraception in 1937. Failure to do so earlier did not imply consensus: local gynecological societies, the AMA's Obstetric, Gynecology and Abdominal Surgery Group, and the Medical Women's National Association had endorsed contraceptives years earlier, as had doctors working in clinics. The AMA joined them in 1937 not due to a belief in a woman's right to control her fertility but due to doctors' calls to curb the dispersal of ineffective or dangerous contraceptives that had emerged to satisfy consumer demand. The FDA answered this call in 1937 by regulating and inspecting condoms. Medical school curricula incorporated contraceptive training, and many doctors now viewed birth control as a means to avoid VD and protect women's health from incessant childbearing. Rights to distribute contraceptives meant that some doctors benefited economically from a booming business. Clinics multiplied, although many doctors favored hospital clinics over freestanding clinics because they viewed lay staff as possible rivals.[48] These changes did not usher in a golden age of birth control. The 1930s saw increased publicity about and access to contraceptives compared to earlier decades. Nonetheless, many women and men still had no access to and/or little knowledge of birth control.

Judicial sanction also led to federal involvement in contraceptive distribution, albeit on a small and quiet scale. In 1937 the Farm Security Administration (FSA), which dealt with migrant camps and was particularly concerned with maternal and infant health programs, acknowledged that many women requested information on contraceptives. Such initiative on the part of indigent women dispelled the notion that this group lacked the desire to control their family size. FSA staffers worked with the ABCL to distribute provisions in southern and western migrant camps, mainly in California. ABCL nurses instructed FSA agents in viable contraceptive methods, and by March 1939 350 FSA workers were distributing supplies. These efforts faltered in the South for a number of reasons: some husbands opposed birth control; some women lacked necessary information; some women disliked the methods available, especially those not suited to homes or camps without running water; and some women trying to procure supplies without a prescription encountered resistance once the ABCL's free sample kits ran out. These programs remained intact in California throughout World War II. Despite the popularity of this plan, Washington bureaucrats refused to make known their work with the ABCL and withheld any mention of contraceptives in their reports. The decline of the FSA—due to wartime economic prosperity, migration of farmers to urban defense jobs, increasing opposition in Washington to New Deal legislation, and tensions between the FSA and the AMA over government involvement in health care delivery services—brought an end to federal involvement in mainland birth control distribution until the 1960s.[49]

State-Funded Clinics

The increased national acceptance of contraception contributed to the emergence of publicly funded clinics. They first appeared in the South, where the unemployed swelled relief rolls. North Carolina established the first state clinic in 1937 under Dr. George M. Cooper, director of Maternal and Child Health and assistant director of the state board of health. Cooper received support from Dr. John Norton, a public health officer who was "one of the earliest people in the country to come right out for birth control and to institute state-supported services" in 1937.[50] Cooper was willing to incorporate contraception into the public health system, if he could secure outside funding.[51] Clarence J. Gamble, longtime advocate of contraceptives, agreed to contribute $4,500 to finance the first year. Four years later, 75 percent of state public health units offered contraceptive services, although few women successfully obtained information—only 4 percent by 1940. Gamble withdrew his money the same year because officials kept the program quiet.[52] Still, it gained notoriety in some national publications as well as in state newspapers.[53] In 1939 South Carolina made contraception a public health service. Initiating a campaign in 1936 to reduce maternal and infant death tolls, the resulting March 1939 program also intended to reduce high fertility of the poor and those on relief. One official reiterated the familiar axiom, "The people least equipped to provide for them have the biggest families." These services met no public opposition, perhaps due to the lack of a strong Catholic presence. Alabama followed in 1941, as did Florida, Georgia, Mississippi, and Virginia by the end of the decade.[54]

Government involvement in contraception also emerged in Puerto Rico during the mid-1930s. Between the world wars, birth control on the island became a complex issue fought over by contending factions. Hard-line eugenicists advocated it to limit people of color, public health workers and reformers promoted it to reduce maternal and infant mortality, and many women fought for it to control family size. The Catholic Church, on the other hand, opposed it, as did the Nationalist Party, which saw contraception as an imperialist and genocidal plan.[55] While advocates managed to open voluntary organizations such as the League for the Control of Natality, established in Ponce in 1925, and the 1932 Birth Control League in San Juan, they ultimately failed because of church pressure. As the Depression worsened, colonial bureaucrats believed overpopulation exacerbated growing joblessness, destitution, malnutrition, and social turmoil.[56] In May 1935 the Puerto Rico Emergency Relief Administration allowed contraceptives to be dispersed for maternal health at fifty-three clinics; social workers referred individuals on relief. Mainland Catholic officials quashed this plan. The following year, Ernest Gruening, director of the Division of Territories and Island Possessions of the Department of the Interior, attempted to incorporate contraception into Puerto Rican Reconstruction Administration projects that dealt with infant and maternal health. Because 1936 was an election year, the government buckled to Catholic opposition, especially from Cardinal Francis J. Spellman of New York.[57]

After *One Package*, however, the Puerto Rican legislature acted. A 1937 law allowed doctors to dispense contraceptives not only for medical reasons but for poverty and "bad social conditions," and it legalized both eugenic and contraceptive sterilization. Two years later the Insular Health Department Program incorporated contraceptive services. Twenty-three privately funded clinics opened in Puerto Rico. In 1939 a case challenging the Puerto Rican law reached the federal courts. The judge sustained the legislation but, in line with *One Package*, barred economic and social justifications. Mixed reactions ensued. While many feminists fought for the right to birth control, the Catholic Church continued its opposition. Moreover, the Puerto Rican Nationalist Movement viewed contraception as a means by which imperialists could ignore the socioeconomic problems on the island.[58] Nationalist aversion to contraception resembles mainland black nationalists' position during the 1930s.

The Response of the Black Community

Birth control was not new to the black community during the Depression. Many black newspapers had advertised methods since the late nineteenth century, Black Belt pharmacies had stocked contraceptives, and many blacks had practiced birth control prior to the introduction of clinics in the South.[59] Nevertheless, contraceptive programs brought mixed reactions from black leaders. Some of them opposed these programs because of race suicide theories. Dean Kelly Miller of Howard University used arguments analogous to those employed by Teddy Roosevelt and others earlier: upper-class blacks, the intellectual elite, were heading toward extinction, while the masses were multiplying. Although he desired a reduction of births among the poor, he believed access to contraceptives would only increase an already widening differential between the birthrates of upper- and lower-class blacks.[60]

Some black nationalists also opposed liberalization. They believed the survival of the race and the augmentation of its power depended upon increased numbers. W. Montague Cobb, a black anthropologist, feared that in the future the white majority might eliminate a black minority. He advised the black American to "maintain his high birthrate. . . . This alone has made him able to increase in spite of decimating mortality hardships. If the tide should turn against him later," he continued, "strength will be better than weakness in number."[61]

This "power through numbers" rhetoric did not attract a large audience during the 1930s. W.E.B. DuBois criticized those who were "led away by the fallacy of numbers" and "cheered by a census return of increasing numbers and a high rate of increase." DuBois advised black Americans to learn that "among human races and groups, as among vegetables, quality and not mere quantity really counts." George Schuyler, columnist for the *Pittsburgh Courier*, agreed: it was "far better to have less children and improve the social and physical well-being of those they have." Dr. Charles H. Garvin argued that contraception would not lead to "race suicide" but to "race preservation and advancement." Racial improvement would be realized with "fewer and stronger babies, higher quality, low quantity production."[62]

Some leaders opposed contraception on religious grounds. Marcus Garvey and his followers believed it interfered with God's will. At the Seventh Annual Convention of Garvey's Universal Negro Improvement Association, held in Jamaica in 1934, members unanimously adopted a resolution recommending that blacks not "accept or practice the theory of birth control such as is being advocated by irresponsible speculators who are attempting to interfere with the course of nature and with the purpose of the God in whom we believe." Garvey's religious background was Catholic, and these views reflected the dictates of the church.[63] Most black ministers did not agree with this moral objection. Many spoke of family limitation from the pulpit and distributed pamphlets among their congregations.[64]

Other prominent blacks not only endorsed contraceptives but supported them on feminist grounds. DuBois, for example, contended as early as 1919 that the "future woman must have a life of work and future independence. . . . She must have knowledge and she must have the right of motherhood at her own discretion." Three years later he criticized as "reactionary barbarians" birth control opponents who desired women to fulfill their biological function. Garvin wrote that it was the "inalienable right of every married woman to use any physiologically sound precaution against reproduction she deems justifiable." Disputing Dean Miller's contention that black women had too few children, journalist J. A. Rogers declared: "I give the Negro woman credit if she endeavors to be something other than a mere breeding machine. Having children is by no means the sole reason for being."[65] Similar themes are also apparent in the writings of some black women. In plays published after World War I, female authors criticized the lack of accessible birth control.[66] Black women's fiction also dealt with birth control as a significant aspect of their lives, especially Jessie Fauset's *The Chinaberry*

Tree and Nella Larsen's *Quicksand*. Black women, according to historian Loretta J. Ross, "saw themselves not as breeders or matriarchs but as builders and nurturers of a race, a nation."[67] Such feminist themes, noticeably absent among white advocates of contraception, gained support from some women and men in the black community.

Black newspapers generally supported contraception. They argued that birth control could reduce the number of black women dying from bungled abortions. Newspapers offered respectful coverage of black doctors arrested for performing safe, albeit illegal, abortions. Stories reported that such abortions were the result of women's efforts at reproductive control, not of "poor health or sexually transmitted diseases." Mainstream white newspaper coverage differed greatly: neither abortionists nor women tended to be portrayed sympathetically. While supportive of birth control, black newspapers criticized any policies that promoted population control.[68] Individual autonomy was paramount, especially in light of white population control rhetoric calling to reduce the fertility of the "inferior," a term easily construed by the black community to apply to them.

Many black activists considered contraception as part of a comprehensive health program. Most participants distributing contraceptive information were also active in health clinics and black women's clubs. They believed contraceptives could help improve the health and status of their neighbors as well as bring racial uplift. In rural areas home demonstration agents (similar to settlement workers in urban areas) visited homes to spread information on a host of health issues, including birth control. Unlike many whites who saw contraception as a panacea for the poor, many blacks considered it one aspect of a larger agenda. It could help eliminate one cause of socioeconomic stress, but real progress could only be achieved if society insured equal economic, political, and social opportunities.[69] Black activists stressed the health aspects of contraception and avoided any mention of free sexuality, an understandable tactic in light of white stereotypes surrounding black sexuality, that is, that women were promiscuous and men hyperpotent.

The black community, therefore, was fairly receptive to birth control. The Colored Women's Club Movement championed it, as did the National Urban League, the National Association for the Advancement of Colored People (NAACP), the National Council of Negro Women, and leading black newspapers such as the *Pittsburgh Courier* and the *San Francisco Spokesman*. The Reverend Adam Clayton Powell, Jr., pastor of the Abyssinian Baptist Church in New York City, toured publicly to advocate birth control. The minutes and newsletters of the Bureau of Social Hygiene and the Division of Negro Service (DNS), a department established within the Birth Control Federation of

America (BCFA) in 1939, showed strong support for contraceptives among the black community.[70] The national advisory council of the DNS included DuBois; Mary McLeod Bethune, founder and head of the National Council of Negro Women; Walter White, executive director of the NAACP; Adam Clayton Powell, Jr.; and Professor E. Franklin Frazier. A. Philip Randolph, president of the Brotherhood of Sleeping Car Porters, lent his support, and the National Medical Association (the black counterpart to the white AMA) endorsed contraception in 1941.[71]

Loretta J. Ross has argued that historians have often portrayed the contraceptive movement as having been "thrust upon reluctant African-Americans by a population control establishment anxious to control black fertility." Instead, Sanger's early feminist arguments for birth control helped to galvanize black women's "covert support for and use of family planning into the visible public support of activists in the club movement."[72] Historian Johanna Schoen asserts that in many locales white officials hindered black access to birth control because white women often refused to use an integrated clinic or because officials did not believe the government should provide health services for blacks.[73] African American activists formed their own clinics, a feat some white population control advocates hailed as an effective check on black fertility. When the International Union for the Scientific Investigation of Population Problems claimed at its 1931 meeting that the black population would increase in the United States because of immigration restrictions, higher wages, improved hygienic and social conditions, and reduced infant mortality, American delegates refuted this conclusion based on the opening of contraceptive clinics, which were being "considerably used by the negro population."[74] Despite these intentions, black women benefited from and helped to spread such services.

The involvement of the black community can be seen in the establishment of neighborhood clinics. In 1925 the National Urban League worked with the ABCL to establish a clinic in the primarily black Columbus Hill area of the Bronx. Four years later the Urban League and the BCCRB opened a clinic in Harlem, endorsed by the black newspaper, the *Amsterdam News*. When restrictions on contraceptive information loosened during the 1930s, blacks opened and operated clinics in numerous cities, including Baltimore; Richmond, Fredericksburg, and Lynchburg, Virginia; Nashville; and Berkely County, South Carolina. Kentucky had a number of clinics, as did Oklahoma and Washington, D.C. West Virginia opened the first statewide birth control clinic operated by blacks in 1938. Little organized resistance to these clinics within the black community emerged, and black urban birthrates declined noticeably during the 1930s, mimicking a trend that had begun in the 1880s.

The national black TFR fell from 7.5 in 1880 to 2.87 in 1940. That this decline was part of a conscious attempt by blacks to limit their fertility is no longer in dispute. The health thesis posited by earlier historians—that the decline in black fertility was a result of poor health conditions and diseases—has been convincingly refuted by historian Carole R. McCann and others.[75]

The Case of Rhode Island

The grassroots activism witnessed in some black communities and in white volunteerism in clinics such as the Cleveland Maternal Health Association was also apparent in Rhode Island. The situation here was unique in several ways. Not only did the clinic serve all races, religions, and ethnicities, but it was the only one in New England. Despite a large Catholic presence, the legislature did not restrict access to birth control, nor did it close the clinic. Some claimed that this lack of regulation was a legacy of free expression and civic liberty by state founder Roger Williams.[76] The clinic staff followed the national discourse on contraceptives closely but rejected the eugenic and classist rhetoric of Sanger's ABCL, although they did share the aversion to feminist justification for birth control. The clinic emphasized instead the connection between contraception and women's health, a tactic that helped quiet opposition to its program.

The Rhode Island Birth Control League (RIBCL) opened on 31 July 1931 in Providence with an annual budget of five thousand dollars. The president of Brown University, the dean of Pembroke College, four Protestant clergymen, forty-three physicians, and "civic-minded citizens" sponsored the clinic, lending it a sense of authority in the community. The staff included a male doctor, a trained female social worker, and a registered female nurse. The executive officers over the next two decades were women, with a few exceptions; the doctors were all men, ostensibly to gain legitimacy. The RIBCL worked closely with physicians: of 80 honorary members, 39 were doctors, and the RIBCL received endorsements from 119 "prominent" physicians. Dr. Edward S. Brackett, chief of staff of Providence Lying-In Hospital, became the medical advisor. Thus, the tension between doctors and clinics experienced in other studies does not apply to Rhode Island. Moreover, the clinic opened six years prior to AMA endorsement of contraceptives, demonstrating that physicians did not speak in one voice on this issue. As white elite men, their support may have been part of the population control agenda, but the records make no such reference.

In some ways the clinic mirrored developments in other regions. Most if not all of the officers and board members were Protestant: records mention unsuccessful attempts to induce local Catholic leaders to join the board of directors. While the clinic worked with black community leaders, staff and board members appear to have been white. The RIBCL opened two extension clinics, one in Newport in February 1935 and one in Washington County in June 1940.[77] All three gave advice only to "properly accredited married women" who "because of mental or physical disability cannot safely bear children" and charged fees on a sliding scale. A referral to the clinic had to be made by either a private physician, a hospital, a clinic, or a "recognized agency." The founding women boldly printed "Birth Control Clinic" on the door. The "more conservative members of [the] medical staff," however, were not as willing to publicize their work. When *Life* magazine sent a reporter to write about the clinic, staff "would allow none of it."[78] Doctors realized the fine line they were walking and that they stood to lose respect and socioeconomic status if they were portrayed in a negative light in the national media, especially in the context of AMA silence on the issue at this point.

A legal battle ensued following the clinic's opening. The board of aldermen voted eight to three to condemn the clinic based on Antonio C. Ventrone's argument that it was illegal and "morally wrong." The *Providence Visitor*, a Catholic newspaper, joined "the fray in desperate fury" and published a front-page picture of RIBCL president Mrs. Henry Salomon that portrayed her as "a malevolent old witch scurrying about and carrying a most sinister looking black bag." A month later the aldermen reversed their decision because Rhode Island had no law that regulated such a clinic and no statute that denied an individual's right to birth control. Ventrone responded that "if a physician were to attempt an abortion, he would be found guilty of murder in the first degree. This is one step earlier." His colleagues disagreed. One defended birth control on the basis of freedom of choice: "It is not for me to decide for others whether . . . birth control . . . is right or wrong. . . . It is best left to the conscience of each individual," an argument in line with Roger William's philosophy of civic liberty. Another argued that the nation was inundated with "repressive, prohibitory legislation" that resulted from "intolerance, bigotry, [and] fanatical frenzy" and that contradicted the American heritage of "personal freedom." Women's health was also a concern, one best left to the medical, not legislative, arena: "There can be nothing immoral in a doctor giving a patient information which may later save a mother's valuable life."[79]

With no legal obstacles, the clinic primarily served Rhode Islanders, but it was open to other New Englanders as well. The "majority of the patients" were "from families living on extremely limited incomes." Thirty-two percent of women had unemployed husbands "entirely dependent upon charity." The remainder labored under "economic handicaps" that made the "addition of another mouth to feed . . . a real calamity."[80] The records attest to women's determination to control their fertility. They were not pushed by agencies to visit the clinic, despite the stricture that women be referred; instead, the majority came "on their own initiative." Of the first eight hundred clients, 78 percent had unsuccessfully tried contraceptives before seeking aid. By 1935 that percentage was 84.3 and by 1939 91 percent.[81]

Such statistics are important for several reasons. First, they confirm Andrea Tone's argument that most Americans obtained contraceptives from bootleg trade, pharmacists, and the like.[82] Second, they confirm that lower-income couples desired to control their fertility; access, not ignorance and reticence, as population controllers contended, was often the barrier. Clinics in other areas found similar results. Dr. Sarah Marcus's clinic on Cleveland's South Side among immigrants and working-class women made her aware of the desperate demand for safe and reliable contraception. Dr. Marie Kopp analyzed ten thousand cases from New York City collected by the BCCRB in 1932 and found that nearly all of the sample came from the poorer classes.[83] The average applicant was between thirty and thirty-five years old, had been married eight years, and had a family income of less than twenty dollars a week. Before seeking medical advice, 93.3 percent had attempted some form of birth control (excluding abstinence). A similar 1933 investigation in a Newark, New Jersey, clinic determined that 91.5 percent of the clients had employed family limitation before visiting the clinic.[84] While these studies have an urban bias, they still testify to lower-income women's motivation to control their childbearing.

Who were these women? Historian Jimmy Elaine Wilkinson Meyer's study of the Cleveland Maternal Health Association lacked racial or ethnic data on clients, but the RIBCL kept such records. From August 1931 to December 1933 RIBCL staff recorded the ethnic/racial identity of 776 women (see table 4.1). In the early years "Americans" comprised 52 percent of the clientele and immigrants and second generation 48 percent. While the ethnic background of clients generally matched that of the state, discrepancies were apparent with the English, Irish, and French Canadians. As WASPs, British immigrants may have faced less discrimination and thus were sounder financially. For the Irish and French Canadians, Catholicism could have been a determining factor, although it did not seem to affect Italians significantly. In 1935 the staff listed only three categories: American, 69 percent; Italian, 9 percent; and other, 22 percent. The increase in Americans was due to the elimination of the second-generation division. The following year the Italian separation disappeared, leaving American, 70 percent, and other, 30 percent. Had the RIBCL been swept up in the racist rhetoric prevalent at the national level,

Table 4.1. Ethnicity of RIBCL Clients and State Residents

	RIBCL clients	% state population
"American"	404 (52.06%)	—
Italian	110 (14.17%)	19.7
Italian second generation	31 (3.99%)	—
Portuguese	30 (3.86%)	4.3
English	29 (3.73%)	12.7
Canadian	21 (2.70%)	4.2
Armenian	17 (2.19%)	0.8
"American Negro"	17 (2.19%)	1.4
Russian	14 (1.80%)	2.9
Jewish	12 (1.54%)	—
Irish	11 (1.41%)	14.9
English second generation	11 (1.41%)	—
Scotch	9 (1.15%)	3.2
Irish second generation	4 (0.51%)	—
Polish	4 (0.51%)	4.8
Canadian second generation	4 (0.51%)	—
Nova Scotian	4 (0.51%)	—
Portuguese second generation	3 (0.38%)	—
Jewish second generation	3 (0.38%)	—
German	3 (0.38%)	2.2
Austrian	3 (0.38%)	0.4
Swedish	3 (0.38%)	3.0
French Canadian	3 (0.38%)	19.6
French Canadian second generation	2 (0.25%)	—
French	2 (0.25%)	0.9
French second generation	2 (0.25%)	—
Lithuanian	2 (0.25%)	0.5
Russian second generation	2 (0.25%)	—
Brazilian	2 (0.25%)	—
"Roumanian"	2 (0.25%)	0.2
Swedish second generation	2 (0.25%)	—
Danish second generation	1 (0.12%)	—
Dutch	1 (0.12%)	—
Norwegian	1 (0.12%)	0.3
Syrian second generation	1 (0.12%)	—
Finn	1 (0.12%)	0.2
Belgian	1 (0.12%)	0.3
Polish second generation	1 (0.12%)	—
German second generation	1 (0.12%)	—
Armenian second generation	1 (0.12%)	—
Greek	1 (0.12%)	0.5
Indian	1 (0.12%)	—

Sources: Monthly reports of social worker, files 1932, 1933, PPRI Records; U.S. Bureau of the Census, *Fifteenth Census of the United States: 1930*, vol. 3, pt. 2 (Washington, D.C.: Government Printing Office, 1932), 762.

the staff would have lamented that the majority of clients were American, not immigrants, but no such criticism is evident. The average client age was twenty-nine.[85] Of the 2,221 clients between 1931 and 1938, 43 percent had not finished grammar school, and only 11 percent had graduated high school (versus a national average of 30 percent).[86] These low educational levels did fit population controllers' target groups, but the RIBCL records do not hail as successful their work to reduce fertility among the poor and uneducated. While they may have discussed this aspect amongst themselves, they left no written evidence.

RIBCL staff did record the motivating factor for clients. Between August 1931 and December 1933 32.48 percent of the women came with a physician's referral; 31.33 percent came of their own accord despite restrictions on self-referrals. Medical and social agencies referred 11 and 6 percent, respectively, while 3.09 percent fell among "others."[87] These statistics are telling. First, despite the AMA's silence prior to 1937, private physicians were recommending contraceptive services for patients. That they referred rather than dealt with women could be a result of lack of training in contraceptives, fear of being affiliated with a controversial topic, or a recognition of patients' needs for subsidized devices, a service they were unwilling to provide. Second, physician and agency referrals could reflect the white elite establishment's attempts to reduce the fertility of the poor and uneducated. Third, against the national rhetoric that low-income women were unwilling to employ contraceptives, RIBCL clients demonstrated marked determination to gain access. Their resolve increased as the Depression continued (see table 4.2). Most self-referrals heard from other patients and sought advice even though they knew "they [were] expected to bring a physician's statement."[88] Self-referrals were not turned away; patient confidentiality would have prevented outsiders from discerning whether the staff adhered to clinic referral policy.

Self-referrals were more committed than women who had been referred. RIBCL social worker Sophie R. Gordon often called referrals "non-cooperative patients" who refused to return for follow-ups. Social workers instituted a home visitor plan to reach them, but it was ineffective: some argued that their husbands or clergymen opposed contraception or that contraceptives were too "troublesome."[89] That referred women were noncompliant is not surprising. They may have visited doctors or social agencies for problems unrelated to birth control. To have an outsider suggest a need to reduce family size could have been construed as a criticism of existing family norms. Doctors and agencies may have referred families they considered "unfit" or "inferior," a distinction these women would have rejected. The staff offered no understanding of the dilemma these women faced but simply labeled them

Table 4.2. Referral of Women to RIBCL, 1935–1939

Year	Self-referral	Physician referral	Community agency
1935	37%	33%	30%
1936	38%	36%	26%
1937	45%	34%	21%
1938	59%	25%	16%
1939	53%	28%	19%

"uncooperative" because they rejected advice that agencies and staff members believed was in the referred women's best interest. The latter may have interpreted such suggestions as coercion as they came from those with power and status.

Some of the "noncooperative patients" complained about the methods prescribed. Similar to national trends, the most prescribed method was the diaphragm with jelly (93.43 percent, versus the condom with jelly, 4.37 percent, the sponge with foam, 1.87 percent, and the cervical cap with jelly, 0.31 percent).[90] Some referred women refused the diaphragm because either it was too cumbersome, or it caused irritation, or they lacked the confidence to use it properly. One social worker concluded, "Fortunately there is a very large group of very cooperative and appreciative women who more than 'make up' for those few patients" who, once referred, did not return.[91] These appreciative women came of their own volition rather than being forced to do so, an important distinction social workers failed to make. Ninety percent returned regularly, and they experienced a 97 percent success rate from 1934 to 1941.[92]

The husband's role in contraceptive decisions was mixed. The social worker claimed that "with very few exceptions, the applicants have talked over with their husbands the advisability of seeking advice and the decision is, therefore, one which has been reached by those most interested." The husband's consent, however, was not mandated. Some accounts reported husbands' refusal because a woman's duty was to bear unlimited children. A twenty-seven-year-old woman with seven children found pinholes in her diaphragm. The clinic doctor gave her a new one and told her to hide it and place the old one in the usual spot.[93] While his action encouraged marital deception, it demonstrated concern for the patient's well-being over socially accepted norms of patriarchy in marriage.

These records demonstrate birth control's impact on married women. "My husband has worked on and off for the last five years," declared one woman. "We love our children dearly, but when you are unable to provide for those you already have, I don't think it fair to bring more into the world." One woman with four of her six children living and her husband unemployed told Gordon, "You can't imagine what a change has taken place since my instructions here. For the first time in our 16 years of married life we are living naturally. The worry, the dread, and the tension has disappeared and I feel young again." Similarly, another client remarked, "I was sick and discouraged to death of married life. I thought all of the time about divorcing my husband," but now, "without any fear of getting pregnant it seems as if we are living a new life—free from worry." Birth control also contributed to successful childrearing. As one woman concluded, "The Birth Control Clinic has changed me from a cross, irritable woman who worried herself sick from the fear of having another baby to a cheerful, happy, contented mother, with all fear gone." Another woman claimed, "I have regained my strength and can care for my children as I should."[94]

The RIBCL cited this humane aspect more than the ABCL. At a fundraiser Dr. Brackett argued that birth control was important but "should not be expected to take the place of other relief measures: . . . there is demonstrated beyond a doubt the need for every form of efforts which can contribute to the general welfare." President Eleanor Jones of the ABCL, on the other hand, advised the crowd that without clinics, "birth control would not spread in the right directions." It must spread quickly in "city slums" among those who "would have children that would be a burden to society and a detriment to the race." Jones endeavored to persuade RIBCL staffers that the reduction of the "socially inadequate" was "worth any amount of trouble, any amount of money. For reduction of the fertility of the unfit . . . means that there will be fewer people born, *good-for-nothing*, for welfare agencies to struggle with in vain and the rest of us to support."[95] As ABCL president, Jones was responsible for raising funds from a broad public sector, a goal she presumably believed could be achieved with race suicide theories and welfare savings ideas. Such propaganda was missing from RIBCL records with two exceptions: the RIBCL spoke of "physical betterment of the race" and the burden of "public charges" in letters to convince Rhode Island's national representatives to support legislation in 1932 and 1934.[96] Such arguments were more persuasive to legislators concerned with national security and budgetary issues than were those based on women's health. The latter argument was more likely to attract mothers, not male legislators.[97]

The RIBCL was similar in some ways to clinics around the country. First, it opened during a transition time for women activists, after the suffrage movement but before World War II drew large numbers of women into the paid workforce. Second, it operated prior to AMA endorsement of birth control. Meyer argues that clinics demonstrated the public demand for reproductive services, which could have served as a catalyst for the AMA to act or get left behind. Third, between 80 and 90 percent of clients had practiced contraception prior to seeking out a clinic. The RIBCL and other clinics, however, moved in the opposite direction of pharmacists and the black market, placing contraceptives in women's hands with diaphragms rather than in men's hands with condoms. Fourth, female staff pushed the edge of respectability in pursuing their middle-class activism within the disreputable realm of sexuality.[98] Although birth control was not illegal in Rhode Island, any association with sex was still suspect. They situated their activism within the larger context of health for both mothers and children, thereby diminishing the sexual nature of contraceptives and avoiding notions of sexual liberation for women, either married or single. Feminist notions were absent from the records. These middle-class founders of the clinic served primarily working-class clients in much the same way that other middle-class volunteers benefited working-class mothers and children in movements for milk stations, settlement houses, child labor laws, and mandatory school attendance.

Illegal Abortions

The Depression led to an expansion of abortion services. Economic circumstances often led officials to look the other way, allowing abortions to occur with less threat of penalty. Some doctors, according to Leslie Reagan, "specialized" in abortion and "ran what may be called abortion clinics." Her study of a Chicago clinic found eighteen thousand abortions occurring between 1932 and 1941. Most of the women were married, in their twenties, and from varied class backgrounds. Approximately half came to the clinic with a physician's referral, demonstrating the collusion of respected professionals in answering women's demands for abortion. The clinic was able to operate through regular payments to the police.[99] Such open practices occurred in many regions of the country as increasing numbers of women sought abortions.

Although Rhode Island had no overt abortion clinic, abortions were prevalent nonetheless. In the RIBCL's first month of operation, 37 percent of clients came to obtain an abortion; the next month, 18 percent; the next, 15 percent. The decreasing percentage resulted from quick word of mouth that the clinic would not provide abortions. Upon rejection, one woman self-induced and returned for medical assistance, demonstrating her determination both to abort and to gain clinic assistance. Elmer Wright, social worker, found that women sought abortions "in spite of the possible consequences. In fact, for the average number of living children of each patient we find a long list of self-induced abortions." A thirty-three-year-old mother of four told Wright of eleven self-induced abortions, the last of which landed her in the hospital. RIBCL staff estimated that three thousand abortions occurred annually in Rhode Island and that 16.2 percent of maternal deaths in 1930 and 21.2 percent in 1932 resulted from abortion. From their own sample, the first 800 clients reported 3,617 pregnancies: 613 ended prematurely—450 miscarriages and 167 abortions. But, as their report concluded, "figures for miscarriage are always deceptive as few women will admit abortion; referring to it as a miscarriage and maintaining it was accidental." Staff pointed to 1934 statistics from Rhode Island Hospital that reported 189 women hospitalized for bungled abortions; 109 had previously been hospitalized for abortion complications. Yet the staff argued that their contraceptive services were decreasing the incidence of abortion: at Rhode Island Hospital 28.9 percent of gynecological admissions in 1932 resulted from bungled abortions, 23.4 percent in 1934, 18.6 percent in 1935, and 11.9 percent in 1936. The staff failed to consider rising hospital births during the 1930s, which could explain the relative drop in the percentage but not the numbers of admissions for abortion complications. While their statistics may have helped in fund-raising activities, the data do not reflect the reality regarding abortion. In fact, abortion continued to be a widespread recourse. Twenty-two percent of new patients in 1936 reported self-induced abortions, 23 percent in 1937, 22 percent in 1938, and 18 percent in 1939. The latter year saw an additional twenty-six women who came to the clinic seeking an abortion, totaling 27 percent who obtained or hoped to obtain an abortion.[100]

While the RIBCL data set dealt with married women who self-induced, Rhode Island newspapers confirmed that both married and young single women sought paid services. The majority of abortionists investigated were women. Officials continued to arrest and prosecute men involved in procuring abortion. One man, a thirty-three-year-old marine, impregnated a nineteen-year-old woman, confirming fears of the sexual threat sailors and soldiers posed to Rhode Island women.[101]

The RIBCL hoped contraceptives would eliminate abortion, but at least one doctor saw this stand as cowardly. Dr. A. J. Rongy, a Russian Jewish immigrant, radical, and AMA member, contended that no matter how hard contraceptive advocates endeavored to separate abortion from birth control, the two were "intimately and indissolubly linked" because women who expected to delay or forgo childbearing would often resort to abortion if their contraception failed. He criticized Protestant churches that supported birth control while condemning abortion as "sinful" and "obscene": "It requires a gargantuan imagination to conceive of abortion as indulged in for its obscene gratifications." Even worse was the Catholic Church, which aggravated the "basic causes of abortion . . . by its insistence on the sinfulness of contraception." Rongy claimed that a "counterrevolution" in Western society had restored birth control to individual choice but lamented that the "same rationality . . . is not yet employed toward abortion."[102]

Rongy's sympathy for women and feminism is clear. The lack of access to safe abortions forced them to resort to unwanted children or to underground and sometimes fatal procedures. A physician providing abortion services was "regarded as a sort of benign Robin Hood who defies the law to help the needy" and thus was "not stamped with a stigma of shame." The "organized profession" could not "fly too boldly in the face of the public standards of right and wrong," but in private many physicians favored "some sort of liberalization" because "no matter how callous the average physician appears to be, he is not left unaffected by the pathetic and often pitiful pleadings of the woman to whom a new pregnancy is a genuine cause of distress." Increasing economic participation of postwar women was "part and parcel of the emancipated femininity," but women could not manage both career and childbearing. Rongy condemned laws that forced women to seek abortions in "haste and fear and secret." Compelling women and abortionists to break the law increased contempt for the law in the same way that Prohibition did.[103] The AMA based its opposition to abortion in part on the Hippocratic oath, yet Rongy argued that Hippocrates did not personally oppose abortion; he endeavored to prevent male physicians from "encroaching on a field already possessed by . . . female doctors of Greece who were experts in abortion. The utterances of Hippocrates . . . may mean that this was a subject more expertly handled by the sages-femmes of the period."[104] Rongy's interpretation of Hippocrates matched well with the AMA's nineteenth-century portrayal of abortionists as primarily women.

Abortion, similar to contraception, was part of supply and demand in the private sector. Compiling hospital statistics, Rongy found that for every one hundred women treated for abortion complications, forty-three had had at least one prior abortion, thirty-four had had two, and eleven had had three. Since World War I, Rongy concluded, the "demand of women to have abortions . . . has become so insistent that the entire medical profession has, in essence, been revolutionized." While his statement was an overgeneralization, young doctors were especially involved in the abortion trade: young women "reluctant to go to their family doctor" sought a physician starting a practice and offered him "tempting fees."[105] Pharmacists controlled some of this networking: women made a "beeline for the drugstore" because the druggist was in an "unusually effective position to spread the reputation of a neighboring abortionist." With abortion so "widespread," laws against it were ineffective because public opinion favored "greater freedom in the matter of childbearing."[106]

Rongy recommended a law that foreshadowed 1960s legislation. Abortion should be allowed in cases of rape and incest and to preserve the physical and mental health of women. This latter aspect was a considerable expansion of existing legislation that allowed abortion to save the life, not preserve the health, of a pregnant woman. He stipulated that illegitimacy, desertion, and widowhood should be grounds for abortion. Married couples with living children should be able to avoid an additional birth to protect the well-being of existing children. Rongy argued that "either parent" should "have the right of invoking" abortion.[107] While his law would greatly ease restrictions, it did not protect all women's right to choose. A healthy married woman in an economically secure household would have no legal recourse to abortion. Furthermore, he did not clarify how a husband could invoke a right to abortion. This stipulation conflicted with a woman's right to control her body. Rongy did not argue the inverse, that is, that the husband should have the ability to prevent his wife from aborting, as late-twentieth-century antichoice activists did. Both, however, promoted third-party control over the decision to abort in some instances.

Rongy's endorsement of legal abortion reached a limited audience. Most magazines and newspapers refused to advertise his book. Even though many doctors were performing or referring women for abortions, the profession refused to push for liberalized laws because of abortion's association with radical groups with whom conservative doctors did not wish to collaborate.[108] Feminists also did not push for reform. As adamant as population controllers were to achieve their agenda, even they did not advocate abortion to shape the population. Congress, reluctant as it was to liberalize contraceptives, steered clear of any discussion of abortion. With no groundswell for legislative change, abortion remained illegal unless performed to protect the mother's life.

Sterilization

While population controllers stayed away from abortion, the same is not true of sterilization. In fact, sterilization gained increased attention as the Depression worsened. The economic situation and the emphasis on population control led to a push for sterilization of the "unfit" in public institutions. Paul Popenoe, who had rejected sterilization in the 1920s, became one of its most vocal advocates. Annual sterilizations reached new heights as state hospital budgets decreased. Lacking the finances to erect additional facilities, discharging the mildly retarded to make room for the more severely retarded seemed acceptable, especially once the parolee was sterilized. As Molly Ladd-Taylor argues, officials portrayed compulsory sterilization "as a bargain for taxpayers, who would otherwise have to pay for charity or the costs of institutionalizing the 'unfit' and their children." Between 1907 and 1927 8,500 institutionalized individuals were sterilized; during the 1930s the annual number peaked at 4,000.[109]

To bureaucrats, sterilization provided a cost-effective means to deal with undesirable reproduction.[110] The Human Betterment Foundation (HBF), founded by Popenoe, stressed the humane aspects: sterilization "removes no organs or tissues from the body, interferes with no blood or nerve supply, produces no physical changes. It does not in any degree unsex the individual, except in making parenthood impossible."[111] The HBF estimated that 18 million Americans were in some way physically and mentally defective. The "economic burden" they posed was "tremendous and steadily growing worse. A billion dollars a year would be a low estimate of the cost of caring for these unfortunates." Many eugenicists estimated that of 125 million Americans, at least 25 million were socially maladjusted or unadjusted, including the unemployed and unemployable, deaf, deformed, blind, delinquent, mentally deficient, degenerate, and infectious.[112] Such arguments helped increase the acceptance of the procedure among bureaucrats and legislators.

Leaders of the sterilization cause often overlapped with contraceptive liberalization activists. In Providence Sanger asked the crowd, "What are we to do with these defectives?" No one wanted to bear the burden of their expense: "Even the Catholic Church . . . will not take care of its own mental defectives, but puts them back on the State or nation." If society did not adopt drastic measures, future generations would be forced to carry the expanding debt of the mentally and physically impaired. "The time has come," Sanger insisted, "to demand something be done to curb the increase" among "defectives." The permanent solution of sterilization, according to Sanger, was preferable to the temporary and often uncertain methods of contraceptives.[113]

By 1936 twenty-seven states had either compulsory or voluntary sterilization laws. Harry H. Laughlin of the Eugenics Record Office, who was "an enthusiastic supporter of Nazi Germany," justified these laws because the state had no qualms imposing the death penalty or denying individual freedom through military conscription.[114] Both cases were acceptable because "in the long run, the welfare of the commonwealth is of vastly more importance to the sum total of human happiness than is the temporary freedom and personal security of the individual." The same ideology could be applied to reproduction: "By all means aid . . . the poor, the unfortunate and the suffering, but permit only those individuals most splendidly endowed by nature, with socially valuable physical, mental and moral qualities to reproduce."[115] In other words, only upper- and middle-class white Anglo-Saxon Protestants should replicate themselves.

Between 1907 and 1936 23,118 people were sterilized under state law; most of them were mentally deficient, idiots, insane, epileptics, or imbeciles. But some states stretched the interpretation of "undesirables" to include prostitutes, persons convicted of two crimes, drug addicts, and sodomites. Hardliners employed racial doom propaganda to convince society that laws should be compulsory, not voluntary, as a "necessary step to prevent racial deterioration" and to protect the government from "mentally abnormal . . . voters."[116] All mental institution inmates must be sterilized before release: "After all, the real risk to society comes from hereditarily dangerous people who are at liberty." Their sterilization would remove "a burden from society" because they not only threatened racial purity but could not be responsible parents. The CMH agreed: all "feeble minded and insane persons in institutions" should be sterilized before returning to "community and family life."[117] Social Darwinist notions abounded: the charity, welfare, education, medicine, and technology of the modern state interfered with natural "survival of the fittest." Before a House committee on destitute citizens, Dr. Lee Stone of Madera County testified about "Oakies." He believed that "to give these people a bed and a mattress would be like putting a blanket over a pig. . . . If you come down to me," he continued, "I would say, sterilize the whole bunch of them."[118] Popenoe stated: "In modern civilizations, where the weak and helpless are protected so carefully, it is not possible to depend on Nature to solve this problem of the survival of the unfit." These arguments, coupled with economic distress, increased sterilizations: between 1930 and 1933 50 percent more sterilizations occurred than over the preceding twenty-five years.[119]

By the 1930s few eugenicists still believed that aberrant social behavior was genetically transmitted to offspring. While still intent on sterilizing those with genetic defects, many officials now emphasized preventing childbirth among parents considered socially and economically inadequate to care for children. This transformation, according to historian Philip Reilly, brought an increase in female sterilization. In 1927 53 percent of people sterilized were men; between 1927 and 1932 67 percent were women. Welfare agents and doctors encountered more women than men and were more inclined to target women than men for sterilization. Many mildly retarded women were institutionalized specifically so they could be sterilized and then released. The HBF boasted that 75 percent of the "feebleminded" girls sterilized under California law were actually "sex delinquents" likely to rely on public funds if they became pregnant; "only one in every twelve" resumed sexually delinquent behavior following the procedure. The HBF's goal was twofold: save money and curtail women's sexuality. The sex discrepancy in procedures continued even though males exceeded females in institutions for the retarded by 10 percent and a vasectomy was easier and safer than a tubal ligation. Braslow argues that another reason for this skewed gender ratio was that by the 1930s "physicians lost their faith in the restorative powers of male sterilization." In his study of Stockton Hospital male sterilizations fell from 1,064 between 1910 and 1926 to 537 between 1930 and 1950; the number of female sterilizations in the same periods rose from 460 to 588. Allison C. Carey finds a similar national trend: professionals attacked the rationale for male sterilization but continued to tout the benefits of female sterilization for both women and society. The primary justification for female sterilization, according to Ladd-Taylor, was the savings in cost to the state.[120]

Sterilization proponents looked to Nazi Germany as the model for programs targeting the "unfit." Ironically, the Germans modeled their eugenic law, passed on 14 July 1933, on Laughlin's draft. In reaction to the German law, Leon F. Whitney, secretary of the American Eugenics Society, claimed: "Many far-sighted men and women in both England and America have long been working earnestly toward something very like what Hitler has now made compulsory." American eugenicists boasted of their influence on German law and became energetic promoters of it. Kopp studied German policy and recommended its implementation in the United States because it was "imperative to correct conditions undermining the health of the nation." Kopp praised the German law because it applied not only to people in institutions but to the population at large.[121]

The 1935 International Congress for Population Science in Berlin marked the height of international sanction of Nazi race policies. The conference's two vice presidents were Americans: Laughlin and Clarence G. Campbell. The latter lectured that Hitler had synthesized the works of American eugenicists "to construct a comprehensive race policy of population development and improvement that promises to be epochal in racial history. It sets the pattern which other nations and other racial groups must follow." When Campbell returned home, he campaigned to sterilize at least 10 percent of the population to prevent race degeneration.[122] His plan met resistance.

Aversion to Sterilization

Many Americans rejected sterilization. Some held a "deep-seated repugnance" for any "meddling with the sexual organs." Numerous scientists objected because of the scarcity of reliable data that showed that defects were hereditary. While the BSH concluded that eugenics had "attracted persons of unequal attainment and scientific standing . . . they numbered in their ranks idealists whose zeal prompted them to formulate programs based on stronger claims than the known facts seemed to warrant." Similarly, the American Neurological Association (ANA) reported in 1936 that legislation was based "more upon a desire to elevate the human race than upon proven facts." Although they understood social Darwinists, who resented measures that allowed the "sick, the weak, and the unfortunate to survive and propagate," they criticized overzealous eugenicists who recommended sterilization of the "ugly" and "asocial." While agreeing to sterilize some of these groups, they believed more research was necessary before turning to mass sterilization because madness could breed genius, as in the case of Hans Christian Andersen, Ludwig van Beethoven, and others who were offspring of quasi-mad parents.[123]

Some scientific and political organizations also expressed doubt over hard-liners' views that feeblemindedness was more prevalent among blacks and Italians. Geneticists Walter Landauer and Hermann J. Muller reviled the "scientific basis" of Hitler's anti-Semitism and Aryan supremacy and discrimination against blacks and other minorities. While Muller, who would win the 1946 Nobel Prize in Physiology or Medicine, and others rejected hard-line eugenics, they supported reform eugenics. The American Eugenics Society became the focus of the eugenics movement; it followed a more temperate path, especially in its rejection of unfounded racist and classist theories. Dr. Abraham Myerson, a Lithuanian immigrant, psychiatrist at Boston Psychopathic Hospital, and later professor of neurology at Tufts College Medical School, demonstrated that feeblemindedness occurred equally among the classes, not overwhelmingly among the lower classes, as hard-liners argued. Psychiatrists in elite psychiatric hospitals such as Butler Hospital in Providence reached the same conclusion. Myerson also led an ANA investigation into sterilization among the institutionalized mentally ill. The June 1935 report renounced the eugenic principle that mental disease was increasing and ruining the race; commitment rates had increased but as a result of up-to-date treatment at modern institutions and increased longevity, leading to more cases of senility.[124]

Catholic editors of *Commonweal* added this scientific position to their moral condemnation of sterilization. Church leaders argued that insufficient concurrence among authorities existed to warrant "drawing the lines about a whole group as to be restrained by law from reproducing their kind." Once governments adopted such programs, the line could be stretched from "pathologically insufficient" to "merely very dull or very simple," all to ensure that society was "spared the results of their sexual indulgence." No one had license to maim another based on societal considerations. *Commonweal* also charged that the "sexual mutilation of the pauper feeble-minded [was] a piece of arrant class discrimination" that contradicted the nation's democratic foundation.[125]

Such arguments appealed to the legacy of individual rights in Rhode Island. A new senate measure emphasized the "welfare of society" as justification for the procedure but added that the "health of the individual" would also benefit. It applied only to institutionalized clients suffering from "insanity, idiocy, imbecility, feeble-mindedness or epilepsy." The bill revealed economic concerns in language similar to that heard at the national level: "The state has in custodial care and is supporting in various state institutions many defective persons who if now discharged or paroled would likely become, by the propagation of their kind, a menace to society, but who, if incapable of procreating, might properly and safely be discharged or paroled and become self-supporting, with benefit to themselves and to society." The eugenic strain was also more evident, again reflecting the national discourse: if a state superintendent found that an inmate "by the laws of heredity is the probable potential parent of socially inadequate offspring likewise afflicted . . . and that the welfare of the inmate and of society would be promoted by sterilization," the state could order the operation.[126] While such arguments worked elsewhere, they fell on deaf ears in Rhode Island, leaving sterilization unregulated for the remainder of the century. While Catholic pressure could have been responsible for the measure's defeat, the scenario was unlikely; similar pressure could not convince the General Assembly to ban birth control. With no legal restrictions, doctors could set their own standards, and voluntary sterilization did take place.[127]

Sterilization laws in other states drew criticism because of their compulsory nature. Hawaii experimented with contraceptives and sterilization to curtail "antisocials" and those on relief, a program with class and racial implications. Work in the cane fields attracted immigrants from Puerto Rico and the Philippines, but officials claimed that the "melting pot of races here had produced something detrimental to the community." Dr. Nils Paul Larsen of Queens Hospital in Honolulu found that the reproductive rate among reliefers, the insane, the neurotic, and the feebleminded was much higher than that of "normals." As a result, Hawaii passed a compulsory sterilization law for those deemed by psychiatrists to be "unfit" for procreation.[128] This law left psychiatrists, most of whom were elite white men, with a great deal of power to determine who in their view was fit or not. The Catholic journal *America* denounced the compulsory aspect of the law as an "intrinsically immoral invasion of the human person." Omitting any discussion of church policy, the editors argued the state had no right to destroy the "capacity of an innocent person to procreate." Economic justification was dangerous to the freedom of individuals: "Once we adopt materialistic 'social utility' as an overriding standard of public morality, mercy-murder of 'social misfits' will be the logical next step." The law was also class biased: it subjected public institution patients to compulsory sterilization but exempted financially secure feebleminded patients.[129]

How did the black community respond to sterilization? While Schoen found some black physicians advocating access to it as an effective method of birth control, most blacks opposed sterilization. The Colored Women's Club Movement criticized its excessive use on black women. DuBois wrote in the *Pittsburgh Courier* that "the thing we want to watch is the so-called eugenic sterilization" because the burden of such programs would "fall upon colored people and it behooves us to watch the law and the courts and stop the spread of the habit." Editorials in the *Courier* rejected sterilization because eugenicists advocated it for the "weak and oppressed" and for those on relief who were "having a large number of children." Some sterilization advocates proposed candidates who were homeless, unemployed, or on relief. Because blacks often found themselves in these situations, many feared they would become the prime target. As the *Courier* concluded, "With the Negro disfranchised, what will he be able to do about it?"[130]

By the late 1930s, as news spread of the perverted Nazi program, calls for moderation in population policy intensified. The *Population Bulletin*, earlier an advocate of eugenic sterilization, now criticized "alarmists" who advocated the sterilization of hundreds of thousands or even millions of the mentally or physically impaired. The editors also opposed "voluntary" sterilization as the price of a marriage license for certain "undesirable" elements of society. During depression or war, when people attributed their troubles to scapegoats, civil liberties were at risk; "Hitler-type demagogues" could "whip up resentment against a minority group." Society must be on guard against plans to improve the race, they warned, lest the United States follow the path of dangerous dictators in other countries.[131]

Nazi population policy contributed to the decline of hard-line eugenicism in the United States, but not until the 1940s. Adherents were slow to acknowledge Nazi abuse; some continued to travel to Germany early in the war to meet with sterilization program leaders. The latter convinced the former that the Nazis were implementing "a large scale breeding project, with the purpose of eliminating from the nation the hereditary attributes of the Semitic race."[132] These Americans carried back positive impressions of Nazi programs, negating information from Jewish and German émigrés who endeavored to alert the American public to the inhuman devastation. Not until after the war did American eugenicists claim they were critical of Nazi programs. This attempt was too little too late.[133]

Other events also led to the demise of hard-line eugenics. Henry Fairfield Osborn and Madison Grant—prominent eugenicist and author of *The Passing of the Great Race*—died, Charles Davenport retired, Harry Laughlin was ousted from important political and scientific posts, and the Carnegie Foundation ceased funding the Eugenics Record Office in 1939. Mainstream society opposed overt anti-Semitic assertions. Genetic breakthroughs undermined the unsubstantiated assertions of eugenics. More people turned to sociology to answer problems associated with poverty. The therapeutic value of sterilization fell out of favor as new technologies and treatments, such as electroshock therapy, lobotomy, and occupational and recreational therapy, became available to treat mental illness. Eugenicists and geneticists continued to study individual genetics, but coercion and promotion of programs to save the race declined. Instead, some scientists turned to new technologies—genetic counseling and prenatal diagnosis—to help individuals make choices that were right for them. As Diane B. Paul concludes, researchers "shifted from concern with the welfare of populations to the welfare of the individual families, as determined by the families themselves." Regard for patients' rights, previously ignored by many eugenicists, became a consideration following the war.[134] Professional concern for individual rights did not extend to all, then or now. New technologies have been used primarily to help middle- and upper-class white couples experiencing fertility problems, not lower-class racial and ethnic minorities. Still, the overt calls to sterilize the "unfit" did subside.

In the early 1940s the Supreme Court acknowledged the class bias in sterilization laws. The Habitual Criminal Statute of Oklahoma allowed the state to sterilize some repeat offenders until Jack T. Skinner, accused again of armed robbery and chicken larceny, challenged it. In *Skinner v. Oklahoma*, 316 U.S. 535 (1942), the Court invalidated the statute because it contradicted the equal protection clause by stipulating sterilization for some criminals but not others. Embezzlers (white-collar criminals), for example, were exempt. Unlike Holmes in *Buck v. Bell*, Justice William O. Douglas argued that the "power to sterilize, if exercised, may have subtle, far reaching and devastating effects [and in] evil or reckless hands, it can cause races or types which are inimical to the dominant group to wither and disappear."

Although hard-line eugenics fell out of favor, mainstream eugenics, according to Wendy Kline and Laura Briggs, lasted longer than most historians assume. The *Journal of the American Medical Association* published Clarence J. Gamble's eugenic articles during the 1950s and wrote editorials in support of eugenic family planning as late as 1961. Eugenics shifted from a strict hereditary explanation of degeneracy to incorporate environmental factors.

Mothers came under increasing scrutiny because they shaped children long after pregnancy; thus, mothers must be "fit" not only to bear but also to raise young children. With this new emphasis, eugenics continued well into the 1960s. Kline concludes that "continuity, rather than discontinuity, characterizes" eugenics between the 1930s and the postwar period.[135] This continuity can be seen in welfare officials' treatment of white versus black mothers on Aid to Dependent Children (ADC) and in continued population control agendas in the postwar period. Involuntary sterilization may have fallen out of favor in the immediate aftermath of Hitler's genocide, but it reemerged relatively quickly, rearing its head once again in the 1960s as welfare agents targeted indigent black and white women for coerced sterilization procedures.

Conclusion

As the nation concentrated on World War II, the population discourse that had raged during the 1930s subsided considerably. What had been accomplished? Doctors could now prescribe contraceptives in all states except Massachusetts and Connecticut, and seven southern states incorporated contraceptives into their public health programs. The discussion that brought about these changes generally lacked any feminist rationale. Instead, positive and negative eugenic arguments based on the "fit" versus the "unfit," race, and class dominated. White elite population controllers' cries of racial degeneracy superseded any assumption of a woman's right to control her body. The push for change came predominantly from white upper- and middle-class men and women concerned with the composition of the population. Ironically, the movement benefited middle- and upper-class women with access to safe and regulated contraceptives through their doctors, a choice not affordable to many low-income and indigent women. Clinics such as the RIBCL helped bridge the gap in access for lower-income women. These clients either ignored or were unaware of the classist and racist rhetoric of population controllers: women availed themselves of contraceptive services to fulfill their own agenda, namely, to control their family size and protect their health.

Liberalization of contraceptives did not extend to abortion. No groundswell for reform emerged among feminists, doctors, or population controllers. A few radicals such as Rongy did promote change, but they received little or no attention. Not surprisingly, then, the courts and legislatures ignored the issue, and abortion remained illegal except to save the mother's life.

Sterilization, on the other hand, was central to the discourse on population policy. During the Depression population controllers advocated it as the answer to both state budgetary problems and race degeneration. The procedure burgeoned in number, targeting far more women than men compared with earlier decades. Welfare measures allowing officials to determine who was "unfit" brought more women to officials' attention as generally women, not men, applied for assistance through programs such as ADC. While association with Hitler's genocide quieted overt calls for sterilization, this situation was only temporary. By the late 1950s and 1960s officials once again turned to sterilization as a simplistic answer to perceived problems of population.

5

World War II, the Baby Boom, and the Population Explosion, 1939–1963

During and after World War II Americans had greater access to contraceptives than previous decades. The military dispensed condoms to soldiers as part of a campaign against venereal disease. Birth and population control advocates capitalized on the national preoccupation with the war to promote contraception's contribution to national health, soldiers' fitness, the wartime economy, and women's ability to undertake war work. While abortion remained illegal unless the woman's life was at stake, officials often ignored the practice, as it helped maintain a stable defense workforce. Sterilization did not disappear, but in the wake of Nazi abuse population controllers no longer publicly touted it as the solution to societal problems. The dramatic loss of life at war's end led to pronatalist attitudes similar to those of Dr. Horatio Storer in the post–Civil War period: while not as blatant as Storer, population controllers worried over who would replace the war dead. The postwar baby boom, which affected women in all socioeconomic classes, quieted but did not erase population controllers' anxieties over differential fertility rates between the educated and uneducated. They turned their efforts to the "population explosion" in the Third World. By the 1950s researchers had developed a new technique—the pill—that could be readily dispensed to low-income and indigent women overseas, and they began testing its effectiveness on "human guinea pigs" in Puerto Rico. Concern over the "quality" of the population both at home and abroad continued to dominate the national discourse. Generally untouched by these trends, the RIBCL evolved into a comprehensive health care facility, which brought it in conflict with PPFA. At the same time, this expansive health care program led to a strong rapport with the local black community. A microlevel analysis of developments at the Rhode Island clinic in the 1940s and 1950s shows the impact of grassroots activists on the lives of individual women determined to control their fertility.

World War II

War led to concern over not only the composition of the population but, specifically, the quality and health of men in the armed forces. Thomas Parran, appointed surgeon general in the spring of 1936, contended that the rejection or deferment of 40 percent of draftees was a "national disgrace." In an article in Washington's *Sunday Star*, Blemont Farley, director of public relations of the National Education Association, stated: "We have lost more men in World War II because of educational and physical deficiency than we had under arms in World War II." As of 1 February 1945, according to Farley, 5,704,000 men had been rejected for military service. Appalled, Guy Irving Burch of the Population Reference Bureau wrote that continued proliferation among the "wrong groups of people" was ruining American defense capability. "Uncontrolled human reproduction," he contended, favored the "survival and multiplication of the least gifted members of society" and endangered "human liberties and any chance for a world at peace."[1] Former domestic concerns now had international and national security implications.

A year later President Harry Truman addressed Congress regarding declining mental and physical standards. Selective Service exams "revealed the wide-spread physical and mental incapacity among the young people of the nation." The approximately five million men between the ages of eighteen and thirty-seven classified as unfit for military service had cost the nation dearly; "mental cases" occupied more than half of hospital beds at a cost of $500 million a year, "practically all of it coming out of taxpayers' money." In addition, more than 1.5 million soldiers had been discharged due to physical or mental disability, exclusive of wounds, and an equal number had been treated for diseases and defects that existed before induction.[2]

This rhetoric did not necessarily reflect reality. An ignored government survey found that the three primary reasons for deferral were "defective vision," "insufficient teeth," and syphilis. A navy report produced similar data and added that the often-quoted "defective physical development" generally referred to men who were over- or underweight, over or under a certain height, or too small chested. While height and weight standards were a safety issue, other deferments were the result of a "desire to protect the taxpayers from the treasury drainage of pensions and rehabilitation of unfit candidates. . . . We will have enough pensioners after a national emergency without recruiting defective individuals."[3] Prophets of racial doom failed to differentiate between medically valid defects and defects deemed so by the government to save money.

VD, on the other hand, was a serious medical "evil" that cost the armed services in lost duty and diversion of medical resources despite rapid and effective treatment with sulfa drugs and penicillin by 1944. Prior to the war, Parran labeled VD the primary public health problem and called on the federal government to provide funds to battle it. Congress responded with the National Venereal Disease Control Act in May 1938, allocating federal grants to state boards of health to expand programs and investigate new remedies. Yet Congress did not appropriate money for chemical prophylactics and condoms, the most important safeguards, due to the influence of sexual conservatives and the Catholic Church.[4] The acute level of infection among troops and its impact on American fighting power changed the government's position. The military's main concern was combat readiness, not sexual mores and political wrangling with the church. The army initiated a VD campaign and in 1942 established the Venereal Disease Control Branch in the Preventive Medical Division, with Lt. Col. Paul Padget as its head. Films, posters, and pamphlets urged men to avoid illicit sex. Men who could not remain abstinent should use mechanical and chemical prophylactics provided in their supplies so that, as Padget said, soldiers "drew condoms at the same time they drew their soap and brushes." The army also scattered prophylactic stations around popular leave areas.[5]

Controversy arose over whether similar tactics should be used in the newly formed Women's Army Corps (WAC). Its establishment heightened anxieties about changing gender norms. Women in the formerly all-male military assumed the traditional male roles of primary breadwinners and defenders of the nation. Many civilians and even the mainstream press depicted military women as sexually adventurous, a characteristic condoned in male GIs but not in women. In reaction, WAC Director Oveta Culp Hobby attempted to portray WACs as celibate. The military support of condom distribution to men did not extend to women.[6]

On the domestic front, population control advocates feared a widespread campaign encouraging patriotic women to have children to replace men lost overseas. Liberalized contraceptive policies seemed threatened. To counter this anticipated baby drive, they adapted their oratory to the national preoccupation with war. They argued for quality versus quantity as a source of national strength and contended that immediate additions to the population would be of no direct value in winning the war. A 1943 article in *American Mercury* by Mildred Gilman claimed that "too many subnormal people, too many 'borderline' cases, are breeding too high a proportion of our infants," thereby "filling our asylums, juvenile courts and hospitals." Others were quick to emphasize that the rejection of 40 percent of draftees left the healthy, fit, and intelligent to serve and die; the "billion dollars" spent annually to support the "feeble minded and mentally diseased" should be diverted to wartime efforts.[7] Cutbacks in social and relief programs to pay for the war made free contraceptives crucial for low-income and indigent women. In a vein similar to that employed by Storer after the Civil War, population controllers argued that replacements for the war dead should come from the healthy, educated, middle- and upper-class population, not from uneducated, low-income families. Population controllers touted contraceptives to limit "unfit" progeny and strengthen the family and thus national stability: planned pregnancies led to happy unions, while the stress and drain of an unplanned child led to marital discord. Loving couples were less likely to be tempted by enemy rhetoric.[8]

The anticipated pronatalist wave did not materialize, however, and new wartime roles for women increased acceptance of contraceptives. The Industrial Division of the United States Public Health Service in May 1942 sanctioned *family planning* for married women in war industries. A public relations specialist concocted the term to place contraception within the safe confines of marriage. Not an acknowledgment of a woman's right to control her body, this move expressed concern for a reliable labor force in vital war industries. Managers reported that work days lost to pregnancy and even abortion caused shortages that could worsen if the nation had to rely heavily on female workers. Doctors who faced women suffering from bungled abortions began to view the practice as a "public health problem." Suddenly, contraceptives became a patriotic symbol.[9] By January 1943 married women could obtain information on family planning at 795 clinics: 219 in hospitals, 272 in health departments, and 304 extramural. The medical profession jumped on the bandwagon: twenty-one medical schools gave instruction in contraceptive techniques, and 97.8 percent of doctors surveyed by Dr. Alan F. Guttmacher of Johns Hopkins School of Medicine approved of contraceptives for the mother's health; 79.4 percent approved for economic reasons.[10]

Public opinion also supported contraceptive use. A Gallup poll found that 77 percent of Americans favored teaching contraception through government health clinics.[11] In an August 1943 *Fortune* survey 84.9 percent of women agreed contraceptives should be available to married women; 69.8 percent believed the same for unmarried women. In a further breakdown, 92.6 percent of college-educated women, 70.2 percent of grammar school–educated women, and 69 percent of Catholic women approved of contraceptives for all married women; 78.5 percent of college-educated, 55.3 percent of grammar school–educated, and 58.9 percent of Catholic women approved for unmarried women.[12] Thus, Americans' break with church policy began well before the publicized gap in the 1960s.

The White House moved with the flow. Eleanor Roosevelt broke her silence and renewed her support following FDR's reelection in 1940. A year later she organized a White House conference on contraception, with activists and representatives from the Children's Bureau, the Public Health Service, and the Department of Agriculture. The resulting "Negro Project" targeted blacks suffering from inadequate public health services. The proposal for this project claimed that "birth control, per se, cannot correct economic conditions that result in bad housing, overcrowding, poor hygiene, malnutrition and neglected sanitation, but can reduce the attendant loss of life, health and happiness that spring from these conditions." A Division of Negro Service was established within the National Health Council, with an advisory council that included W.E.B. DuBois, Mary McLeod Bethune, Adam Clayton Powell, Jr., and other black ministers, doctors, and educators. Mrs. Roosevelt organized a second White House conference for December 1941. Two months later Parran endorsed state family-planning projects for married couples.[13]

The new emphasis on family planning was obvious in the 1942 transformation of the ABCL into the PPFA. Dr. Kenneth Rose, appointed national director in 1940, met with male leaders of various population control groups and engineered the name change over Sanger's objection. "Planned parenthood" conveyed married couples planning and spacing children, while "birth control" carried a negative image of people enjoying sex. Under Rose, PPFA followed a pronatalist path throughout the war and played down any feminist affiliation with birth control.[14]

Rhode Island during the War

RIBCL evolved into the Rhode Island Maternal Health Association (RIMHA) in 1939 because the term *birth control* was "obsolete." The new title reflected comprehensive health care and served as a disguise in a predominantly Catholic state. The new name brought a 25 percent increase in contributors. Still, RIMHA fell short financially because of new premarital and marital counseling programs and evening clinics to meet working women's demands. It opened a new clinic in Washington County in 1940. In 1941 leaders contemplated offering infertility services to answer client requests, augment RIMHA's legitimacy, and undercut Catholic opposition, but lack of funds prevented this expansion.[15]

During the war RIMHA worked with national organizations. It was one of thirteen states to send a delegate to a BCFA conference in New York City in May 1940 that stressed financial incentives to solicit physicians' support: "The idea must be sold that contraception under medical care will mean money in the physician's pocket." RIMHA disagreed: cooperation with physicians could ensure total health for clients, not profits for doctors. Still, RIMHA did elect a delegate to the BCFA board.[16] Both BCFA and RIMHA adopted "planned parenthood." RIMHA had employed the term in reports and memos as early as 1938. Two years later RIMHA circulated letters to clergymen asking them to mention "planned parenthood" in their Mother's Day sermons. The 1941 fund-raising manual emblazoned "Planned Parenthood for Healthy Mothers and Healthy Babies" on its cover. Thus, when the national organization changed its name to PPFA in 1942, RIMHA president Dorothy Hegeman applauded the move while simultaneously affirming RIMHA's title: "We in R.I. are holding to this emphasis. . . . [W]e are stressing the health, both in mind and in body, of our patients."[17]

Despite their congruence over planned parenthood, RIMHA and PPFA did not always see eye to eye. First, PPFA continued to stress the quality of the race in its propaganda, while RIMHA emphasized women's and children's health. Its fund-raising manual instructed volunteers that if people asked, "Does birth control mean race suicide?" they should answer, "The purpose of birth control is not fewer children but a better chance in life for more children." Missing was any comment regarding the race, ethnicity, religion, or class of the children common in PPFA rhetoric. As for queries regarding shirking motherhood, RIMHA staff pointed to a client with five sons. Second, RIMHA refused to buckle to pressure from PPFA in 1944 to change from a Class B affiliated local committee to a Class A state league of PPFA. RIMHA maintained control over clinic programs: national policy often had no bearing on local needs and little understanding of state politics.[18]

During the war, for example, RIMHA found itself in a bind between growing public acceptance and decreased government empathy: a Catholic administration governed Rhode Island in 1941. RIMHA's board set a policy of "very little publicity" because of the "precarious position with the present Catholic administration in the state." Officers felt particularly vulnerable due to their "proximity to Connecticut and Massachusetts," where laws prohibited clinics. RIMHA did not participate in PPFA's fund drive because officers received "warnings from people close to the State House that we must be extremely careful." The inability to publicize the Washington County clinic led to its closure in May 1943.[19]

Fortunately, RIMHA was able to connect contraception to the war effort. RIMHA worked with the Women's Defense Committee on joint press releases and emphasized "defense in our publicity." In 1943 Hegeman argued that "family planning is as much a part of any complete program for National Defense as the numberless other steps we are taking to preserve our nation. Millions of mothers are going into war work—the American woman is now facing heavy responsibilities and her health is paramount when she is doing the triple job of homemaker, production worker and breadwinner." Facing these responsibilities "without the fear of pregnancy" provided the "security" women coveted.[20]

This focus on health care led to a relationship between RIMHA and local black leaders. RIMHA prided itself on its long-standing rapport with the black community. The clinic had been integrated since its beginnings and experienced an increase in black clients from 2.19 percent in 1931 to 10.8 percent in 1941, even though blacks constituted just 1.3 percent of Providence County and 1.4 percent of the state in 1930 and 1.5 percent of both county and state in 1940.[21] This increase differs from Jimmy Meyer's study of the Cleveland Maternal Health Association, where the staff accepted black clients but labeled them "socially and economically handicapped and inferior," leading to a drop in black patrons from about 30 percent to 12 percent during this same period.[22]

The Urban League of Rhode Island (ULRI) considered RIMHA a "major" contributor to the health and well-being of the black community. The ULRI distributed pamphlets advertising clinic services and touting black leaders' views on contraceptives. A. Philip Randolph, the president of the Brotherhood of Sleeping Car Porters, believed that "better schools, better employment, better medical and recreational facilities will do much to produce a better generation, but planning for health must begin at home and if possible even BEFORE the next generation is born. Family planning is the first step in attaining this goal." Mary McLeod Bethune, president of the National Council of Negro Women, contended that "we, the organized women of America, have a special responsibility in creating a greater understanding of the significance of planned parenthood. Our welfare activities as well as our social contacts have made us aware of the many problems that arise from ignorance of child spacing and family planning." Mrs. Estelle Massey Riddle, consultant to the National Nursing Council for the War, remarked, "It is strange that in a country where education and training count for so much, we have been so long in realizing the great need for sound information and careful planning in the creation of our families." ULRI leaders described birth control as "preventive medicine," allowing women to "undertake pregnancies when they are physically equal to the task."[23]

Black churches also endorsed RIMHA, inviting RIMHA staff to address their congregations. RIMHA's board worked with Mrs. Walter C. Wynn, a black activist, to prioritize health problems among blacks. For the remainder of the war RIMHA held "well-attended" educational meetings at black churches, parsonages, and club gatherings. RIMHA was honored to play "an important role in the community" during such difficult times.[24]

The war posed difficulties for both RIMHA clients and staff. Many new clients had husbands in the service or had physically or mentally injured husbands; all wished to "postpone further pregnancies." The staff also felt the effects of war. Four of six doctors had entered the service by October 1942, leaving the remaining two to "find some women doctors"—a feat they failed to accomplish. Either no women doctors lived in the vicinity or a woman doctor was unwilling to risk her reputation at a controversial clinic. By 1944 one of the two remaining doctors had entered the war, but the clinic did not turn patients away. When gas shortages curtailed the home visitor program and women's ability to travel to the clinic, the staff mailed supplies home. The clinic had its own trouble procuring supplies; sometimes "inferior" materials arrived when not delayed by Railway Express strikes.[25]

Despite these barriers, RIMHA continued to provide service to the tristate area.[26] Despite Catholic policy, the majority of women were Catholics (47.9 percent), followed by Protestants (44.96 percent), Jews (6.35 percent), and "others" (.68 percent). Between 93.4 and 96.5 percent of women received a diaphragm and jelly, despite available instruction in the rhythm method to suit Catholic clients. Both statistics confirm a gap between Catholic policy and practices well before the 1960s. Some women came for abortions: eleven in 1940, fifteen in 1941, seven in 1942, and nineteen in 1943, a "marked decrease" from an annual average of fifty-five in the 1930s. Access to effective birth control or increasing economic opportunities could explain this reduction. Patients' annual income increased with the war, from $16.07 in 1939 to $29.58 in 1943. As economic prospects brightened, new patients decreased from 305 in 1941 to 258 in 1942 to 232 in 1943. Economically stable families could afford either "planned" children or private contraceptive care; as more physicians received training in birth control, the demand on clinics eased. The decline could also be a result of the decreased publicity due to political considerations. Friends were the main source of referrals (65 percent), followed by physicians at Quonset Naval Air Station. Between 20 and 25 percent of new clients during the war were wives of servicemen.[27]

As the war wound down the number of patients surpassed prewar levels, with 318 new clients between April 1944 and April 1945. An "unprecedented number" were service wives, reflecting the economic uncertainty of the war's end as well as returning injured veterans. Discharged physicians serviced this growing clientele: one doctor in 1945 grew to seven by 1947, all male. The staff found "an earnest acceptance" among the public of the "fact that child spacing" would help foster stable families. Ruth B. Lubrano, RIMHA social worker, concluded that "many homes have been saved from a separation because of the help obtained at the center."[28] Contraception helped prevent divorce; stable families, in turn, could ward off the threat of Communism.

The Postwar Period

With the war's end, selective-growth proponents resumed their drive to decrease "undesirables." Drafting doctors during the war had decreased sterilizations; as doctors returned, sterilizations increased but did not attain pre-war levels.[29] Contraceptive distribution offered the more acceptable solution to the "population problem," reflected in a pronouncement from the Federal Council of Churches in 1946: "The irresponsible who propagate recklessly" would soon "be represented in disproportionate numbers," unless society encouraged contraception to discourage parenthood among those "unfitted" to reproduce.[30] Their main concern was differential birthrates. A study by the Milbank Memorial Fund and Scripps Foundation for Research in Population Problems suggested that lower economic and social groups had the highest birthrate because they did not possess "as reliable [a] means of controlling their fertility as their more well-to-do neighbors." These researchers concluded that the "equalization of size of family among the various economic groups is . . . essential to the welfare of the nation." Burch contended that without an effective "humane selection of the fittest," the population would "deteriorate both physically and mentally."[31] Such a trend could damage American military and scientific competition with Communists.

The 1945 publication of the 1940 census confirmed that educational levels impacted women's prolificity. White American-born women between the ages of forty-five and forty-nine with four years of college had fewer than 1.25 children—a 45 percent replacement failure. With four years of high school, the corresponding figures were 1.75 children and a 21 percent replacement failure. Women with one to four years of grade school had 4.33 children and a replacement surplus of 95 percent. For white American-born women between the ages of thirty and thirty-four the fertility differences were even sharper: women with four years of college had .7 children; with four years of high school, 1.2 children; and with one to four years of grade school, 3.1 children. National discourse failed to note that the lower rates for the second group could be explained in part by their younger age: some probably had not completed their families. In addition, they experienced their fertile years during the Depression, when the fertility rate declined. Population control advocates contended that these birthrate differences were the "most serious population problems which the nation must face." If the trend continued for three generations, descendants of the lowest educational and economic level would outnumber the top third at least nine times. Society would deteriorate because "to understand and be able to help solve the complex problems of a modern democracy requires at least a high school education if not a college education." To reverse this trend, educated women must stop "shirking motherhood," and contraceptives must be dispersed among lower educational and economic levels.[32] These advocates looked to Sweden as a model. By implementing free obstetric services, nursery schools, and pediatric dental clinics to lower the cost of bearing and rearing children, Sweden's wealthy and educated were "scoring the highest birth rates," while women with less education and financial resources were bearing fewer children because nationwide they had access to contraceptives. *Colliers* called on Congress to investigate European models to reverse the American birthrate "shrinkage." They were not beneath Red-baiting: the Russians and the Chinese had too many people; the United States was falling far behind. To be a powerful international force, the "downward population spiral" must be reversed.[33]

Other factors exacerbated their fears. Many women who entered the workforce during the war hoped to advance in or at least maintain these higher-paid skilled jobs. Many observers predicted a drastic decline in fertility if women remained employed. Large-scale female employment was acceptable for emergencies, but the defeat of Germany and Japan led many Americans to expect women, particularly white middle-class women, to return to their "rightful place" in the home. Returning male GIs needed the jobs that some women occupied.[34] No call emerged for ethnic and minority women to return home: employers desired their cheap labor, and population controllers rejected them as suitable mothers for American citizens.

The Baby Boom

By 1947 the transition to private life and economic prosperity had produced an unprecedented national phenomenon, one that allayed temporarily the oracles of genetic ruin as it captured American "hearts and minds." The decline in fertility that had characterized American society since the early nineteenth century halted in the late 1940s. The TFR rose from between 2 and 2.5 for the Depression to between 3 and 3.7 for 1947 to 1964.[35] Catholic and black fertility rose proportionally faster: 3.7 for whites versus 4.3 for Catholics and blacks. Although both blacks and Catholics traditionally had higher fertility rates than white Protestants, in the 1930s blacks' fertility had fallen to all-time lows.[36] This decline accentuated the rise in black fertility a decade later.

What caused this aberration? Demographic observations include the increased number of women having at least two children; the decrease in women remaining single and childless and their average age at marriage; and the shorter interval between marriage and first and succeeding births. Unprecedented economic growth from the late 1940s to the early 1960s along with the GI Bill and veterans' benefits economically supported the boom. The abundance of jobs for the Depression cohort males may have encouraged couples to marry young and have several children. The psychological reaction to the loss of life and the separation of families during World War II led to a desire for a stable family life and the resurgence of promarriage, pro-housewife, and pronatalist ideologies. Childbearing and childrearing within marriage returned as one of the only acceptable avenues for women entering adulthood.[37]

The surprising rise in white fertility among all socioeconomic classes caught selective-growth proponents off guard. Unsure if the rise in fertility was a short-term aberration, government and business leaders continued to exert pressure to oust women remaining in the higher-paid, skilled jobs of wartime. Defying such pressure, women increased in the workforce during the 1940s more than any previous decade, albeit in mostly traditional pink-collar jobs. The *American Journal of Sociology* claimed this trend would decrease the birthrate. *Newsweek* blamed the impending doom on educated women: "For the American girl books and babies don't mix . . . ; it is the higher-educated wife, rather than the husband, who brings down the birth rate."[38] *Ladies Home Journal* concurred: educated women generally had one child, while women with a fourth-grade education were "almost certain to have at least four." "Danger of outright decline in the physical and mental makeup of our population" loomed, because children of college-educated parents have a "higher average intelligence than children born into noneducated homes." Educated women were "guilty of squandering their genetic inheritance" and "lowering the standards of future generations."[39] Yet the sharpest increase in the birthrate occurred among the most highly educated women.[40] Absent in these critiques was any condemnation of educated men's behavior. Prophets of genetic doom blamed women, implying that their selfishness and power over their husbands were the causes of national ruin.

One tactic to legitimize contraceptives during this period was to change activists' image. The Margaret Sanger Research Bureau (MSRB), for example, opened an infertility clinic in 1946 under the direction of Dr. Abraham Stone. Elizabeth Cohen Arnold, registered nurse and later clinical MSRB supervisor, asserted that new infertility services "made it easier to raise money from some people. It opened up doors and was a threshold to respectability." It also reduced Catholic opposition because the MSRB helped couples have babies. The choice of a male director increased the clinic's legitimacy. The MSRB accepted only married couples with a copy of their marriage certificate. Concern for its image also influenced the clinic's decision to avoid abortion referrals.[41]

Similarly, PPFA sought legitimacy in part by incorporating male leaders and members. Dr. Mary S. Calderone, medical director of PPFA (1953–64), claimed that PPFA wanted a man for her position, "but most male physicians would not risk their reputations." Because she had "none to risk" she accepted, but her public health colleagues "pitied" her for "professional suicide." Nevertheless, she helped win a place for family planning in American medical and public health establishments. In 1959 Calderone, along with Martha Eliot, head of the Children's Bureau, helped persuade the American Public Health Association to endorse planned parenthood. Calderone also convinced the National Health Council to accept PPFA as a member. In 1964, her last year as medical director, she persuaded the AMA to issue a statement on contraception, its first since 1937: "Family planning is not only responsible parenthood, it is responsible medical practice." In spite of her significant contributions, Calderone faced "sexist attitudes" within PPFA. When she left, PPFA replaced her with two male physicians, the younger of whom received a higher salary than Calderone had in eleven years. Planned Parenthood activist Beatrice Blair noted the enormous pressure to hire male executive directors and to have men on local Planned Parenthood boards. Such men were concerned over the "awful population explosion" in Third World countries. Calderone recalled that Cass Canfield's appointment as president represented the acknowledgment of the population explosion in underdeveloped countries in the face of decreasing fertility in the developed world. Canfield received male and big business support previously lacking for PPFA.[42]

The entrance of large numbers of men angered many women long active in the movement. Dr. Sarah Marcus stopped working at Planned Parenthood in Cleveland because it "had already started putting men on, a lot of men on." She resented them because they discriminated against women and because, unlike female activists concerned with birth control, men were interested in population control. Racism and classism were apparent among many new PPFA benefactors. As Blair concluded, they hoped PPFA would help reduce undesirable groups. Loraine L. Campbell contended that Doris Duke gave substantial contributions for "the wrong reason" as part of an "anti-black" cause.[43] While Blair and Campbell objected to this emphasis, it was not new: the ABCL had promoted the control of undesirables since its beginning.

The International Population "Problem"

By the 1950s a number of private organizations, such as the Hugh Moore Fund, the Population Reference Bureau, and the Committee to Check the Population Explosion, had engaged in a national discourse on the world population "predicament." No clearly organized movement emerged until John D. Rockefeller III founded the Population Council in 1952. The council helped establish an international population agenda and programs and legitimize the burgeoning field of demography. Rockefeller chaired the board, and Frederick Osborn was executive vice president while simultaneously president of the American Eugenics Society. The council gave professionals a reputable foundation to underwrite a "problem-oriented approach" to population.[44] Major foundations supported it because it sought to control population overseas, not fight for a woman's right to contraceptives at home. Campbell considered the establishment of the council a "striking blow at Planned Parenthood," which had been receiving financial support from the Rockefellers.[45] PPFA was "considerably weaker" than population organizations and in fact lost clients, workers, and local affiliates in the 1950s.[46] Unprecedented postwar prosperity undermined the economic justification for contraceptive dispersal so popular during the Depression, and the end of the war eliminated the emergency arguments used during the conflict.

While PPFA continued to focus on domestic issues, cold war zealots such as Hugh Moore, author of "The Population Bomb," splashed attention on the Third World "problem." Moore argued that poor nations needed contraceptives because a starving population was ripe for Moscow's rhetoric. The cold war attracted supporters to the population lobby among white elite businessmen who argued that investment could solve privation and halt the spread of Communism in Asia, Latin America, and Africa.[47] Much of this "problem," according to them, was located among these people of color.

By 1959 the federal government had examined the population "problem" and commissioned Gen. William H. Draper to study the United States Military Assistance Program, prompted by Senate accusations that the United States spent too much money overseas on military assistance rather than economic development. The Draper Report, made public on 23 July 1959, concluded that overpopulation hindered financial progress and recommended that U.S. foreign aid programs incorporate contraception.[48] Reaction varied. The World Council of Churches, the United Presbyterian Church, the Union of American Hebrew Congregations, and the American Baptist Convention endorsed the report in 1959. Catholic bishops objected. As a result, President Dwight D. Eisenhower ignored the report's recommendations, stating at a press conference: "I cannot imagine anything more emphatically a subject that is not a proper political or governmental activity or function or responsibility. This government has not, and will not . . . have a positive political doctrine in its program that has to do with this problem of birth control. That's not our business."[49] This speech came more from political considerations than personal convictions. In fact, a year earlier Eisenhower had asked the National Security Council how foreign aid could succeed if population growth continued at its present rate. When Draper asked Eisenhower years later why he had rejected the recommendations, he said he did not want to divide the nation on the eve of a sensitive election.[50]

Ironically, the earliest presidential endorsement of population control came from the country's first Catholic leader. John F. Kennedy involved over-

seas population control as part of his Third World program for economic development. In a special message on foreign aid in 1961 Kennedy warned that
the world population problem was "staggering. In Latin America, population
growth is already threatening to outpace economic growth . . . and the problems are no less serious or demanding in other developing parts of the world."
Kennedy directed his staff to revise outdated reports on population control.
In addition, Secretary of State Dean Rusk appointed Robert A. Barnett as a
full-time officer to the undersecretary for economic affairs "to maintain a
continuing review of the foreign policy implications of the world population
problem and to take such actions as are called for in the national interest."[51]
Barnett consulted Draper, Robert Cook of the Population Reference Bureau,
Canfield and Fred Jaffe of PPFA, Oscar Harkavy of the Ford Foundation, and
Rockefeller III. By late 1961 a small group of population control advocates in
the State Department had changed the Agency for International Development (AID) policy, allowing AID public health technicians to give reproductive information on request.[52]

The following year Sweden announced that population control would be
a major component of its foreign aid and placed a resolution entitled "Population Growth and Economic Development" on the UN General Assembly
agenda. The most controversial paragraph stated that the United Nations
should "give technical assistance, as requested by governments, for national
projects and programs dealing with the problems of population."[53] The Kennedy administration supported it, but Catholic leaders denounced the inclusion of "technical assistance." Kennedy compromised: the United States
supported the resolution in its entirety but abstained from the vote in committee. Despite its defeat, Richard N. Gardner, deputy assistant secretary for
international organizational affairs, described the resolution as a "turning
point" in world recognition of the population "problem."[54]

In April 1963 the National Academy of Sciences released *The Growth of
World Population,* a study initiated by private-sector scientists who believed
that if they did not research this topic, government scientists would not be
allowed to act. Their report claimed that "either the birth rate of the world
must come down or the death rate must go back up." It called for increased
private and government spending for biomedical, demographic, and social
research and training in the area of population control. At a subsequent press
conference Kennedy asserted that Americans should "know more about the
whole reproductive cycle and . . . this information [should] be made more
available to the world so that everyone could make their own judgment."[55]
Draper praised Kennedy's "wise leadership." On 20 July 1963 the Senate Foreign Relations Committee amended the Foreign Assistance Act of 1963 offered by Senator William Fulbright (D-AR) to authorize "research assistance

to cooperating countries in carrying out programs of population control" based on the "profound impact of population growth on economic development." This amendment, along with a similar one to the Food for Freedom Act, appropriated U.S. funds for overseas population control programs.[56]

Once Kennedy endorsed population control to "help" Third World nations, other prominent leaders followed suit. Eisenhower recanted his early statements, became an honorary cosponsor with Harry S. Truman of the Planned Parenthood–World Population campaign in 1965, and made an about-face on the government's role in reproductive matters. In a letter to Senator Ernest Gruening (D-AK), Eisenhower contended that contraception was an "obligation resting upon every enlightened government." If governments ignored the plight of unborn generations, "which, because of our unreadiness to take corrective action in controlling population growth, will be denied any expectations beyond abject poverty and suffering, then history will rightly condemn us."[57] The National Institutes of Health—research arm of the United States Public Health Service—published in January 1963 a catalog of 382 contraceptive projects financed by government and private agencies at an annual cost of $6 million.[58]

Contraceptive Experimentation

To implement population control, contraceptives had to be easily distributed and highly effective. Researchers devised an oral contraceptive and tested it on women of color and/or low-income women. PPFA provided some funding, but the bulk came from individuals such as Clarence Gamble and especially Katherine Dexter McCormick, heir to the McCormick reaper fortune. Gregory Pincus of the Worcester Foundation for Experimental Biology in Massachusetts teamed up with John Rock, a faculty member at Harvard Medical School and devout Catholic, to develop a contraceptive of which society and the Catholic Church would approve. They concentrated on a pill for women because it reflected advanced medical technology. The responsibility for taking a pill would be in women's hands, where Sanger and McCormick believed it should be, and Pincus and Rock believed it was easier to control one ovum than millions of sperm.[59]

Historian Laura Briggs has shown that researchers knew the key to preventing ovulation by 1940. No urgent need existed, however, to develop a contraceptive with expected side effects that could harm healthy women. Not until Third World overpopulation became a "problem" in need of a quick fix did clinical trials begin. As Briggs argues, by 1955 "the dangers of overpopulation were construed as life threatening and hence worth a great deal of risk." Supporters of this technology looked to Puerto Rico for volunteers.

Feminists on the island who had long fought for better contraceptive care found themselves caught between liberals advocating birth control to save women from the hazards of and poverty associated with constant childbearing and conservatives promoting population control to save society from the economic burden and racial implications of large Puerto Rican families.[60]

Prior to the pill, population controllers had looked to sterilization to solve the island's perceived population problem. In the 1940s U.S. industries located there, enticed by tax-free financial opportunities and a cut-rate workforce. With women a large part of this workforce, many employers considered contraception necessary. It was much cheaper than on-site day care. The International Planned Parenthood Federation, Gamble, and others advocated free or low-cost sterilization.[61] Many physicians promoted it because they believed low-income and indigent Puerto Rican women could not practice reliable contraception. Facing this type of pressure and with other contraceptives either too costly, ineffective, or inaccessible, one-third of Puerto Rican women of childbearing age had been sterilized by the 1960s—the largest proportion in the world.[62]

At face value, this statistic seems to imply an effective population control agenda, but Briggs has demonstrated a much more complex picture. Although the 1937 law legalized sterilization for eugenic or contraceptive purposes, the majority of operations were done in the latter category during the 1940s and 1950s. While nationalists and the Catholic Church condemned sterilization as a genocidal and imperialist plot, many island feminists supported it as an effective means for women to control their fertility. While population controllers, especially Gamble, wanted to extend eugenic sterilization, this plan failed: the medical infrastructure was not sufficient to handle the procedure done en masse; and doctors lacked access to the majority of women, who lived in rural areas where home births predominated. Moreover, Briggs found that women traveled far to hospitals that offered sterilization and reported satisfaction with the operation. Thus, while population controllers promoted it as a quick fix to the population problem, women ignored such rhetoric and demonstrated agency in accepting funding from Gamble and other zealots to shape programs that benefited women.[63]

With sterilization available primarily in urban areas, rural women, the majority, had limited access. Many population controllers continued to deplore Puerto Rico's "population explosion." Five births for every death and a declining infant mortality would not decrease unemployment. Although emigration provided a solution, population controllers desired to reduce "the flow from the faucet" to New York for racist reasons.[64] Gamble argued that Puerto Rico's population problem was "direct and immediate" because immigrants exhausted "medical services and relief funds."[65] The pill seemed a logical solution.

Developers of the pill tested it on two hundred animals, but they had to confirm their findings on human subjects. McCormick stated that for research to continue, developers must find "a cage of ovulating females." Because of their marginalized and racial status, Puerto Rican women were perfect subjects; researchers could perform experiments in Puerto Rico that would be difficult to do on the mainland. Puerto Rican women gave researchers an advantage because they now had "guinea pigs who could talk." Many Puerto Rican women again ignored such racism and volunteered to participate in experiments, hoping that their actions would bring an effective alternative to sterilization.[66]

Some historians have argued that these experiments were "not at all inconsistent with contemporary clinical research practices." While true, McCormick's statements and the lack of informed consent demonstrate disregard for the subjects in much the same way that researchers viewed the Tuskegee participants. Although not enforced, the Nuremberg Code's ten-point mandates regarding human experimentation had been passed and applied to these experiments. These scholars also conclude that Pincus and Rock chose Puerto Rico for reasons unrelated to race: they had professional connections with researchers at the University of Puerto Rico and with clinics staffed by respected physicians; the geographic isolation of the island sheltered experiments from prying media eyes and allowed researchers to monitor participants, because it was difficult for them to leave the island; and Massachusetts, Rock's and Pincus's home state, still had laws against birth control.[67] If laws were a concern, however, Pincus and Rock could have conducted their experiments in Rhode Island, where no legislative prohibitions existed. To ward off Catholic opposition there, Pincus and Rock could have emphasized the health aspects of their experiments, as RIMHA had done for decades. RIMHA had respected physicians with whom Pincus and Rock could have worked. Moving their headquarters less than an hour down the road to Rhode Island would have been easier than relocating to Puerto Rico. In Rhode Island, however, there were no captive island population of women of color and no protection from media exposure. Researchers chose Puerto Rico primarily because there were no drug-testing restrictions and because minority groups historically have been targeted for "unethical research and medical practices." As Ruth Macklin argues, mainland experiments would not have occurred "without informing women that they were involved in a research project or about the side effects they might experience, including the chance of becoming pregnant." Even though federal guidelines regulating human experimentation had not yet been passed, "the scruples of research-ers prevented their doing the same study on more educated women in the United States." Researchers chose Puerto Rican women because they were easily exploited and less likely to protest than mainland women, not because their subgroup had any direct bearing on the research. They were healthy, not ill with a disease from which these experiments would benefit them. Lastly, population controllers had long targeted Puerto Rico as "problematic" be-cause of poverty and overpopulation.[68]

Experiments began in the 1950s under Edris Rice-Wray, a local public health physician and medical director of the Puerto Rican Family Planning Association whom Gregory Pincus had met in San Juan. By this time there were sixty-three contraceptive clinics on the island. Rice-Wray conducted the experiment at one situated in Río Piedras, a poor suburb of San Juan. Whether or not these trials seem exploitive in hindsight, at the time many women were willing to try the pill because they did not want to be steril-ized and few other reliable options were available. Rice-Wray collected data on 221 women: although none became pregnant, 25 percent dropped out because of noxious side effects—nausea, vomiting, fluid retention, and diz-ziness. Lowering the dosage helped while retaining a high rate of effective-ness. Dr. Adaline Pendleton Satterthwaite, a gynecologist at Ryder Memorial Hospital in Humacao, thirty miles from San Juan, conducted a second experi-ment, collecting data from 243 women. Pincus used these findings to argue for the approval of Enovid before the United States Food and Drug Admin-istration (FDA). Approval came in 1957 for gynecological disorders, not for contraceptive purposes. Still, 500,000 women were using it by 1959.[69]

Pincus, however, did not report to the FDA Rice-Wray's conclusion that despite effectiveness in preventing pregnancy, the pill was unacceptable be-cause of adverse side effects. One woman died of congestive heart failure, and another developed pulmonary tuberculosis, but developers dismissed findings linking the pill to circulatory disorders. Dr. Satterthwaite expressed concern that the pill worsened cervical erosion, but such concerns were dis-missed. As late as 1970 Garrett Hardin claimed that "the woman's mind was involved.... [T]he expectation of unpleasant side effects increased the prob-ability of experiencing them. What we see here is what is called a *self-fulfill-ing prophecy.*" Pincus's concern for effective population control rather than women's health led him to accept psychological over physiological explana-tions.[70] He and others attempted to gain PPFA's endorsement, but Calderone refused in 1958 and 1959 because the FDA had not accepted the pill for con-traceptive purposes.[71]

Yet as early as the 1950s PPFA was circulating information on an oral con-traceptive to clinics. At that time RIMHA prescribed the diaphragm and jelly to nearly 100 percent of its clients; staff members counseled a few Catholics in the rhythm method. Physicians at RIMHA adopted a policy in 1952 that if patients asked about the "pill form of contraceptive," they would be told that there was "no proven method of contraceptive that can be taken by mouth." The following year Mrs. C. Tracy Barnes, secretary of the PPFA board, informed RIMHA's annual meeting that the failure to reach more low-income women resulted from the lack of a "simple effective method of contraception." Reports published in 1953 claimed that a pill would soon be perfected. In 1954 PPFA persuaded RIMHA to participate in a new project: "This experiment calls for the use of a new tablet called FOMOS." RIMHA had to "get twenty-five patients to try the new tablet" within six months. RIMHA agreed. By 1955 three "cooperating" women had reported "favorable" use of FOMOS. The annual PPFA meeting that year emphasized the importance of perfecting a "more simple method of contraception" in order to reach "a section of the population, which because of ignorance, required the utmost simplicity."[72] Such class bias led PPFA to support experiments not only in Puerto Rico but also in Rhode Island.

Why target Rhode Island? Investigations found high approval for contraception. A Brown University Sociology Department survey in 1957 of one hundred low-income families in Providence found no noticeable difference in attitudes toward contraception between Catholics and non-Catholics: although seventy-two of the one hundred were Catholic, 87 percent approved of "some type" of birth control, and 58 percent had employed contraception "but with varying success." Population controllers took advantage of this grassroots demand. In 1957 G. D. Searle and Company convinced some physicians to prescribe Enovid to low-income patients. RIMHA did not participate because its Medical Advisory Committee rejected Enovid based on "theoretical and practical concerns," including "possible side effects." RIMHA officials deemed the pill too dangerous, although they had buckled to PPFA pressure three years earlier with FOMOS. Over the next several years Charles Hachadorian and David Gleason, medical representatives in Rhode Island for G. D. Searle, reported no complaints from participating doctors about adverse reactions to the pill among their patients.[73] Gleason claimed the most serious side effect was "morning sickness" caused by Enovid's "close duplication of the hormonal complex in a real pregnancy."[74] Such conclusions are suspect. Physicians willing to experiment with low-income women's bodies as part of a larger plan to promote selective population growth might hesitate to report or even take seriously complaints lodged by patients.

In 1960 the FDA approved the pill as a contraceptive for no more than two years because its long-term safety was uncertain. Two years later Searle was made aware of more than one hundred cases of thrombosis and embolism related to pill use, including eleven fatalities. These problems led the World Health Organization (WHO) in 1965 to study the pill, but, as a task force member told a reporter, "the people who were concerned with population problems had already decided that we were going to deliver a whitewash."[75] The "population explosion" outweighed concern for the health of women seeking reliable birth control.

In addition to the experiments based on the pill, the Sunnen Project took place in Puerto Rico during the 1950s. Joseph Sunnen, a Protestant, Republican contraceptive manufacturer from St. Louis, Missouri, believed population control was an economic necessity in Puerto Rico. He offered financial encouragement for sterilization. For rural people who could not commute to urban clinics for the procedure, he distributed Emko, a vaginal foam, at no charge. Close to fifteen hundred volunteers, some from the company that produced Emko and others from Puerto Rico, brought the product to rural women and returned to restock supplies. Ironically, close to 80 percent of these volunteers did not use Emko themselves. As with the pill, Emko was experimental and possibly ineffective or dangerous.[76] Reaction was mixed. Most people whom volunteers encountered supported birth control. Yet most women had access only to experimental and/or dangerous methods, such as the pill and Emko, or to permanent methods, such as sterilization. The primary opposition came from the Catholic Church and Puerto Rican nationalists who opposed birth control itself, not specific methods. Pedro Albizo Campos, head of the Nationalist Party, exalted the peasant woman who bore children for the homeland. Macho men were also antagonistic to contraceptives because they believed their virility was called into question if their wives and mistresses were not bearing their children.[77]

In the end, contraception on the island was a complex issue. Women demonstrated agency in their willingness to participate in experiments that required them to keep records, to show up for testing, and to reject ineffective or harmful contraceptives. Some women rejected programs due to spousal antagonism or to church and/or nationalist opposition. Feminists and working women desired effective contraception; sterilization answered that demand.[78] While the population agenda pushed sterilization to solve the "problem," and while many women were exploited in the system, others utilized programs to control their fertility.

Abortion

The postwar era witnessed transformations in abortion. While the misery of the Depression and the dire need of women workers in World War II covertly condoned abortion, the postwar years, according to Leslie Reagan, witnessed the "harshest" crackdown on illegal abortions. This siege, she argues, "was part of the repression of political and personal deviance that took place in the 1940s and 1950s." The postwar offensive against abortion clinics undermined a reproductive health care system that many physicians had supported through referrals. Ross argues that white officials disproportionately targeted black physicians and midwives during this crackdown.[79] Rhode Island officials joined the siege. An amended abortion law allowed dying declarations as admissible evidence at trial—a trend Reagan found in other parts of the country. Police busted a decade-old abortion network that served northern Rhode Island, primarily the towns of Cumberland and Woonsocket. Every abortionist arrested in the crackdown was male. Either men began to dominate what they considered a lucrative enterprise or women were more subtle in plying their trade. Women could have been more competent than men: the court cases evolved from medical complications that forced the patients into local hospitals.[80]

Despite this onslaught, women continued to seek abortions. The demographics remained fairly constant. The majority continued to be married, not single, women. As Dr. Charles Potter, RIMHA's medical director, told a group of Brown-Pembroke students in 1948, "abortions are not most usual in single girls, as is popularly supposed. Ninety per cent occur in married women." That same year, a married woman visited RIMHA for reliable contraceptives because she had already resorted to three illegal abortions.[81]

The illegal nature of abortion makes precise assessments difficult. Marie Kopp's study of a New York clinic in the early 1930s found that women aborted one of five pregnancies. Illegal abortions increased during the war, especially in large cities. In June 1942 the National Committee on Maternal Health sponsored a conference at the New York Academy of Medicine entitled "The Abortion Problem." In April 1955 a committee appointed by the Conference on Abortion at Arden House, New York, concluded that between 200,000 and 1.2 million abortions occurred per year. By the mid-1950s PPFA's Dr. Calderone addressed RIMHA concerning increasing abortions. In 1956 she placed the annual number at 750,000. In *Pregnancy, Birth and Abortion* (1958) Paul Gebhard estimated that two thousand abortions occurred daily, mostly among married women. Alfred Kinsey found that 22 percent of his sample of married women had experienced an abortion. In the tail end of the baby boom, police experts believed abortion to be the third largest crime behind narcotics and gambling.[82] One means to estimate illegal abortions was the incidence of women seeking assistance at emergency rooms. Just as women turned increasingly to hospitals for childbirth in the postwar years, the same was true for complications from abortion.

Legal abortions also occurred. By the late 1940s doctors were performing legal abortions "often and routinely." Therapeutic justifications included cardiovascular conditions, kidney dysfunction, neurologic diseases, toxemia, respiratory disease, orthopedic problems, and blood diseases. Some doctors even performed abortions if the mother suffered from serious mental illness. In the early 1950s, however, the situation changed. Therapeutic abortions decreased from 5.1 to 2.9 per 1,000 live births between 1943 and 1953.[83] This drop may have resulted in part from increased medical technology, which eliminated some problems that had earlier proved dangerous during pregnancy. Hospital abortion committees also contributed to the decrease. Established as early as 1939, most hospitals had them by the 1950s. Their goal was to provide legal and moral impunity to physicians performing therapeutic abortions and reduce an individual doctor's power to grant a therapeutic abortion; the case had to come before the committee.[84] A 1955 policy at Providence Lying-In Hospital mandated the diagnosis of seven senior staff physicians that psychiatric, medical, or genetic indications were clear.[85]

Nonetheless, Reagan argues that demand actually increased. When hospital committees refused women's requests, some threatened suicide. Doctors generally acquiesced but punished the woman with sterilization: women inimical to fulfilling their destiny as mothers should not have another opportunity. Such tactics curbed legal abortions but did nothing to contain illegal abortions. Between hospital and state efforts to curb abortions women paid more for procedures that were increasingly difficult to procure. Secrecy intensified: many women were blindfolded and led to the abortionist. The death rate from abortions rose, doubling for New York City between 1951 and 1962. For women of color the death rate quadrupled. Psychologically, the back-alley abortion seemed worse to women who had grown to expect medical treatment in a sterile environment.[86] Some were able to find what Carole Joffe calls "physicians of conscience," who performed about one-third of annual illegal abortions in the 1950s. These doctors were competent, held medical licenses, and faced imprisonment and forfeiture of their licenses, source of income, and reputation, yet they continued because they believed denying women abortions was wrong.[87]

For women without such access, other options were available. Wealthy women could fly to Puerto Rico, England, Switzerland, and Mexico. They generally obtained a referral from their private doctors, who agreed to a follow-up visit to ensure recovery. Women lacking financial resources could be referred to domestic underground services, but even these services were generally out of reach for lower-income women. Black women could sometimes rely on black physicians or midwives, although officials disproportionately targeted these providers. While hospital services had supplanted midwifery practices among most other minorities by the 1950s (90 percent of births occurred in hospitals by 1948), black midwives continued to operate in the rural South, offering both abortions and contraceptives to thousands of women, both black and white.[88]

Medical opinion, therefore, was not united toward abortion. Some doctors called for liberalization of restrictions at the same time their colleagues were closing legal loopholes. Some pushed for reform because they witnessed firsthand women who came to hospitals following bungled abortions. Dr. Calderone organized an abortion symposium in 1954 that was attended by physicians, psychiatrists, anthropologists, religious leaders, and legal experts who recommended easing restrictions on therapeutic abortions and contraceptive dispersal.[89] Yet no reform occurred for over a decade, leaving desperate women scrambling for the safest and most accessible illegal abortions.

Rhode Island in the Postwar Period

By the late 1940s the baby boom had hit New England, yet it did not lessen the need for contraceptives. Local and state activists continued their reform efforts. In Massachusetts Loraine Leeson Campbell, a member of PPFA's board of directors (1941–69) and later its president (1956–59), joined with the League of Women Voters in the 1940s to petition for change but collided with the Catholic Church, which had a great deal at stake in this campaign. It had lost much of its hold over its parishioners' economic well-being with the New Deal and the welfare state, which also undermined the political machine in Massachusetts, with which the church was strongly connected. Contraception became the church's last-ditch effort to assert its political and religious power.[90] In Rhode Island, on the other hand, the church was unable to close RIMHA. Several factors explain the difference. First, in Massachusetts the church had only to maintain the status quo, while in Rhode Island the church would have had to campaign to close an established clinic. Second, Massachusetts activists were pushing solely for liberalization of contraceptives. RIMHA emphasized women's health, of which birth control was only one aspect.

In the postwar years PPFA attempted to influence local affiliates. It recommended that RIMHA augment its respectability by employing only college-educated married women at least thirty-five years old. RIMHA agreed but rejected the male-led model of the PPFA. Since the 1930s the presidents, officers, and 96 percent of the board had been women. This trend continued until 1955, when the clinic, perhaps succumbing to PPFA pressure, encouraged men to sit on the board: "Maternal Health in all its aspects is of interest to men as well as to women." By 1959 seven men were sitting on the board, but aside from the treasurer and assistant treasurer, the officers remained women. Even with these adjustments RIMHA was still out of step with PPFA. It twice "unanimously" rejected PPFA recommendations to change its name to Planned Parenthood League of Rhode Island, insisting that RIMHA more accurately reflected its goals, but finances also played a role: national affiliation required clinics to turn over 25 percent of membership fees.[91] Planned Parenthood League of Massachusetts and Planned Parenthood League of Connecticut gave in, but neither could operate a clinic. RIMHA also apportioned less campaign funds to PPFA than the latter expected.[92]

RIMHA and PPFA also clashed over the role of contraception. PPFA's 1948 fund-raising pamphlet argued that "the cost of unplanned families, of broken homes, of delinquency, disease and broken health is always paid for by the community in tax-supported courts and institutions, in contributions for welfare and rehabilitation in all its forms." RIMHA spurned this "Human Betterment" philosophy, contending that it smacked of "Fascism, Hitler, Mussolini, Stalin, etc. [who] were or are in favor of high birth rates" for certain groups while eliminating the reproductive choice of others. RIMHA instead believed first that *"parents should be the ones to decide how many children they will have"* and second in comprehensive health care. Its goal was "to educate the public in medical, social, economic, democratic, and scientific aspects of voluntary parenthood as a part of a well-rounded state program of public health."[93]

To that end, RIMHA expanded its health care services. In April 1947 the clinic instituted annual pelvic exams, and in October 1950 it offered annual breast exams. Female executive officers advocated an instructional program on breast self-examination; the male medical committee argued that women were incapable of learning such techniques but acquiesced in the face of executive pressure. RIMHA expanded health care further in 1953 with Pap smears as a cancer preventive measure for women over thirty-five. RIMHA staff members considered themselves the "definitive health service to these mothers, many of whom we know, would otherwise be neglected." As a result, they continued offering Pap smears and breast and pelvic exams to older patients who no longer needed contraceptives. They extended Pap smears in 1955 to new patients and returning patients over thirty.[94] These programs detected potentially life-threatening medical problems that otherwise would have gone untreated, referring between 10 and 21 percent of patients to specialists.[95]

The time and expense of these tests raised controversies among RIMHA leaders. Its Medical Advisory Committee recommended in 1957 that the clinic participate as one of seven states in the federal cytology program for detecting uterine cancer in women over twenty. The board hesitated because it would pose a financial "strain" and place an "added burden" on already inundated doctors. In fact, the "doctor situation [was] not healthy already" because large private practices limited their time, and "unfortunately most of the new GYN men coming to start practice are Catholic and so not available to us." Dr. Potter countered with the "lifesaving importance of early detection of cancer." The board voted to participate, but by late 1958 the clinic was running a deficit. The board restricted testing to Rhode Islanders: federal payments did not cover out-of-state women, who by that time constituted one-third of the clinic's clients. A battle must have raged behind the scenes, as the next month saw the board "empower our doctors to perform such tests on out-of-state patients" because "a lot of our patients are afraid of the thought of a cancer Clinic, but will come to us." While health care was important, some board members recognized the practical value of cancer testing, which provided the clinic with "an enormous leg to stand on if we should ever get any criticizm [sic] from those who might oppose us." Others realized that the program was "a wonderful money raiser." Some saw cancer tests as "another 'drawing card' for attracting new patients": clients stated they preferred to have a pelvic exam and cancer smear at the same time rather than at two clinics.[96]

This program again brought RIMHA into conflict with the national organization. PPFA wrote to RIMHA in 1956 that Pap smears were not to be rendered at clinics. RIMHA countered, "We feel that this is one of our most important services . . . and we will continue it as long as our doctors feel it is the thing to do." The following year, a PPFA directive reiterated that yearly pelvic exams were not necessary or the domain of a clinic. RIMHA refused to buckle, responding that "although birth control is our primary function very few of our patients would go elsewhere for a pelvic examination and we consider this and our Papanicolaou smear program two of our most important beneficial services." Dr. Potter defended RIMHA's position at a Chicago meeting of Planned Parenthood doctors and won them over. RIMHA's president reported that "just recently the Medical Committee of National has decided that yearly examinations are valuable and should be continued in planned parenthood clinics. We are pleased that they agree with us." Other conflicts continued. PPFA in 1958 wanted the RIMHA executive director and social worker to "receive orientation at National Headquarters" and to "improve our campaign and see that it is more in line with National practices." RIMHA, however, rejected the "constant emphasis" of national on "the international aspects of the population problem." In 1959 PPFA again tried to compel RIMHA to change its name. Dr. Potter took issue: "Maternal Health in toto has caught on locally, but not nationally. No enthusiasm there about total product of maternal health. There is a feeling that it is a diversionary type of thing, taking energies away from the principal purpose." The board agreed to keep "*Maternal Health* rather than Planned Parenthood because we have always felt that we wanted to be *more* than a birth control Clinic."[97]

These new services increased clients. By 1948 the clinic had experienced a 22 percent increase. Clients' average monthly salary was $35.12 in 1946; it fell to $32.00 in 1947 as recession hit the state and increased to $40.83 with economic recovery in 1948. Many clients were wives of veterans who were either injured and/or unemployed or delaying families while attending college on the GI Bill. Patients' average age fell slightly, reflecting a national trend. The only decrease in patients (6 percent) occurred between 1951 and 1952, during the state's economic boom. The upswing returned in 1953 and continued for the remainder of the decade. Two factors explain this increase. First was a recession: "Old patients are returning because they can no longer afford private doctors—new patients are coming because they cannot afford a larger family." This circumstance burdened the clinic, as patients could pay less, if at all, especially in light of the enhanced health services. Rejected as a member of the Community Chest, RIMHA depended on private funds, which ebbed and flowed with the economy. Second, women came because of "excellent and complete examinations." Before Medicaid, RIMHA health services were one of the few available to low-income women. Many earned too much to qualify for welfare and public health programs but too little to afford private physicians. By 1960 RIMHA was caring for more than 3,800 women per year, remarkable in light of little publicity. Only 5 percent of clients were referred, reflecting caution by "key" officials: in 1955 RIMHA applied for Providence United Fund membership but was rejected because the agency feared withdrawal of its Catholic sponsors. Approximately 77 percent of clients heard of the clinic by word of mouth, including financially secure women whose "private doctor will not . . . give contraceptive advice." Other referrals came from private physicians and ministers sending couples for premarital counseling.[98]

Clients' characteristics did not change significantly from previous years. Despite religious doctrine, 55 percent were Catholic, 36 percent were Protestant, and 9 percent were listed as "other" (primarily Jewish). One exception occurred in 1959 following edicts by Catholic bishops reaffirming church opposition to artificial contraceptives. That year alone Protestants dominated (51 percent), with Catholics close behind (44 percent) and a small number of "others" (5 percent). Clients were married, with most between the ages of twenty-one and thirty. Most clients were Rhode Islanders, with 17 percent outsiders in the 1940s, increasing to 23 percent in 1951 and 43 percent by 1959.[99] While a few came from Nova Scotia and Quebec, almost all were from Massachusetts and Connecticut. These women refused to allow the Catholic hold on state laws to dictate their family planning; they traveled to Providence for the services they desired.

The clinic also continued to attract black women. By this time physicians and researchers had rejected early-twentieth-century racial doctrines to explain the difference in mortality rates between blacks and whites. Instead, according to historian David McBride, "the nation's medical community had discovered that the roots of improved health care for American blacks lay . . . in greater access to medical care for families, especially maternal and child populations."[100] Black health experts had reached similar conclusions earlier and welcomed contraceptives to alleviate health risks among children and mothers. RIMHA's additional health services were especially attractive to black women who lacked affordable access to Pap smears and pelvic exams. At an open house in November 1946 ULRI representatives constituted the largest contingency. The following February ULRI invited RIMHA staff to a ULRI social. In April the RIMHA annual luncheon found Mr. Andrew Bell, president of ULRI, at the head table. Mathild C. Smith, executive director of RIMHA, worked closely with ULRI to disseminate information about clinic services. By 1948 the RIMHA could report that "an excellent group of leaders in the Negro Community has been found. . . . They have also arranged exhibits on Family Planning at the Urban League during Negro Health Week." RIMHA worked with ULRI in subsequent health campaigns and on suitable speakers to sponsor. RIMHA also collaborated with the Junior Service League, a "group of about 10 young married colored women, who were most enthusiastic about our work," and with the John Hope Community Center.[101] RIMHA's black clients increased from 6 percent in 1945 to 13 percent in 1955, when blacks constituted only 1.8 percent of Providence County and 2.13 percent of the state.[102] Two factors explain this increase: the augmented health services and the dissemination of information by black leaders among the Roxbury, Massachusetts, community.[103]

The clinic's experience with the black community helped shape national policy. In 1949 PPFA mailed a long-range planning questionnaire to affiliates asking, "Should the Federation have a special program for work with minority groups?" Such a program had been in place since 1940, with separate funds for two professionals and one secretary "for them." RIMHA criticized this segregationist policy, recommending PPFA "eliminate [the] special program for work with minority groups. Minority problems should be dealt with through already established channels. . . . Qualified negro personnel should work on all problems in [the] Field Department." This integrationist approach led PPFA to follow suit in 1949.[104]

Other conflicts persisted. By the early 1950s PPFA was active in what it considered "The World's Most Pressing Problem." William Vogt, its national director, spoke in Providence in 1952 about the "population explosion." In a speech at RIMHA in 1956 Dr. Calderone underscored the importance of controlling population growth internationally: "For too long now I have been taking the easy way of not facing up to our basic problem today; overpopulation can no longer be assessed in terms of the individual family, as it was in Margaret Sanger's day, but in terms of our total world." The RIMHA president's report reflected dismay at this obsession: "At the Rhode Island Maternal Health Association, we are not so much concerned with over-population as we are with helping the women of our state and many from Massachusetts and Connecticut so that they and their families may lead happier and more fruitful lives."[105] Local women's health and choices took precedence over the crusade to control women overseas.

By the late 1950s retirements among longtime officers and staff had brought a turnover. In 1959 the first female medical director, Dr. Evelyne L. Slabey, assumed office.[106] The board commented that the clinic seemed "to be entering a new regime," one with a different vision. Mrs. Burgess Green, newly elected president in 1959, argued a line the PPFA had used several years earlier: she was "distressed because our cancer detection program has seemed to receive more attention and a greater reaction from this board than our Birth Control Program. I am not deprecating our cancer program. I, personally, feel that each member of this board needs to be more aware of how Birth Control has helped individual patients rather than how many preinvasive cancers we have detected." Mrs. David Kennedy, newly elected executive director in 1960, also adopted a PPFA stance: "World population is growing much too rapidly for world resources as we know them . . . ; we must assume the responsibility that has been thrust upon us as the only co-ordinating agency that is doing something about human fertility." The following year saw Mrs. John L. Clark elected as president. She argued that with increased Blue Cross coverage, many patients could receive medical care elsewhere; comprehensive health care was not the clinic's responsibility. Tension between new and old leaders came to a head in the early 1960s; the latter won the debate and convinced officers to expand cancer detection programs. Both sides ultimately achieved their objectives. New leaders recognized the fundraising potential of increasingly popular population control rhetoric, but the board and the Medical Advisory Committee convinced them that the respectability the clinic gained from its health services was also "a wonderful money raiser."[107]

RIMHA imitated the national trend in appealing to men for campaign contributions. It sought "men, especially a businessman," to serve on the board and included in the campaign "a men's division." It hailed a new film, *The Costly Crowd*, because it was "suitable for showing to many groups, especially men's." While the president, executive director, four vice presidents, and the secretary remained women, the board included eight men and twenty-nine women by 1962. One RIMHA representative commented that "we are no longer just a ladies organization. We are facing an economic problem which is most meaningful to men and which motivates them to collect larger contributions than ladies concerned with women's personal problems had been able to elicit."[108] Following the national strategy of targeting men and emphasizing population control quieted Catholic opposition and increased community acceptance. RIMHA was entering a new stage. Whereas earlier leaders fought to maintain the local character of the clinic, new leaders tried to bring the clinic more in line with national policies and tactics.

Conclusion

The 1940s and 1950s saw significant changes in reproductive health. The war years witnessed government endorsement of condoms and industrial support for contraceptives for women war workers. Abortion, while illegal unless the woman's life was at stake, covertly continued with little state interference. The postwar period experienced a crackdown that posed barriers to abortion, but it did not decrease: desperate women continued to resort to "back alley," overseas, or self-induced abortions. Because this issue divided the medical profession, some women were able to seek care from what Joffe calls "physicians of conscience." While the baby boom mentality permeated popular culture, many women postponed or limited their childbearing, taking advantage of local birth control clinics and abortion to achieve their goal. The rise in middle-class fertility rates temporarily alleviated population doomsayers, although concerns over the quality of the race remained. To that end contraceptive experimentation burgeoned, with testing done primarily on low-income women of color, the very subgroup most disturbing to population controllers. Overall, the message of previous decades continued: white middle- and upper-class families should procreate, while the reproduction of low-income women and women of color should be curtailed. Most of the pressure for intervention came from organizations preoccupied with the "population explosion" in the Third World among people of color. The postwar period kept contraceptive programs primarily in the hands of private individuals and organizations. The federal government embarked in this arena on a small scale, first with wartime military policy allowing condom distribution to male soldiers and later with international policy underwriting population control programs in countries that asked for assistance. On the domestic front, the federal government remained aloof from any association with contraceptives. Doomsayers' predictions of the declining quality of the American population failed to convince the government to take action. Government expenditures in the following decade would lead to a dramatic shift in policy, with government funding of all three realms of reproductive control: abortion, contraception, and sterilization.

Who Pays?

Contraceptive Services and the Welfare State, 1963–1975

The Great Society introduced new programs that intervened in the private lives of citizens, from Medicaid and Medicare to contraception. Rather than a crime, contraception became a major ingredient of public policy. What brought about this transformation? Some groups fought for contraception as an individual right, but their influence was inconsequential. Apprehension over "breeding ourselves to death" had a significant impact on population policy, but many people cared more about *who* was breeding rather than the numbers bred.[1] Population controllers continued their quest to limit the fertility of the low-income and indigent, uneducated, and racial/ethnic minorities while no longer overtly calling them "undesirables." Employing rhetoric similar to that heard during the Depression, population controllers attracted fiscal conservatives by calling for laws and programs to decrease welfare dependents and curtail the escalating costs of tax-supported programs. National organizations and individual lobbyists touted this popular, cost-effective argument. The press played a dual role, providing supportive coverage that swayed public opinion toward government intervention but also reporting cases of abuse. PPRI benefited from national attention to family planning, particularly with increased private and government funding that allowed the clinic to expand while continuing to offer comprehensive health care. With health and choice its priority, the clinic avoided the genocide accusations faced by some clinics and continued its rapport with the local black community.

Developments in Contraceptive Research

Searle Pharmaceutical Company marketed Enovid-10, the new oral contraceptive pill, in late 1960. Cheap and reliable, it did not disturb the flow of sexual intercourse but prevented accidental pregnancies because of its high rate of effectiveness. Many population control advocates considered it the cure-all for social and economic ills, yet some women condemned it because of the exploitive tactics used in its development. As Patricia Maginnis, an abortion reform activist, stated: "I resented the pill. I felt that the women were guinea pigs used for the pill, and we were being denounced for any failures of the pill, [which] made me bitter." Dr. Calderone asserted that while most people in the population control movement "naively thought that if we could have 'the pill,' all problems relating to over-population . . . would automatically resolve themselves," she disagreed because of "hangover cultural beliefs" in the value of children as free labor and a source of security in old age. Moreover, she contended that women who needed and wanted the pill would not have access to it due to lack of funds.[2] The initial and annual doctor's visits and the pill's expense led primarily middle-class women to use it.

Unequal access and safety was a concern at RIMHA. While RIMHA had refused to participate in Enovid experiments in the late 1950s, once the FDA approved it in 1960, the board allowed physicians to offer it with monthly monitoring of women. The board established a pill fund for indigent patients and hoped manufacturers would develop a lower-dose pill that would be safer and less expensive.[3] Thus, when asked to join several other affiliates in a five-year study of a 5-milligram Enovid pill organized by Searle and PPFA, RIMHA agreed. Participants had to remain on the pill for two years or more and be examined every six months. By October 1961 47 women were using it, "most successfully," but the method of choice remained the diaphragm.[4] By February 1962 134 women and by year's end 316 women were on it. When national news cited "Enovid in the deaths of some women from thrombophlebitis," 131 (41 percent) of the 316 discontinued its use. Within several months, however, demand "was back to normal" and increased rapidly during 1963; "favorable press and publicity" created an "air of confidence."[5]

Late 1963 and 1964 proved a watershed in new pills. Johnson & Johnson marketed Orthonovum, a 2-milligram pill, in November 1963; the competition forced Searle to lower Enovid-5's price. Both were "100%" effective and available at RIMHA. In early 1964 Searle introduced Ovulin, a 0.5-milligram pill, to be tested at RIMHA beginning in June, as long as patients were "made aware" that the drug was in an investigative phase.[6] RIMHA also participated in Mead Johnson & Company's Megestrol study: patients took estrogen for fifteen days, followed by Megestrol and estrogen for five days. This method eliminated progestin, the expensive part of the pill, and continued the menstrual cycle. Mead provided the pill free for two years, which granted indigent patients access to it, and contributed $110 a month to the clinic to defray the clinic's costs.[7] By the summer of 1964 the clinic could offer an "a la carte menu of pills." The staff had read Lee Rainwater's *And the Poor Get Children* and supported its recommendation to "offer a *choice* of methods" to suit women's individual needs.[8]

RIMHA still bristled at PPFA's "constant emphasis" on how the pill could ameliorate "the international aspects of the population problem" and the "overcrowding, juvenile delinquency, etc." in American cities rather than on how it improved women's health and choices. RIMHA representatives returned from an annual PPFA meeting astounded that "the pervading thought throughout the sessions was that sexual energy is just as dangerous and powerful in the modern world as atomic energy." PPFA stressed the "importance of population control" and the "economic and business consequences of the population explosion" more than the impact of new contraceptives on women's daily lives.[9]

By 1965 physicians could hail three modern contraceptive techniques: the pill, injectables, and the IUD. The third annual meeting of the American Association of Planned Parenthood physicians in 1965 gave oral contraceptives "top honors for the method considered surest, safest, and soundest." Second place went to "injectable progestin given intra-muscularly once a month." In 1965 PPRI joined fifty-eight other affiliates in a two-year study of a monthly injectable called Deladroxate sponsored by the Squibb Institute for Medical Research. The thirty-eight PPRI women were "enthusiastic about the shot," but others rejected it because they had either prolonged menstrual cycles or monthly childcare and transportation difficulties. PPRI also joined an IUD investigation; in one year 322 women chose IUDs with "no serious complications," although two pregnancies occurred.[10]

Despite other options, the pill remained paramount and launched a pharmaceutical revolution. It replaced condoms and douches as the most used contraceptive and thereby transformed consumerism. Individuals no longer relied primarily on drugstores or mail-order catalogs for supplies. Women's reactions to medical care, especially contraceptive care, changed: many visited a physician's office with a clear set of demands. Placing the pill, IUD, and injectables in physicians' hands brought to fruition Sanger's plan for a medical monopoly over contraceptives. Although most doctors had little training in chemical contraceptives, Andrea Tone argues that these methods "created widespread doctor patient acceptance of medical birth control." Part of the reason women were so knowledgeable was the media blitz surrounding the pill. When it first emerged, the media hailed it as the first significant progress in contraceptive technology in half a century. Stories extolled its ease of use. As the decade progressed, some questioned its impact on morality, while others began to probe its safety.[11]

The pill's safety had become an issue by decade's end. While medical professionals had debated its connection to thrombosis, cancer, and neurological problems, no consensus had been reached. The turning point came in 1967 when the *British Medical Journal* linked the pill to increased risk for blood clotting. Two years later, the FDA reported that women on the pill were 4.5 times more likely to experience thromboembolism. Scientists documented other risks, although a clear connection to cancer was difficult to discern; Senate investigations in 1970 found the pill had been marketed without adequate testing of its long-term impact. Although the Senate acknowledged the impracticality of banning the pill, it mandated full disclosure because 66 percent of women had not been informed of possible side effects. The resulting packet inserts, according to Elizabeth Siegel Watkins, made the pill "the first orally administered drug to carry a detailed warning directed at patients." With widespread coverage of Senate hearings, 87 percent of women became aware of safety concerns; 18 percent stopped taking the pill. Physicians continued to prescribe it because it was easier than fitting an IUD or diaphragm and women continued to demand it.[12]

Congressional hearings on the pill's safety spurred research into new contraceptives. Researchers tested a postcoital vacuum tampon that would stimulate the Fallopian tubes to close as well as a skin implant and a tampon, both of which contained a synthetic steroid compound that would provide a year of contraception. "Sunday pills," a weekly steroid dose, disrupted the normal pattern of the endometrium and prevented nidation. A new female sterilization procedure used "transvaginal injections of Quinacrine of carbolic acid" to "obliterate the tubes," but it was "not as effective as [the] surgical procedure." The morning-after pill was effective but required physician supervision. PPRI staff made it clear that women could only use it twice; choice had its limits. By 1973 PPFA recommended that all affiliates discontinue its use because malpractice insurance refused to cover it due to lack of FDA approval. PPRI complied. In a new abortion method, physicians gave prostaglandin intravenously to "increase uterine and tubal mobility," which worked well in the eighth to twelfth weeks of pregnancy. Researchers also pursued three forms of male contraception. An intravasational device provided temporary sterilization; it rendered spermatozoids ineffective. A "sylastic implant of androgens" stopped sperm production but potentially damaged the prostate gland and increased cholesterol levels. Lastly, a substance prevented the "maturation of the spermatozoids on the epididymis."[13] Research into male methods was half-hearted at best, leaving pharmaceutical contraceptives a female responsibility. No new methods challenged the primacy of the pill. Despite safety concerns, many women continued to rely on it because of its effectiveness.

Contraception and the Federal Government

During the 1940s and 1950s waves of rural southern blacks and Puerto Ricans in search of better jobs and living conditions migrated to urban centers in the Northeast and Midwest. Job competition, overcrowding, and racial tensions led to unrest and a rise in welfare rolls, making the low-income and indigent more visible to society. Critics asserted that high fertility contributed to the cycle of poverty. Many of the same groups involved in international population control programs in the 1950s and 1960s began to lobby for a domestic agenda. Federal and state officials' search for a means of control helped lead to the dispersal of government-subsidized contraceptives.

Federal actions began in the early 1960s. Congress approved the District of Columbia Health Department budget in 1962; it included $25,000 to provide contraception to public health maternity patients and public welfare clients.[14] When Lyndon B. Johnson assumed office, he declared a "War on Poverty" and created a number of new agencies. The Economic Opportunity Act of 1964 established the Office of Economic Opportunity (OEO) to alleviate problems among less advantaged groups. In response, the *New York Times* editorialized that the only way to win the battle would be "to tackle a root cause of poverty—the present explosive growth of population." Statistics on increasing numbers of dependents indicated that "the cost of maintaining such an enlarged burden of nonproducers could of itself add millions of families to those which today are unable to adequately support themselves."[15]

The Johnson administration considered broadening government investments in domestic contraceptive programs. Two cabinet officials publicly supported contraception because of its economic advantages: Secretary of Labor Willard Wirtz and Secretary of the Interior Stewart Udall, who oversaw health care for Native Americans and the Pacific territorial islands, two groups targeted by population controllers. The population lobby, spearheaded by the Population Council and PPFA, worked to convince Johnson to incorporate family planning in his War on Poverty and to address the gravity of overpopulation in his State of the Union address.[16] In four separate statements during 1965 he proclaimed that the government would seek to solve population problems. Governments, he asserted in an address to the United Nations, should "act on the fact that less than $5.00 invested in population control is worth $100.00 invested in economic growth."[17] Although in May 1965 the National Academy of Sciences called birth control a "basic human right," economics, not women's rights, sparked the Johnson administration's endorsement of contraceptives. Johnson wanted to move quickly but without eliciting Catholic opposition, which prevented the population lobby from convincing him to create a president's commission on population.[18] Donald Critchlow argues that Johnson buried family planning within existing agencies, especially health and welfare programs, rather than establish a centralized agency solely for contraception. The lack of an effective national distribution method, exacerbated by the lack of nationalized health care, left the government dependent on private organizations for contraceptive dispersal.[19]

In December 1964 the government cautiously began to underwrite contraceptive projects. The OEO provided the first federal funds directed solely at contraception with a nine-thousand-dollar grant to Corpus Christi, Texas, a site chosen, according to congressional testimony, because of its new clinic's success in reducing "unwanted births and bungled abortions among charity patients." Most observers of this program hoped that "low-income poorly educated adults" would use contraception "to limit their families to supportable sizes and achieve independence of the welfare system."[20] The OEO approved similar programs in Austin, St. Louis, Buffalo, Nashville, and Oakland.[21] A leading OEO deputy concluded: "If all the poor had the same number of kids as the non-poor, we would have fifteen to twenty percent of poverty licked right there. Birth control could do more than any other single poverty project." The Council of Economic Advisers estimated that for 1964 more than one million children lived in families with more than six siblings and an annual income less than $2,000; 25 percent of all children (about fifteen million) lived in poverty. In 1965 alone Aid for Families with Dependent Children (AFDC) ran up a bill of $1.5 billion.[22]

That year saw a rapid succession of federal activities. In January the Children's Bureau, a branch of the Department of Health, Education and Welfare (DHEW), allotted $5.5 million to clinics that dispensed contraceptives to low-income and indigent married women. The OEO targeted funds for family planning to fight poverty in early 1965. Soon after, the National Academy of Sciences' Committee on Population suggested the government "promptly" increase its population control efforts. The White House Conference on Health in November 1965 concurred, calling for government services to indigent women. Congress amended the Social Security Act to require state health departments to extend family-planning services within ten years and to authorize federal grants for distressed areas that could not meet this goal.[23]

At the same time, the Supreme Court struck down the antiquated Connecticut Comstock Law in *Griswold v. Connecticut*, 381 U.S. 479 (1965). In November 1961 the Connecticut Planned Parenthood League, with Estelle Griswold as executive director (1954–65), challenged the statute by opening a clinic. The police arrested Griswold and Dr. C. Lee Buxton of Yale Medical

School; the circuit court found them guilty, as did the superior court and the state supreme court. In a seven-to-two decision the United States Supreme Court declared the Connecticut law unconstitutional.[24] The "zone of privacy" established by the Court to protect individual access to contraceptives, however, extended to married couples only. Justices were unwilling to sanction premarital sexuality.

This restriction to married women did not reflect public opinion. A 1965 national poll found 80 percent approved of birth control for "anyone who wants it," 13 percent disapproved, and 7 percent did not know. By religion, 83 percent of Protestants, 70 percent of Catholics, and 88 percent of "all other" approved. A Population Council–initiated Gallup poll the same year found that 63 percent favored federal funding of state and city contraceptive programs; 28 percent opposed. In an October 1965 poll 59 percent of Catholics approved of federal aid to family-planning clinics. Dr. William V. D'Antonio, associate professor of sociology at Notre Dame, established the Catholic Committee on Population and Government Policy to inform the government that not all American Catholics agreed with church doctrine on birth control.[25]

With increasing support for government funding, some politicians drafted legislation. Representative James Scheuer (D-NY) introduced two bills in 1965 to repeal Comstock; neither passed until 1971, when they were combined into Public Law 91-662. Several other 1965 bills called for the creation of Offices of Population Problems in the DHEW and State Department, the organization of a White House Conference on Population, and the allocation of funds for contraceptive distribution to clinics across the country.[26] Hearings on S 1676 came before a subcommittee chaired by Senator Ernest Gruening in the summer of 1965. He observed that the government was moving too slowly: the United States had the "highest rate of population growth, the highest rate of unemployment, and the highest rate of public dependency of any industrialized nation in the world." Part of the problem, he argued, was that the government, through its welfare regulations, had "unwittingly" implemented a "pronatalist" policy. He concluded that the facts had become "so overwhelming and the need so apparent" that the government must reevaluate its policies and make contraceptives available to low-income and indigent people.[27]

Testimony at the hearings confirmed that the government's slow response was a leading cause of mounting welfare expenditures and problems associated with poverty. Senator Milward Simpson (R-WY) argued that all levels of government "must take a more active role . . . to promote population control" because the situation had reached a critical impasse:

We are all familiar with the problems caused by the needy families
who have too many unwanted children. Our welfare departments are
plagued with the poor who continue to have children when they can't
afford to feed the ones they have. And many of these, unfortunately, are
born out of wedlock. The cost of maintaining children of the poor has
climbed to more than a billion dollars a year in welfare funds. One child
in every twenty-five receives welfare aid, and the number may double
in the next 10 years.

He concluded that "a direct correlation between poverty and uncontrolled
births" existed.[28] Senator Robert Byrd (D-WV) pointed to the lack of contraceptives to explain the leap in AFDC recipients: "The problem is the spiraling
birth rate among those who are incapable of adequately providing for their
offspring." Byrd claimed that every dollar spent on family planning saved $25
in AFDC benefits. James R. Dumpson, New York City welfare commissioner,
testified that only federal aid would help in "reducing welfare costs." Walter
Kuralt of the North Carolina Public Welfare Department testified that subsidized contraceptives could reduce male family desertion by allowing couples to limit their offspring; if husbands remained and contributed to family
income, AFDC expenditures would decrease. F. A. Schumacher of Planned
Parenthood asserted that government assistance to clinics would "ultimately
reduce illegitimacy, abortions, delinquency, welfare costs, [and] taxes."[29] Despite support, the bill failed to be reported out of committee, primarily due
to the testimony of John Gardner, DHEW secretary. Gardner argued that it
was unnecessary because funding was available for contraceptives from the
DHEW, the OEO, and the amended Social Security Act. Gruening countered that his proposal not only earmarked special funds but demonstrated
congressional concern. Gardner remained unconvinced, leaving DHEW and
OEO in the forefront of federal programs.[30]

These two agencies launched the first major federally funded campaign in
1965. Grants from DHEW, OEO, and the Ford and Rockefeller foundations
established a family-planning clinic in poverty-stricken rural Lincoln Parish
in northern Louisiana. One in thirteen Louisiana residents was on relief, and
the illegitimacy rate among the indigent had reached 30 percent versus a
national average of 21.3 percent. Of the women who used this new clinic, 85
percent were black. While Louisiana had more poor blacks than whites, officials found whites reluctant to use an integrated facility. This program met
with success despite high numbers of Catholics. In one year, births among
low-income families declined 32 percent, illegitimate births 40 percent, and
second illegitimate births 41.5 percent. When some pushed to make this
project compulsory, Dr. Joseph D. Beasley, director of the Louisiana Family

Planning Program, criticized "tax-payer vigilantism" that favored coercive contraception to reduce welfare and illegitimacy.[31]

Press accounts of such successes led to pressure for increased government activity, and the government responded. In January 1966 Gardner issued a DHEW policy allowing contraceptives to both married and unmarried women. OEO Director R. Sargent Shriver, however, restated his limitation of federal subsidies to married women living with husbands. Why did divergent policies exist? DHEW provided funds through its maternal and child health plans, which serviced mothers, both married and single, while OEO funneled aid through community action programs. Single mothers and single women were two very different groups. Because OEO was new and sometimes controversial, Shriver may have decided to follow a conservative path. In the spring of 1966, however, OEO raised the amount available for contraceptives from twelve to twenty dollars for each woman and eliminated the one-year eligibility limit. Commenting on growing government involvement, Shriver observed that until the mid-1960s, contraception was "like syphilis—politically you couldn't talk about it." In 1966 the government spent $25 million on contraceptive services, yet with nearly five million indigent women of childbearing age, this money made only a small dent.[32] The welfare costs continued to grow. Critics failed to acknowledge that increases resulted in part from expanded services and eased eligibility requirements, emphasizing instead the large families of welfare mothers. OEO research deemed contraception the most "cost-effective" antipoverty measure available. Similarly, the Public Health Service asserted that a contraceptive program funded at $90 million over five years would decrease infant mortality and be seven times more effective than the expensive maternity programs.[33]

In 1966 Senator Joseph D. Tydings (D-MD) along with Gruening and others introduced a bill calling for congressional funds specifically earmarked for contraception. It appropriated $15 million for fiscal year ending 30 June 1967, $30 million for 1968, $45 million for 1969, $60 million for 1970, and $75 million for 1971. The bill included guarantees against coercion or loss of services in other financial or medical programs. Although Tydings's proposal gained widespread support, it failed because Gardner deemed it unnecessary. He pushed for measures that fit his agenda. First, Gardner supported a Senate bill that would increase funding for public health programs, which indirectly would fund contraceptive services. While his approach could have been a means to disguise government's outright involvement in birth control, it could also have been an attempt to ensure that contraception remained part of comprehensive health services. Second, Congress passed his Comprehensive Health Planning and Public Health Services Amendments, giving state and local governments authority to finance family-planning services. Third,

Gardner established a new post in DHEW—deputy assistant secretary for science and population—to augment the federal government's role in family planning. Population control advocates believed contraception warranted a post of its own. Gardner disagreed. Fourth, he evaluated regional and state clinic service requirements and training needs. Last, he set up a departmental committee to coordinate all federal family-planning programs.[34]

Program budgets also increased. Appropriations for Title V of the Social Security Act for fiscal year 1966 equaled $45 million and, for 1967, $50 million. The Children's Bureau allocated $30 million (fiscal year 1966) to meet up to 75 percent of program costs for women in low-income areas. Yet PPFA studies indicated that about 5 million medically indigent women wanted assistance; only about 500,000 received services. Such data led Tydings to promote legislation for additional government assistance.[35]

He and Gruening cosponsored a bill in 1967 to expand domestic family-planning services. They believed that "at least $100 million" per year was necessary and would be "the wisest investment . . . in combating poverty" because "each dollar spent for provision of family planning services repays itself many times over in savings for welfare costs."[36] As with the two earlier bills, the 1967 proposal received wide support. Representative George Bush (R-TX) told the Senate subcommittee that he was "strongly in favor of a more active program in this field." In his opinion,

> this Congress should press vigorously for the most direct approach possible. When the Salk vaccine was discovered and approved, it was widely disseminated by Public Health Officials. With the pill and other devices, we have made great strides in this field. But even though all Government programs in this field, to my knowledge, are voluntary, I get the feeling that we are still tiptoeing cautiously around the edge of the problem. . . . Birth control, often misunderstood, is an answer to an increasingly important public problem.[37]

Bush seemed to call for a quasi-compulsory program or at least more vigorous advocacy. His equation of the pill with the polio vaccine as a solution to poverty was a unique contention, one that seemed to liken indigent children to a disease in need of eradication.

These hearings exposed the rift between bill sponsors and Gardner. The former criticized DHEW for not "recognizing the need for greatly expanded Federal assistance in the delivery of family planning services." Tydings contended that Gardner was ignoring Johnson's calls for action; by 1967, LBJ had made forty-one such statements. Representative Scheuer concluded from the record of the "pusillanimous and faint-hearted administration" that DHEW lacked "effective leadership, drive, direction, and forward thrust in getting

Table 6.1. Estimated Number of Illegitimate Births and Illegitimacy Ratios, United States, 1920–1968

Year	Illegitimate births			Ratio per 1,000 births		
	Total	White	Nonwhite	Total	White	Nonwhite
1920	86,365	38,490	47,875	29.3	15.0	125.0
1930	90,800	42,296	48,504	34.7	18.6	141.1
1940	102,996	43,473	59,523	40.3	19.8	166.4
1945	128,190	58,670	69,520	44.8	23.6	179.3
1950	148,372	54,353	94,019	40.9	17.5	179.5
1955	189,733	64,812	124,921	46.2	18.6	202.4
1960	230,428	83,333	147,095	53.4	22.9	215.8
1965	297,055	124,196	172,859	78.6	39.7	263.2
1968	343,815	155,200	188,615	97.8	53.3	312.0

Source: Phillips Cutright, "Illegitimacy in the United States: 1920–1968," in *Demographic and Social Aspects of Population Growth*, ed. Charles F. Westoff and Robert Parke, Jr. (Washington, D.C.: Government Printing Office, 1972), 383.

the services to where the action is in the neighborhoods of America." Others reproved its slow response to community needs, its lack of flexibility in funding, and the dearth of funds allocated specifically for family planning. The panel agreed that the optimum federal funding came from OEO, not DHEW. OEO designated family planning a "National Emphasis," while DHEW expanded its role, perhaps in response to the panel's sharp criticism. Gardner elevated family planning to one of six special priorities and finally created a post to deal specifically with this area, appointing Katherine B. Oettinger to fill it. Perhaps the most controversial 1967 policy was congressional removal of the restriction against federal funds for unmarried women.[38] Illegitimacy rates among women on welfare had consistently risen during the 1960s (see table 6.1). One means to reduce these numbers was to give single women free devices.

To save AFDC money, Congress proposed changes in the welfare system in 1967. HR 12080 obliged mothers and teenagers over the age of sixteen on AFDC to take jobs offered them, regardless of wages, working conditions, or the needs of their children or other dependents. It also refused payment for children born after an unwed mother had enrolled for benefits. When the House proposal reached the Senate Finance Committee, two black women—Mrs. Johnnie Tillmon of Watts and Mrs. Alice Nixon of Pittsburgh—led sixty women under the auspices of the Poverty Rights Action Center to Washington. When the Senate Finance Committee refused to hear them, they turned to the media.[39] In the end, the Senate did not pass the proposal, but House action demonstrated the popularity of programs designed to reduce welfare, regardless of the impact on recipients. Amendments to the Social Security

Act did pass in 1967. Introduced by Bush and Herman Schneebeli (R-PA), both of the House Ways and Means Committee, these amendments mandated no less than 6 percent of funds appropriated for Maternal and Child Health services and Maternal and Infant Care be devoted to family planning. They required state health departments to include contraceptives and make them available to welfare recipients and the indigent.[40]

Congress took further action on the international front. Johnson's 1967 State of the Union message claimed: "Next to the pursuit of peace, the really great challenge to the human family is the race between food supply and population increase. That race tonight is being lost. The time for rhetoric has clearly passed. The time for concerted action is here, and we must get on with the job." In March Senator Fulbright introduced Title X to the Foreign Assistance Act, which earmarked $35 million annually for three years to overseas contraceptive programs. Title X allowed the president to subsidize government, United Nations, and international private nonprofit population programs, including the production and distribution of contraceptives. In May Congress allowed AID to finance contraceptives. By late 1967 population control was an integral goal of U.S. economic programs abroad.[41]

Public response affirmed federal efforts to decrease poverty and welfare costs. In a 1967 Harris poll on LBJ's Great Society programs, welfare and relief payments headed the list of desired cutbacks along with farm subsidies. The same year a PPFA national survey found that most respondents approved of publicly funded contraception to combat poverty and curb welfare expenditures.[42] Yet services to low- or no-income women remained inadequate. A 1968 OEO survey found that nearly 85 percent of the 5.4 million American women estimated to need subsidized services received none. Less than one-third of local health departments and one-fifth of hospitals with large maternity services provided any family planning for indigent patients.[43]

Radical population controllers ranted that the government was not doing enough. At a welfare hearing in New York in early 1968 some suggested that the government pay every impoverished woman of childbearing age $500 a year not to have a baby. An article in *Redbook* argued that if the indigent could not decide whether they could afford children, the state should establish a licensing board for them.[44] Such sentiment may have led individual welfare workers to coercive measures. Although federal and state family-planning policies were voluntary, some social workers apparently told clients to use contraceptives or lose their benefits. These reports are suspect: they originate in a Catholic periodical and could have been an attempt to discredit federal involvement in contraception. Still, reported incidents prompted the government to reassert its opposition to compulsion and to establish a grievance board to ward off coercion.[45]

Table 6.2. Percent Pregnant, 1968, by Age and Race

Age	Black	White
15	2.1	0.2
16	3.9	0.3
17	5.8	1.4
18	7.2	0.3
19	5.0	0.5

Source: Melvin Zelnik and John F. Kantner, "Sexuality, Contraception and Pregnancy among Young Unwed Females in the United States," in *Demographic and Social Aspects of Population Growth*, ed. Charles F. Westoff and Robert Parke, Jr. (Washington, D.C.: Government Printing Office, 1972), 372.

By the late 1960s population controllers were continuing to propagandize that public contraceptive funding would solve a host of social and economic problems that swelled the welfare rolls, namely, unwanted pregnancy, teenage pregnancy, and illegitimacy. Studies showed that abused children later abused their own offspring and that lower-income couples had more unwanted children than middle- and upper-class couples. Unwanted children often ended up in foster care at an average annual cost of $2,400 to $8,000 a year.[46] Teenaged childbirth also increased state costs. In 1968 600,000 births, or 17 percent of all births, occurred to women under age twenty; more than 200,000 were seventeen years old or younger. Black teens were more likely to become pregnant than whites (see table 6.2). Many children born to teen mothers ultimately ended up on AFDC.[47] A high percentage of teen pregnancies were also illegitimate. The illegitimacy rate had been increasing steadily from 7.1 in 1940 to 24.1 in 1968. Studies concluded that 75 percent of nonwhite and 31 percent of white increases in illegitimacy between 1940 and 1960 resulted from improved health conditions that reduced miscarriage. Young, unmarried, white women legitimated their conceptions more than their nonwhite counterparts, accounting for the higher rate of black illegitimate children on AFDC—a difference that increased during the 1960s (see table 6.3). In 1961 24 percent of AFDC children were illegitimate, of whom 38 percent were black; by 1969 the corresponding figures were 31 percent total, of whom 46 percent were black. AFDC's estimated expenditure on illegitimate children in 1969 was $1.1 billion, one-third of the entire AFDC bill for 1969.[48] Population controllers used such data to justify their push for clinics in predominantly black neighborhoods and for teen access to government-subsidized contraception.

Some members of the black community saw illegitimacy in a different light. Many black teens did not consider pregnancy as ruining their life chances; they already lived in poverty and felt trapped there. Raising ba-

Table 6.3. Legitimate, Illegitimate, and Total Out-of-Wedlock Conceived Birthrates per 1,000 Unmarried Women by Color and Age, U.S. 1964–1966 Annual Average

Age of mother	All mothers	White	Nonwhite
15–44			
Legitimate	18.7	17.3	27.4
Illegitimate	22.4	11.3	88.2
Total OWCB	41.1	28.5	115.6
15–19			
Legitimate	20.2	18.8	29.4
Illegitimate	16.4	7.8	72.4
Total OWCB	36.6	26.6	101.8
20–24			
Legitimate	33.3	28.9	58.6
Illegitimate	38.4	21.5	137.3
Total OWCB	69.6	50.5	195.9
25–29			
Legitimate	7.5	8.6	2.7
Illegitimate	46.7	23.4	146.2
Total OWCB	54.2	32.0	148.9
30–34			
Legitimate	1.8	1.5	3.7
Illegitimate	35.6	16.1	121.6
Total OWCB	37.4	17.6	125.6
35–44			
Legitimate	0.5	0.6	0.0
Illegitimate	9.7	4.8	34.9
Total OWCB	10.2	5.4	34.9

Source: Phillips Cutright, "Illegitimacy in the United States: 1920–1968," in *Demographic and Social Aspects of Population Growth*, ed. Charles F. Westoff and Robert Parke, Jr. (Washington, D.C.: Government Printing Office, 1972), 404.

bies as teens allowed them to draw on their mothers and grandmothers for support. Moreover, job opportunities were minimal for black teens; staying home to raise a child did not interfere with their economic advancement. Pregnancy did not deter their continuation of high school; most black teens who became pregnant had already dropped out of school.[49] None of this is to say that black teens purposely became pregnant. But if pregnancy did occur, they did not see it as the problem decried by population controllers and economic conservatives.

Teens desiring birth control could face difficulties procuring it. Planned Parenthood, fearing for its public image, refused contraceptives to women under eighteen without parental consent. Dr. Sadja Goldsmith of San Francisco's Planned Parenthood found this policy absurd. She saw thousands of teens who needed contraceptive care flocking to Haight-Ashbury, yet Planned Parenthood turned them away. In 1967 Goldsmith opened a clinic for teenagers that served as a national model by the late 1960s.[50]

Population controllers hailed this development but called for more government action. They lamented that by early 1969 more than two million AFDC recipients were either single mothers or their illegitimate children, and 79.6 percent, or 4.3 million women, still had no access to publicly funded devices. DHEW and OEO officials advocated the extension of contraceptive services. In 1969 the National Academy of Sciences in *Resources and Man* urged that "efforts to limit population increase in the nation and the world be intensified by whatever means are practicable.... Ultimately this implies that the community and society as a whole, and not only the parents, must have a say about the number of children a couple may have."[51] This last statement implied coercion or licenses for parenthood, but DHEW and OEO rejected such tactics.

When Richard M. Nixon assumed the presidency, he expanded the federal role in population control. On 28 January 1969 the government called for a plan "to prevent or reduce the incidence of births out-of-wedlock." Such a program "must be extended progressively to all appropriate adults and youths, with initial priority for mothers who have had children born out-of-wedlock . . . and for youths living in conditions immediately conducive to births out-of-wedlock." Later that year Nixon delivered the first presidential address solely directed at the "problem of population." Claiming that the White House considered the population dilemma "perhaps the most singular problem we face today" except disarmament, he called for expanded programs: "Unwanted and untimely child bearing is one of the several forces which are driving many families into poverty or keeping them in that condition.... [I]t needlessly adds to the burdens placed on all our resources by increasing population.... The federal government makes only a minimal effort in this area. The efforts of state and local governments are also inadequate." Nixon set a goal to make contraceptives available to all low-income families by 1975. The short-term cost of $30 million a year, according to Nixon, was worth the long-term savings in welfare. He was careful to tip his hat to the Catholic Church by guaranteeing that his program would not "infringe upon . . . religious convictions."[52]

To fulfill his goal, the Nixon administration implemented new policies. In the fall of 1969 DHEW answered Nixon's call for a National Center for Family Planning Services, quite a change from its earlier slow response to the appointment of a deputy secretary for family planning. On 2 February 1970 the administration passed an increase of $13 million in the budget for contraceptive research, totaling $28.5 million.[53] Later the same year Congress finally passed and Nixon signed into law the Family Planning Services and Population Research Act to provide services to all low-income and indigent women; it was the first of its kind to deal solely with family planning. It al-

located $382 million over three years to nonprofit organizations to estab-
lish and expand such services as pill distribution, consultations, supervision,
instruction, and referral to other medical services. The act also established
the Office of Population Affairs and provided grants for "acceptable" forms
of contraception; abortion was not included.[54] Congress expanded contraceptive services with the Social Security Amendments of 1972, which reim-
bursed 90 percent of state contraception expenses.[55] While Nixon hailed
this "landmark legislation," PPRI was critical. The 1970 act was a "watered
down" version: the original Senate bill allocated $967 million over five years;
the House allocated only $267 million over three years. Nonetheless, the
compromise bill of $382 million was "still a long step in the right direction."
Although grateful for federal funding, PPRI questioned the constant criticism of indigent women as responsible for overpopulation, arguing that the
"more affluent in this country" should practice family planning because the
"greatest growth of population is from this segment of our society."[56] Federal officials were not concerned with overpopulation per se, only with large
families who financially burdened the state.

The 1960s witnessed a revolution in federal policy. A topic considered
taboo in the early part of the decade, birth control dispersal and research
became an integral part of government attempts to combat poverty, illegitimacy, and, most important, mounting expenditures. Touting contraceptives
as the cure-all allowed the government to push easy and publicly accepted
solutions to much more complex socioeconomic problems plaguing society.

State and Local Actions

Local governments experimented with contraceptive programs in poverty-
stricken areas in the early 1960s. In Chicago inner-city programs resulted in
a 25 percent decline in the birthrate between 1960 and 1964. Dr. Elizabeth
Corkey initiated one of the first mass pill programs in 1960 in Mecklenburg
County, North Carolina. Welfare officials reported that the number of children on AFDC rolls had not increased since implementation.[57] A program
in Wolfe County, Kentucky, brought a 50 percent decrease in the birthrate by
1965.[58] Such success increased pressure for more government involvement.
Similar to federal efforts, the driving force behind state and local actions was
economic: contraceptives were an easy way to reduce expenditures on low-
income and indigent populations.

State funding increased in the early 1960s. North Carolina health and welfare departments combined forces in 1960 to supply oral contraceptives to
indigent women. To avoid accusations of government-sponsored immorality,

an unmarried woman had to have already given birth. Wallace Kuralt, Mecklenburg County welfare director, estimated that his county saved $250,000 in AFDC grants between 1960 and 1964. Although he supported birth control as a woman's right, he instead touted economic savings in his public speeches. Publicly funded clinics in South Carolina reported similar welfare savings.[59] Neither North nor South Carolina encountered resistance to publicly funded contraception, perhaps because the most influential opposition, the Catholic Church, exerted little influence in most southern states.

Similar programs in Illinois, on the other hand, encountered opposition. Dr. Lonny Myers, an anesthesiologist at Michael Resse Hospital in Chicago, discovered that mothers on relief could not be given contraceptives at public health facilities in Cook County: she had "heard all these complaints about high welfare costs and how the ADC's going way up, and at the same time those very same people deny these people the right to have birth control." She argued that tax dollars should be used to help "poor people who *don't want* babies" and to relieve the tax burden on citizens who did not want to support these children. As a result, Myers founded the Illinois Citizens for the Extension of Birth Control in 1961 in cooperation with Don Shaw, an Episcopal priest, Ralph Brown, a lawyer, and Norman Lazarus, a Chicago businessman.[60] Since the plan had been privately funded, public reaction was muted. The same was not true when Arnold H. Maremont, chair of the state public aid commission, and Harold O. Swank, director of the Illinois Department of Public Aid, worked to cut the state's welfare budget. Maremont identified the cause of the jump from $285 million in 1955–57 to $628 million in 1961–63 as an "out-of-control" birthrate. Fifty percent of the welfare budget went to AFDC; three out of four relief recipients in Illinois were black. Many taxpayers resented this expense, especially in view of high illegitimacy among welfare families. Within a six-month period, for example, 78 percent of births to AFDC mothers at Cook County Hospital were illegitimate. Maremont and Swank proposed to supply contraceptives at state expense to both married and single women on relief; $600,000 for contraceptives could save $1.2 million a year in AFDC payments.[61]

Reaction was mixed. The board of health contended there was no medical need for contraceptives, and, according to Myers, the AMA, the Chicago Medical Society, and the Illinois Medical Society "just stood by" because of Catholic opposition. Others argued that the legislation promoted immoral behavior. Attorney General William G. Clark, for example, argued that it would make the state "an accessory to sexual promiscuity and prostitution." Benjamin S. Adamowski, Republican candidate for mayor of Chicago, claimed it "subsidized immorality with the taxpayers' money." Dr. Myers responded: "We all agree that the ideal way for women who do not live with their spouses to avoid pregnancies is to abstain from sex and divert their sexual drive into more constructive and socially acceptable channels, such as bridge parties, teas, and great book clubs. But what chances has an AFDC mother to attain this ideal? The result of our naive desire to settle for nothing less than abstinence is random reproduction and irresponsible parenthood." Her argument failed to overcome objections.[62]

In the summer of 1963 the Illinois legislature established a committee to determine whether the department of public health should fund contraceptive services for all clients; the committee voted "yes, 100%." Yet when the bill passed it restricted state-funded contraception to married women living with their husbands. By eliminating single females the new program disqualified 80 percent of women receiving AFDC and undermined the goal of reducing illegitimacy and welfare. It also forbade social workers to initiate the topic of contraception. Myers blamed the Catholic Church, which "simply wanted to show how much power it had," and politicians who would rather "put up with hundreds of thousands of unwanted kids and complain and complain about giving them support money" than acknowledge premarital sex and risk Catholic censure.[63]

News of the Illinois plan traveled. When Maremont and Swank proposed their initial plan, the *New York Times* called for a similar plan in New York. The state legislature, however, passed a compromise bill in 1964 that authorized the state to fund contraceptives for married relief recipients only. Social workers could not initiate the topic. Little opposition emerged because of these restrictions.[64] By 1965 twenty-nine states and the District of Columbia provided publicly funded contraceptive services through either their welfare or their public health departments.[65]

The issue of force versus choice emerged as some states allowed social workers to initiate the topic of contraception with welfare clients. Maryland adopted such a policy in September 1962. Privately funded clinics had existed there for decades. The state board of welfare adopted an affirmative position on funding and referrals because births to indigent women had been steadily increasing since 1950. Widespread acceptance of this policy, according to Dr. John Whitridge of the Maryland Department of Health, reflected a "rapid shift in public attitude" due to growing irritation with mounting welfare expenditures. After three years of public contraceptive funding, births decreased significantly. Although a national 6 percent decline in fertility occurred at the same time, the Baltimore rate decreased by 9 percent.[66] Other states followed Maryland's example—Ohio in 1965 and New York in 1966. North Carolina increased its program fourfold between 1963 and 1965. The impetus for expansion, according to Kuralt, was "the ever-increasing number of children . . . the public did not wish to support."[67] By late 1967 thirty-four states not only paid contraceptive costs for AFDC families but also allowed public welfare department staff to initiate discussion, counseling, and referrals for family planning.[68]

Catholic Opposition

The Johnson administration's endorsement of family planning left the Catholic Church in an awkward position. Critchlow analyzes the nuances of the behind-the-scenes wrangling among hard-liners, liberals, and moderates within church leadership to devise an acceptable position with regard to federal involvement in contraception. In the end they agreed not to adopt an official policy of opposition as long as all programs were voluntary and offered instruction in the rhythm method. Individual priests could take any action that suited their consciences.[69] Some criticized federal involvement. In November 1965 Monsignor George C. Higgins of Chicago contended that the War on Poverty tried to solve poverty and growing relief rolls by urging the indigent to have fewer children—a policy of "defeatism and despair" aimed primarily at poor blacks.[70] Following a fall 1966 meeting in Washington, D.C., Catholic bishops denounced the family-planning actions of the Johnson administration. "Far from merely seeking to provide information in response to requests from the needy," they contended, "government activities increasingly seek aggressively to persuade and even coerce the underprivileged to practice birth control." This trend threatened "the free choice of spouses" to determine family size and seriously endangered the "inviolability of the right of human privacy."[71] Rather than retreat to a moral condemnation based on Catholic doctrine, they harped on traditional fears of government infringement on individual rights.

New state programs that allowed social workers to initiate the topic of contraception ignited additional criticism from some Catholic leaders. They insisted that the caseworker's mentioning of contraceptives could influence people and eliminate their freedom of choice. As *America* argued: "The State, on whom [the welfare recipient] depends for his subsistence, tells him through a social worker that he has 'too many' children and 'advises' him to get contraceptive information. No one threatens him with legal penalties, it is true. But how free is he, psychologically, to refuse to accept the advice?" A similar argument appeared in *Commonweal*.[72] The editorial staffs of these two Catholic journals feared that as welfare expenditures mounted, the pressure to convince the indigent to use contraception would also increase. This fear was legitimate in light of increasing pressure to solve growing government expenditures with the distribution of the pill.

Most other religious groups supported government actions, hailing them as a humane response to dire family situations. In a letter to Johnson, Gardner, and Shriver, influential Protestant leaders labeled the bishops' charge of coercion "completely unfounded." Even some prominent Catholics criticized the bishops' statement.[73] Many Catholics ignored their leaders' criticism and used contraceptives, hoping that the Vatican's silence signaled an easing of the church's position. They were mistaken. In 1968 the papal encyclical *Humanae Vitae* again denounced all artificial means of contraception.[74] This pronouncement did little to curb contraceptive use among American Catholics.

Birth Control and the Black Community

Some blacks became skeptical of the increasing push for contraceptive dispersal in inner-city neighborhoods. Although the black community had generally supported birth control since the 1930s, some members rejected it as a white plot to decimate the black race. This controversy continued in a low-key manner through the 1940s and 1950s.[75] By the 1960s the fear of genocide had heightened, much of it rooted in centuries of abuse. Slave rape, breeding, and genital mutilation provided a strong basis for mistrust of any program dealing with black sexuality. Although most blacks, especially black women, rejected the notion of birth control as genocide, black suspicions were not unwarranted.

In general, black nationalists and revolutionaries raised genocidal fears. The more estranged from the government blacks felt, the more likely they were to distrust state-sponsored contraception. Whitney Young, leader of the National Urban League, revoked his group's support of contraception in 1962. Several local NAACP chapters followed suit. Marvin Davies, head of the Florida NAACP, argued that black women needed to have large numbers of babies until the black population comprised between 30 and 35 percent of Americans. Only then would blacks be able to affect the power structure. At a meeting of the Council of Philadelphia Anti-Poverty Action Committee in 1965, Cecil Moore, president of the local NAACP chapter, condemned a Planned Parenthood program for northern Philadelphia because 70 percent of the population was black. Labeling the plan "replete with everything to help the Negroes commit race suicide," Moore convinced the committee to table the proposal. These decisions show a key transformation from prior decades, when these organizations hailed birth control as a vehicle for racial improvement. Around the same time, Donald A. Bogue, a Chicago activist, reported that the black birthrate in Chicago had fallen from 39.4 per 1,000 in 1960 to 29.1 per 1,000 births in 1965. Although Bogue deemed this decline a breakthrough in family planning, some blacks considered it evidence that contraception was a front to eliminate the black population.[76]

Opposition among some blacks escalated as the 1960s progressed. Most objections came from inner-city lower classes; the middle class generally accepted family planning to increase their mobility. The two groups associated with genocide were the Black Panthers and the Black Muslims. The Black Panther Party considered contraception only one part of a government scheme: drugs, venereal disease, prostitution, coercive sterilization bills, restrictive welfare legislation, inhuman living conditions, "police murders," rat bites, malnutrition, lead poisoning, frequent fires and accidents in run-down houses, lack of a comprehensive sickle-cell anemia program, and overrepresentation among Vietnam soldiers all contributed to a malicious plan to annihilate the black race.[77]

Black Muslims opposed contraception for three reasons. First, the Koran condemns it. Second, women's primary role was to breed. As Muslim leader Elijah Muhammad stated: "The woman is man's field to produce his nation." Third, contraceptives were a genocidal plot devised by the "white devils." Muhammad warned against the "disgraceful birth control laws now aimed exclusively at poor, helpless black peoples who have no one to rely on." He compared the contraceptive campaign to Pharaoh murdering the first-born boys of Israel. Malcolm X also suspected genocide: "It's easy to see the fear in their mind," he declared, "that the masses of dark people . . . will continue to increase and multiply and grow until they eventually overrun [other peoples] like a human sea, a human tide, a human flood." *Muhammad Speaks*, the Muslim weekly, published stories on the "deadly" and "diabolic" nature of birth control.[78]

A primary genocide theorist was Dr. Charles Greenlee, a respected black physician from Pittsburgh who opposed the state contraceptive program. In December 1965 Pennsylvania allocated public funds for contraceptive dispersal and allowed social workers to initiate the topic with clients. This policy, however, was controversial among state legislators. While many approved, others feared it would encourage immorality and/or accusations of coercion. After months of battling, the new law prohibited caseworkers from initiating the subject and limited public funds to married women.[79] Public reaction varied. Planned Parenthood Center of Pittsburgh (PPCP) criticized it, arguing that states that allowed caseworker initiation showed "concern and progress for humanity."[80] Greenlee, on the other hand, believed the law provided insufficient guarantees against caseworker coercion.[81]

Greenlee raised the issue of black genocide in 1966 and kept it alive in the press. Although he did not oppose birth control per se, he objected to the "pill-pushing in black neighborhoods," arguing that public assistance workers carried contraceptive "propaganda" into poor black homes and forced people to use contraceptives or risk losing benefits. He contended that free clinics constituted "genocide"—a conscious conspiracy by whites to achieve a Hitlerian solution to the "black problem" in the United States. The best way to improve the plight of poor blacks was to multiply into a powerful army and demand a fair share of the American pie. As he told *Ebony*, "Our birth rate is the only thing we have. If we keep on producing, they're going to have to either kill us or grant us full citizenship." In a Pittsburgh television panel he accused the white power structure of using clinics to "decimate the black population in America within a generation." The only answer to this genocide, he argued, was to convince black women to have more babies.[82]

In July 1966 OEO allocated funds to PPCP to expand its services in eight poverty areas, six of which were predominantly black.[83] PPCP initiated a "home visitor" program to acquaint women with available services and OEO contraceptive funds.[84] Greenlee's opposition attracted William "Bouie" Haden, a controversial civil rights militant whom the *Pittsburgh Post Gazette* regarded "as the most violent of Pittsburgh's black leaders."[85] He became a leader of the Homewood-Brushton Alliance, founded in 1967, to "consolidate the latent strength of the Negro community into an effective force for the betterment of the community."[86] Another supporter was the Reverend Charles Owen Rice, a white Catholic priest at the predominantly black Holy Rosemary parish in Homewood-Brushton. On 17 November 1966 Rice appeared with Greenlee on WQED, Pittsburgh's public broadcast television station; both men voiced their opposition to OEO contraceptive funding.[87]

Rice seldom employed traditional Catholic rhetoric in his public statements, relying instead on genocide. In his *Pittsburgh Catholic* column he criticized government attempts to mingle contraception with welfare: this "tie-in is not only an unwarranted intrusion of public power into private life but it is also subtly anti-Negro."[88] He lambasted the *Village Voice* for an article that supported contraceptive subsidies for the poor. "Do you not realize that the Pill is pushed in black & Puerto Rican areas in a manner entirely different from its promotion in other areas?" he asked. "Here in Pittsburgh," he continued, "Planned Parenthood & the OEO have a humming Pill Mill in Negro poverty areas. They send lay people around with all manner of contraceptives from door to door to Negroes." He maintained that blacks such as Greenlee and Haden were "just waking up" to the reality of the situation.[89]

The Pittsburgh NAACP, with Greenlee chairing the Medical Committee, condemned the PPCP home visitors as worse than army recruiters because they "invade[ed] the privacy of the individual" without an invitation and inaugurated a "session of brain-washing." It alleged that PPCP had promised

OEO officials to "recruit" clients for these federally funded clinics. "The evidence indicates that they not only kept their promise to the OEO," claimed the NAACP, "but improved their methods by adding a 'go out and get them back' arm to their operation." PPCP solicited "women from every house in every predominantly black neighborhood where the O.E.O. out-reach clinics" were located and operated a "military police for the purpose of keeping the females in their anti-parenthood clinics." This "birth control operation is black genocide." The local stand conflicted with the national organization's support of birth control, but Greenlee chaired both the board and the health committee of the Pittsburgh NAACP.[90]

These public denunciations of PPCP-OEO programs led to investigations. The Health Advisory Council of Community Action Pittsburgh (CAP), a local agency that worked with other private and public agencies to combat poverty, unanimously gave PPCP a clean record.[91] For unknown reasons, the report was not made public. In addition, Planned Parenthood flew Dr. Douglas Stewart, its national director of community relations, to Pittsburgh to investigate the matter. Stewart, a black man, accused Greenlee of doing "nationwide harm" with false accusations of genocide. PPCP also examined the program and denied all charges, asserting that 80 percent of PPCP clients were white and that both races received identical treatment.[92]

Despite criticism by black militants and Rice, the clinics continued to operate. The board of the Homewood-Brushton Citizens Renewal Council, one of eight target neighborhoods, approved the renewal of OEO funding for PPCP programs in May 1967.[93] By this point PPCP operated seventeen branch clinics. Between 80 and 90 percent of clinic funds in poverty neighborhoods came from OEO.[94] By 1968 Haden was determined to eliminate OEO funding in the Homewood-Brushton neighborhood, including "blowing up" clinics. To aid his cause, Rice convinced the Catholic Diocese of Pittsburgh in July 1968 to fund Haden's United Movement for Progress, an organization to bring "a more militant position into the civil rights arena."[95] The diocese gave the United Movement for Progress a grant of $12,000, $10,000 of which was earmarked for Haden's salary.[96] Public response was fast and furious: the *Pittsburgh Courier* labeled Haden a "Salaried Militant"; hate mail and abusive calls poured into Holy Rosemary rectory. One parishioner summed up: the church supported a "criminal militant" for no reason other than that he opposed "the giving out of birth control pills." Church contributions fell, and Bishop John J. Wright was hanged in effigy at Saint Paul's Cathedral with a sign reading "Bishop Wright, puppet of Bouie Haden."[97]

Many Homewood-Brushton residents were no happier. Haden was from Garfield and used his new church money to relocate to Homewood-Brushton. David Epperson, executive director of CAP, labeled Haden an "outsider."

The "standard-bearers" of the community looked upon him as a "rabble rouser." Sarah Bradford Campbell, a Homewood-Brushton community leader through the 1950s and 1960s, claimed that Haden came to her neighborhood "seeking power." She believed the church relocated him so he could challenge the "status quo," which, in this instance, was the Homewood-Brushton Citizens Renewal Council, one of the longest-running neighborhood organizations in Pittsburgh. Members of this community, according to Epperson, had a "strong, solid, very responsible neighborhood-based organization. . . . They worked hard and they did good things." Then "out of the woodwork" came Haden, who endeavored to challenge the "older folks who had been in power." Rice, Greenlee (who was also not from Homewood-Brushton), and Haden, according to Campbell, "felt that they could wrest power from us by using this genocide issue." They sought "any issue to try to divide the group and that was why the genocide issue came up."[98]

Haden's target during the summer of 1968 was the new Homewood-Brushton Medical Center, financed with the help of $1.5 million from OEO. PPCP, with both OEO and private funds, planned a permanent clinic there. Haden threatened PPCP representatives with bodily violence if they did not cease activities in Homewood-Brushton and warned there would be riots and fire bombings "if anyone tries to operate a birth control project in the area."[99] Haden's terror tactics were widely criticized. One citizen berated him for labeling birth control genocide but, in the next breath, threatening to bomb a black neighborhood clinic. Another wrote that "this seems to me to be the most bold-faced affront to our black neighbors' intelligence," because Haden was essentially saying that "'you people don't have sense enough to think or choose for yourself so I will choose for you.'" Under such threats, PPCP temporarily suspended operation in Homewood-Brushton.[100]

Many Homewood-Brushton women, however, protested this suspension. Admonishing Haden to "mind your own business," seventy predominantly black women, led by Georgiana Henderson, requested PPCP to continue. Henderson stated, "We're getting tired of statements by Mr. Haden. . . . He is only one person—and a man at that—and he can't speak for the women of Homewood. . . . Birth control is none of his business." Another woman asked, "Why should I let one loudmouth tell me about having children?" With regard to Haden, Greenlee, and Rice's indictment of the home visitor program as black genocide, Betty Morris, the nurse in charge of contraceptive services in Homewood, answered that PPCP personnel visited poor white areas but with little success because the majority were Catholic. Morris explained that visitors avoided wealthy areas where women could afford a private physician.[101] Women gained support from the session, the governing body of the black congregation, Bethesda United Presbyterian Church. PPCP services were not genocide: "To label such a program of family planning 'genocide' is patently false. . . . No strictures are too harsh in calling to task those persons who would thus mislead and inflame the public on this important issue." The session affirmed couples' right to birth control and PPCP services.[102]

The Homewood-Brushton Citizens Renewal Council held a meeting on 14 August 1968 to discuss neighborhood contraceptive services. Greenlee and Haden continued to claim that government-sponsored contraception perpetuated "black genocide." Henderson, leading seventy women, maintained that these men had no right to dictate the needs of women, who could speak for themselves, and they demanded the continuation of services. The women prevailed: the mostly male council unanimously supported their demands.[103] Haden refused to accept this decision. While the "status quo" leaders of the Homewood-Brushton community considered Haden an outsider, those outside the established circle of power saw Haden as a "folk hero." Many of his followers were low-income, young black males, heavily influenced by Black Power ideology, and some young females whom the "standard organization" viewed as "really on the outside because of dress and behavior." Haden's support base was in the eastern section of the community, where most people were on welfare. He attracted younger people who "were desirous of leadership roles but had no notable credentials for them." Basically, the disenfranchised gravitated toward him.[104] Throughout the fall of 1968 and early 1969 Haden maintained a steady barrage of propaganda against contraception. Not only did he label black supporters of the program "Uncle Toms," but he accused black CAP board members of "selling out" to keep their positions within the federal bureaucracy. Greenlee espoused similar arguments during a television appearance in early 1969, while Rice kept the debate alive in his weekly column.[105]

This persistent pressure led the CAP board to consider the issue at their meetings in February and March. Byrd Brown, president of the local NAACP and chair of the CAP subcommittee on planned parenthood, "flip flopped" on the issue, according to Campbell, and "reluctantly" introduced the proposal to maintain funding. Members of the Welfare Rights Organizations of Allegheny County, which included both black and white women, supported funding, informing the press: "We cannot help but notice that most of the anti–birth control pressure is coming from men, men who do not have to bear children. We're speaking for the women and we want the Planned Parenthood Centers to stay in our neighborhoods."[106] During the CAP meetings Haden reiterated that contraception was "black genocide." Greenlee called it an "international conspiracy" to diminish the "darker races" in the world.

Another Haden supporter questioned the lack of facilities in white poverty neighborhoods; PPCP answered that strong Catholic opposition kept clinics out.[107] The opposition quickly lost steam.

Advocates for funding appeared before CAP in full force. Approximately two hundred mostly black women, organized by Sarah Campbell, demanded the continuation of PPCP services. Prior to the hearing Campbell and her supporters had "collared Bouie Haden" and informed him that they "were not going to accept this business of genocide." At the meeting he attempted to discredit them by claiming they spoke only for the middle class. Instead, they undermined his stance by insisting on their right to decide birth control issues without the intervention of domineering men. Others pointed out that PPCP operated services besides contraception, such as infertility clinics and marriage and child-spacing clinics, which benefited large numbers of women. These women, according to Epperson, believed family planning constituted a positive addition to health care services in addition to securing their right to control their family size.[108] In the end, the women persuaded CAP to reinstate federal funds. Haden chose the wrong community to target, yet Epperson argued that Haden did raise "certain points of view that were valid." The only way to guarantee against coercive or genocidal plans was to have black citizens, particularly women, direct family-planning programs in black communities.[109]

The issue of genocide also emerged on the national level. In the summer of 1967 the male-dominated Black Power Conference in Newark, New Jersey, passed an anti–birth control resolution that equated birth control with "black genocide."[110] The following year the Third Annual National Conference on Black Power in Philadelphia called on blacks to "resist the increasing genocidal tendencies of American society." Resistance ranged from a small California group called Efforts to Increase Our Size to groups in Pittsburgh and Cleveland that protested Planned Parenthood programs to the ultramilitant group in New York known as the Five Percenters. These organizations asked two questions: "Is birth control just a 'white man's plot' to 'contain' the black population?" and "Is it just another scheme to cut back on welfare aid or still another method of 'keeping the black man down'?"[111] The *Thrust* questioned why blacks could not get a free aspirin for a headache, "yet when you're a Black woman old enough to look sexy you can get a truck loaded down with [birth] control pills free. . . . The whole plot makes Hitler look like a Boy Scout."[112] By the late 1960s a survey found 28 percent of blacks agreed that "encouraging blacks to use birth control is comparable to trying to eliminate this group from society." In Cleveland, Ohio, militant blacks burned down a contraceptive clinic after labeling its activities "black genocide."[113] Genocide arguments attracted mostly northern, urban young men, not women. A 1973 study found younger blacks feared genocide more than older blacks, northern more than southern blacks, less-educated more than higher-educated blacks, and males more than females. The study concluded that despite genocide fears among young black men, there was "considerable evidence that black women . . . are even more positively inclined toward family planning than white women."[114]

Many black women criticized Black Power ideology regarding women. They especially objected to the conclusion not only that white society had castrated black men but that black women had "contributed to this emasculation." Frances Beal, New York coordinator of the Student Nonviolent Coordinating Committee Black Women's Liberation Committee, argued that black women "are not resentful of the rise to power of black men. . . . Nevertheless, this does not mean that you have to negate one for the other. . . . It is fallacious reasoning that in order for the black man to be strong, the black woman has to be weak." The apparent "need to affirm manhood" among Black Power men led many to assign secondary roles to women. As Angela Davis stated in 1967: "I was criticized very heavily . . . for doing a 'man's job.' Women should not play leadership roles, they insisted; a woman was to 'inspire' her man and educate his children" and, as black commentator Linda LaRue noted, rear "warriors for the revolution."[115]

Most black women rejected this assigned role as revolutionary womb. They disagreed with the "brothers" over birth control and genocide. LaRue asked these men about the "potential revolutionary warriors . . . abandoned in orphanages." Similarly, author Toni Cade countered genocidal accusations by asking black men, "What plans do you have for the care of men and the child? . . . How do we break the cycle of child-abandonment-ADC-child?" Although she supported the "need to produce," she rejected the "irresponsible, poorly thought-out call to young girls, on-the-margin scufflers, every Sister at large to abandon the pill." The pill would allow couples to control the spacing and number of children born to carry on the fight.[116] The Black Women's Liberation Group claimed that women took the pill "because of poor black men" who refused to "support their families" and would not "stick by their women." The group realized that "a lot of black brothers" were asking women not to practice contraception because it was "a form of Whitey's committing genocide on black people." For women, however, the pill symbolized "the freedom to fight genocide of black women and children. . . . Having too many babies stops us from supporting our children . . . and from fighting black men who still want to use and exploit us." Dara Abubakari, vice president of the Republic of New Africa—a separatist movement to establish a new black nation in Mississippi, Louisiana, Alabama, Georgia, and South Carolina—wrote, "Women should be free to decide if and when they want children. . . . Men shouldn't tell us. Nobody should tell us."[117]

This attitude prevailed in the black community. In a 1970 Chicago study Donald Bogue found that 80 percent of black women approved of birth control and 75 percent used it. A 1971 public opinion poll found that the majority of blacks, both men and women, supported government subsidy of contraceptives. In *Genocide?* Robert Weisbord concluded that "the black masses are no more responsive to the genocide notion than American Catholics are to papal encyclicals on artificial contraception."[118] Martin Luther King, Jr., supported family planning and received the Margaret Sanger Award in Human Rights in 1966 for his efforts. He argued that "intelligent guides of family planning" were a "profoundly important ingredient" in the black quest for "security and a decent life." Stability for a black man would result from "easy access to the means to develop a family related in size to his community environment and to the income potential he can command." Walter R. Chivers, chair of the Department of Sociology at Morehouse College, embarked on a speaking tour to promote contraception as a means to strengthen, not destroy, black families. Other prominent blacks also supported family planning, including Carl Rowan, former U.S. ambassador to Finland and syndicated columnist; James Farmer, national director of the Congress of Racial Equality (CORE); Bayard Rustin, chief organizer of the 1963 March on Washington; Jerome Holland, distinguished black sociologist and educator; Ron Dellums, California Democrat and member of the congressional black caucus; and Representative Barbara Jordan of Texas. In addition, the NAACP, CORE, and the National Medical Association endorsed family planning.[119]

Although the majority of blacks supported birth control, some wondered if the only motivation behind the white power structure was to help blacks improve. Jesse Jackson did not oppose birth control, yet he did question the "timing" of the population control hysteria in the 1960s: "That this issue should surface simultaneously with the emergence of blacks and other nonwhites as a meaningful force in the nation and the world appears more than coincidental." Langston Hughes, American poet and novelist, wondered why the government suddenly had millions of dollars for contraceptives for people of color in India, China, Africa, and Harlem. Urelia Brown, a black social worker, told the *Reporter* that "Negroes don't want children they can't take care of, but we are afraid to trust you when your offered help has so often turned out to be exploitation."[120]

Some family-planning activists acknowledged that many contributors were racist. Beatrice Blaire worked to establish a clinic in Rochester's Baden Street neighborhood, a predominantly black area, and she "knew damn well that many people, in their minds, made the connection, well, we're going to keep the blacks down." Blaire "took the money anyway" because she believed women needed and wanted a clinic. She and her supporters were "sensitive enough to make sure we had a black person to work with black people." Lonny Myers had a similar experience in Chicago. When asked if she was bothered that some money came from racists, she said yes but concluded that "any cause has strange bedfellows." The financial backing and the "votes of the racists" who supported contraceptives "just to decrease the number of blacks in the city" were crucial to bring about change to benefit women.[121]

Events in Rhode Island

The RIMHA experienced rapid client growth from 2,873 patients in 1961 to 4,932 in 1964. Several factors explain this increase. First was the mailing of "Dear Mother and Father" letters to new parents; these letters brought about 15 percent of new clients. Second was the health program. The Rhode Island Foundation for the detection of uterine cancer gave RIMHA an annual grant of $3,000 beginning in 1960 and increased it to $5,000 in 1965. The Medical Advisory Committee extended Pap smears to all patients, and the clinic sent more slides to be processed "than any other single source including the cancer clinic."[122] Third was the "tremendous amount of public information on the population problem and on . . . the Pill." As the staff concluded, "Suddenly things have changed and very rapidly." Catholic clients increased from 52 percent in 1962 to 61 percent in 1963, which paralleled the 60 percent Catholic representation in the state. By 1963 "the news blackout which had always surrounded us began to come to an end." By 1964 staff members were giving television and radio interviews and receiving front-page coverage in the *Providence Journal*. While appreciative of "remarkable free publicity," some staff members were worried that some women would not realize that RIMHA services included birth control. After years of defying PPFA, the executive committee voted in July 1964 to become PPRI in order to benefit from national publicity in fund-raising and patient loads.[123]

Despite increasing public acceptance, Rhode Island did not join other states in using public funds for contraception. Clinic reports claimed that the 60 percent Catholic population prevented such implementation. Executive Director Anne Wise tried in 1963 to convince Augustine W. Riccio, director of the Department of Social Welfare, that the state's failure to pay for contraceptives for indigent and welfare recipients constituted class discrimination: "Giving citizens the right to plan children is just as valid a health service as any other legitimate public health service. Family planning is a matter of personal choice and those who must receive their medical care through pub-

lic aid should have this same right of choice as our more fortunate citizens."
When this line of reasoning failed, Wise adopted the economic argument
more palatable to many administrators: "Surely the constantly rising costs
of ADC and other aid programs, to say nothing of the toll in human misery of unwanted children make it necessary that a careful evaluation of this
policy . . . be undertaken." This argument succeeded: Riccio invited the clinic
to provide an exhibit at the Rhode Island Conference of Social Work, and in
1965 the Department of Social Welfare allowed caseworkers to refer clients
to PPRI on request.[124] Cost-cutting rather than class discrimination arguments transformed state policy. The impact of this decision was immediately
evident: in 1963 only 53 patients were on welfare; in 1965 286 were.[125] While
the state allowed referrals, it did not provide PPRI funds to defray the cost of
welfare clients.

In search of new revenues, PPRI courted the business community. For the
first time, two of the five vice presidents were men in 1964.[126] The staff organized a series of "Business Men's Dinners" and a "Men's Team of solicitors"
and brought in John Nuveen, chair of the national campaign fund, to speak
to men about the "economic consequences of the population explosion." They
consciously employed different rhetoric when dealing with the business community, emphasizing population control rather than health and choice. For
some, the rhetoric was not important; the main point was to raise money. It
bothered others that people would associate PPRI with PPFA's population
control obsession. They argued that PPFA should "work on polishing its image. . . . Too many people believe that P.P. espouses a negative philosophy of
too many children in the world to make it an evil place." Despite strategic
differences, money flowed from businessmen. Combined with other contributions, the budget jumped from $62,273.46 in 1963 to $144,548.40 in 1966.
Although the clinic enjoyed increased acceptance, especially in the wake of
Griswold, the United Fund rejected PPRI, fearing reprisal from the state's
Catholic hierarchy.[127]

With *Griswold*, clinics opened in Massachusetts and Connecticut, yet
many women continued to come to PPRI, complaining that "the services offered were not what they had come to expect after coming to [PPRI]." Cancer
detection remained "one of the most valuable" services at PPRI; the Rhode
Island Foundation doubled its annual contribution in 1967 to $10,000, and
the Council of Community Services finally accepted PPRI the same year. The
staff launched a publicity campaign "to find more patients from hard core
poverty areas, where the greatest needs not only for birth control but comprehensive health services remain." PPRI expanded health services to include
blood pressure tracking for all, not just pill takers, as well as vitamin therapy
and diet advice. They also handled minor vaginal problems because patients

found referrals hard to fulfill while juggling jobs, child care, and other responsibilities.[128]

In 1967 Rhode Island joined the majority of states in funding contraceptives. The Rhode Island Conference on Social Work again invited PPRI to
exhibit at the 1966 convention and held a session on family planning at its
Spring Institute. In June 1967 the Department of Public Welfare followed
new federal Social Security amendments to pay for contraceptive prescriptions, "an important step," according to PPRI, because it placed "birth control
in the same position as other vital health services in the state." The following
year the public welfare department allowed caseworkers to initiate birth control discussions with clients.[129] These changes affected PPRI's patient load:
welfare clients increased by 31 percent, and no-fee, nonwelfare patients increased by 17 percent.[130]

The patient load strained the clinic, still the only one in the state. To ease
access, PPRI opened a supply center in South Providence in June 1966. Regular PPRI patients could pick up contraceptives here rather than travel to the
downtown clinic. In its first six months more than 250 women took advantage of the "convenience of a neighborhood office." Women also benefited
when Providence Lying-In Hospital opened a clinic in January 1967 to serve
ward patients. A grant of $35,000 from DHEW in 1968 allowed Lying-In to
expand the clinic to nonpatients. South County Hospital agreed to open a
clinic under PPRI supervision in 1967, and PPRI established a clinic in Newport. South County had a steady caseload, but the Newport facility competed
with a new IUD program run by the navy for sailors' wives.[131]

By the late 1960s PPRI carried an annual caseload of 6,600 clients—an
increase of 1,000 since 1966, despite the drop-off of out-of-state clients and
the opening of other clinics. Approximately 27 percent could pay no fee, and
18 percent of these were welfare clients. Catholics constituted the majority,
despite the 1968 papal encyclical. New and old clients benefited from health
care services, with 10 percent referred for further treatment. Most clients
were between twenty and forty years old, although some were in their fifties,
and some parents brought in teens. By the late 1960s the clinic saw increased
Spanish- and Portuguese-speaking clients, reflecting immigration patterns
in the state.[132]

Although the clinic offered various contraceptive options, there was "no
question about the supremacy of the 'Pill.'" With twelve pills from which to
chose, 79 percent of new clients went with oral contraceptives. Doctors often
switched pills to find the least side effects; they did not dismiss women's complaints as psychosomatic. Dr. Slabey reported five serious problems among
patients in 1967. One woman died, but she had been treated for hypertension, renal necrosis, and disseminated vascular thrombosis. The other four

were thromboembolic episodes; they recovered and were placed on different contraceptives. In all five cases "there was discrepancy in the history they gave and in the reporting of symptoms." Some patients were "reluctant to admit the presence of side reactions for fear that the doctor will not prescribe the pill."[133] As informed consumers, these women knew what type of birth control they wanted, and they knew the medical complications that contraindicated its use. IUDs were second behind the pill; 552 used it, with only 4 cases of pelvic inflammation. In "each of these patients," however, "a history of prior inflammation was finally elicited and admitted." Just as with the pill, patients withheld information to ensure their choice of contraception. Barrier methods such as condoms, diaphragms, jellies, and foams were "limited" in use. The once-sought-after diaphragm decreased in popularity except when adverse publicity on the pill occurred. Following Senate hearings in 1970, for example, 13 percent of PPRI women stopped taking the pill (versus 18 percent nationally).[134] After a "cooling off period" 65.3 percent returned to the pill.[135] By 1968 70 percent used the pill, 13 percent IUDs, 14 percent diaphragms, and 3 percent some other method. Dr. Slabey closed the rhythm clinic for lack of use.[136]

The availability and testing of cutting-edge contraceptives at PPRI made it an educational center. The clinic had trained 426 individuals by the late 1960s: 50 percent were student nurses; others included sixth-year medical students at Brown University, students majoring in social work or health and education from seven area colleges, social and welfare workers from state agencies, and area physicians. The classes for which students gained college credit filled "a gap in the nursing and medical education in this area." Although 39 states accepted federal funds for birth-control educational programs, Rhode Island refused them. PPRI's program therefore fulfilled an important function in the state.[137] Still, clients exposing their intimate lives and body parts must have felt some embarrassment at the poking and prodding of students.[138]

Public funding continued to increase in the late 1960s. In 1969 PPRI received from the state health department $10,700, which covered approximately one-third of PPRI's cost for low-income women. The health department increased its payments over the next several years, but the welfare department refused until 1973, when, after seven years of negotiation, it agreed to pay $13 per visit for welfare clients.[139] PPRI received federal money as well, but, as Critchlow has shown, the relationship between private organizations and federal bureaucracies was not always smooth. An unexpected freeze in federal family-planning projects in 1973 raised concerns among the staff: "The proposed federal budget may result in a sky-rocketing case load for us if other clinics are unable to keep functioning."[140] State welfare payments kicked in just as federal funding became less assured.

Federal funding stirred controversies, as it had in Pittsburgh. In this case, religious, not racial, tension hit Pawtucket, Rhode Island, when neighborhood groups requested that OEO offer contraceptive services, specifically, a mobile unit to serve the Blackstone Valley area, including Pawtucket, Cumberland, Lincoln, and Central Falls. The board of the Blackstone Valley Community Action Program (BVCAP), including some Catholic clergy, unanimously approved the program, and the government awarded a grant of $12,791. Because PPRI's Anne Wise was to oversee the program, women served in the mobile unit would receive total exams, including a uterine cancer test. Pawtucket Mayor Robert F. Burns, however, publicly opposed the program because birth control would be available to single women and because he did not "believe a municipality should be as closely identified with a birth control program." He insisted that the BVCAP board return the grant or vacate their offices in city hall. City Councilman John J. Coleman backed Burns, vowing to rescind BVCAP's designation as the antipoverty agency for Pawtucket if it did not return the grant. Central Falls' mayor and Cumberland's town administrator backed Burns and Coleman. BVCAP voted twenty to nine with two abstentions to comply with Burns and Coleman because failure to do so would jeopardize other important antipoverty programs for Blackstone Valley.[141]

This decision drew sharp criticism. The *Providence Journal* lambasted Burns:

> When Mayor Robert F. Burns can issue ultimatums demanding conformity to his views on threat of eviction from city premises and thus successfully coerce the Blackstone Valley Community Action Program, Inc. into allegiance to him rather than to the poor for whom the program is set up, the future seems anything but promising. . . . In our view, Mayor Burns' heavy-handed action to kill not only a valid but a much needed program of family planning for impoverished people was improper. He has exploited his position as mayor to exert powerful personal influence where none was called for, by use of threat rather than reason, and without due regard to the best interests or the rights of Pawtucket's poor.

PPRI officials believed Burns engaged in a power struggle. Under OEO legislation, poverty programs remained outside local governments. The latter "can become sensitive to those poverty programs which are successful in that they may reflect a lack of programming for the poor under regular government functions." The Green Amendment to OEO legislation gave local governments the option to control community action programs, but the Pawtucket city council voted that CAP remain separate. Burns resented this decision: the city council "vote immediately preceded the mayor's violent reaction to the birth control program."[142]

No local protest to Burns's actions ensued. The fact that the grant would have established a new service may explain the silence. Had Burns dismantled a long-standing service, the reaction would have been different. The community may also have feared losing other new programs benefiting the poor. Moreover, women in this community had met Wise and others from PPRI during the proposal process. Blackstone Valley is in northern Rhode Island, not far from Providence. While a mobile clinic would have been more convenient, Blackstone Valley women could make the trip to PPRI without too much difficulty.

That the outcome in Pawtucket was so different from the controversy in Pittsburgh can be attributed to the long-standing activism of women in Homewood-Brushton who had been fighting for years for better contraceptive services. No matching groundswell occurred in Pawtucket, where many Catholics may have been unwilling to come out publicly to fight for birth control. Visiting an established clinic was much less brazen than protesting for new services. Women in Homewood-Brushton had the public backing of neighborhood churches, while Pawtucket women did not.

The controversy in Pawtucket constituted the only upheaval over birth control in the state. Unlike the racial politics that reverberated through Pittsburgh, Providence remained unscathed. In the mid-1960s PPRI worked with CORE and the University of Rhode Island to establish Citizens of Concern programs to assist residents in the Roger Williams housing project. The "interest was great" enough to establish family-planning services in South Providence, a predominantly black area, to save clients the trip downtown. ULRI staff concluded that "the idea of opening this branch office was sound; . . . participation was high and interest was keen."[143] When PPFA told PPRI that national had to work to combat "the feeling among some Negroes that Planned Parenthood activity has racial overtones," PPRI staff responded that they faced no such problem. The ULRI continued to invite PPRI to open houses, and "CORE invited us to set up a supply station on Camp Street," which served "to indicate a repudiation locally of those groups who claim Planned Parenthood has racial overtones." The board discussed genocide and understood the depths of despair that some minority groups felt: "Minority groups have inadequate housing, education, are hungry, poor, and often ill—they lack economic, social and political power—they are advised to have fewer children when around them on all sides are affluent, well educated, well fed and politically powerful people who are raising large families." Hoping to instill this empathy in the people trained at PPRI, they provided a questionnaire for trainees: "You're on duty at [Providence Lying-In]. Negro post partum patient . . . You mention the availability of family planning services and are accused of preaching black genocide. How would you handle this upset patient and this accusation?"[144] Although no answers were provided, the question is telling. PPRI was aware of genocide fears and wanted to ensure that its trainees would handle them in a manner congruent with PPRI's emphasis on women's health and choice.

This priority dominated PPRI through the early 1970s. New leaders came and went, including the first male vice president in 1968 and then first male president in 1969 and 1970; women resumed the presidency for 1971, 1972, and 1973.[145] Through these changes the medical director's reports showed the "kind of concern for the individual for which our medical program is known." By 1970 Wise was disgusted with "the rhetoric coming from the overpopulation prophets" who played a "numbers game." PPRI refused to play, rejecting national emphasis on a two-child family: "No policy on family size best." The staff worked with Brown medical students to remind them that "clinic patients are also human beings."[146]

In the early 1970s Rhode Island women benefited from expanded clinics, partly as a result of federal funds. By 1972 there were eight clinics outside Providence; joining PPRI within the city were ten Progress for Providence Health Centers and the Lying-In clinic. PPRI no longer served the majority of state citizens, and the characteristics of women coming to PPRI changed. Most new clients in 1970 had incomes of $49 or less per week (versus $75 to $100 in 1966); they were between twenty and twenty-four years old (versus twenty to twenty-nine in 1966); 49 percent had no children (versus four children in 1966); and only 6 percent had four or more children. By 1972 most new clients were between the ages of eighteen and twenty-five; 80 percent of new clients and 66 percent of all clients had no children. The patient load increased to 8,664, despite other clinics. With a burgeoning caseload of clients less able to pay, PPRI relied on fund-raisers and government subsidies.[147]

PPRI used federal funds to offset the expanding costs of health services. In 1970 the clinic began testing for VD and pregnancy and the following year added granulosa cell (GC) cultures and urinalyses. In 1972 the staff considered incorporating sickle-cell anemia testing but decided not to only because "many other agencies do it." Although the staff no longer recorded clients' racial/ethnic backgrounds, the consideration of sickle-cell testing affirms a significant percentage of black women. The staff also initiated genetic screening, in line with the national trend toward genetic counseling. The staff believed these new programs brought "more complete health care" for patients. Community support surged, with a 25 percent increase in donors, allowing their operating budget to jump from $197,560 in 1970 to $444,265.56 by 1976.[148]

Although more people sought contraceptive care, many still expressed anxieties about it. "Patients' fears" included "refusal or denial of help; too costly; illegality or immorality of birth control; pelvic exam; jeopardize public assistance status; loss of sexual enjoyment; being sterilized or losing capacity for future pregnancies." This list is revealing. Despite government assurances that welfare payments were not tied to contraceptive use, media coverage of coercion convinced many women they were connected. The fears of sterilization reflect national coverage of coerced sterilization of welfare clients at federally funded family-planning clinics. For men, the concerns in ranked order were "loss of stature as head of household; loss of self-esteem, self-confidence; loss of respect of peer group; capacity to give sexual pleasure; sickness or disease resulting from the use of contraceptive; mate's opportunity for infidelity; taboos on discussion of sex with outsider as too personal a matter; ignorance of language."[149] The first three deal with undermining traditional male authority. Also noteworthy is the fear men expressed concerning the sexual freedom women could gain from contraceptives; birth control equaled sexual liberation.

With younger women seeking contraceptives, PPRI built on the model set by Dr. Goldsmith in San Francisco and opened the Teen Age Center in 1970. "The growing number of minors referred by agencies and individuals or brought by parents . . . pointed out the need for a special youth services program," according to Wise, who saw it as part of a "comprehensive health service for teenagers." Once again, PPRI was in the vanguard in its region: "There is no such type of service available in the state—there is much talk about the poor situation of many of today's teenagers but no action—we should take action, take the lead in this field." As late as 1971, according to Elizabeth Siegel Watkins, the "majority" of clinics "still required proof of marriage."[150] While the staff was very enthusiastic, the board avoided publicity so as not to alienate potential contributors. By 1971 34 percent of patients were nineteen and under; the following year saw "increases nearly every month." Only one of 728 teens became pregnant. Wise concluded: "It is not just the availability of contraceptives which prevents pregnancy, since drug stores are open to all. We give education and counseling. We neither condemn nor condone. Most important, we provide a place where young people can discuss their concerns about their sexuality in a non-judgmental atmosphere." The staff also stressed the importance of communication with parents. By 1974 923 "youth patients" had been served, and as late as 1975 PPRI was the only clinic in the state that allowed minors access to contraceptives without parental consent. The majority of teens were from "middle-class, close-knit families that share many things except talk about sex, which is a no-no." Confidentiality and the ability to relate to teens appeared to be keys to the Teen Age Center's success.[151]

Conclusion

The first decade of government cooperation with private organizations in contraception reduced some social and economic "problems" associated with the indigent and low-income clients. Katherine Oettinger of DHEW reported that in 1964 only thirteen states allowed health departments to provide contraceptive services, but by 1967 forty-six states did so. By the end of the decade the birthrate for all nine geographic regions in the country had decreased. Moreover, DHEW was "encouraged" that these declines were registered "in areas of the lowest educational attainment—the highest incidence of poverty—the highest rates of illegitimacy—[and] the largest number of children per family." A 1970 Senate report claimed that the "economic effects of the oral contraceptives on such matters as decreased family size, increased disposable family incomes, [and] decreased public welfare costs" were evident in American society.[152] By that point, both state and federal governments had incorporated contraception as a principal component of public policy. This evolution resulted primarily from a desire to decrease mounting welfare expenditures. Between 1965 and 1975 the government saved an estimated minimum of $1.1 billion due to its investment in contraceptives. In 1975 alone, for every dollar spent on contraception, the government "saved" $2.50 in 1976 by averting the births of children who presumably would have depended on the welfare system for survival. The long-term savings ranged from $26 to $100 for every dollar spent on contraceptives.[153]

Whatever the motivation for government involvement, individual women on the local level benefited from expanded clinic services and research into safe and effective methods of birth control. National researchers generally remedied the medical effects of the pill, lowering the amount of estrogen and thus reducing some side effects. PPRI clients especially benefited from top-notch comprehensive health care.

While population controllers hailed government efforts in contraception, many pushed for further changes. Permanent methods of control such as sterilization not only would save money but also could provide a final solution to the perceived population problems. The younger the age at which women are sterilized, the more childbirth costs the government can save. The apparent success of the contraceptive programs prompted many social critics to promote additional policy alterations in the areas of abortion and sterilization.

Who Pays for What?

Abortion and Sterilization, 1960–1975

In the early 1960s illegal abortions continued unabated, with underground services proliferating as the decade progressed. A number of influential organizations pushed for change, including Nixon's Commission on Population Growth. A number of factors triggered growing acceptance of abortion and sterilization: environmental concerns, scarcity of world resources, greater openness about sex and contraception, and the availability of relatively safe and simple procedures. Women increasingly called for reproductive rights, a demand that held little sway over state and federal legislators. Fiscal conservatives, population controllers, and demographers' pressure to reduce government expenditures, especially AFDC, did influence state and federal decisions not only to legalize but also to fund abortion and sterilization procedures. State reform provided statistics demonstrating the impact of legalization, namely, declines in illegitimate birthrates, teenage births, maternal mortality, and the fertility rate of indigent women. Although population controllers hailed these statistics as proof that abortion could help solve the population "problem," Nixon opposed abortion. Concern for the Catholic vote led him to reject abortion but not sterilization, despite official church rejection of both procedures. Of the two, Catholic opposition was much stronger to abortion than sterilization. The latter provided Nixon an opportunity to keep elite white population controllers' support without losing the Catholic vote—a win-win situation for him. As with earlier reform, the rhetoric used to justify liberalization was not as important to individual women as the reproductive freedom many gained. While middle- and upper-class women enjoyed more choice, many lower-class and indigent women faced coercive tactics by white officials who believed they should choose who ought to be allowed to procreate. As it had during the genocide accusations with the pill, PPRI remained unscathed by the coercion controversy. The clinic adapted its programs to suit client demands, offering abortion services and opening the first vasectomy clinic in New England.

The Push for Abortion Reform

During the early 1960s illegal abortions rose 10 percent, reaching an estimated 1.5 million annually. A study of urban North Carolina found 14.9 illegal abortions per 100 conceptions for whites and 32.9 per 100 conceptions for blacks. It also found a high rate of illegal abortions for women of both races who had five or more pregnancies.[1] Growing numbers of abortions among single women concurred with rising illegitimacy rates. Both trends demonstrated increased premarital sexual activity. While arguing that contraception could prevent these pregnancies, some social critics contended that abortion laws should be reformed to terminate unwanted pregnancies that did occur. Demographer Charles Westoff claimed that between 800,000 to 1 million unwanted births took place annually, most among the indigent and low-income women who burgeoned welfare costs. He asserted that 20 to 25 percent of all pregnant women each year sought abortions. In almost all cases, the wealthy secured legal operations (approximately 10,000 per year) because they either had a trusted doctor or traveled abroad.[2]

While indigent and low-income women might encounter a sympathetic doctor willing to help them, they often experienced unsanitary conditions and painful, botched procedures. A twenty-four-year-old married woman with three children paid Mrs. Dorothy E. Furtado of Providence $150 for an abortion performed in Furtado's apartment. The woman developed an infection and had to be hospitalized. Such stories did not prevent other women from seeking illegal abortions. In fact, women protected abortionists. When thirty-year-old Anthony Altieri was arrested for performing an abortion on a twenty-two-year-old Providence woman, the latter refused to cooperate with police and testified in court that she did not see the abortionist. With legislative immunity still in place, she stood to lose nothing from refusing to identify the man. Her testimony forced the state to dismiss the charges against Altieri.[3]

Several events in the 1960s brought the legal status of abortion to a head. First, in 1962 Dr. Helen Brooke Taussig of the FDA investigated thalidomide, a European narcotic marketed as a sleeping tablet, tranquilizer, and miracle aid to combat morning sickness, and found it caused fetal malformations, especially in early pregnancy.[4] Sherri Finkbine, a television personality and mother of four in Arizona, had taken thalidomide after her husband brought it from England to ease her morning sickness. Her doctor recommended she terminate the pregnancy, but state officials refused; she traveled to Sweden.[5] Sarah Weddington, the lawyer who argued *Roe*, contended that Finkbine "had a great impact" because she was a middle-class woman who "had other children she loved very much, and she was very articulate about simply not wanting this particular pregnancy." The American public agreed: 52 percent supported her, 32 percent disapproved, and 16 percent had no opinion.[6]

Second, after four years' work at the behest of physicians concerned with ambiguous abortion laws, the American Law Institute (ALI) affirmed abortion when the woman's physical or mental health was endangered; the fetus was physically or mentally defective; or the pregnancy was the result of rape, incest, or other felonious intercourse.[7] The mental health inclusion was important: as medical advances eliminated conditions dangerous to pregnant women, physical health justifications decreased. Psychiatrists increasingly recognized the impact on a woman's mental health if she was forced to carry an unwanted pregnancy to term.[8]

Third, German measles swept the nation from 1962 to 1965, posing a 50 percent chance of fetal deformity to infected women. Many sought abortions. Sympathetic doctors in California ignored the law and performed them. Patricia Maginnis argued that these doctors came under scrutiny because the state was "heavily dominated by Catholic politicians." The inquiry suspended further abortions, but indictments raised a public outcry, and many physicians came to the defense of the accused.[9]

Fourth, the 1967 European introduction of vacuum (or suction) aspiration made abortion more acceptable to many physicians. Earlier, the primary method was dilation and curettage (D & C), a bloody procedure many doctors found troublesome.[10] Vacuum aspiration done in the first trimester was a relatively easy and painless procedure that reduced aversion to abortion among some doctors, just as vasectomy had earlier replaced castration as a more acceptable medical practice.

As abortion demands increased, abortion referral services emerged to help women secure safe, albeit illegal, abortions. The New York Clergy Consultation Service on Abortion (NYCCSA) was established in 1967 under the leadership of the Reverend Howard R. Moody, pastor of the Judson Memorial Baptist Church in Greenwich Village. The church administrator at Judson, Arlene Carmen, became NYCCSA director, motivated by her belief that abortion laws were designed to keep women "in their place. It had nothing to do with our safety or protection at all." As Carmen concluded, the church affiliation of NYCCSA lent a "certain appeal . . . for the public, which I'm sure the authorities shared." Even the Catholic Church made no efforts to "do anything" about the NYCCSA, perhaps because it was not calling for the legalization of abortion. It simply assisted women who "were going to have abortions anyway." The NYCCSA operated from May 1967 to July 1970.[11] Sadja Goldsmith organized a clergy counseling service at the San Francisco Planned Parenthood in 1967, believing that the clergy affiliation gave the service an "umbrella of respectability." Goldsmith encountered resistance from conservative Planned Parenthood board members who argued that involvement with abortion would damage fund-raising for contraception. When she refused to abandon the project, some board members resigned, and some foundations withdrew financial support, but the service continued to operate. In Los Angeles Hugh Anwyl organized a similar group, and in Chicago underground services were available through "Jane," who arranged approximately eleven thousand abortions. The National Clergy Consultation Service, founded in November 1968, operated affiliates in twenty states, involved thousands of ministers, rabbis, and laypersons, and counseled over 300,000 women by 1970. Most National Clergy Consultation Service clients were middle class.[12]

Low-income and indigent women often faced back-alley abortions. Warren M. Hern, physician and staff member of OEO's family-planning program, wrote that these women suffered and sometimes died because they could not afford safe abortions, "obtained with relative ease by the more affluent. . . . A disproportionate number of the women who die are Puerto Rican, black, Mexican American, or members of some disadvantaged group." Magazines such as the *Christian Century, Pageant,* the *Saturday Evening Post, Parents Magazine, Atlantic Monthly, Redbook,* and the *New York Times Magazine* ran articles decrying the bungled criminal abortions to which low-income and indigent women had to resort because safe, antiseptic operations were available only to the affluent.[13]

While referral services and some journalists were concerned with women's health and safety, population controllers and fiscal conservatives pushed for reform to manipulate demographics and to save money. The hazards of back-alley abortions scared many low-income and indigent women into carrying a pregnancy to term, often resulting in additional AFDC expenditures. Women in poverty accounted for 60 percent of white and 80 percent of nonwhite illegitimate births. Demographers asserted that within eight years legal abortions might reduce illegitimacy by 50 percent and eliminate the cost of maintaining defective offspring.[14]

Public opinion also supported reform.[15] Studies in 1965 and 1970 asked six identical questions regarding abortion and found a substantial change (see table 7.1).[16] The percent favoring abortion for couples who could not afford a child more than doubled in every group. The increase was even greater for those in favor of abortion for unmarried mothers and seemed to correspond with mounting illegitimacy rates and AFDC costs. In 1965, for example, AFDC expenditures totaled $1.5 billion; in 1969 they reached $3.3 billion, and 31 percent of all children on AFDC were illegitimate. Critics argued that legalized abortion would give these mostly young mothers an alternative and save taxpayer dollars.[17]

Table 7.1. Percent of Wives Who Approve Different Reasons for Abortion, 1965–1970

Year and reason for abortion	Total	White Non-Catholic	Black	White Catholic	Black
Mother's health endangered					
1965	88.7	88.7	89.3	93.4	76.9
1970	89.8	90.3	86.3	93.0	82.2
Difference	1.1	1.6	-3.0	-0.4	6.3
Pregnancy result of rape					
1965	52.8	54.0	43.3	58.5	43.1
1970	71.0	72.1	64.3	75.3	62.8
Difference	18.2	18.1	21.0	17.8	19.7
Probable deformity of child					
1965	50.9	52.4	37.2	57.5	40.2
1970	69.4	70.6	59.5	74.3	59.2
Difference	18.5	18.2	22.3	16.8	19.0
Mother unmarried					
1965	12.3	12.6	10.4	14.1	9.1
1970	32.1	32.6	27.4	36.1	22.3
Difference	19.8	20.0	17.0	22.0	13.2
Couple cannot afford child					
1965	11.0	11.0	12.7	12.3	7.9
1970	25.3	25.3	29.4	28.4	16.5
Difference	14.3	14.3	16.7	16.1	8.6
Couple do not want child					
1965	7.3	7.3	7.9	8.4	4.7
1970	21.6	21.6	23.9	24.2	14.0
Difference	14.3	14.3	16.0	15.8	9.3

Source: Elise F. Jones and Charles F. Westoff, "Attitudes toward Abortion in the United States in 1970 and the Trend since 1965," in *Demographic and Social Aspects of Population Growth*, ed. Charles F. Westoff and Robert Parke, Jr. (Washington, D.C.: Government Printing Office, 1972), 572.

By the late 1960s cost-cutting arguments, combined with concern for women's health and safety, led various organizations to support reform. The United Presbyterian Church, Unitarian-Universalist Association, ALI, American Civil Liberties Union, American Medical Women's Association, New York Academy of Medicine, local affiliates of PPFA, National Council of Women of the United States, and YWCA called for liberalization. A survey of 2,285 gynecologists in New York found that 87 percent favored a new law.[18] The Citizens' Advisory Council on the Status of Women, established under Kennedy, argued in its 1968 report that the government should be removed from a private decision and called for outright repeal rather than reform because proposals that "permit abortions under certain circumstances while penalizing all others deny the right of a woman to control her own reproductive life in light of her own circumstances, intelligence, and conscience." Yet the report spent more time discussing overpopulation and the environment than women's right to choose.[19]

Feminists attempted to shift the discussion to women's rights. Redstock-ings, founded in 1969, defined abortion as integral to women's autonomy and called for the decision to be in the hands of women, not doctors, lawyers, or courts.[20] The National Organization for Women (NOW) called for "the right of women to control their own reproductive lives" and removal "from the penal code laws limiting access to contraceptive information and de-vices . . . and governing abortion."[21] NOW's attempt to redirect the abortion movement from health, economic, and population concerns to individual freedom was not successful. Lucinda Cisler, national cochair of NOW's task force on abortion, acknowledged that this line of reasoning was the least popular. She criticized "those who caution us to play down the women's-rights argument" because the feminist perspective was a "really disturbing idea." She resented that the growing popularity of abortion reform stemmed not from a women's rights standpoint but from "improved health, lower birth and death rates, freer medical practice, the separation of church and state, happier families, sexual privacy, [and] lower welfare expenditures."[22] Femi-nists gained support when the American College of Obstetricians and Gy-necologists (ACOG) stated that abortion should not be used "as a means of population control." In 1969 the Group for the Advancement of Psychiatry, an organization of 280 psychiatrists with abortion rights activist Lawrence Lader as one of its major representatives, recommended repeal because "a woman should have the right to abort or not, just as she has the right to marry or not."[23]

Such feminist arguments held little sway with legislators. Fiscal conten-tions on decreasing welfare expenditures were much more persuasive to these overwhelmingly white men than any notion of women's reproductive rights. Burgeoning state budgets, not feminist demands, were key to abortion reform.

Reform of State Laws

Some states began to alter laws and looked to legislation in other countries. In 1920 the Soviet Union authorized abortion on request during the first trimester. Japan legalized it for socioeconomic reasons in 1948. Between 1956 and 1958 Czechoslovakia, Hungary, Yugoslavia, Poland, and Bulgaria legalized abortion on request. Population controllers and fiscal conserva-tives pointed to the 30 to 50 percent decline in the illegitimacy rates in these nations.[24] Abortion reform in the United States, they argued, could bring similar results and thereby reduce welfare expenditures.

One of the first states to reform its law was California. Efforts had begun in the early 1960s but failed, according to Maginnis, because of "Catholic Church influence on legislation." In 1962 Maginnis formed the Society for Humane Abortion, a tax-exempt educational body, and the Association for the Repeal of Abortion Laws as a parallel for lobbying and other political activities.[25] The association tried to defeat a reform measure, the Bielenson Bill, but it passed in 1967. It allowed women to petition a committee of three to five physicians for an abortion, but applicants did not have the right to meet with this committee, which could grant abortions for rape or incest or grave impairment to women's physical or mental health. To meet the mental health criterion a woman needed two psychiatrists' letters, a time-consuming and expensive mandate. Moreover, insurance companies often deemed such women suicidal and canceled their policies. Women in teaching or other sensitive occupations found their jobs on the line because these letters entered their permanent medical records as signs of mental instability.[26]

Feminists resented such paternalism. Many male legislators believed women should have no say in "when they should be bred and not bred." The procedure to fulfill the rape or incest condition struck many women as an "absolute, *shocking* insult." Many legislators claimed that "girls" would use the mental health stipulation to "get even with their husbands." There was a "huge distrust of women" and contempt for them among these legislators. They "always" referred to women as "girls," and "*fetuses* were, just as now, incorrectly called babies." Some legislators described women desiring abortions as "sluts . . . irresponsible . . . self-serving . . . and selfish." In the end, male legislators designed the law "to keep women under control" (a statement heard repeatedly at the hearings) and to make a woman "crawl on her belly with an immense lump of cash in her hand."[27]

Illinois activists attempted to avoid the problems associated with the California law by calling for repeal rather than reform. Lonny Myers established the Illinois Citizens for the Medical Control of Abortion (ICMCA) in 1966 as the first state group to call for repeal on grounds that abortion was a private matter between a woman and her doctor. This reasoning attracted conservatives as well as liberals because it placed abortion within the context of individual freedom and responsibility. Myers chose the name to attract physicians, but this tactic failed. She then sought the support of professional men, "the most prestigious people." Although she also attempted to enlist women, "there just weren't that many prestigious women who were willing to come out for abortion in Chicago." Hugh Hefner endorsed ICMCA, and *Playboy* did all its printing. The endorsement of a man and magazine that treated women as sex objects did not fill the credibility gap left by physicians. Between 1967 and 1968 the ICMCA unsuccessfully lobbied the legislature for repeal. While the Committee on Public Welfare supported the measure to reduce expenditures, Governor Otto Kerner vetoed it, fearing strong Catholic opposition.[28]

In other states some reforms were so complex that few women could meet the criteria. North Carolina allowed licensed doctors to perform abortions in hospitals for life and/or health endangerment; deformed fetus; incest; and rape, if reported within seven days. The law also stipulated a four-month residency requirement except in case of emergency and written consent from three doctors not engaged in private practice together.[29] The latter aspect posed an insurmountable financial burden for most women. The restrictive nature of this and other measures led ICMCA to sponsor the First National Conference on Abortion Laws in Chicago in 1968, which led to the formation of the National Abortion Rights Action League (NARAL) in 1969 to pursue legislative repeal and judicial change. By 1970 Alaska, Arkansas, Delaware, Georgia, Hawaii, Kansas, Maryland, New Mexico, New York, Oregon, South Carolina, Virginia, and Washington had altered their statutes. Most laws adhered to ALI restrictions, but legal abortions still increased from 5,000 in 1963 to more than 200,000 in 1970.[30]

The most significant change occurred in New York, where Constance Cook, a Republican representative, led the repeal effort in 1970. She rejected requirements that women go before a doctors' committee and hospital committee and consult with psychiatrists. Cook was "bothered" that "the speeches were so outrageous, and so male-oriented," with men making "the whole decision as to what women's lives shall be." She gained the support of liberals concerned with women's reproductive rights and conservatives who believed repeal would reduce welfare rolls, especially AFDC. To ensure enough votes, Cook compromised, stipulating that abortions be performed by a doctor within the first twenty-four weeks. New York health law already required that doctors carry out the procedure; she backed down "reluctantly" on the time limit but did not believe she "sacrificed the basic principle." Cook refused amendments mandating veto power for the husband and parental consent for minors. Groups working for the bill's passage included the New York branch of NOW, NYCCSA, NARAL (a group Cook considered "radical"), and the Association for the Study of Abortion, a group formed by doctors tired of "playing God" when determining if a woman qualified for a therapeutic abortion. New York's AMA did not endorse repeal because many of its members were Catholic; and, according to Cook, doctors feared that abortions would "hurt the profession economically" by reducing pediatric care. Planned Parenthood affiliates in Syracuse, New York City, and elsewhere endorsed the Cook Bill, but PPFA took no stand because it feared loss of its tax-exempt status if politically involved. This concern did not dissuade the Catholic Church. The bill carried by a single vote, surprising everyone but Cook. First, she had downplayed feminism so as not to alienate male politicians. Second, as Cook recalled, there was "a whole group . . . who thought this would be a good way to cut welfare." Third, as Alan Guttmacher remarked, the law passed due "to mounting concern about U.S. population growth and pollution."[31]

The new law was the most liberal policy passed by 1970. New York left the decision to the patient and her doctor. It required no residency, no parental permission for teenagers, no consultations with other doctors, and no justification of the procedure. In the first six months 69,000 abortions were performed in New York City alone: 45 percent of clients were city residents, 4 percent were from other parts of the state, and 49 percent were out-of-state residents. Within the first year, according to department of health statistics, 181,821 legal abortions occurred in New York City—a figure that surpassed the expectations of reform proponents.[32]

The impact was clear. Birthrates declined, and illegitimate births dropped for the first time since 1954. Teenagers accounted for 13.8 percent of live births but 16 percent of abortions; of these, 33 percent were girls seventeen years old or younger. "All" shelters in New York City that cared for unmarried pregnant girls reported a "sharp decline" in applicants.[33] This abatement suggests that legal abortions did not merely replace underground operations; rather, teenagers terminated pregnancies that would otherwise have resulted in births. As Representative Shirley Chisholm (D-NY) noted, New York policy before 1970, intentionally or not, served "to maximize illegitimacy"; the new law would help alleviate the problem of illegitimate children, who were usually "the most unwanted of the unwanted."[34] It also reduced the fertility rate of indigent women. Women difficult to reach with contraceptives were likely to resort to legal abortion. Between 1 July 1970 and 31 March 1971 ward patients accounted for 46 percent of live births but 55 percent of abortions. In addition to hospital services, Carmen and Moody established the nonprofit Center for Reproductive and Sexual Health in New York City in 1970 to offer low-cost abortion services. The center charged only $25 for an abortion and set aside 25 percent of abortions for indigent women. Fifteen months of legalized abortion brought a 7.5 percent decline in out-of-wedlock births and cut the maternal death rate in New York City by more than half to two deaths for every ten thousand live births, the lowest rate in city history.[35]

Black women comprised a sizable percentage of women seeking abortions. Nonwhites were more likely than whites to abort when the operation was legal. Nonwhite residents of New York City, for example, accounted for 32 percent of live births between 1 July 1970 and 31 March 1971 but 42 percent of abortions (see table 7.2). In a follow-up study black women accounted

Table 7.2. Characteristics of Women Having Abortions, New York City, 1970–1971

Characteristics	Legal abortions per 1,000 live births
Poor	775
Nonwhite	594
First births	590
Age nineteen or less	527
White	422

Source: Jean Pakter and Frieda Nelson, "Abortion in New York City: The First Nine Months," *Family Planning Perspectives* 3 (July 1971): 1–15.

for 47.6 percent of abortions versus 39 percent for white women, although more than twice as many white women lived in New York City.[36]

This high incidence of abortion among black women renewed genocide arguments of militant black males. Carmen confirmed that some white elites donated money "for all the wrong reasons," but this goal did not reflect clinic staff attitudes, and black women realized the difference.[37] Many black women argued that illegal, not legal, abortions were tantamount to genocide. Frances Beal asserted that "rigid laws concerning abortions" were a means of "outright murder," because 80 percent of abortion deaths in New York City during the 1960s were among black and Puerto Rican women. Editor Renee Ferguson of the *Washington Post* contended that the New York law would have a "positive effect on halting the heretofore growing rate of New York hospital emergency cases of black and other minority-group women" who self-induced abortions.[38] Shirley Chisholm worked actively for the repeal of remaining laws for the same reasons. She argued that 49 percent of pregnant black and 65 percent of pregnant Puerto Rican deaths resulted from criminal abortions. She concluded that "to label family planning and legal abortion programs 'genocide' is male rhetoric, for male ears. It falls flat to female listeners and to thoughtful male ones."[39] Genocide arguments did not stem the flow of women seeking abortions.

In fact, abortion on demand gained wide support. The Women's National Abortion Coalition supported abortion as a civil right; 2,500 demonstrators, mostly women, marched in Washington, D.C., to demand repeal of restrictive laws.[40] In June 1970 the AMA House of Delegates voted 103 to 73 to allow doctors to perform abortions for social and economic as well as medical reasons as long as the doctor was licensed, the abortion was performed in an accredited hospital, and two other doctors were consulted. In response, Dr. Gino Papola of Pennsylvania, president of the 6,000-member National Federation of Catholic Physicians Guild, resigned from the AMA and urged the 35,000 Catholic doctors to do the same.[41] Despite Catholic opposition, most doctors favored a liberalized policy. The ACOG called for abortion to be left to the woman and her doctor. In addition, close to two hundred doctors and medical professors wrote a friend of the court brief to the Supreme Court in August 1971 claiming that abortion restrictions were unconstitutionally interfering with their right to practice medicine; these constraints led to "anti-social" results, such as unwanted children and dangerous illegal abortions.[42]

Public opinion also favored reform. In a 1965 poll 91 percent opposed liberalized policies, but a 1971 survey conducted by Nixon's Commission on Population Growth and the American Future found that 50 percent believed the decision should be left to the woman and her doctor, 41 percent claimed abortion should be permissible in certain circumstance, 6 percent stated it was unacceptable under any conditions, and 3 percent had no opinion. A further breakdown found that 33 percent of blacks but 51 percent of whites approved of liberalized policies; 45 percent of women but 53 percent of men approved; 45 percent of those over age thirty but 58 percent of those under age thirty approved; and 39 percent of Catholics, 48 percent of Protestants, and 91 percent of Jews approved of reform. A second question asked if abortion was acceptable for parents who had all the children they desired or could afford: 49 percent approved, 42 percent disapproved, and 9 percent had no opinion. Another survey by the American Council on Education found that 83 percent of first-year college students favored legalized abortion.[43]

In early 1972 three influential groups added their support. First, the ABA's 307-member House of Delegates approved a statute permitting abortions "on demand" during the first twenty weeks. Beyond twenty weeks, the ABA approved if the mother's mental or physical health was threatened, if the fetus was gravely deformed, or if the pregnancy resulted from rape or incest. Only thirty members dissented in this traditionally conservative body. The liberal tone of their statute was startling: of laws in effect at that time, only New York's was more permissive. Perhaps their stand derived less from a liberal belief in women's rights than from a conservative, elite concern with population composition, government expenditures, and government intervention in private and/or medical matters. Second, the UN's population division reported that abortion "may be the single most widely used method of birth control in the world" and that death rates among women undergoing legal abortions were "very low." Third, Nixon's Commission on Population Growth and the American Future, with John D. Rockefeller III as chair, made public conclusions reached after a two-year investigation of population policy: the majority of the commission believed abortion should be left to the woman and her doctor. The commission called for laws "creating a clear and positive framework for the practice of abortion on request," recommended government funding for it among the indigent, and urged health insurance companies to cover its costs. The commission also asserted that contraceptives and sex education should be available to minors and that state laws impeding full access to these services should be reformed.[44]

Abortion and the Federal Government

Despite Nixon's strong support of contraceptives for population control and welfare savings, he refused to endorse abortion. Mindful of Catholic voters, he argued that "nothing should be done on the Federal level"; he preferred abortion laws "be considered by each State, and . . . acted upon by each State depending upon the opinion in that State."[45] Nevertheless, the early 1970s saw numerous bills introduced to Congress. Senator Robert Packwood (R-OR) sponsored S 3501, a bill to liberalize abortions in the District of Columbia, in February 1970 to serve as "an example to the rest of the country as to what the States should pass." Because overpopulation was the "most important problem" facing the nation, he supported a policy to "control, restrain, and plan the population in this country." He also introduced S 3502 to provide tax incentives for family limitation: a tax deduction of $1,000 for the first child, $750 for the second, $500 for the third, and none for subsequent children. Neither proposal received much attention.[46]

The following year, on 31 July 1970, an administrative memorandum allowed physicians at military hospitals to perform abortions at government expense. This policy may have been connected to chemical warfare in the Vietnam War. In 1961 the military launched Operation Hades (later renamed Operation Ranch Hand), poisoning and defoliating Southeast Asia for at least ten years. By 1970 the United States had destroyed more than 5 million acres in South Vietnam by spraying nearly 23 million gallons of defoliants. The United States assured South Vietnam that this spraying was harmless to animals and humans, yet not until 1966 did the National Institutes of Health study the impact on pregnant animals. Results showed that a pregnant Vietnamese woman who drank water from a sprayed area had a 90 percent rate of fetal malformation.[47] In June 1968 South Vietnamese newspapers reported a "remarkable rise" in deformed babies as a result of American defoliation. In December an American C-123 with engine trouble jettisoned a thousand gallons of defoliant on Tanhiep, twenty miles north of Saigon; the village later reported malformed infants.[48] By February 1969 officials knew that Agent Orange (2,4,5-T) caused fetal deformity: it was 100,000 times more potent than thalidomide as a cause of birth defects. Yet no government agency safeguarded American servicemen or Vietnamese civilians. That summer, law students affiliated with consumer advocate Ralph Nader investigating the FDA discovered a report that found that "all dosages, routes, and strains" of Agent Orange resulted in a threefold increase in abnormal fetuses and an almost 80 percent fetal mortality rate. The study was unable to achieve a "no-effect" level—every dosage level produced deformed fetuses.[49]

On 29 October 1969 Dr. Lee Du Bridge, Nixon's science advisor, announced that the government would restrict the use of 2,4,5-T in domestic food crops and military operations. White House officials would give no further information because the government did not want "wild speculation" similar to that over the birth control pill, which had "caused millions of women to get hysterical with worry." The following day, however, the Pentagon announced that military use of 2,4,5-T in Vietnam would continue and refused to acknowledge that it caused fetal deformities. Continued use opened the United States to charges of "callous disregard for innocent human life" and war crimes involving genetic damage to American GIs and Vietnamese civilians. By late 1969 both WHO and the UN General Assembly condemned American use of chemicals in Vietnam. Not until 15 April 1970 did the deputy secretary of defense ban Agent Orange use in Vietnam. By that point the military had sprayed forty million pounds of it there. The offspring of Americans involved in Operation Ranch Hand as well as GIs on the ground displayed birth defects and genetic damage.[50]

Knowledge of fetal abnormalities presumably influenced the decision to allow and subsidize abortions at military hospitals. In San Antonio, Texas, the Wilford Hall Air Force Medical Center performed 135 abortions on service wives within a four-month period.[51] This trend stirred abortion opponents in Congress. In October Representative John G. Schmitz (R-CA), former national director of the John Birch Society, unsuccessfully introduced a bill to reverse the July policy.[52] Some doctors on bases refused to perform the operation. The Pentagon stipulated that in such situations the servicemen's wives could go to a civilian hospital with government funds as long as abortion was legal in that state.[53] This stance outraged Schmitz, who told Congress that the "Federal Government should not be in the forefront of the baby elimination movement." He introduced HR 4257 to require military hospitals to abide by state laws in which they were located, but again Congress took no action.[54]

The controversy spilled into the 1972 presidential race. In March 1971 Senator Edmund Muskie, the leading Democratic candidate and a Catholic, contended that abortion within the first six weeks of pregnancy was acceptable but "beyond that point" posed a moral dilemma because he believed the fetus had "quickened." Despite his support for family planning, he opposed abortion as a remedy to reduce welfare.[55] Paul N. McCloskey, Jr. (R-CA), a Republican challenger, asserted that the "rights of a woman to determine whether she bears a child" deserved a "heavier weight in the scales of justice in 1971 than the rights of the fetus to life."[56] His stand conflicted with the majority of his fellow Republicans, especially Nixon. In April Nixon broke his silence, maintained since his 1968 campaign. He reiterated that the issue was for the states, not the federal government. "Partly for that reason," he stated, "I have directed that the policy on abortions at American military bases in the United States be made to correspond with the laws of the States where those bases are located."[57] With most bases in states where abortion was illegal, Nixon's directive substantially lowered abortion access for military women. Bella Abzug (D-NY) criticized Nixon for invoking states' rights when the armed forces had no choice in their military assignments.[58]

Nixon took this opportunity to present his views. He stated that "from personal and religious beliefs I consider abortion an unacceptable form of population control." Moreover, he claimed that "unrestricted abortion policies, or abortion on demand, I cannot square with my personal belief in the sanctity of human life—including the life of the yet unborn. . . . A good and generous people will not opt, in my view, for this kind of alternative to its social dilemmas. Rather, it will open its hearts and homes to the unwanted children of its own, as it has done for the unwanted millions of other lands."[59] Critics pointed out that Nixon's abortion view conflicted with the doctrine of his family's church, the American Friends Service Committee, which stated that "no woman should be forced to bear an unwanted child" and that "abortion, performed under proper conditions, is preferable to the birth of an unwanted child."[60] His Southeast Asia policies also clashed with Quaker pacifism and the "sanctity of human life." Nixon took no action to aid the ten to fifteen thousand children fathered by American servicemen in South Vietnam: the government had "no authority" over or "responsibility" to children fathered by GIs. Servicemen attempting to bring their offspring into the United States encountered numerous obstacles, not the "open hearts and homes" to which Nixon referred.[61]

Editorials proliferated in reaction to Nixon's speech. Dr. E. James Lieberman of the National Institute of Mental Health questioned Nixon's "selective reverence for life": "By tightening the military hospital abortion policy while softening the Mylai court-martial verdict, the President appears more concerned with the survival of the unwanted fetus than with the murder of those unlucky families who had to face Lieutenant Calley's guns."[62] A letter to the *New York Times* argued that if Nixon would "generalize his deep personal conviction 'on the sanctity of human life' beyond the abortion issue to one of universal life and limb," then he would order a withdrawal from Vietnam and bring the "senseless carnage" to an end.[63] A *New York Times* editorial concurred: "Issues affecting the 'sanctity of human life' are far more involved in the Vietnam war than they are in the removal of legal obstacles to abortion."[64] NARAL claimed that Nixon "seemed more concerned with the survival of the unwanted fetus than with the heartbreaking waste of American and Vietnamese lives in Southeast Asia."[65]

Nixon also drew criticism for interjecting his personal opinion into the public arena. Some accused him of playing politics by endorsing the "Catholic position" when the Supreme Court and state legislators were deciding whether the state had jurisdiction over a pregnant woman's body and her physician's professional judgment.[66] The *New York Times* argued that any federal or state actions to make Nixon's personal views "the basis for public policy would be both cruel and regressive." The editors also critiqued Nixon's claims regarding unwanted children: "Astonishing, indeed, is the President's assertion that America 'will open its hearts and homes' to these unwanted children. He, more than most, has reason to be aware that the nationwide conservative revolt against the cost of welfare is centered on the tens of thousands of children born out of wedlock in welfare homes." They concluded that "to deny mothers in these homes the same freedom of choice as wealthier women . . . is an act of inhumanity and social irresponsibility."[67]

This perceived threat to reform ignited increased activism. Senator Packwood introduced a bill in May 1971 that authorized abortions in the first twenty weeks if performed by licensed physicians and after that time if continuing the pregnancy endangered the woman's health.[68] In July 1971 Abzug introduced a bill to provide consistent quality medical care, including abortion, to all military women regardless of the state in which they resided.[69] The following May Abzug introduced the Abortion Rights Act of 1972. It would "finally and completely affirm the right of every American woman to choose whether or not she will be the mother of a child." Abzug argued that restrictive policies discriminated against the indigent, who "most often" experienced the "problem of unwanted children." These women had "been compelled to bear their unwanted children and to subject them to the deprived environment of poverty."[70] The Women's National Abortion Action Coalition, NOW, and Zero Population Growth promoted this act. Once again, however, the bill received little attention. Dr. George S. Walter, an advocate of Abzug's bill, claimed that resistance to legalized abortion was a holdover of male desire to dominate women: "The pregnant woman symbolized proof of male potency, and if the male loosens his rule over women and grants them the right to dispose of that proof when *they* want to, the men then feel terribly threatened lest the woman can, at will, rob them of their potency and masculinity."[71]

Three days after Abzug introduced her bill, Nixon reiterated his aversion to liberalized policies. Expressing gratitude to his commission for their population study, he repudiated their primary recommendations: "I want to reaffirm and reemphasize that I do not support unrestricted abortion policies" and "unrestricted distribution of family planning services and devices to minors."[72] Rumors circulated that Nixon's concern over the population problem was supplanted by his fanatical drive to win reelection—a goal he believed he could achieve by appealing to southern conservatives and Catholics. White House Chief of Staff H. R. Haldeman recalled Nixon arguing in fall 1971 that "the place for us is not with the Jews and the Negroes, but with the white ethnics and that we have to go after the Catholic thing."[73] Nixon walked a fine line between paying lip service to the population movement backed by business elites, which promoted both contraception and abortion, and opposing abortion and teen access to contraceptive information to woo the Catholic Church.

By 1972 abortion was a political football. The National Women's Political Caucus unsuccessfully tried to place abortion on the Republican platform. Democratic presidential hopeful George McGovern personally opposed abortion, while the caucus wanted an abortion rights plank in the platform. Gloria Steinem offered a modified resolution that prohibited government "interference in the sexual and reproductive freedom of the American citizen." Shirley MacLaine, actress and liaison between McGovern and women's groups, omitted it because she believed it undermined McGovern's chances. Steinem reviled Gary Hart, McGovern's campaign manager: "You promised us you wouldn't take the low road, you bastards."[74] With abortion rejected by both political parties, some feminists feared a repeal of rights already won in some states.

The Supreme Court Legalizes Abortion

On 22 January 1973 the Supreme Court handed down its decision in *Roe v. Wade*, 410 U.S. 113 (1973). Attorney Sarah Weddington had met Jane Roe, an unmarried pregnant high school dropout, through her law school friend Linda Coffey. Roe, who lived in Texas, had challenged her state's law prohibiting abortions. In 1970 the case came before a federal court in Dallas, which declared the abortion statute unconstitutional because it denied women their Ninth Amendment right to decide when and if to procreate. The court failed to interdict the district attorney from indicting physicians, assuming the state would comply with the court's decision. District Attorney Henry Wade, however, announced he would pursue such prosecutions, giving Weddington and Coffey the basis for an appeal to the Supreme Court.[75]

With approximately twenty-five abortion cases pending, the Court chose the Texas and Georgia (*Doe v. Bolton*, 410 U.S. 179 [1973]) cases, planning to dispose of them in one hearing. Weddington argued her case twice, first on 31 December 1971, but the retirements of John Harlan and Hugo Black left the Court "hesitant on such a key kind of case to decide it with only seven judges." She reargued in 1972 after Nixon had appointed Lewis Powell and William Rehnquist, men he believed would reject a liberalized federal abortion policy. Weddington contended that the real justification for the delay was Nixon's reelection concerns: "Burger, being a Nixon appointee, thought that it would be very embarrassing to the President for the Nixon court to come out with a decision in favor of the right to choose during the time he was campaigning." Justice Harry Blackmun's notes confirm a similar suspicion. The Court announced its decision on the first Monday after Nixon was inaugurated to his second term.[76] In *Roe*, Blackmun, also a Nixon appointee, wrote the critical opinion establishing women's right to choose but not mandating access to abortion. *Doe* asserted that the state cannot interfere with the exercise of a woman's right by prohibiting or limiting access to abortion. Following *Roe* and *Doe*, state laws allowed women to procure abortions without third-party interference.

Women's sovereignty over abortion was not absolute. Blackmun placed the power in the first trimester in the "medical judgment of the pregnant woman's attending physician." The Court limited abortion in the second and third trimesters, allowing for state interest in promoting women's health and for "appropriate medical judgment." In sum, abortion was, "primarily, a medical decision."[77] While privacy was important, medical sovereignty was key. Many physicians transformed this sovereignty into profit. Carmen argued that, following *Roe*, "cutthroat competition" emerged among doctors "out to make a buck." They quickly established clinics such as Park Medical Center in New York City, where some doctors made $500,000 a year performing abortions "part-time." Goldsmith claimed that even conservative doctors changed their stance and began to perform abortions because "they realized that abortion was going to become a very lucrative new part of their practice."[78] While women benefited from safe abortions offered by physicians, the Court restricted services to the discretion and availability of doctors.

Roe represented the culmination of efforts by many state legislators and political leaders to curb large families among single mothers on welfare. As historian Rosalind Petchesky concluded, the state "carefully avoided concessions to feminist ideology about reproductive freedom. To accommodate popular pressure without legitimating feminism, . . . state and population planners subsumed abortion politics under the rubric of population control." The push for abortion reform, while a feminist plank, was truly "spearheaded by a coalition of private and family planning organizations, foundations, and corporate interests organized around the population issue."[79] Federal and state governments financed abortions for indigent women through Medicaid and other public health bills, allowing easy access to services for women deemed responsible for increasing welfare expenditures. Regardless of the motivation of population controllers and the limits of the decision, individual women at the local level benefited from safe abortions. Female mortality from abortion decreased with its legalization.[80]

Abortion in Rhode Island

Rhode Island failed to liberalize abortion in the 1960s, despite attempts beginning in 1966. PPRI supported abortion reform but heeded PPFA's recommendation that any endorsement come from staff members as individuals, not as representatives of PPRI.[81] The Rhode Island Medical Society argued, to no avail, that abortion was not a legislative problem but a medical one.[82] Catholic leaders blocked reform and pushed, unsuccessfully, for legislation to eliminate the century-old exemption to save the woman's life.[83]

With only therapeutic abortions available, PPRI counseled and referred women elsewhere. The medical director spent 75 percent of her time in abortion counseling. In 1971 610 women requested abortions. The staff put clients in touch with Clergymen's Advisory Committees in Rhode Island and Massachusetts or referred them to legal New York clinics. PPRI board members traveled to clinics to ensure their safety and were often disappointed by the disparity among them: "Unfortunately there is a good amount of financial exploitation of abortion patients and incredibly high profits being made in some facilities." Technically, PPRI violated state law by participating in referrals.[84] Walking this fine line was dangerous, especially in light of a "worsening climate in Rhode Island" as the Catholic Church did all it could to hold back state reform.[85] The church lost the battle with *Roe* in 1973.

Following *Roe*, the PPRI executive committee felt a "sense of urgency" to establish "a free standing abortion clinic as soon as is feasible." Anne Wise argued that "PPRI owes its existence to the fact that people risked community censure to offer a service in which they believed and for which there was a desperate need. Feeling against birth control in 1931 was stronger and more widespread than is feeling against abortion in 1973. We have the highest law of the land and the majority of American citizens behind us." Even with Supreme Court sanction, PPRI realized that the church's power in the state would make widespread acceptance "highly unlikely." By the summer of 1973 PPRI was conscious of increasing opposition to the Supreme Court's decision and "a growing movement in Congress toward a constitutional amendment to prevent abortions."[86] PPRI continued to help women procure abortions out of state, but this assistance became difficult. Following *Roe*, New York curtailed its abortions for no-fee, low-income women because of the decreased demand as other states offered the procedure. By April 1973 some New York clinics reported a decrease in daily abortions from 130 to 30: "For this reason most clinics can no longer afford to do $25.00 or free abortions." As a result, "Rhode Island's low income women have no access to legal abortion and therefore are the victims of unequal protection of the law."[87]

The summer of 1973 saw plans begin for a clinic. After Lying-In opened a facility in August, Pelham, a New York group, informed PPRI that if it did not open a clinic, Pelham would. The staff believed Pelham was interested only in profits. A freestanding clinic at PPRI would offer lower cost and a more sympathetic atmosphere, and, most important, "it would be far less traumatic for patients that already established a relationship with Planned Parenthood if they were able to remain here after counseling." In September all but one board member voted to incorporate abortion.[88] Yet health department regulations posed a barrier: an anesthesiologist must be present, the operating room must be equipped for abdominal surgery, blood must be stored, and death certificates must be filed. Wise objected to the latter as "an invasion of privacy." These restrictions would "make operating an out-patient clinic impossible." In order to comply, PPRI needed a new building.[89]

During the interim, PPRI noticed a shift in the national discourse regarding abortion. "Population seems to have lost popularity as a topic; abortion is the subject of most concern." Few people continued to tout abortion as a means of population control and welfare savings in the face of antiabortion rhetoric that equated abortion with murder. The explosion from antichoice groups drowned out prochoice advocates. PPFA "warned" PPRI that "antiabortion forces in the country are organizing for a spring offensive . . . and have started a growing movement to appeal [Roe]." PPRI believed the vehemence of the opposition "gave us the opportunity to realize that we cannot remain complacent."[90]

By 1974 a new building had been secured and plans were under way for the clinic. The staff estimated that each year 22 percent of clients (about two thousand women) would seek abortions from PPRI, a number that fell within the PPFA national directive that abortions "not exceed 25% of the total patient load." No explanation was given for this national policy, but perhaps national was concerned that the public would perceive abortion as a regular method of birth control, a belief that could damage financial contributions to the organization. The staff planned to charge $150 and expected that 15 percent would be unable to pay. Even with this "bad debt," they projected the abortion clinic would be "economically advantageous," with an annual profit of $103,212 to defray other health care costs.[91] No one mentioned the irony of PPRI's earlier criticism of Pelham's interest in profits associated with abortion.

In the spring of 1975 the abortion clinic opened. Within two weeks "Right to Life" groups picketed the entrance, and Catholic pressure made finding doctors to staff the clinic difficult. Women and Infants Hospital informed PPRI that no new residents wanted to work at PPRI, and two doctors slated to perform abortions "decided not to do so." National polls demonstrating doctors' approval of abortion did not necessarily translate into their willingness to perform abortions. The shortage of physicians meant the clinic was only able to perform 25 percent of expected abortions. Moreover, increased lab fees, a "jump in professional fees," and other unanticipated costs brought estimated profits down to $28,000.[92] By summer the situation looked "grim indeed." Francine S. Stein, administrator of the PPFA abortion loan and technical assistance program, visited PPRI and "had the unhappy feeling that in a variety of ways, perhaps unconscious or unexamined, the program was not fully accepted by the Affiliate. The staff verbalized dread, fear, even nervous flippancy about abortion." Stein found that some volunteers believed "too much effort was being expended on abortion." She recommended that staff who could not "whole heartedly . . . support the program" be "given a choice of new job assignments . . . or of resignation." Similar problems occurred with college interns. A University of Rhode Island professor wrote the clinic concerning an "older, mature student (Protestant)" seeking a fall internship but only if she could avoid the abortion program. This student "very much wants to work in a family planning agency—*contraception, sex education*, et al.—but . . . has not yet come to terms with her feelings about abortion."[93] Supporting abortion in the abstract was easier than providing abortions to women.

PPRI managed to expand its services while not sacrificing the humane aspect central to its identity. Stein found that the staff spent too "much time with each patient" and that "pre-abortion clinic procedures appeared terribly cumbersome . . . because everything is done individually." She recommended pamphlets to replace one-on-one counseling when possible and organizing groups of four or five women with a counselor for a "brief 20/30 minute group discussion about what will happen." PPRI resented this criticism of "too much TLC" and refused to follow her suggestion that the staff be "Brief, Concise, Write Little, less TLC." Their decision paid off. As one patient told the *Providence Journal*, "This place is right. Women are treated as humans here. They are given support. They are never intimidated."[94]

National Trends in Sterilization

In the face of a well-funded, well-organized, and highly visible antichoice movement, few population controllers continued to tout abortion as a solution to the social and economic "problems of population." Instead, emphasis shifted to more acceptable and permanent means of government-funded fertility control, in particular, sterilization. Many people considered this operation less "offensive" than abortion because it prevented rather than terminated pregnancy. A marked increase in contraceptive sterilization occurred in the late 1960s. By the early 1970s sterilization as a means of voluntary family planning had become popular. Unfortunately, coerced sterilization had increased as well.

A number of reasons explain the popularity of sterilization. First, the ACOG relaxed its guidelines for eligibility in 1970. Earlier, ACOG prerequisites required consultation with two doctors and a psychiatrist. Second, advances in medical technology made the procedure relatively easy and risk-free. Third, for growing numbers of two-income families and female-headed households, sterilization guaranteed against work interruptions due to pregnancy and childrearing. Fourth, Catholics increasingly turned to sterilization because it constituted one "sin" rather than the constant turmoil over contraceptives and church doctrine. Fifth, population controllers touted this option as a more reliable answer to the population explosion and mounting welfare expenditures than contraception and abortion. Individual philanthropists and public officials provided funds to encourage indigent women to undergo sterilization, hoping to end permanently high fertility among them.

Early sterilization bills targeting the indigent occurred in the South. In the early 1960s Virginia twice attempted to reduce welfare costs with compulsory sterilization for women with illegitimate children. Although both attempts failed, the legislature passed a voluntary sterilization law in 1962, the first in the nation to accept economic hardship as a pretext for the operation.[95] A Mississippi bill in 1964 authorized jail terms for unwed mothers with two or more children unless they agreed to sterilization. The dual intent of this proposal was to reduce welfare and run unwed mothers out of the state, which would also save the state money. The uproar from civil rights leaders over this "genocide" legislation led to its defeat.[96]

In California police arrested twenty-one-year-old Nancy Hernandez on a superficial drug charge. Santa Barbara municipal court judge Frank P. Kearney sentenced her either to six months in jail or immediate probation if she agreed to sterilization. With no attorney present, she chose the latter. Later, her public defender labeled this action "unreasonable, capricious, illegal, and unconstitutional." Hernandez revoked her coerced consent and was freed within three hours.[97] Hernandez had two children, one from her estranged husband and one from her current partner, Joseph Sanchez. Kearney told a press conference that she was an "unfit mother . . . in danger of continuing to lead an immoral, dissolute life endangering the health, safety and lives of her children." To charges of racism he answered: "I'm not trying to be a Nazi. It seemed to me that she should not have more children because of her propensity to live an immoral life." Conservative critic William F. Buckley contended that "the original ruling of the judge ought to remain as a permanent exhibit in our judicial chamber of horrors."[98] Sterilization was irrelevant to the crime committed.

Not all sterilization abuse received as much attention as the Hernandez case. Dr. Julius Paul of the Walter Reed Army Institute of Research in Washington, D.C., told a meeting of the Population Association of America in the spring of 1966 of his reservations regarding sterilization of unwed mothers on welfare or sometimes of both parents of illegitimate children. He warned that current emphasis on compulsory sterilization as a means to protect the public from its "unfit" members, a term now used to denote social and economic undesirables rather than mental and physical "defectives," echoed the 1930s eugenic movements. Between 1960 and 1965 seven states—Delaware, Georgia, Illinois, Maryland, Mississippi, North Carolina, and Virginia—considered legislation to sterilize parents of illegitimate offspring. Although none passed, Dr. Paul warned that they indicated that the country had "come full circle" to the punitive attitudes of the early twentieth century, when many states sterilized criminals and other "undesirables."[99] Most of these laws remained in effect: twenty-six states authorized sterilization for the "mentally ill or mentally defective," fifteen did so for epileptics, and twelve for certain criminals.[100] The 1960s campaign differed in that it had racial and economic rather than physical and mental overtones. Part of this change can be explained by the rising level of concern for the mentally and physically handicapped, a movement fueled by family members. They established the National Association for Retarded Children; with chapters in each state by the 1960s, it was an influential pressure group.[101] Protection for this group previously defined as "unfit" did not extend to the socially and economically "unfit" of the 1960s and 1970s. Dr. Paul even warned against voluntary sterilization, because "consent" might be a price paid for something in return, such as release from jail or continued welfare benefits.[102]

Yet voluntary programs did emerge. Fauquier Hospital in Warrenton, Virginia, established a free sterilization clinic for indigent women primarily to reduce the county's tax burden. By September 1962 sixty-three women had been sterilized, 66 percent of them black. This program drew national attention; many considered it the best solution to poverty and its costs to society.[103] The opposition stemmed from concern over coercion. The *New York Times* believed this policy raised profound questions: "The almost feudal disparities between landlord and tenant, millionaire and poor man" in Fauquier could not be solved with "free medical care for the indigent or sterilization." *America* criticized the program as "an adroitly aimed slap in the face of the poor." Its "'voluntary' aspect" was a "mere anodyne. . . . It is no secret that people, perhaps the poor most easily of all, can be cunningly trapped between their own legitimate personal pride and the external forces of social pressure." Once an official suggested sterilization because of a woman's economic status, her freedom to choose became tainted. Not surprisingly, some women had "'voluntarily' knuckled under in the face of such pressure."[104] Church officials again employed a social critique rather than moral condemnation. Archbishop Patrick A. O'Boyle of Washington, D.C., objected to paternalism and racism: those taking part in the program—mainly blacks—were "treated as irresponsible children" who did not possess "enough intelligence to lead a normal existence." In addition, he charged that the "crudely selfish" purpose was "to reduce the tax rate in Fauquier County." Baptist evangelist Billy Graham and *Commonweal* concurred.[105] Some black women also criticized this program. Frances Beal contended that county officials pressured "poor and helpless black mothers and young girls" into undergoing sterilization "in exchange for a continuation of welfare benefits." Although the world denounced Nazi sterilizations, "no one seems to get upset by the repetition of these same racist practices today in the United States of America—land of the free and home of the brave."[106]

Clinic officials, however, hailed sterilization to relieve indigent conditions and to reduce welfare. Other regions followed Fauquier's example. A 1963 North Carolina law permitted a patient to choose sterilization if two physicians agreed it met a family need. In Berea, Kentucky, part of depressed Appalachia, Dr. Louise Gilman Hutchins, long active in providing contraceptives to combat poverty, received $25,000 from Jesse Hartman, a Manhattan investor, to offer sterilization to prevent the chronically unemployed from bearing children they could not afford. With Hartman's money Hutchins sterilized 140 women and 50 men. Once Hartman's funds ran out, the Mountain Maternal Health League maintained this service because Hutchins argued that sterilization reduced welfare payments. Because the state paid a fifty-dollar delivery fee plus hospital expenses for each birth to indigent women, officials claimed this program saved the state thousands of dollars in six months.[107]

The success in reducing welfare led to increased support for sterilization. A national poll in 1966 found that 64 percent approved of sterilization for "women who have more children than they can provide for properly," 24 percent disapproved, and 12 percent had no opinion. Some groups pressured the federal government to fund this service. The Association for Voluntary Sterilization literature stressed government-subsidized sterilization as one answer to the waste of "billions more of our tax dollars . . . on relief" and to the "critical need to control the population explosion."[108] The association joined the American Civil Liberties Union (ACLU) in protesting the ban on using OEO funds to sterilize low-income men and women. Although OEO underwrote contraceptives in 1966, sterilization funding seemed too risky. At the same time, however, federal money poured into the Population Council for projects bureaucrats believed were too controversial for federal involvement, including sterilization.[109]

By 1970 social acceptance of sterilization had grown considerably among physicians, mainstream periodicals, and federal officials.[110] Federal bureaucrats advocated incorporating federally funded sterilization into clinics. Eighty percent of OEO clinics wanted it as an option. Nixon's Commission on Population Growth recommended that "all administrative restrictions on access to voluntary contraceptive sterilization be eliminated so that the decision be made solely by physician and patient." Although Nixon had rejected this commission's recommendation regarding a similar medical context for abortion, he supported its stand on sterilization. Federal funds became available in 1971.[111]

As sterilization became an accepted method of family planning among white middle-class couples, some doctors sterilized women "whose fertility patterns offended their values" or indigent and low-income women, especially ethnic and racial minorities.[112] Many physicians misled women about the dangers or permanence of tubal ligations. Health care officials sometimes coerced women during labor or abortion or convinced them that their welfare services would be rescinded unless they consented. Some women did not even know they had been sterilized.

These acts of coercion were joined by attempts to pass another wave of legislation to reduce welfare. The Senate considered a bill to sterilize any woman on welfare with two illegitimate children. In Oregon legislators discussed sterilizing wards of the state. A Maryland proposal called for the sterilization of mothers of illegitimate children on relief rolls. Georgia welfare director William Benson suggested sterilization to contain welfare expenditures. Louisiana followed the Georgia example. In 1970 William Shockley, cowinner of the Nobel Prize for Physics in 1956, stated that racial quality was declining in part because the average black IQ was lower than that of whites; he endorsed a "Sterilization Bonus Plan" to pay "intellectually inferior" peoples of both races to undergo sterilization.[113] His plan echoed Hitler's.

Classism and racism prevailed in these discussions. Bruce Hilton, director of the National Center for Bio-Ethics, contended that racism as well as paternalism led to coercion in sterilization. He stated that "otherwise decent, God-fearing, church going people still feel that God has given them the black man as a responsibility. And that kind of paternalism says that if this woman isn't smart enough to stop having children, then it is my responsibility to help her." This type of "help" was just an unspeakable wish to control blacks. Susan LaMont of the Women's National Abortion Action Coalition believed the sterilization campaign resulted from hatred of the poor, both black and white.[114] Doctors' attitudes substantiated these arguments. A survey of teaching hospitals in the late 1960s found 53.6 percent made sterilization a condition for obtaining an abortion among indigent women, deeming welfare women incapable of using contraception effectively. In two surveys in the early 1970s 6 percent of doctors said they discussed sterilization with private patients, while 14 percent recommended it as the best choice to indigent women. Moreover, 94 percent of obstetrician-gynecologists approved of compulsory sterilization of welfare mothers with three illegitimate children.[115]

The impact of such attitudes can be seen in sterilization trends. The National Abortion Action Committee found that fourteen states had considered legislation "designed to coerce women receiving welfare to submit to sterilization." In South Carolina Representative Lucius N. Porth proposed in 1971 to force female welfare recipients with two children to choose sterilization or forfeiture of welfare payments because such families were not only a threat to society but an expense the public should not have to bear.[116] Women dependent on public funds were sterilized more than others, and minority women on welfare were sterilized more than whites in the same situation. Sixty percent of black postpartum women in Sunflower County, Mississippi, had been sterilized by 1965 without their knowledge or consent. In North Carolina the proportion of blacks sterilized by the state increased from 23 percent during the Depression to 64 percent by 1966, mainly due to new ADC regulations that included blacks in welfare programs. Once they came under the scrutiny of social workers, their chances of involuntary sterilization increased. Sterilization rates inflated for both races with the number of children born to welfare mothers. While this increment could reflect women achieving their desired family size, more likely they faced pressure from welfare officials to limit their families. Welfare officials targeted women, despite the fact that tubal ligation is more complicated and recuperation more difficult than vasectomy. Popular culture promoted female sterilization under the guise of sexual liberation, but coerced sterilization of welfare mothers had little to do with liberation.[117]

Involuntary sterilization came to a head in the summer of 1973. In June newspapers revealed that federal funds had been used to sterilize black children on welfare. The Montgomery Family Planning Clinic, an OEO-funded facility, had given the Relf sisters Depo Provera, an experimental contraceptive. When the FDA banned its use for birth control, the Relf family caseworker insisted that the girls lacked the "mental talents" to take contraceptive pills. Because "boys were hanging around" the girls, she recommended sterilization. The clinic presented Mrs. Relf with a consent form. Believing the girls were receiving a replacement contraceptive, their illiterate mother placed an X on the signature line. Although one sister refused to undergo the procedure, the clinic sterilized twelve-year-old Minnie Relf. A Senate investigation found that the Relf family had not asked for family-planning assistance. Instead, welfare officials had sought out the girls. Newspapers revealed that eleven other girls might have been involuntarily sterilized at the same clinic.[118]

While population controllers looked favorably on these actions, the black press was outraged. The *Chicago Daily Defender* called the Relf case "a blatant infringement on human rights" as well as "a clear and revolting instance of Southern race prejudice intruding itself into the private lives of illiterate blacks bereft of either power or influence." The *Black Panther*, the party newspaper, argued that it demonstrated the true intention of the Montgomery family-planning clinic—the premeditated murder of a race. *Muhammad Speaks* considered the incident "a deliberate act of genocidal sterilization" and declared that the "demonic advocates of 'population controls' had escalated their war against the nonwhite people" with two new lethal weapons, abortion and sterilization. The *New York Daily Challenger* believed the situation demonstrated "the low esteem in which Black life is held and the genocidal nature of programs supposedly designed to help Blacks." The *Pittsburgh Courier*, the paper that had earlier supported black women's access to OEO-funded contraceptives, asserted that the Relf incident was "another case of a white director of a white-run institution deciding what is 'best' for blacks in the long run." Columnist Vernon E. Jordon wrote in the *Afro-American* that the Relf case was "an act that makes the blood run cold in its callous disregard for the most fundamental rights of the individual."[119]

One month after the Relf story broke, Nial Ruth Cox, an unwed black mother, charged that she had been coerced to undergo sterilization in New Bern, North Carolina, at age eighteen. State law allowed the parent of a "mental defective" under the age of twenty-one to sign consent forms for this procedure. State officials deemed Cox a "mental defective" because she had given birth to a daughter at age seventeen, just as Carrie Buck's mother had been labeled in the early twentieth century. Similar to the 1930s, some bureaucrats used the ruse of teenage sexuality, especially that resulting in illegitimate births, to be sufficient evidence of mental instability to warrant sterilization. Cox's mother, a widow with nine children, signed the consent forms after the caseworker informed her that if she refused, her family might stop receiving welfare checks. No one explained that the procedure was permanent. As Nial Cox told a reporter, "Nobody explained anything. They treated us as though we were animals."[120]

That same summer Mrs. Carol Brown, a welfare mother pregnant with her fifth child, visited three doctors in her hometown of Aiken, South Carolina, to find one who would deliver her baby. All three refused unless she consented to sterilization. In the same town another doctor, Clovis H. Pierce, refused to deliver the third child of welfare mothers unless they first agreed to sterilization. In a six-month period in 1973 Pierce performed twenty-eight sterilizations: eighteen were welfare mothers, of whom seventeen were black. Yet his nurse claimed, "This is not a civil rights thing, or a racial thing, it is just welfare."[121]

Events in Aiken became controversial. Black newspapers criticized the violation of black women. The *Black Panther* believed the Aiken incidents were part of a "racist, genocidal extermination directed at poor Black girls and women." The *Afro-American* contended that Pierce's ultimatum sounded similar to "some sinister un-American horror story unraveling." Yet many whites in Aiken supported coerced sterilization of welfare mothers. The executive director of the Chamber of Commerce, Bryan McCanless, argued that both black and white "trash . . . should be sterilized." Others circulated petitions that justified compulsion when welfare mothers did not voluntarily use subsidized contraceptive devices. Other petitions rationalized coercion because taxpayers maintained the right to dictate the medical treatment of welfare recipients. Doctors in Aiken claimed they did what was "best for society."[122] As elite white men, they believed they should control the reproductive choices of indigent women.

Other groups reacted strongly to coercion. Black congresswomen Shirley Chisholm, Barbara Jordon, Yvonne Burke, and Cardiss Collins wrote letters of outrage to DHEW secretary Caspar Weinberger warning him that sterilization abuse "raised doubts in the minds of minority citizens concerning the voluntary nature of federally funded family planning programs." NAACP and Urban League officials also made heated speeches. Fourteen national groups condemned further use of public funds until Congress drafted "comprehensive statutory prohibitions" for this procedure.[123] Some feminists condemned coerced sterilization. Gloria Steinem told *Ebony* that sterilization "affects all of us but . . . especially minority women. The government thinks it not only has the right to tap our phones but to interfere in all areas of our personal lives, including governing our very bodies." Some women organized groups against abuse, such as the West Coast Committee Against Forced Sterilization and New York's Committee to End Sterilization Abuse.[124] The feminist critique, however, was muted and slow in coming, perhaps because population control groups that supported sterilization among the indigent had been strong allies of the prochoice movement. Moreover, the issue of coerced sterilization did not affect the feminist movement, which was dominated by white middle-class women. In fact, they were the very group population controllers encouraged to procreate.

Most of the immediate reaction came from legal and government sources. The ACLU brought additional abuse cases to public attention. Eleven Chicanas filed suit against the Los Angeles County Medical Center, charging they were either coerced or deceived into signing consent forms during labor or under the influence of medication. One mother had anesthesia withheld until she agreed to sign. Others had not signed any form at all. Few of these eleven spoke more than minimal English, and all were indigent; four were unaware the procedure had been performed until they asked for contraceptives; one woman only found out four years later during a routine medical exam. The Chicana case was particularly traumatic not only because doctors decided who should not reproduce but because traditional Mexican American society often judged women on their ability to bear children. Judge Jesse W. Curtis was unsympathetic: he decided against them in *Madrigal v. Quilligan* No. 75-2057, Ninth Circuit U.S. District Court, 1978, because he believed the situation was "essentially the result of a breakdown in communication between the patients and the doctors."[125] The white male establishment united against abused women of color.

Following this case, the Health Research Group investigated surgical sterilization in 1973 and concluded that consent forms were a "farce" because hospital staffs pressured women to consent while in labor. This study also found that coercion of indigent white and black women was widespread, especially in the South. Research by Barbara Caress at the Health Policy Advisory Center concurred. "Sterilization abuse is not the exception but the rule," she wrote. "It is systematic and widespread. . . . Such abuse is the most widespread example of medicine as an instrument of social control."[126] The lack of strict federal regulations facilitated the injustices many indigent women faced.

Native American and Puerto Rican women were especially victimized. The Indian Health Service (IHS), part of the federal government, sterilized so many women that, according to one observer, it could have eliminated all pure-blood tribes within fifteen years. Every full-blooded Oklahoman Kaw woman had been sterilized. Between 1973 and 1976 the IHS sterilized 3,406 Native women. By the end of the decade nearly 25 percent of women of childbearing age had undergone tubal ligations. Officials did not inform them about the irreversibility of the operation. Investigations concluded that the cause of abuse was the cultural insensitivity of doctors: they pushed a middle-class family norm of two children and believed single, indigent women should not procreate. Similar to the Chicanas, many Native American women were ashamed that they could no longer have children. This loss undermined their sense of tribal identity.[127] In Puerto Rico more than one in three women in their childbearing years were sterilized, yet legal abortions were essentially unavailable.[128]

Although funding for abortions had decreased substantially since *Roe* and private insurance companies generally refused to cover contraceptives, both public and private funds for sterilization remained intact. A survey of thirty-seven private insurance companies found that one paid for the pill and two paid for IUDs, but thirty-four covered female sterilization, while twenty-seven covered vasectomies. Sterilization was much more cost-effective and efficient than contraception.[129] Moreover, it provided a permanent solution to population concerns.

Outcry over abuses led to government investigations. A 1973 survey of federally funded programs revealed that two-thirds of clients were white and one-third black, yet blacks constituted 43 percent of those sterilized. A DHEW report concluded that from the summer of 1972 to the summer of 1973, 25,000 adults were sterilized in federally funded clinics. Of these, 153 females were under eighteen. Another report found that of 1,620 sterilizations in North Carolina between 1960 and 1968, 63 percent were performed on blacks, 55.9 percent of whom were teens. In Alabama more than 50 percent of involuntary sterilizations authorized by the state health department in 1973 were performed on black women.[130] White middle-class health officials used their power to shape the population along lines they deemed acceptable.

A small part of the blame for these abuses rested with the federal bureaucracy. Officials drafted guidelines in 1972 for federally funded sterilizations. Although OEO had 25,000 copies ready for distribution, the White House "suppressed" them: 1972 was an election year, and Nixon did not want his administration openly linked with sterilization for fear of losing Catholic votes. The guidelines sat on the shelf, while the federal government financed sterilization without safeguards until 1974. By that point the most blatant abuses had occurred.[131] Whether guidelines would have prevented abuse is debatable: officials could have ignored them the way doctors ignored the Nuremberg Code in medical experiments. These abuses violated women's constitutional rights. They were not allowed to choose a method of family planning; others chose for them. Because officials did not apply the same coercion to self-supporting women, Relf, Cox, and others in the same situation were denied equal protection under the law.

What action did these women take? Cox sued North Carolina for $1 million. The Relf family retained prominent attorney Melvin Belli to sue clinic officials and federal health officials for $5 million. The civil suit against then-DHEW secretary Casper Weinberger alleged that the "intrusion into the plaintiffs' bodies and personal lives" was an infringement of their basic constitutional rights. When investigators discovered the White House connection, Belli amended the suit to include former White House aides John W. Dean III and John D. Ehrlichman.[132] The National Welfare Rights Organization also brought suit against Weinberger for failing to establish clear-cut guidelines within DHEW for federally funded sterilizations.[133]

In March 1974 Judge Gerhard Gesell of the United States District Court for the District of Columbia handed down *Relf et al. v. Weinberger et al.* He stated:

> Over the last few years, an estimated 100,000 to 150,000 low-income persons have been sterilized annually under federally funded programs.... Although Congress has been insistent that all family planning programs function on a purely voluntary basis, there is uncontroverted evidence in the record that . . . an indefinite number of poor people have been improperly coerced into accepting a sterilization operation under the threat that various federally supported welfare benefits would be withdrawn unless they submitted to irreversible sterilization.

Gesell observed that the "dividing line between family planning and eugenics is murky" and ruled that the lack of guidelines to protect patients was "both illegal and arbitrary because they authorize involuntary sterilizations, without statutory or constitutional justification." Federally funded sterilizations were permissible only with the "voluntary, knowing and uncoerced consent of individuals competent to give such consent." What had occurred in Alabama, according to Belli, was "the kind of thing Hitler did." Not only racism but paternalism played a role, according to Howard Phillips, ex-director of OEO: "This is a classic example of the mentality that 'the social worker knows what's best.'"[134] Although Phillips excluded doctors from his condemnation, they too believed they were in a position to make such life-altering decisions.

On 6 February 1974 DHEW issued guidelines for federally funded sterilizations. They imposed a moratorium on sterilizing patients under the age of twenty-one, prohibited obtaining consent during labor, mandated a waiting period, and ordered women be informed that no benefits would be lost if they refused sterilization. DHEW also required a review committee of five to approve the operation and insisted upon a court ruling that sterilization was "in the best interest of the patient." Moreover, DHEW decertified Dr. Pierce of Aiken and barred him from providing obstetric services for Medicaid money. His private practice, however, continued to flourish.[135] These guidelines drew criticism. Some groups wanted all federal funding of sterilization eliminated.

Others believed the guidelines did not protect individuals against coercion because the government provided no enforcement mechanism. As Richard Babcock, Jr., of the Center for Law and Social Policy in Washington, D.C., stated, "The H.E.W. regulations are . . . wholly inadequate. . . . As the incidents which were exposed last summer illustrate, welfare recipients in this country can be threatened, lied to, or misinformed until they consent to be sterilized. The H.E.W. regulations . . . in fact do nothing to prevent such coercive tactics." The guaranteed voluntary nature of all family-planning services before *Relf* did not prevent the abuses reported in the summer of 1973. Without adequate police power, the new stipulation for a signed consent would do little to stop further abuse. "Obviously, agreeing to something with a gun at your head is not really agreeing at all," argued Babcock. Similarly, accepting an offer "you cannot refuse" would be equally involuntary. These objections, however, brought no change in DHEW guidelines.[136]

Studies confirmed the persistence of abuse. One investigation discovered that 76 percent of hospitals did not comply with DHEW guidelines, while another claimed 94 percent were noncompliant. One-third did not even know guidelines existed. A follow-up study in 1979 discovered that 70 percent of hospitals involved with Medicaid sterilizations continued to breach the 1974 regulations.[137] Part of this noncompliance was a result of doctors' attitudes. Dr. Hutchins agreed that sterilization should be voluntary but believed DHEW guidelines were too rigid as a result of government overreaction to the uproar surrounding *Relf*. Doctors should be given latitude in deciding who should be sterilized.[138] Doctors in the Northeast agreed. Boston City Hospital as well as hospitals in New York City performed unnecessary hysterectomies on black women, ostensibly to train interns in the procedure.[139] The fact that white doctors targeted black women implies that physicians believed that they, not women, had the right to decide who procreates.

Despite the sterilization controversy, Congress amended section 19 of the Social Security Act in 1975 to allow federal funds to pay 90 percent of its cost for indigent patients. Concurrently, federal funds covered only 50 percent of abortions. These revisions enticed health care officials to promote sterilization.[140] Not only did these financial inducements decrease return patients at clinics, but federal coverage could be viewed as a blanket endorsement of sterilization. The Committee for Abortion Rights and Against Sterilization Abuse, founded in 1976, argued that population controllers purposefully funded sterilization but not abortion to force indigent women, many of whom were also women of color, to end their fertility permanently.[141]

In September 1977 the National Conference on Sterilization Abuse brought delegates from fifty organizations to Washington, D.C., including feminists, health reformers, family planners, minority women, Native Americans, and church social action groups. They conferred with DHEW representatives and demanded stricter regulations. In response DHEW issued a new policy in 1978 that required a translator where needed, prohibited gaining consent during any other medical procedure (abortion or birth), limited sterilization to those twenty-one or older, and extended the waiting period from three to thirty days. Many feminists saw the latter as paternalistic: women did not need thirty days to make up their minds.[142] While a woman seeking sterilization might not need this time, indigent women facing pressure from officials could use it to investigate their rights. With new guidelines in place, most abuse watchdog organizations disbanded.

The unethical use of sterilization as a form of population control led many indigent groups, particularly ethnic and racial minorities, to mistrust family-planning services. A survey of 1,890 blacks in one northern and one southern city found that 47 percent rejected sterilization as a means of birth control. Yet Dr. Emily Hartshorne Mudd of Pennsylvania found that a surprising number of black women chose sterilization following the completion of their last wanted pregnancy. Because of the genocide issue, Mudd required that a married woman obtain the consent of her husband. Although men were leery of sterilization for themselves, they agreed to it for their wives, especially if their economic situation was desperate. Most blacks preferred less permanent birth control. Ninety percent of those polled agreed that contraception should be taught in junior and senior high schools, and 87 percent approved publicly financed contraceptive clinics.[143]

Sterilization in Rhode Island

While sterilization abuse was common in many areas, PPRI remained unscathed: no accusations of genocide or coercion occurred. The staff differed from welfare officials in recommending sterilization for men, not for women. As a private nonprofit organization, it had no budgetary connections to the concern over welfare costs. With no laws regulating sterilization in Rhode Island, the decision was left to doctors. Most physicians refused to sterilize single men or first-time fathers upset by the disruption of a new baby, and most required a consent form signed by both husband and wife. The late 1960s saw a growing grassroots demand from men for easier access to vasectomies.[144]

PPRI responded with the first vasectomy clinic in New England on 30 September 1970. From the start it had a "long waiting list." Married men met with the medical director; the clinic encouraged but did not mandate wives' attendance. To ease male embarrassment the clinic hired a male aide. PPRI continued to serve as a training center, allowing male student nurses to attend each vasectomy clinic. By November PPRI had received over 175 applications, and 122 men were waiting for appointments. PPRI experienced problems staffing the clinic because of "an acute shortage of urologists." While demands for tubal ligations also increased, PPRI emphasized the relative ease of vasectomy.[145] The emphasis on male versus female procedures was due to concern for women's health, but economics may have played a role as well. PPRI could not perform tubal ligations but could perform vasectomies.

For the remainder of the decade the number of vasectomies mounted. In early 1971 "the demand for vasectomies far surpass[ed] our ability to perform them." More than 150 men were on a waiting list, leading the Lying-In to open a vasectomy clinic in August 1971; it was immediately booked, with "a long waiting list." PPRI hired five urologists to cut the wait time.[146] The clinic allowed low-income men the same reproductive control as middle- and upper-class men who could afford private physicians.

Dr. Rudy K. Meiselman, a Providence urologist, cited two factors for the grassroots demand. First, both men and women "routinely discussed" all available methods of contraception. Second, the widespread use of the pill "promoted the notion of spontaneity in sexual relationships." Whenever negative publicity surfaced concerning side effects from the pill, Meiselman and PPRI experienced an increased demand for vasectomies. Dr. Nathan Chaset, chief of urology at Lying-In, concurred but added that "Women's Liberation [brought] pressure for a reassigning of responsibilities." Chaset argued that researchers should develop male methods: "There ought to be some way of getting to the male. The average woman is ready to quit (having children) at 30, and to put her through all that (the pill, etc) for another 20 years doesn't make sense."[147]

Yet Wise found targeting men was not always successful because of remaining "hangups." Wives would come to PPRI and "get all the information for their husbands," but then men failed to follow through on the procedure. Dr. Charles Potter of PPRI found male reluctance rooted in "fears" of "reduction in his (sexual) drive." Dr. Meiselman concurred, contending that it perhaps explained the residual social stigma attached to the procedure. He had some patients who "preferred to pay out of their pocket (rather than put in for Blue Shield) because they don't want people around their office to know. There's still a cloud over it."[148]

Those men who did undergo vasectomies were satisfied. One man's account was revealing: "In less time than it took my wife to have a cup of coffee with a friend . . . I was sterile. . . . It would be nice to say that the Zero Population Growth movement had gotten to me, that I had undergone a vasectomy from a sense of social and ecological responsibility. But the truth is, the choice was purely selfish. We had just had our fourth child." Ten weeks after the operation "arguments and discussions over the Pill, the Loop, the Foam, and other contraceptive methods would seem as remote from my new lifestyle as the horse and buggy."[149]

Conclusion

How successful were family-planning programs during the 1960s and 1970s? The 1970 census suggests that during the late 1960s the birthrate in families with less than $5,000 annual income declined sharply. The number of births fell almost twice as far in indigent as it did in wealthy families: births to indigent women dropped thirty-two per thousand, while the rest of the population dropped seventeen per thousand. The largest decrease occurred among black women—a decline of forty-nine per thousand. *Newsweek* claimed that the "chief cause" for this reduction was "the increase in government sponsored birth control clinics." Another study found that subsidized family-planning services lowered the pregnancy rate among teenagers and that access to abortion substantially reduced the incidence of illegitimate childbirth.[150]

In order to lower illegitimacy, break the cycle of poverty, and reduce welfare expenditures, the government subsidized services, including contraceptives, abortion for a short time, and sterilization. Government action in this area had little to do with women's right to control their bodies but rather with concerns over mounting welfare expenditures and perceived uncontrolled fertility among the indigent, especially ethnic and racial minorities. To resolve these "problems" the federal government increased financial support for family planning by 1,300 percent between 1967 and 1973. This involvement coincided with the welfare explosion of the late 1960s and the escalating costs to society of programs for the indigent. Through subsidized contraception white elites in powerful positions attempted to shape the racial and socioeconomic quality of the population along lines suitable to them. While many women faced coercive tactics, others were able to take advantage of new subsidized services to govern their life choices. At PPRI these choices included a full range of contraceptives, abortion, and vasectomy.

8

Backlash, 1973–2000

Government subsidies and population control advocacy of contraception and sterilization continued through the end of the twentieth century. By 2000 female sterilization was the most common contraceptive, especially among women of color and lower economic means. The use of public funds for abortion, on the other hand, came under increasing attack. The battleground shifted from efforts to legalize abortion to organized and sometimes violent attempts to recriminalize or restrict access to it. The modern antichoice campaign resembles nineteenth-century efforts to undermine women's demands for equal rights by forcing them to revert to the traditional role of mother. While both campaigns portrayed aborting women as selfish and unnatural, few in the nineteenth century debated the legal status or personhood of the fetus. The post-*Roe* opposition, on the other hand, prioritized the legal and constitutional protection of the fetus over the mother. The vocal antiabortion camp led population controllers to emphasize instead sterilization and long-acting contraceptives, especially Depo Provera (DP) and Norplant, as the answer to perceived population problems. As abortion became too politically charged to promote as a cost-saving method for governments, state and federal funding dried up. Funds for sterilization and long-acting contraceptives, on the other hand, remained intact. These methods better suit the population control agenda as they are permanent, or semipermanent, and thus avoid any accidental pregnancies that indigent women could not afford to abort.

Contraceptive and Abortifacient Developments

Population controllers latched on to new contraceptive technologies, especially DP and Norplant, to prevent socially and economically "unsuitable" women from conceiving, while avoiding the abortion issue. Abortion restrictions disproportionately affected indigent or low-income women, often minorities and teenagers, the very groups white conservative elites targeted for decreased fertility. They hoped to correct the consequences of abortion limitations through the dispersal of new, long-lasting contraceptives.

DP, manufactured by Upjohn Company, is an injectable contraceptive, effective for three months and cheaper than the pill. Most clinical trials were conducted on women of color, especially in Kenya, Mexico, and Thailand. In 1967 Upjohn applied to the FDA, but not until 1972 did DP gain approval, and then only for inoperable cancer treatments because of its possible carcinogenic qualities. The following year Congress received assurances from Upjohn that the company would not distribute DP for unapproved purposes. Upjohn reapplied in 1978 for contraceptive use, but the FDA refused. Nevertheless, Upjohn marketed DP as a contraceptive in developing nations and demanded a hearing before a public board of inquiry consisting of non-FDA members. The Center for Drugs and Biologics informed the board that "never has a drug whose target population is entirely healthy people been shown to be so pervasively carcinogenic in animals as Depo Provera has been." DP failed tests in three species: dog, monkey, and mouse. The 1984 board report concluded that DP was unsafe and could not be approved for marketing. One board member dissented but urged approval for only two groups of women, the mentally retarded and drug abusers. In 1986 Upjohn withdrew its application from the FDA.[1]

Studies discovered other side effects. Permanent sterility was possible; even supporters of the drug urged that it not be used on women who had not completed their families. DP could also cause irregular bleeding, cessation of periods, miscarriages, stillbirths, birth defects, or damage to a nursing infant, and it could cause or aggravate heart disease, stroke, or lung complications. It could also lead to severe depression and sometimes suicide, but doctors dismissed this side effect as "trivial," as they did with the pill in the early 1960s. Dr. Gary Richwald of the UCLA School of Public Health found that serious depression, not mood swings, occurred among 15 to 40 percent of users. Other reports indicated that DP's effect on the immune system was unclear, possibly leaving women more susceptible to tuberculosis, AIDS, and other diseases.[2]

Despite these problems and the FDA ban, congressional investigations in 1987 uncovered misuse of DP among indigent and low-income, often minority, women. Upjohn failed to keep its promise to Congress and shipped DP to family-planning clinics, county health departments, student health centers, private physicians, and the IHS. The IHS ignored FDA safety determinations and prescribed DP to Native American women, the majority of whom were mentally retarded. The IHS justified its actions by arguing that such women could not be relied upon to take other contraceptives, yet it gave the shot to healthy Natives as well, almost all of them on welfare. The IHS had no written informed consent, and it failed to mention that the FDA had not approved DP. It prescribed a potentially carcinogenic drug with other serious side effects to physically healthy women without guaranteeing they were aware of the possible consequences.[3]

Congress also discovered that doctors gave the shot to women who "would not" take other contraceptives. ACOG's policy "strongly recommends that Depo Provera be used as a contraceptive in those women who are unable or unwilling to use other contraceptive methods"; WHO, International Planned Parenthood Federation, the American Academy of Pediatrics, and the AMA agreed with ACOG's position. The literature on DP listed groups of women for whom DP was recommended: women who would not use another method; had refused sterilization; were "unmotivated," "unreliable or irresponsible," "less competent or incompetent," "illiterate," "retarded," or "of low intelligence"; were "problem women" or had "problem families"; were psychiatric patients; were "promiscuous," especially if young; or could not understand English. The list ended by hailing DP as a significant aid in population control. The National Women's Health Network testified regarding the registry it kept of DP users from 1979 to 1987. Ninety percent received no information regarding the drug's unapproved status, and none were told that it was the only contraceptive method linked to cancers in all animals tested.[4]

Karen Branan, a white middle-class woman, confirmed DP abuse. She telephoned six clinics that catered primarily to indigent women of color to ask for DP. Each told her to come in for the shot. When she asked if problems existed with it, they assured her no; none told her that the FDA had not approved DP. Branan then called six private doctors' offices catering primarily to white middle- and upper-class women; they expressed shock that she had heard of DP and strongly recommended against taking it. One doctor informed her that DP was for retarded women and women who could not care for themselves. All six revealed that the FDA had not approved it.[5] Branan went on to produce a documentary entitled *The Ultimate Test Animal*. She sent one black and one Native American woman into clinics serving welfare clients where they asked for birth control, not DP. In every case the staff recommended DP. One woman told clinic officials she had diabetes, a contraindication for DP, but the doctor offered her the drug anyway. Some clinics provided DP free of charge, but no other contraceptive method was gratuitous. Black and Native American women told Branan that DP was the only method to which the doctor introduced them. Branan blamed the "paternalism and racism of the doctors who, almost without exception . . . were enthusiastic about it, spoke of women's ignorance and inability to be responsible for their own contraception." Health officials targeted indigent, low-income, and minority women with an unapproved and potentially dangerous drug for purposes of population control. PPFA favored DP and urged removal of the FDA ban.[6] The FDA approved it in the summer of 1992.

Since FDA approval DP has continued to be controversial. Side effects persist. Upjohn's studies found that 60 percent of the women using it experienced weight gain of up to fifteen pounds. Questions regarding its possible link to breast, liver, and cervical cancers remain unanswered, although some research indicates that this link may not be as strong as previously thought. The shot's duration means side effects are prolonged: the average woman needs six to eight months to expunge the drug from her system; for some, the effects last eighteen months or longer, even after a single shot. Women therefore experience a longer delay before conception than those who discontinue use of pills, IUDs, or barrier methods. This delay limits their control over reproduction and makes DP all the more attractive to population controllers and medical professionals. Moreover, DP could be used for the "chemical castration" sentences that some judges have considered for clients they deem unworthy of motherhood.

Similar controversy emerged over Norplant, a contraceptive surgically inserted in the arm that lasts at least five years and as long as eight. Many considered Norplant—developed by the Population Council and approved by the FDA in 1990—to be the best contraceptive innovation since the pill. Norplant offered indigent and low-income women, who have more unplanned pregnancies, a very reliable, nonpermanent option to meet their intended childbearing goals. Testing began in 1968 and, similar to the pill and DP, was conducted primarily on women of color in underdeveloped nations. More than one million Indonesian women who have used it since the early 1980s have indicated that they received incomplete information and that health officials pushed this option over others and deterred women from early extraction. Population control policies and medical research results, not women's health and choice, directed Norplant's availability.[7]

Numerous side effects plagued Norplant users. Irregular bleeding, prolonged periods, headaches, acne, weight gain, dermatitis, nausea, nervousness or mood swings, mastalgia, changes in appetite, ovarian enlargement, and infection at the site of implantation were common. Problems also existed with removal, including difficulty locating and extracting the device, which sometimes required surgery under general anesthesia and resulted in scarring and long-term pain. Most primary care physicians were not trained in removal, forcing women to seek specialists available at Planned Parenthood or large teaching hospitals.[8] Other problems existed. Norplant's high cost—$350 for the device and $150 each to embed and extract it—made officials reluctant to comply with requests for early removal. Medicaid defrayed the cost in all fifty states, but because payment for other contraceptives varied, this universal coverage exerted economic pressure on the indigent to choose Norplant. Norplant, similar to DP, made women dependent on medical expertise for insertion, but it also required them to seek medical attention for its removal. Both Norplant and DP led to a decreased use of condoms, which may have increased AIDS among users.[9]

As with DP, health officials targeted minority, low-income, and indigent women for Norplant. In June 1991 IHS began offering it to clients. The Native American Women's Health Education Resource Center (NAWHERC) investigated IHS use in South Dakota and published its findings in 1992. Norplant was a poor choice for average Native Americans on reservations because they had the highest rates of diabetes and gall bladder disease—two contraindications for Norplant use. Other contraindications included hypertension, cancer, smoking, and cirrhosis. Yet IHS continued to encourage its use in medically at-risk women. Two women with family histories of breast cancer on South Dakota's Rosebud Reservation were given Norplant; no one informed either of them of the association between Norplant and breast cancer. A heavy smoker with high blood pressure also was not warned of the risks. NAWHERC found that IHS had no protocol for informed consent and no guidelines about removal. IHS clinicians sometimes ignored demands to remove the device if women had not kept it in long enough to offset the cost of implantation. By 1992 dozens of Native American women reported that their requests for removal were discouraged or refused by physicians.[10]

The National Black Women's Health Project (NBWHP) initially hailed Norplant but grew concerned with health conditions affecting black women. Similar to NAWHERC, NBWHP concluded that many women of color lacked the necessary health care to evaluate whether Norplant was safe for them. NBWHP questioned the punitive and racially motivated use of Norplant: "Because it's the closest thing to sterilization, folks have seized on this and tried to impose it on the women who have the least power in our society. . . . They see it as social control for those women who they believe are responsible for all of our social issues." One means of imposition was incentive programs: while incentives were not a "bad thing," the distinction between inducement and compulsion in state packages was obscure because officials only offered them to certain women—indigent, usually single mothers on relief who were often women of color.[11] These women were the very group population controllers did not trust to reproduce in socially desirable ways.

Baltimore was a case in point. With one of the nation's highest adolescent birthrates, 10 percent of all fifteen- to seventeen-year-olds gave birth at a government cost of $222 million in 1990. In 1991 23 percent of all city births were to teens. Critics hailed Norplant as one solution. Health department family-planning clinics made Norplant available to adolescents in the summer of 1992, but officials believed the best distribution method would be in already existing school-based health centers in six high schools. The city instituted a pilot program for the 1992–93 school year in Paquin School, a combined middle and high school for parenting and pregnant teens chosen because teens who gave birth were at a higher risk of pregnancy than others. Opposition had emerged by January 1993 among a small but vocal group. They argued that the city used Norplant to target inner-city black teenagers, which was tantamount to genocide: Paquin was 90 percent black. They also contended that Norplant had not been sufficiently tested on black teens and had dangerous side effects. Its users were less likely to use condoms and thus placed themselves at a higher risk of STDs and AIDS. A city council hearing in February 1993 responded to charges of genocide, arguing that all contraceptives were available in school-based programs. The majority at the hearing supported the program as long as it was not coercive. Baltimore continued to make Norplant available at Paquin and three other high schools with plans to expand to the remaining two.[12]

Fears of genocide may have been justified in light of the ease of coercion with Norplant. Some argued that its involuntary insertion did not necessarily violate a woman's right to privacy, as fertility returned rapidly upon removal. Such arguments depicted mandated insertion as more acceptable than sterilization because Norplant's reversibility did not permanently deny women their right to reproduce, yet it reasserted judicial and legislative control over some women's reproduction. Legislators concerned with population control proposed mandatory use of or incentive plans for Norplant, claiming that society should be able to avoid public expenditures associated with births among certain groups, including the indigent, mentally or physically handicapped, and HIV-positive. Supporters touted Norplant, as they had the pill earlier, as the cure for teenage pregnancy, welfare dependency, child abuse, and drug-addicted mothers.[13]

This simplistic answer to complex problems subjected Norplant users to the population agenda of some health professionals. Medical officials who wished to curtail certain women's reproduction either deliberately or subliminally encouraged them to accept Norplant by downplaying its side effects and framing other choices in a negative light. Reports confirmed that physicians continued to judge certain women incompetent to employ effectively other options, such as the pill. Moreover, women relying on public funds, who constituted more than half of Norplant users by 1994, faced difficulty convincing health officials to remove Norplant before the five-year period was complete unless they experienced severe medical problems: a patient's desire to become pregnant or complaint about "minor" side effects was dismissed. Many indigent women did not seek early removal despite side effects because of the cost.[14] In this framework Norplant served well the interests of traditional population control politics.

Examples of coercive tactics abounded. The *Philadelphia Inquirer* ran an editorial entitled "Poverty and Norplant: Can Contraception Reduce the Underclass?" proposing that Norplant be used as "a tool in the fight against black poverty." The Philadelphia Association of Black Journalists attacked the editorial as a "tacit endorsement of slow genocide." Numerous states suggested that indigent women, often women of color, be forced or financially enticed to accept Norplant.[15]

Between 1991 and 1992 legislators introduced twenty bills in fourteen states offering cash incentives to indigent women for using Norplant or making it a condition of eligibility for AFDC. In Kansas Republican Representative Kerry Patrick called for welfare mothers to be paid $500 to be implanted; the state would pay for the implant and for annual medical follow-ups and give the woman a fifty-dollar annual bonus for keeping the implant. He justified his proposal by contending that "it's time we stopped worrying about the rights of the mother and started worrying about the rights of the children she's bringing into the world." He also claimed that "we, the community, have a right to be spared unnecessary costs . . . to provide welfare payments and education . . . if that kid is born drugged." The legislature defeated the bill. In Michigan in 1992 the legislature approved $755,600 for family-planning programs, $500,000 of which was earmarked for Norplant because it was the most cost-effective. Supporters maintained that "the program not only costs less [than pills] but saves money when it comes to the hospital costs for an unwanted crack baby born to an addict who could have opted for Norplant." In Mississippi legislators tried but failed to pass a bill in 1992 mandating Norplant for all welfare women of reproductive age as well as women with four or more children who received government support.[16]

Twenty-one states considered such proposals between 1993 and 1994. South Carolina discussed requiring welfare women to use Norplant. Governor William Schaefer of Maryland called on the legislature to require welfare women with illegitimate children to use Norplant. Although most attempts failed, a South Dakota law stated that if Medicaid paid for the insertion, it would not pay for removal unless a clear medical reason existed. One woman in a shelter gained sixty-five pounds in six months and experienced trouble with her knees and blood pressure, but still doctors informed her they would not remove the implant unless she agreed to a tubal ligation, a procedure she did not request or want. Although debated, no state laws passed mandating the use of Norplant or offering financial incentives for implantation.[17]

Coercion was also employed in certain criminal sentencing, especially child abuse and drug cases. Advocates argued that if child abusers could be sentenced to jail, where they were denied many liberties, including procreation, then denying them the right to bear children with Norplant while on probation rather than in jail was the lesser punishment. This line of reasoning is problematic. Mandating Norplant was gender biased: it restricted the reproductive rights of only the mother, while abusive fathers were not legally prohibited from having children. No studies showed that Norplant made women less violent mothers. The state's concern for a mother's inability to care for her children properly was not served by probation. Rather than Norplant, officials should have offered child abusers services such as counseling, job assistance, and pre- and postnatal care. In extreme cases, removal of the child might have been necessary.[18]

Still, judges used their powers to mandate Norplant for some women. The first case occurred in California in 1991. Judge Harry Broadman sentenced Darlene Johnson, a twenty-seven-year-old black mother of four, to Norplant for child abuse. Johnson had beaten two children with a belt and electrical cord after she caught them smoking. Broadman contended that state interest in protecting the rights of the woman's future children, including those not yet conceived, outweighed her right to privacy and reproductive choice. Furthermore, society had the right to protect itself from future social and economic costs associated with such abuse. Yet Johnson's status as an indigent black woman had as much to do with her sentencing as her crime. Her case fits the historical framework of reproductive policies aimed at those considered "undesirable."[19]

In the wake of this case various states considered legislation to mandate Norplant for certain female convicts as a condition of sentencing or parole. In Ohio Senate Bill 82 deemed bearing a drug-addicted child second-degree aggravated assault. Punishment for a woman with no prior child abuse conviction was either a drug addiction program or Norplant, with an agreement to abstain from drugs for five years. For a woman with previous child abuse convictions the punishment was mandatory Norplant paid for by the woman. In South Carolina Bill 986 required physicians to test newborns for drugs if they suspected drug abuse by the mother. A positive result was grounds for sterilization or Norplant. Kerry Patrick of Kansas introduced legislation mandating Norplant for all women of childbearing age convicted of possession or distribution of cocaine, crack, or heroin. A Texas court sentenced Cathy Lanel Knighten to Norplant as part of her plea bargain following her conviction for smothering her infant daughter. The prosecutor claimed that "it was a question of whether someone like this goes to prison and gets out and reproduces, or we do something like this." Ida Jean Tovar, also of Texas, agreed to Norplant instead of prison after her child abuse conviction.[20] No one explained how this punishment protected her child.

This misuse of Norplant had a race and class bias. Studies showed that black women were ten times more likely to be prosecuted for drug abuse than white women, despite proportional drug use among pregnant women of both races. As a result, many black female drug users avoided prenatal care and drug treatment, fearing criminal prosecution. Dorothy E. Roberts argues that "punishing drug addicts who chose to carry their pregnancies to term burdens the constitutional right to autonomy over reproductive decisions." The only way to avoid prosecutorial action was abortion, which suited the agenda of population controllers and fiscal conservatives. Other studies conclude that indigent minority women faced higher rates of arraignments and sentencing for child abuse than wealthy whites and therefore of forced sterilization, albeit temporary, by the state.[21]

Poignant similarities exist between earlier sterilization injustices and the coercive potential of Norplant. In both instances proponents grasped new medical technology that appeared more legally and socially acceptable than earlier methods to solve perceived social and economic problems. State legislation, judicial sentencing, and administrative actions indicate that elite biases against indigent and minority women remained relatively constant throughout the twentieth century.[22] Norplant simply replaced earlier, grosser attacks on certain women's fertility. Officials used it, as they did sterilization, to avoid reproduction considered socially and economically irresponsible.

Parallels are also apparent between Norplant and abortion. The extension in the Norplant debate of legal recognition to children not yet conceived, as in the Kansas and California cases, is similar to that given fetuses in the abortion controversy. With Norplant, however, officials attempted to safeguard a child who did not exist in any sense. If the state mandated Norplant, then the "child" it sought to protect would never exist. To protect this child the state must nullify its possibility. Thus, state interest in Norplant had little to do with individual rights, despite official rhetoric. Instead, it was concerned with finances, "social control," and the composition of the population.[23]

The search for scapegoats for the economic and social problems of the country converged with conservative and punitive attacks on sexually active women. Norplant moved from increasing women's reproductive freedom to facilitating state repression for certain women. Public opinion supported this government intercession. A July 1991 *Glamour* magazine poll found that 47 percent believed welfare women should be offered economic incentives to use Norplant, and 55 percent favored mandatory Norplant for convicted child abusers. A *Los Angeles Times* survey the same year reported that 47 percent strongly approved of mandatory Norplant for drug-abusing women of childbearing age, while 15 percent "somewhat approved."[24]

A 1995 editorial by nationally syndicated columnist Donald Kaul played on these beliefs. Politicians, he argued, agreed on one clear goal, "to stop incompetent people from having children, incompetent in the sense of . . . extreme youth or poverty or addiction or other circumstances." To achieve this goal he proposed a "sterilization bounty," whereby the government would offer free sterilization and a cash payment of $1,000 to individuals receiving public assistance or living below the poverty line.[25] The government did not adopt his idea, but Barbara Harris established a comparable, privately funded program in California. She offered female addicts $200 if they provided proof from a physician that they were using long-term birth control methods such as Norplant or IUDs or had been sterilized. Similar private programs emerged in Chicago; Minneapolis; Fort Pierce, Florida; and Dallas.[26] While advocates hailed these programs as a "bargain" for society, their voluntary nature was highly suspect. Offering what many young, indigent, or addicted people might consider a great deal of money added an element of unfair bargaining power for those pushing the programs. Moreover, such programs left these women dependent on medical officials for removal. By the 1980s and 1990s women on Medicaid were two to four times more likely, depending on geographic region, to be sterilized than women not on public assistance. Studies showed that 38.5 percent were unaware of its irreversibility, but 45 percent of blacks, 59 percent of Hispanics, and only 24 percent of whites were misinformed, highlighting the racial bias of many welfare officials and physicians.[27]

Norplant and DP were only two of various new female contraceptives since the 1940s, leading much of society to view birth control as a woman's, not a man's, issue. The Today sponge, the female latex condom, the Mirena IUD, the monthly contraceptive injection Lunelle, the Evra contraceptive patch, the contraceptive film, and NuvaRing have provided women with many options, none of which has been misused as DP and Norplant have been. Not surprisingly, no hormonal methods for men will be available for some time, although a bimonthly injection of testosterone and progestin was in clinical trials in April 2005.[28]

Only 8 percent of research funds have been devoted to male contraceptives. Pressure for such research came from two sources: feminists who wanted men to share the burden and governments in India and China interested in curtailing population growth. Experiments with male pills in the 1960s and with Gossypol in the 1970s presented adverse side effects. Further research had dried up by the late 1970s due to liability fears over the woman's pill and the Dalkon shield. Andrology, a male reproductive specialty, emerged in the late 1970s but was viewed as second class compared to gynecology. Pharmaceutical companies turned again to male contraceptives in the 1990s, investigating male injections and male implants.[29] Finding male participants for experiments was difficult: many men did not consider contraception their responsibility, and they feared side effects, in particular impotence and the "loss of male libido."[30] The loss of sexual drive was common in some chemical methods for women, but researchers appeared unconcerned, emphasizing instead the effectiveness of these techniques. Society accepted women's decreased sexual drive because the public continued to see women as sexually dangerous. American culture, on the other hand, accepted virility as integral to male identity. Men demand a "zero-risk" contraceptive, an unrealistic goal and one not expected for women.

The gender inequity in sexual control and funding made headlines in the late 1990s. Viagra, the miracle drug to ameliorate impotency in men, hit the market in 1998 and gained both FDA approval, despite concerns over its health risks, and insurance coverage, despite its significant expense at $10 per pill. Women had for decades been fighting for contraceptive coverage in insurance packages to no avail. In the wake of Viagra women bombarded state houses, arguing for the same economic rights to express their sexuality as men. By December 2005 twenty-three states passed laws covering pills, IUDs, diaphragms, Norplant, and DP.[31]

When contraceptive techniques failed, health professionals emphasized "emergency contraception." Feminists discovered a "conspiracy of silence" surrounding the "morning-after pill." Dispensed to rape victims for more than twenty years, it has a 75 to 89 percent success rate if taken within seventy-two hours of intercourse. Although the morning-after pill is distributed in Canada, England, France, Germany, and elsewhere, antiabortionists in the United States equated it with abortion, and it received little, if any, publicity. Only in the mid-1990s did it become accessible to the public. In addition, a new IUD could be inserted up to five days after coitus to prevent pregnancy. Dr. Paul Blumental of Johns Hopkins argued that if "healthcare consumers were more knowledgeable about emergency contraception, we could avoid about half of the abortions we have to perform every year."[32]

This high rate of effectiveness, however, will not eradicate abortion. Women facing an unexpected or unwanted pregnancy will consider abortion. While 1990 to 1995 witnessed a decline in abortion, this trend can be explained by effective contraceptives such as Norplant and DP, increased use of condoms with AIDS, heightened stigmatization of abortion, and mounting violence at abortion clinics. Yet the number of annual abortions has climbed since 1995. Welfare "reform" pushed many women into the workforce, leaving them little reproductive choice. Increased negative publicity associated with Norplant and DP decreased their acceptability. In the late 1990s more than 3 million unplanned pregnancies occurred annually: half of these women were using birth control; 1.43 million women chose abortion.[33]

As the new century opened, women could choose between surgical abortion or a mifepristone pill, which blocks progesterone and causes miscarriage. Approximately seventy-two hours after taking the pill, a woman vaginally inserts four tablets of misoprostol, which provokes contractions. There are positive aspects to this option. It is 98 percent effective; it can be done earlier in the pregnancy, making it safer; and it allows a woman to avoid antichoice blockades at clinics by visiting her regular physician. In a 1998 poll 45 percent of family practitioners were willing to employ this method, while only 2 percent performed surgical abortions. The pill benefited all women but especially those in rural areas where abortion was practically nonexistent.[34]

Opposition to Abortion

The "new politics" of abortion that emerged following *Roe* affected state and federal governments. Membership in fetal rights groups soared, as did violence at abortion clinics. Prochoice advocates sounded a call to arms but faced an organized, well-funded, and visible antiabortion movement. Both sides built networks and coalitions. Prochoice activists tied abortion to broader issues such as sex education, availability of contraceptives, and watchdog efforts regarding sterilization abuse. Antiabortion advocates allied with right-wing groups concerned with traditional gender and sexual mores.[35]

Although Catholic leaders energized the antiabortion movement, they were joined by the New Right, which emerged between 1974 and 1975 and whose adherents were tied to fundamentalist evangelists. One motivation in the antiabortion campaign was to gain political dominance.[36] Unwilling to appeal to the public with socioeconomic programs, antiabortion rhetoric rallied political support among the less educated. The New Right's abortion stance was not part of pronatalist advocacy: concern for fetal rights ended at birth. Many members promoted denying unwed mothers under the age of twenty-one and their children, many of whom were racial or ethnic minorities, access to public funds as a way to reduce government expenditures and punish single women for their sexuality. The New Right's antiabortion crusade, therefore, was not a single issue. As Faye Ginsburg argues, "opposition to abortion is not the end so much as the means to a larger goal of returning America to 'traditional Christian values.'"[37] It is part of a backlash against feminism and sexual freedom.

The antiabortion movement became increasingly militant. The majority of protesters in the 1980s, according to Ginsburg, were "mostly female moderates . . . for whom abortion signified the cultural devaluing of life and the nurture of others." By the late 1980s and early 1990s they were "mostly evangelical Protestant men" who considered the movement "a vehicle for Christian social action." Part of this transformation came with the founding of Operation Rescue by Terry Randall, an evangelical Protestant, in 1988. Randall galvanized thousands of new, conservative, Protestant protesters to adopt confrontational tactics at clinics and against abortion providers and their families. Such militant tactics undermined the goal of moderates to secure a constitutional amendment to prohibit abortion.[38]

Mounting violence split the antiabortion movement. The American Coalition of Life Activists, founded in 1994, condoned violence and circulated a list of the "Deadly Dozen," twelve American doctors slated for harassment. Supporters targeted not only doctors but their families, friends, colleagues, banks, and other affiliates. Dr. David Gunn, medical director of a Pensacola health care clinic, was fatally shot outside an abortion clinic. Dr. George Tiller survived a bullet wound sustained as he left his clinic in Wichita, Kansas. Paul Hill, a former Presbyterian minister who founded the militant Defensive Action, shot and killed John Britton, a sixty-nine-year-old doctor, and his seventy-four-year-old bodyguard, James Barrett, and wounded Barrett's wife outside Pensacola's Ladies Center despite their bulletproof vests. John Salvi killed two and wounded five in a shooting rampage at a Brookline, Massachusetts, clinic in 1995. The Reverend Matthew Trewhella of Milwaukee instructed his followers to arm and train their children with assault rifles.[39] Facing such risks, 84 percent of U.S. counties offered no abortion services in the 1990s. The federal government responded to this violence with the Freedom of Access to Clinics Entrances Act in 1995. It deemed threats or physical blockades of clinics a federal offense and imposed fines and/or prison sentences.[40]

Moderate antiabortionists rejected violence and joined with some prochoice activists to form the Common Ground Network for Life and Choice in 1994. This diverse group remained ideologically committed to their individual beliefs but, according to Ginsburg, shared a "common interest in making American society more hospitable to women's lives and bodies." Members shared similar backgrounds and a commitment to social and community activism. Common Ground chapters were most active in areas where abortion had been a long-drawn-out battle. Although a small part of the movement, it was important because members cooperated to reduce violence and the need for abortion.[41] Their shared commitment to women dispels the notion that all antiabortion activists are antifeminist. Some supported a feminist agenda but could not support abortion out of personal convictions. They were not, as Ginsburg argues, "reactionary housewives and mothers passed by in the sweep of social change. They are astute, alert to social and political developments." Many drew on images and arguments used by moral reform societies since the nineteenth century: "the dangers of male lust, and the protection of the weak against the depredations of self-interest unleashed." They saw abortion as threatening womanhood, just as some nineteenth-century activists believed suffrage and political participation undermined women's moral foundations. Ginsburg concludes that the abortion controversy was "the most recent expression of a two-hundred-year tradition of female reform movements engaged in defending what activists consider to be the best interests of women."[42]

Prochoice Movement

If not all antiabortionists were antifeminist, neither were all prochoicers cold-hearted, male- and child-hating shrews. Many were mothers and supported better services for pregnant women and children. Ginsburg believes they placed abortion rights within a framework that "identified their efforts with nurturance and domesticity." They contended that "their activism is not for personal gain or individual indulgence but serves the interests of women and social justice."[43] They called for expanded government-subsidized programs to increase socioeconomic opportunities for both women and children. As a bumper sticker proclaimed, "Prochoice/Prochild."

The prochoice movement experienced a transformation in the 1990s. Prior to *Roe*, feminists worked almost exclusively to legalize abortion based on women's rights to control reproduction. From 1973 through the 1980s prochoicers were on the defensive against the growing antiabortion movement and its increasing violence. The election of Bill Clinton and the support of the Supreme Court by the mid-1990s led the prochoice movement to widen its agenda. The conversion of the National Abortion Rights Action League to the National Abortion and Reproductive Rights Action League in 1994 reflected this change. This organization worked not only for abortion rights but for full access to all reproductive choices, including abortion, contraceptives, and birthing healthy babies for all women regardless of socioeconomic status.[44]

Prochoicers sometimes found themselves aligned with strange bedfellows. Population controllers supported birth control, abortion, and sterilization but not as a means to reproductive freedom for women. Coercive techniques to control women, not individual autonomy, drove the agenda of population controllers. Yet their elite power and influence helped keep abortion legal.

The Black Community and Abortion

Mainstream civil rights organizations such as the NAACP remained silent on abortion during the 1970s and 1980s. The National Urban League, however, did sign a legal brief advocating the right to choose. Some blacks marched in the 1986 and 1989 prochoice Marches on Washington, but the march-ers were overwhelmingly white and middle class. The absence of minority groups prompted a letter from Jean Carey Bond, director of publications for the ACLU, and ten black female colleagues: "Where were you?" it asked.

> Minority women need *Roe v. Wade* more than any other women in this country. Why? Because more of us than not are poor—indeed, we are disproportionately represented in the ranks of the poor—and poor women need *Roe* the most. Black and Hispanic women will be the first to end up in the back alleys on the butchers' blocks if abortion is criminalized again. Never mind that certain psychosocial phenomena give the abortion issue some unique spins in minority communities. The bottom line is that black women and other women of color need *Roe v. Wade.*

Although blacks opposed abortion more than the general population, low-income and minority women accounted for a disproportionate number of abortions. Nonwhite women constituted 16.7 percent of the childbearing population but 31.4 percent of abortions; corresponding figures for white women were 83.3 percent and 68.6 percent.[45]

While vocal black prochoice advocates were few, black antiabortion proponents did speak up in the 1980s. They founded Black Americans for Life (BAL), headquartered in Washington, D.C., to "challenge the pro-abortion portrayal of the Black Community." They opposed school-based clinics because they did not offer comprehensive health care to teens; they excluded babies, adults, and the elderly; and their "real agenda [was] to address teen pregnancy" with abortion "offered as a primary tool."[46] BAL compared abortion to slavery, arguing, "On January 22, 1973, seven men on the Supreme Court decided you were not a legal person within that womb. The Supreme Court decided that Blacks were not legal persons either, in the Dred Scot decision of 1857."[47] Another pamphlet harped on the same theme: "1857: If you think slavery is wrong, then nobody is forcing you to be a slave-owner. But don't impose your morality on somebody else! 1973: If you think abortion is wrong, then nobody is forcing you to have one. But don't impose your morality on somebody else! 1857: A man has a right to do what he wants with his own property. 1973: A woman has a right to do what she wants with her body." This pamphlet concluded that society had "once again allowed one class of citizens to be deprived of their rights for the social convenience of others!"[48] Blacks, in their view, had a duty to fight for fetal rights. As an oppressed group, blacks were best suited to empathize with the plight of the embryo.

BAL also resurrected cries of genocide. This time, however, women rather than men associated abortion with genocide: BAL leadership was primarily female. The national organization did not specifically mention genocide, but the undertones were clear: "Tragically, disproportionate numbers of black babies are being killed. . . . It appears that the whole abortion industry is targeting black Americans while most of us are saying and doing nothing." Barbara Bell, president of the chapter Massachusetts Blacks for Life (MBL), did not skirt the issue. She joined the fight "because the BLACK race is being wiped out through abortion. There is a BLACK genocide going on and we as a BLACK people need to stop it now." The MBL accused Planned Parenthood of being "responsible for the *BLACK GENOCIDE*" because "Planned Parenthood's main idea is to get blacks to kill blacks" through abortion.[49] When this pamphlet circulated in 1989, the president of Planned Parenthood and the chairman of the board were both black. MBL resorted to inflammatory rhetoric to gain attention for its cause. One MBL publication, for example, cried, "Yesterday they snatched Black babies from their mother's arms and sold them into slavery, today we cut them out of their mother's womb and use them for experimentation or throw them in the garbage."[50] This group failed to point out that slave mothers had no control over their own and their children's fate, while black women who consciously and freely chose abortion were governing their destiny.

By the 1990s some blacks had become more active in the prochoice movement and had taken the lead in some instances. The African American Women for Reproductive Freedom formed in 1989 to fight for access to complete reproductive options, including abortion, contraception, and birth. In the early 1990s the National Black Women's Health Project dominated the push to repeal the Hyde Amendment, which cut federally funded abortions from about 300,000 in 1977 to fewer than 300 in 1992. By 1994 only seventeen states funded abortions. The lack of funding disproportionately impacted blacks because so many relied on public assistance for medical care. Many activists joined the cause for "full reproductive rights for Black women" because of their previous activism in rape crisis centers or battered women's shelters. Loretta J. Ross argues that "abortion rights has moved from the margins to the center of the dialogue about Black feminist activism." Some blacks worked with the Reproductive Health Technologies Project, which emerged in 1989 as a broad-based coalition to overcome race and class biases in health care.[51]

State and Federal Actions

Government action in the wake of *Roe*, influenced by antichoicers, was fast and furious in the legislative and judicial realms. In 1973 Senator James Buckley (R-NY) introduced the Human Life Amendment to the Constitution to protect the unborn and dismantle *Roe* and *Doe*. His second version, introduced in 1974, defined *person* in the Fourteenth Amendment to include the unborn, except when continuation of the pregnancy would kill the mother. His bill tied the fetus's legal status to the mother's state: if she was healthy, the fetus was a person; if she was critically ill, the fetus had no legal protection. From another viewpoint, his bill valued the woman over the fetus. Senator Jesse Helms (R-NC) eliminated this contradiction with his Human Life Amendment in 1974: it had no exception for the mother's life, valuing the fetus over the mother. Both amendments died in committee.[52] The Roncallo Amendment would have denied Medicare and the Bartlett Amendment Medicaid funds for abortions, but neither passed. The cost-effect argument for subsidized abortion among the indigent still outweighed antiabortion rhetoric at this point. The Church Amendment, on the other hand, became law. It allowed private institutions that received federal funds, especially Catholic hospitals, to refuse to perform abortions.[53]

State legislators joined the fray. As Linda Greenhouse argues, abortion turned "into a kind of legislative guerrilla warfare, with states erecting new barriers as quickly as the Court could strike recently enacted ones down."[54] A 1974 Missouri law mandated written consent from the woman before the abortion, from the husband if she was married, and from a parent or guardian if she was under eighteen. It also stipulated that, after the twelfth week, abortions had to be performed in a hospital rather than in the less expensive and more supportive atmosphere of a clinic. Doctors had to certify that the fetus was not viable. Last, the law prohibited fetal research.[55] Challenges led to *Planned Parenthood of Central Missouri v. Danforth*, 428 U.S. 52 (1976): in a six-to-three vote, the Supreme Court declared the state cannot empower a husband to veto his wife's decision and, in a five-to-four vote, proclaimed that parents of an unwed minor did not have absolute veto over their daughter's decision.

Abortion became an issue in the 1976 election. Hoping to attract the Catholic Church and other right-to-life groups, President Gerald Ford argued that *Roe* had gone "much too far" but that the Human Life Amendments were "too inflexible." His wife, Betty Ford, came out in support of choice: "I am glad to see that abortion has been taken out of the backwoods and been put in the hospital where it belongs." The Catholic Church encouraged parishioners to support antiabortion candidates. Walking a fine line between opposing camps, Gerald Ford signed a bill for states rather than the federal government to decide on abortion.[56] No substantive action followed. Although the Democratic platform included a prochoice plank, candidate Jimmy Carter disagreed with it. He split with his wife, Rosalyn, who stated that she could not undergo an abortion but believed she had no right to prevent other women. With Carter in the White House, the antiabortion movement found an ally. He supported congressional attempts to stop federally subsidized abortion for the indigent because he believed it was "an encouragement of abortion and its acceptance as a routine contraceptive means."[57] Cost-effective rationalization had no impact on this southern Baptist.

Public funding for abortion was a controversial issue during the Carter administration. Following *Roe*, the federal government treated this operation in a way similar to its treatment of other medical procedures, providing coverage for indigent women. On 24 June 1976, however, Representative Henry J. Hyde (R-IL) proposed an amendment to the Labor, Health and Welfare appropriations bill for fiscal year 1977. Its original form stated that no funds appropriated under Title X of the Public Health Service Act could pay for abortions. Although the House accepted it, the Senate amended it to allow funds if the woman's life was in danger. The Hyde Amendment passed both houses in September 1976. In June 1977 the second Hyde Amendment extended coverage to prevent women's serious and long-term health problems and to victims of rape and incest. This version passed each budget until 1981, when Congress conformed to the 1976 guidelines.[58] As the PPRI executive committee concluded, the Hyde Amendment effectively made "abortion unavailable to the poor."[59] The cost-effective rhetoric so popular in the movement to liberalize abortion now fell on deaf ears.

The Supreme Court reviewed these funding restrictions. In *Beal v. Doe*, 432 U.S. 438 (1977), and *Maher v. Roe*, 432 U.S. 464 (1977), the Court held that neither the Social Security Act nor the equal protection clause of the Fourteenth Amendment required federal and state governments to pay for nontherapeutic abortions under programs that funded childbirth costs for the medically indigent. With the vote six to three in both cases, the minority dissented. Justice Thurgood Marshall stated: "It is all too obvious that the governmental actions in these cases, ostensibly taken to 'encourage' women to carry pregnancies to term, are in reality intended to impose a moral viewpoint that no State may constitutionally enforce. Since efforts to overturn [*Roe v. Wade* and *Doe v. Bolton*] have been unsuccessful, the opponents of abortion have attempted every imaginable means to circumvent the commands of the Constitution and impose their moral choices upon the rest of society." For Blackmun, these decisions were "punitive and tragic" for indigent women. In a third case, *Poelker v. Doe*, 432 U.S. 519 (1977), the City Hospital of St. Louis, Missouri, on the mayor's orders, refused to perform abortions unless a pregnancy endangered the mother's life. The Supreme Court found no violation of the equal protection clause and held that the Constitution does not forbid the government from preferring birth over abortion. Several justices again dissented, arguing that the Court had allowed the majority's will to punish the minority and impose its concepts of "socially desirable," "publicly acceptable," and "morally sound" values on a needy minority.

The late 1970s witnessed other restrictive measures. In 1978 Congress passed the Adolescent Health Services and Pregnancy Prevention and Care Act, which promoted contraceptive distribution as well as abortion counseling and referrals to teenagers. *Belloti v. Baird*, 443 U.S. 622 (1979), however, restricted teen abortion rights in some states. In an eight-to-one vote the Supreme Court struck down a Massachusetts law that required parental consent for minors because the statute did not include a judicial bypass. Although the Court had held in *Danforth* that mandating parental consent for minors was unconstitutional, the Court now decided that parental consent was allowable as long as an alternative procedure, such as a judge's approval, was in place.

The following summer the Supreme Court again heard arguments on funding and reaffirmed its stance with *Harris v. McRae*, 100 S.Ct. 2671 (1980). In a five-to-four decision the Court found that neither due process nor any other constitutional provision prohibits Congress from denying public funds for certain medically necessary abortions while funding childbirth. Although the government cannot place obstacles to abortion, it need not remove those it did not create. Indigency, according to the Court, falls into the latter category. Justice William Brennan spoke for the dissenters: "Injecting coercive financial incentives favoring childbirth into a decision that is constitutionally guaranteed to be free from governmental intrusion . . . deprives the indigent woman of her freedom to choose." By cutting off funds for abortion while covering sterilization, the government pressured indigent women to end their reproductive capacity. *Beal, Maher, Harris,* and *Poelker* shifted the abortion controversy from a moral and legal argument to a financial dispute, placing decision making on the states.

How did states respond? Thirty-five ended abortion funding for all but life-endangering situations, three continued to fund "medically necessary" abortions, and twelve plus the District of Columbia assumed the financial burden of abortion programs. The states that eliminated tended to be less urban than those that continued financial assistance. State income level also influenced funding policy.[60] Although economics led low-income states to cut funding, politics also played a role. Many poor states were in the Bible Belt, where the New Right held considerable legislative influence. Catholic Church impact on state policy varied. Some states with high Catholic percentages such as Connecticut, Illinois, Louisiana, and Rhode Island funded abortions only in life-endangering situations, while others such as Maryland and Massachusetts provided full coverage. Overall, the primary factor restricting state funding was the number of Catholics living in the state followed by

Protestant fundamentalists. States with large percentages of NARAL members and with Democrats dominating the state house generally had liberal funding policies.[61]

Similar to state differences, public opinion varied as well. From 1973 to 1980 political and demographic variables seemed the weakest determinants and religious variables the strongest. The degree of religious commitment was more important than denomination, although generally mainstream Protestants and Jews were more supportive of abortion than Catholics and fundamentalists. Women supported abortion rights slightly more than men, and the lower and lower middle classes opposed abortion more strongly than the professional and upper middle classes.[62] Whites in general favored legal abortion more than blacks.[63] The people against whom a class and/or race bias on the part of the white elite might be posited were the most against abortion. These attitudes might have been a backlash against earlier reproductive coercion directed at indigent, particularly minority, women.

By 1980 abortion had polarized political parties. The Democratic platform recognized "reproductive freedom as a fundamental human right" and endorsed public funding for indigent women. Carter again objected. The Republican Party and Ronald Reagan supported a constitutional amendment to prohibit abortion.[64] Reagan, elected with help from abortion opponents, promised to appoint Supreme Court justices sympathetic to the platform.

Under Reagan, prochoice suffered setbacks. The Centers for Disease Control task force in 1981 investigated the prevention of spreading AIDS from mother to fetus but did not recommend abortion. The same year, Congress folded the Adolescent Health Services Act of 1978 into the Maternal and Child Health block grant to the states and enacted the Adolescent Family Life Act, which forbade abortion counseling or referral and supported chastity and adoption but not contraception. This act contradicted the reality of teen culture: Hollywood and television promoted sexually active teens, designers promoted sexually suggestive teen clothing, and music lyrics and videos were sexually explicit. Yet the government promoted abstinence in the face of this sexual onslaught and worked to outlaw abortion. Senator Helms introduced the Human Life statute with Reagan's support, and Congress held hearings on constitutional amendments to return abortion to the states.[65] In *H.L. v. Matheson*, 450 U.S. 398 (1981), the Court upheld in a six-to-three vote a Utah law that required doctors to notify parents of an "immature," dependent minor before allowing her an abortion. Although the 1982 elections brought additional prochoice votes to Congress, abortion continued to be attacked.[66] In January 1983 Reagan confirmed his drive to halt "abortion on demand." Congress cut abortion funding, except life-saving procedures, in health insurance plans affecting ten million federal workers. Senator Orrin

Hatch (R-UT) introduced an amendment to return abortion to state control; it lost by two votes.[67]

In the summer of 1983 the Court struck down some state restrictions and reaffirmed *Roe*. In *City of Akron v. Akron Center for Reproductive Health, Inc.* 462 U.S. 416 (1983), the Court decided, six to three, that states could not substantially limit abortion in the first trimester and could only regulate it during the second trimester if a "reasonable medical basis" existed. Reagan's intervention with a brief demanding the overturning of *Roe*, according to Blackmun, signaled the "real second round of the abortion controversy."[68] The fight continued with *Planned Parenthood of Kansas City v. Ashcroft* 462 U.S. 476 (1983); a five-to-four vote nullified hospital stipulations for abortions, allowing clinics to continue and repealing laws in twenty-two states. The justices also revoked twenty-four-hour waiting periods and informed consent clauses requiring doctors to notify the patient that human life began at conception. The latter aspect was unacceptable to the Court because it interfered with the "discretion of the pregnant woman's physician," giving power to the state rather than the doctor, to whom the Court believed it belonged. Thus, the Court reaffirmed medical control over abortion. Moreover, the Court declared that states could not impose a "heavy, and unnecessary, burden on women's access to a relatively inexpensive, otherwise accessible, and safe abortion procedure."[69]

The 1984 elections saw abortion again divide political parties. Democrats reaffirmed the 1980 plank protecting choice and pledged to work against growing violence toward providers and seekers of abortion. The Republican platform opposed abortion and called for legislation to ensure that "the 14th Amendment's protections apply to unborn children." In a campaign speech Reagan called sexual intercourse "the means by which husband and wife participate with God in the creation of a new human life."[70] This reversion to nineteenth-century notions of sex within marriage for procreation only conflicted with the reality of increasing premarital sexual activity and sex as a means of personal fulfillment, not parenthood.

Although Reagan won, Democrats in Congress kept their pledge to work to end violence. House Committee on the Judiciary investigations led Don Edwards (D-CA), chair of the subcommittee, to question why Republican appointees in the Justice Department had not investigated violence sooner: "The Justice Department has available to it a statute making it a Federal crime to interfere with the exercise of a constitutional right. Reproductive freedoms are constitutionally protected, yet the Justice Department has not intervened here." When Republicans justified their inaction with First Amendment rights of free speech, Patricia Schroeder (D-CO) countered that antiabortion tactics had "gone beyond mere speech . . . ; freedom of speech does not allow breaking and entering, invasion of privacy, bomb threats, and vandalism." In spite of these hearings, pickets harassed 80 percent of clinics by the end of 1985. Antiabortionists picketed homes, churches, and schools of clinic staff and their families; publicized names and addresses of abortionists; identified patients by license plates; made bogus appointments at clinics; and vandalized clinics. They set up mock abortion clinics that offered neither abortions nor abortion counseling but instead inundated clients with gruesome pictures of aborted fetuses and inaccuracies regarding abortion risks.[71]

The Reagan administration did virtually nothing to end such deception and violence and continued its drive to overturn *Roe*. The administration submitted a brief in *Thornburgh v. American College of Obstetricians and Gynecologists* 476 U.S. 747 (1986), asking the Court to dismantle *Roe* and allow states to regulate abortion. A Pennsylvania law comparable to the Akron statute forced doctors to deliver the fetus as if it were being birthed, leading some doctors to employ abortion techniques harmful to the mother. In a five-to-four vote the Court struck it down, claiming the law's intent was to discourage a woman's choice, not protect her health. Justice Blackmun's majority decision defined abortion within a feminist versus his earlier medical framework of *Roe*: "Few decisions are more personal and intimate, properly private, or more basic to individual dignity and autonomy, than a woman's decision . . . whether to end her pregnancy. A woman's right to make that choice freely is fundamental." Following this decision, Chief Justice Warren Burger retired, William Rehnquist replaced him, and Antonin Scalia, a Catholic father of nine, filled the vacancy. Two years later, Lewis Powell, a strong protector of choice, resigned, and Anthony Kennedy filled his seat. Kennedy's law clerks had informed the administration that Kennedy hoped to see *Roe* overturned.[72]

Before Reagan left the White House his administration further restricted abortion. The Department of Health and Human Services adopted regulations in 1988 known as the "gag rule," which prohibited Title X (Public Health Services Act) recipients from providing patients with information, counseling, or referrals concerning abortion, even if a woman asked for information or the doctor believed abortion was medically indicated. Reagan also directed Surgeon General C. Everett Koop to investigate the psychological and physical impact of abortion; the final report was not released because the findings did not fit the Republican political agenda. Congress initiated hearings on abortion's impact at which Koop testified that "obstetricians and gynecologists had long since concluded that the physical sequelae of abortion were no different than those found in women who carried pregnancy to term or who had never been pregnant." As for psychological impact, he claimed his studies "could not be conclusive." More likely, he encountered numerous reports showing depression is far more common following childbirth than abortion and that the most typical feeling after abortion is relief.[73]

When Republican George Bush entered the White House, he continued his predecessor's crusade. In 1989 the FDA banned the importation of RU-486 for safety reasons. Congressional investigations could find no evidence the agency had conducted research on the drug's safety. The hearings concluded that the FDA based its decision on letters from "antiabortion activists and their allies in Congress."[74] Bush then asked the Court to use *Webster v. Reproductive Health Services*, 492 U.S. 490 (1989), to overturn *Roe*. Prochoice advocates responded with the March on Washington on 9 April 1989 with between 300,000 and 600,000 demonstrators, many wearing coat hangers around their necks and chanting "Never Again."[75] Ellen Convisser, president of NOW's Boston chapter, told the press: "We are sending a strong message to the Supreme Court, to the President and to our elected officials that the prochoice majority will not accept any restrictions on our right to safe and legal abortions."[76] While a legitimate argument, it was not persuasive, because abortion reform had not been based on feminist demands for reproductive rights but on cost-effective means to reduce welfare, a population control agenda, and medical autonomy. With sterilization and semipermanent contraceptives answering the first two justifications, only medical autonomy remained as a basis for legal abortions. Feminist arguments were stronger by the late 1980s and early 1990s than they had been two decades earlier, but many rejected them, especially Republican, Catholic, and fundamentalist leaders.

Webster involved a 1986 Missouri law that prohibited state employees from involvement in abortions or counseling, required doctors to test fetuses twenty weeks old or more for viability, and stated that life begins at conception. Harvard Professor Charles Fried argued that the Court need not overturn privacy rights formalized in *Griswold*: "We are not asking the Court to unravel the fabric of unenumerated and privacy rights which this Court has woven. . . . Rather we are asking the Court to pull this one thread. . . . Abortion is different. It involves the purposeful termination . . . of potential life." Frank Susman, lawyer for Reproductive Health Services, argued that abortion could not be banned without affecting contraceptive access and other privacy rights: "I think the solicitor general's submission is somewhat disingenuous when he suggests to this Court that he does not seek to unravel the whole cloth of procreational rights, but merely to pull a thread. It has always been my personal experience that when I pull a thread, my sleeve falls off. . . . I suggest that there can be no ordered liberty for women without control over their education, their employment, their health, their childbearing and their personal aspirations."[77] The justices refused to comment on when life begins but, in a five-to-four decision, upheld other aspects, thereby restricting publicly funded abortions while increasing abortion costs. The minority dissented. Blackmun wrote: "For today, at least, the law of abortion stands undisturbed. For today, the women of this Nation still retain the liberty to control their destinies. But the signs are evident and very ominous, and a chill wind blows." As Blackmun pointed out, *Webster* had serious ramifications. Not only did it represent the first real crack in the legal foundations of *Roe*, but the language of the decision, written by Rehnquist, suggested that the Court hoped to undo *Roe* piece by piece. In addition, the Court encouraged states to devise laws to limit abortion, attempting to force abortion policy out of the judicial and into the political arena.

States discussed 425 bills between 1989 and 1990, 344 antichoice and 81 prochoice. Only sixteen eventually passed: twelve antichoice and four prochoice.[78] By 1990 thirty-two states had passed notification rules. Although intended to allow parents to enter the juvenile's decision-making process, the laws usually affected only troubled or dysfunctional families where interaction was minimal. In the four years Minnesota enforced two-parent notification, the Minneapolis birthrate for ages fifteen to seventeen increased approximately 40 percent and the proportion of teen abortions performed during the second trimester rose to 26 percent: teens attempted to avoid confrontations in the home. Duke University law professor Walter Dellinger concluded that "however well intentioned, parental involvement laws often become a form of state-sponsored child abuse."[79] Nationwide, approximately 40 percent of teens chose abortion, but they had to run the gauntlet of parental consent or judicial bypass.[80]

Antiabortion groups scored another victory with *Rust v. Sullivan*, 500 U.S. 173 (1991). In this case the Court upheld the gag rule in a five-to-four vote. Rehnquist wrote for the majority: "The government has not discriminated on the basis of viewpoint. It has merely chosen to fund one activity [family planning] to the exclusion of another [abortion]." Supporting Rehnquist were Byron White, Scalia, Kennedy, and Bush appointee David Souter, who replaced retired prochoice William Brennan. Blackmun wrote the dissent:

> The purpose and result of the challenged regulations is to deny women the ability voluntarily to decide their procreative destiny. This is a course nearly as noxious as overruling *Roe* directly, for if a right is found to be unenforceable, even against flagrant attempts by government to circumvent it, then it ceases to be a right at all. This, I fear, may be the effect of today's decision. . . . Until today, the court has allowed to stand only those restrictions upon reproductive freedom that, while limiting the availability of abortion, have left intact a woman's ability

to decide without coercion whether she will continue her pregnancy to term. . . . Today's decision abandons that principle, and with disastrous results.

Justice John Paul Stevens argued that *Rust* imposed unconstitutional restrictions on abortion and free speech. Justice Sandra Day O'Connor agreed, asserting that the regulations raised "serious First Amendment concerns."[81] Free speech and medical autonomy, not the abridgement of women's rights, drew the most public criticism of this decision.

Rust affected about four thousand clinics serving roughly 4.5 million, mostly lower-income women. Prior to *Rust*, about 80 percent who discovered they were pregnant chose abortion. Although clinics could not provide federal funds for the procedure, they could refer patients elsewhere. After *Rust*, physicians could not even suggest the Yellow Pages. Instead, they had to state that the clinic "does not consider abortion an appropriate method of family planning." *Rust*, therefore, forced health officials to choose between badly needed federal funds to stay open and a restricted form of counseling they believed to be unsound.[82] Counseling and funding sterilization, DP, and Norplant remained intact.

The timing of *Rust* was also notable. The Court handed down its decision one day after the House voted to permit abortions at military health facilities overseas. Just as antiabortion groups seemed within reach of a solid majority on the Court, especially with the retirement of Justice Marshall and the appointment of Clarence Thomas, choice gained strength in Congress. One month after *Rust*, bipartisan support nullified the gag rule. Representative John Edward Porter (R-IL) broke party rank and proposed an amendment to prohibit the Bush administration from spending funds to implement the regulation. Some legislators believed the gag rule abridged free speech and interfered with the doctor-patient relationship. Others saw the cost of 3.6 million babies to low-income women. On 26 June the House voted 353 to 74 to allow federally funded clinics to continue abortion counseling. Between October 1989 and the fall of 1991, Congress voted five times to liberalize funding of abortions, but Bush vetoed every time, and Congress was unable to override his actions.[83]

In the Supreme Court *Planned Parenthood of Southeastern Pennsylvania v. Casey*, 505 U.S. 833 (1992), challenged four stipulations in the Pennsylvania abortion statute: a twenty-four-hour waiting period, parental consent or judicial bypass, husband notification, and doctors' efforts to discourage abortion by informing women of fetal development and alternatives to abortion. Although choice advocates feared the Court would reverse *Roe*, the right to abortion survived by one vote. O'Connor, Kennedy, and Souter argued that the states should have more power to regulate abortion, and they upheld the restrictions, except husband notification. They reaffirmed, however, *Roe*'s recognition of a woman's right to choose. Blackmun and Stevens wrote that the Court should not uphold any of the Pennsylvania restrictions, while Rehnquist, White, Scalia, and Thomas contended that *Roe* should be overturned.

Two women's groups supported *Roe*'s overturning. Women Exploited by Abortion was a right-wing religious group whose members had earlier chosen abortion. They purported to help women overcome their "guilt" by compelling new members to "admit that YOU chose to let a budding life die."[84] The group Feminists for Life of America, which had been around since 1972, maintained it was continuing the work of feminists such as Susan B. Anthony: it advocated natural birth control and opposed abortion. By the early 1990s the group published a quarterly journal, *Sisterlife*, and boasted thirty-six state chapters.[85]

Bush relied on support from such groups. He opposed all abortions except when the mother's life was threatened or in cases of rape or incest. He supported fetal tissue research from spontaneous abortions, ectopic pregnancies, and cell cultures but opposed it from "deliberately-induced abortions" because it could "encourage abortions, and it raises serious moral questions."[86] He did not clarify if he believed more women would opt for abortions to further the cause of science or if doctors would pressure women to undergo abortions to expand their research. Because the National Institutes of Health Reauthorization Act included funding for fetal tissue research, Bush vetoed it.

In the 1992 election the Republican Party found many of its female candidates not toeing the party line on abortion. Forty-six Republican women ran for Congress, but only Texan Donna Peterson campaigned on a right-to-life platform. The Republican primaries saw prochoice defeating antichoice candidates. Glenda Greenwald founded the Women in the House and Senate List to raise funds for prochoice Republican female candidates. The list signified the deep division within the Republican Party over abortion. A private GOP poll of Republican primary voters in conservative Orange County, California, confirmed this division: 78 percent favored abortion rights despite the opposition of their presidential candidate. At the platform committee meeting, prochoice Republicans urged the party to drop its opposition because the antichoice stand demeaned women, damaged candidates, and did not reflect the attitude of most Americans.[87]

With Bill Clinton's election the pendulum swung toward the prochoice camp. He suspended the gag rule, lifted restrictions on the use of fetal tissue in federally funded medical research, urged the lifting of the ban on RU-486, removed the ban on abortions in overseas military hospitals as long as women used private funds to pay for them, and removed the Reagan/Bush directive that barred U.S. aid to international family-planning programs that included abortion counseling.[88]

Prochoice advocates used this changed climate to employ federal law to enjoin demonstrators from trespassing on clinic grounds. In *Bray v. Alexandria Women's Health Clinic*, 506 U.S. 263 (1993), the Court held in a five-to-four vote that the 1871 civil rights law against the Ku Klux Klan could not be used to protect citizens against lawless activities relating to abortion. The prochoice camp regrouped. NOW filed suit on behalf of the Delaware Women's Health Organization in Milwaukee accusing Operation Rescue, the Pro-Life Action League, Inc., and its leader, Joseph Scheidler, the Pro-Life Direct Action League, Project Life, and others of running a nationwide conspiracy to eliminate abortion clinics with intimidation, bombings, and other violent acts. The Supreme Court agreed to hear this case, with Clinton appointee Ruth Bader Ginsburg replacing White. Ginsburg was prochoice but critical of *Roe* because of its "concentration on a medically approved autonomy idea, to the exclusion of a constitutionally based sex-equality perspective."[89] In *National Organization for Women v. Scheidler*, 510 U.S. 249 (1994), the Court ruled unanimously that clinics can invoke the 1970 federal Racketeer-Influenced and Corrupt Act to sue violent protest groups for triple damages.[90]

That same year elections brought Republican majorities to both the House and the Senate. Republicans introduced more than twelve abortion-related bills; many came directly from the Christian Coalition's Contract with the American Family. One bill would have made doctors liable to criminal and civil charges for performing a "partial-birth" abortion. The accompanying propaganda did not mention that physicians used it in only .04 percent of abortions, usually in cases of severe fetal deformity or if the mother's health was threatened.[91] This tactic left the public with the assumption that doctors performed most abortions in this manner.

The 1994 ascendancy of Republican congressional rule revived notions of who was fit to reproduce and who was not and concerns about burgeoning welfare expenditures. Proponents of welfare reform decried the large numbers of single mothers dependent on public assistance with rhetoric reminiscent of the 1930s and the 1960s. Representative James Greenwood (R-PA) led the fight in 1995 to save a family-planning program targeted by the Religious Right by arguing that "when you prevent unwanted babies, you prevent welfare dependency."[92] Right-wing Republicans such as Senator Lauch Faircloth (R-NC) and Jesse Helms (R-NC) proposed cutting off public funds for unwed mothers under the age of twenty-five. Not only would this proposal save money, in their view, but it would also reaffirm parental control over "wayward" daughters; neither senator mentioned wayward sons.

The mid-1990s witnessed the return of the blame game. Similar to the early twentieth century, educated white women came under attack for the perceived birth dearth. Richard Hernstein and Charles Murray argued in *The Bell Curve* that intelligent women, those best suited for parenting, chose higher education and careers over motherhood. The Religious Right targeted college graduates and professional women for the decline in the birthrate just as race suicide theorists had done at the beginning of the century. Pat Buchanan, Pat Robertson, and other right-wing spokespersons decried rising black illegitimacy when in fact it had peaked and begun to fall by the latter part of the 1990s.[93] The rhetoric may have changed, but the bottom line remained: the wrong types of people were having babies while fit women shirked their duties.

As the decade ended, antiabortionists joined conservative Republicans to control women's choices while simultaneously neglecting millions of children who lived in poverty, lacked health care, and suffered unequal educational opportunities. Some states again tried to ban "partial-birth" abortions.[94] In June 2000 the Court struck down these laws in *Stenberg v. Carhart*, 530 U.S. 914 (2000), because no exemption existed for the mother's life. At the same time, *Hill v. Colorado*, 530 U.S. 703 (2000), stated that a Colorado law prohibiting protesters from within one hundred feet of clinics did not violate free speech.[95]

Conclusion

Race, gender, and class inequality has been rampant in reproductive policies throughout American history. Colonial officials eliminated legal proceedings against unmarried male fornicators 250 years ago but continued to punish unwed mothers.[96] Similarly, female teens in the late twentieth century suffered under abortion restrictions, while male teens were ignored in the debate regarding adolescent sexual behavior and its consequences. The culture of masculinity played a role in early pregnancy: young males encouraged peers to "sow" their "wild oats," especially with as many virgins as possible. For them, pregnancy was proof of their adult, macho, and heterosexual identity. The act of impregnation was about as far as their responsibility went. The decision to terminate a pregnancy fell to the female, while the male was often spared any knowledge of or obligation toward it. The restrictions on abortion were a woman's problem. Doctors, judges, parents, and often the welfare system evaluated the woman's behavior, while male behavior remained unscrutinized. Teenage women became one target group in the abortion back-lash as states enacted regulations that punished them by requiring parental notification or denying abortion unless they could raise the necessary cash. These restrictions were passed, ostensibly, to protect fetal rights, despite the clearly negative consequences for teens and indigent women.

The other group that suffered from restrictions was the indigent, many of whom were women of color. Twenty-four-hour waiting periods posed an in-surmountable barrier to many women. With 84 percent of counties offering no abortion services, many indigent and low-income women had to travel far to clinics. The cost of a hotel, transportation, and missed days of work left them with no real reproductive freedom to choose what was best for them. Lack of federal funding for the procedure itself, even if a clinic was nearby, placed this option out of reach for many women.

The politically charged nature of abortion eliminated the rhetoric regard-ing the cost-cutting impact of abortion for the indigent. Instead, population controllers turned their attention to permanent and semipermanent meth-ods such as sterilization, Norplant, and DP. Government funding of these options but not of abortion curtailed equal access to a full range of repro-ductive choices. Abortion reform, however, was not the result of feminist arguments for equality but of population concerns and medical autonomy. With other options to control the population, the government had no reason to endorse such a controversial procedure, especially in the face of the well-funded, highly organized, and very vocal antiabortion faction.

9

Conclusion

The twenty-first century opened with a presidential campaign in which the Republican candidate, George W. Bush, proclaimed himself to be a "compassionate conservative." His definition of compassion varied from mainstream interpretations. His administration, elected to a second term in 2004, confirmed the continuing lack of regard for the indigent and lower classes obvious in the population control agenda of the last two centuries. Threats to overturn *Roe* and return women to underground services and back-alley abortions grew with the new century as did attempts to equate contraceptives with abortion. The one area population controllers, including Bush, did not attack was sterilization. Funding this procedure while attacking all other options forced indigent and low-income women to resort to this permanent method of fertility control, which suits the population control agenda.

In the nineteenth century the issue of fetal rights had little impact on abortion policy; since *Roe* this topic has been the center of the controversy. Over one hundred years ago activists voiced more concern about the impact of abortion on the composition of the American population than its moral aspects. Nativism, not religion and fetal rights, was the most frequently employed justification in deciding abortion policy. The central issue, they claimed, was that the wrong women—white upper-class Protestants—were having abortions and thereby contributing to the extinction of the Anglo-Saxon "race" in the United States. Such propaganda gained an influential audience and contributed to the banning of the procedure. These activists did not confess their desire to repress middle- and upper-class women during a time when they were asserting their independence and demanding equal rights with men. Similarly, since *Roe* antichoice activists have used fetal rights and morality as their primary justification for restricting abortion and have gained a significant following with such tactics without acknowledging their desire to reverse women's legislative and judicial successes in the political and economic spheres. Clearly stating this aim would have been unacceptable in either century. Thus, activists employed justifications that would appeal to the public and to powerful elites to achieve their goals. Tom Ehrich, an Episcopal priest in Durham, North Carolina, summarized well this attitude. In a

November 2005 editorial Ehrich argued that "abortion is to our society what wearing the veil has become to Islamic fundamentalists—a way to balance a society's moral ledger by forcing something on women." Religious fundamentalists, be they Christian or Islamic, desired to curtail women's "personal freedom, arguing that the future of both religion and state depended on it." Ehrich criticized antiabortion forces for focusing exclusively on women, not the men who impregnate them, on "denying women a personal freedom, and on punishing women who are poor and vulnerable."[1] By limiting funding for abortion, the state pushed "poor and vulnerable" women to choose sterilization, a government-funded and final answer to the perceived problems of the population.

The same holds true for other aspects of reproductive policy and its connection to population issues. Arguing in the early twentieth century that the "best stock" utilized contraception to maintain low birthrates in the face of high fertility among the "less desirable," elite members, including high government officials, condemned birth control as the leading factor in the imminent decline of Anglo-Saxon Protestant hegemony in the country. When the "superior" groups refused to heed these warnings and abandon contraceptive practices, critics changed tactics and began to argue for loosened restrictions on contraceptive distribution among those deemed "inferior" and even resorted to involuntary restraints and state-funded clinics.

The federal government joined the crusade in the 1960s, when continued high fertility among the indigent and dependent led to increased welfare expenditures. Many political leaders considered federally funded contraceptives the most effective means to decrease AFDC costs and other programs aimed at the poor. Beginning with only contraceptive devices, the government ultimately funded sterilization and abortion, the latter only for a time, among the indigent. This policy brought the country full circle, from a nation with few restrictions on reproduction in the early nineteenth century to one with strict regulations in the late nineteenth century and back to one with few guidelines by the early twenty-first century. The biggest push for policy changes occurred in thirty-year cycles directly related to economic issues. During the Depression the cries of "dole babies" sapping limited government resources led to increasing public acceptance of contraceptive dispersal, just as criticism of exploding AFDC costs in the 1960s brought large-scale federal intervention in what once had been a private matter. The 1990s again witnessed critics claiming that the fertility rate among the indigent ballooned welfare expenditures; the simplistic solution, in their view, was new contraceptive technologies, especially DP and Norplant, that could help "reform" welfare.

Welfare changes in the 1990s added to the restrictions indigent women faced in reproductive matters. Congress passed, and Clinton signed, the Personal Responsibility and Work Opportunity Reconciliation Act of 1996 to "end welfare as we know it." Given the misnomer of "welfare reform," this act ended the New Deal protection afforded indigent families with children, leaving thousands of women and children struggling to survive. Some received financial assistance from Temporary Assistance to Needy Families, but its five-year limit left gaps in the safety net established by the New Deal.

As Bush began his second term, for example, 12.7 percent of Americans (37 million people) lived below the poverty line, many of them single women with children.[2] Whereas the prochoice agenda expanded to promote full reproductive options for all women, including the ability to raise children outside the squalor of poverty, the concern among many prolifers and conservative Republicans for the fetus did not extend to these children living in poverty. The emphasis on "compassionate conservatism" allowed Bush and the Republican Party to proclaim their concern for fetal rights while undermining the rights of children and women living in poverty. The budget passed in December 2005 saw Republican senators cut $40 billion over five years. It increased Medicaid fees by requiring copays for pregnant women and children; cut federal funds for child-support enforcement, further shifting responsibility from sexually active men to women; forced state welfare programs to impose work requirements on all recipients; and reduced student loans. The House version went even farther, cutting foster care funds, aid to the disabled, the Food Stamp Program, and the subsidized lunch program for schoolchildren. While justifying these steps as necessary to stem burgeoning government expenditures, the same Republican legislators proposed $70 billion in tax cuts that would benefit the top 3 percent of Americans more than any other group.[3] To sum up, "compassionate conservatism" translated into deficits of unseen proportions for the next generation and cuts in programs for indigent women and children to finance an economic windfall for the wealthy.

These government funding policies discriminated against freedom of reproductive choice for all women. With the reduction of social programs for the indigent and the eradication of welfare, low- and no-income women had no safety net upon which to rely should they become pregnant. Abortion costs were beyond their means. The lack of recourse for lower-class women, many of whom were women of color, led them to submit to sterilization because the government funded this method of control. Forcing women into this box suited population controllers' agenda to end permanently the fertility of the poor. While not as blatant as the forced sterilizations of earlier periods, discriminatory funding policies achieved the same goal. Simultaneously, a profitable business boomed surrounding fertility treatments for wealthy women, most of whom were white. Dorothy Roberts argues that evidence exists that in vitro fertilization programs have attempted to dissuade black couples from seeking technological assistance in childbearing. American culture for centuries has valued white over black motherhood. Devaluing motherhood for women of color has undermined their identity as women of importance to the nation.[4] Thus, the racist and classist component of American reproductive policy continued into the twenty-first century, perhaps not as overtly as earlier, but covert efforts to control population ultimately achieve the same objective—choosing who is and who is not a fit parent.

Abortion politics has plagued the American political landscape since the nineteenth century. First used to prevent WASP women from destroying white Protestant hegemony, population controllers have employed it since the 1970s as a means to suppress women and force indigent women to submit to sterilization by withholding funding for abortions. The issue remained a political football into the twenty-first century. George W. Bush picked up where his father and Reagan left off in attempting to restrict abortion both at home and overseas. In this one arena Republicans reversed their motto that less government is better and insisted on government intervention in a private decision. For all of Clinton's sexual debacles, he was consistent in his protection of women's right to choose, vetoing two attempts in the late 1990s to restrict further women's access to what was a legal procedure. Bush, on the other hand, appointed John Roberts to replace William Rehnquist as chief justice of the Supreme Court in September 2005. Roberts stated that the Court wrongly decided *Roe* and that abortion had no constitutional protection; he did admit that abortion was the settled law of the land. Several months later, Bush appointed Samuel Alito to the Court to replace Sandra Day O'Connor. Alito worked in the Reagan administration to overturn *Roe*.

This newly constituted Court heard its first abortion case in November 2006. A Republican-led House and Senate had passed a ban on "partial-birth" abortion in 2002. While Clinton had vetoed several similar measures, Bush signed the bill into law in 2003. His attorney general, John Ashcroft, subpoenaed medical records from hospitals and university health centers to document whether "partial-birth" abortions were being performed to save women's lives, much in the way Leslie Reagan found state officials in Chicago a century earlier pressuring doctors to enforce the law. An uproar ensued over violations of doctor-patient confidentiality. Lower courts struck down the law because it contained no exemption for the woman's health. In *Gonzales v. Carhart et al.*, 127 S.Ct. 1610 (2007), the Supreme Court upheld the law in a five-to-four vote. Justice Ginsburg, the only woman on the Court, bitterly dissented, arguing that this decision undermined both women's health and physicians' discretion.

Political wrangling has been the mainstay of reproductive policy in the United States since the nineteenth century. Numerous politicians, physicians, eugenicists, and population controllers have used reproductive policy to achieve their larger agenda. In the nineteenth century many doctors pushed for the criminalization of abortion as a means to control reproduction, birth, midwives, women, and population growth. The nativist rhetoric they employed attracted the support of state legislators concerned with the proliferation of immigrant populations that did not conform to the "American" ideal, to wit, they were non-Protestants, often of darker complexion than Anglo-Saxons. In the twentieth century eugenicists latched onto reproductive policy as a means to "save" society from the breeding of the "unfit." The expense of segregation of the "unfit" into institutions and the medical advances in sterilization techniques led the push to sever permanently the reproductive abilities of these groups. Dispersal of contraceptives at government expense served to curtail the "breeding" of indigent and "unfit" not reached with sterilization. State legislators grasped this simplistic answer to the complex socioeconomic problems of the poor. Similar arguments led to federal funding by the 1960s. By the next decade the political football had passed into abortion politics, with Republicans using abortion to attract one-issue voters. This myopic campaigning allowed Republicans to claim to support fetal life while they dismantled policies designed to support indigent children. Frances Kissling, president of Catholics for Free Choice, summed up this attitude in a May 1998 interview when she stated that antichoicers seek to "socialize decision making around reproduction while continuing in a state in which burdens are individualized."[5]

Abusive reproductive policy has been cyclical. History demonstrates that overt pushes for permanent procedures to eradicate the reproductive capacity of the indigent and minorities continue until the press reveals blatant abuses. Population controllers pushed for government intervention from the 1910s through the 1930s, and the government complied with state funding of contraceptive and state laws allowing the sterilization of the "unfit." Not until the abuse associated with Hitler's regime reached the American public did such overt attempts to curtail certain women's reproduction cease. Sterilization did not disappear; it continued quietly under the radar screen until the late 1950s. From that time through the early 1970s a second overt push occurred to sterilize the indigent, especially women of color, without their consent. Once the blatant abuse of Nial Ruth Cox, the Latinas, and others broke in the press, coercive tactics diminished through the later 1970s and 1980s, although they did not disappear. During this same time, federal funding of sterilization but not abortion left indigent women little choice but to accept the former permanent method to control their fertility. With the 1990s the third overt push came, this time with new technologies for less permanent and thus more acceptable means such as Norplant and DP.

The connection that reinvigorates this cycle of overt abuse is economics. Critics were able to convince the public that economic woes, caused in their minds by expenditures associated with the indigent, could be easily solved by halting the reproductive capacity of low and no-income women. In the 1930s critics blamed "dole babies"; in the 1960s AFDC recipients; and in the 1990s "welfare queens," whom the press portrayed primarily as black, drug-addicted women with large families. Racism, therefore, also played a role. Because women of color were overrepresented among the indigent, white elite politicians at the state and federal levels viewed population control as a method both to cut costs and to reduce minority populations in the nation. Thus, the efforts to control the racial, ethnic, and religious content of the population in the nineteenth century with the criminalization of abortion continued throughout the twentieth century with sterilization and contraception dispersal.

The twenty-first century has witnessed a new tactic in the efforts to control women's fertility. All methods of contraception, except sterilization, have come under attack by some groups. The American Life League has argued that contraceptives are equivalent to abortion and has organized efforts to sway public opinion to ban them. Conservative pharmacists have joined the fray, refusing to sell contraceptives. Twelve states have "conscience clause" laws pending that would allow pharmacists personally opposed to birth control not to sell contraceptives; four states have passed such laws. An anticondom campaign, supported by the Department of Health and Human Services, claims that condoms are only 50 percent effective in preventing disease.[6] The morning-after pill, approved by Canada for over-the-counter sales in April 2005, continues to face barriers from the FDA. While the FDA scientific advisory board recommended it for over-the-counter sales in the United States, FDA director Lester Crawford blocked this change.[7] The purpose of this new campaign to eliminate contraceptives is twofold: first, it seeks to control women using moral and religious arguments in ways similar to those of the oft-criticized fundamentalists in other countries; second, it seeks to control the composition of the population. In the midst of this battle no criticism of sterilization can be heard. It continues to be funded by state and federal governments. With both abortion and birth control under attack, indigent and low-income women will have little recourse for reproductive control other than to resort to sterilization. This tactic is the last step in population controllers' attempts to shape the citizenry to suit the agenda of white elites, allowing them to choose who is fit for motherhood.

Appendix A

Henry Miller, "Letter to the President and Councilors of the State Medical Society," 1860

Gentlemen:

At the meeting of the American Medical Association held in Louisville, in May last, by a formal and unanimous vote it was

RESOLVED, That, while physicians have long been united in condemning the procuring of abortion at every period of gestation, except as necessary for preserving the life of either mother or child, it has become the duty of this Association, in view of the prevalence and increasing frequency of the crime publicly to enter an earnest and solemn protest against such unwarrantable destruction of human life.

RESOLVED, That in pursuance of the grand and noble calling we profess, the saving of human lives, and of the sacred responsibilities thereby devolving upon us, the Association present this subject to the attention of the several legislative sasemblies [sic] of the Union, with the prayer that the laws by which the crime is attempted to be controlled may be revised, and that such other action may be taken in the premises, as they in their wisdom may deem necessary.

RESOLVED, That the Association request the zealous co-operation of the various State Medical Societies in pressing this subject upon the legislatures of their respective States; and that the President and Secretaries of the Association are hereby authorized to carry out, by memorial, these resolutions.

In pursuance of our instructions, a memorial, of which a copy is herewith enclosed, has been transmitted to the Governor and Legislature of the State of [name of state], and it now has become our duty earnestly to request of the body you represent, such an early and hearty action in furtherance of the memorial of the Association, as may insure its full success against the common, though unnatural crime it aims to check.

For the Association,
Henry Miller, President

Source: Records of the Rhode Island Medical Society, Rhode Island Medical Society Library, Providence, Rhode Island.

Appendix B

Henry Miller, "Memorial to the Governor and Legislature of the State of Rhode Island," 1860

At the Meeting of the Association held at Louisville in May, 1859, it was formally and unanimously voted, 'to present the subject of Criminal abortion to the attention of the several Legislative Assemblies of the Union, with the prayer that the laws by which the crime is attempted to be controlled may be revised, and that such other actions may be taken in the premises, as they in their wisdom may deem necessary.'

Statistics, reliable and not to be controverted, which are duly submitted in the papers accompanying this Memorial, to prove that an immense number of living children annually are intentionally destroyed in this country, and that besides the serious injury thereby inflicted upon the public morals, a decided and detrimental influence has already been produced upon the rate of increase of the nation and upon its material prosperity.

The moral guilt of Criminal Abortion depends entirely upon the real and essential nature of the act. It is the intentional destruction of a child within its parents; and physicians are now agreed, from actual and various proof, that the child is alive from the moment of conception.

The evil to society of this crime is evident from this fact, that its instances in this country are now to be counted by hundreds of thousands.

Public sentiment and the natural sense of duty instinctive to parents proving insufficient to check the crime, it would seem that an appeal should be made to the law and to its framers.

In many States of the Union, abortion is not yet legally considered an offence, and is unprovided for by statute; in others, the statutes are so drawn as to be easily evaded, or indeed, by their inconsistencies, directly to encourage Common Law, which, by a strange contradiction, fails to recognize the unborn child as criminally affected, whilst its existence for all civil purposes is nevertheless fully acknowledged.

It has therefore become the duty of the American Medical Association, in view of the prevalence and increasing frequency of Criminal Abortion in this country, publicly to enter an earnest and solemn protest against such unwarrantable destruction of human life. The duty would be but half fulfilled, did we not call upon those who alone can check and control the crime, early to give this matter their serious attention. The Association would in no wise transcend its office, but that office is here so plain that it had full confidence in the result. We therefore enter its earnest prayer, that the subject of Criminal Abortion in the State of [name], and the laws in force on the subject in said State may be referred to an appropriate Committee, with directions to report what legislative action may be necessary in the premises.

Accompanying this memorial will be found the Report of the Special Committee of the Association upon this subject, and the papers on which their Report is based.

All of which is respectfully submitted.

For the Association,

Henry Miller, President

Source: Records of the Rhode Island Medical Society, Rhode Island Medical Society Library, Providence, Rhode Island.

Appendix C

Recommended State Statute by Horatio R. Storer

Section 1:

Whoever, with intent to cause and procure the miscarriage of a woman, shall sell, give, or administer to her, prescribe for her, or advise, or direct, or cause, or procure her to take any medicine, or drug, or substance whatever, or shall use, or employ, or advise any instrument, or other means whatever, with the like intent, unless the same shall have been necessary to preserve the life of such woman, or of her unborn child, and shall have been so pronounced (in consultation) by two competent physicians; and any person, with the like intent, knowingly aiding and assisting such offender or offenders, shall be deemed guilty of felony and if such offence shall have been committed by a physician, or surgeon, or person claiming to be such, or by a midwife, nurse, or druggist, such punishment may be increased at the discretion of the court.

Section 2:

Every woman who shall solicit, purchase, or obtain of any person, or in any other way procure, or receive, any medicine, drug, or substance whatever, and shall take the same, or shall submit to any operation or other means whatever, or shall commit any operation or violence upon herself, with intent thereby to procure a miscarriage, unless the same shall have been by two competent physicians (in consultation) pronounced necessary to preserve her own life, or that of her unborn child, shall be deemed guilty and if said offender be a married woman, the punishment may be increased at the discretion of the court.

Source: Horatio R. Storer, *Criminal Abortion in America* (Philadelphia: J. B. Lippincott & Co., 1860).

Appendix D

1861 Rhode Island Abortion Statute

Every person who shall be convicted of wilfully administering to any pregnant woman, or to any woman supposed by such person to be pregnant, anything whatever, or shall employ any means whatever, with intent thereby to procure the miscarriage of such woman, unless the same is necessary to preserve her life, shall be imprisoned not exceeding one year, or fined not exceeding one thousand dollars.

Source: Chapter 371, *Acts and Resolves of the General Assembly of the State of Rhode Island and Providence Plantation* (Providence: A. Crawford Greene, 1861), 133.

Appendix E

1867 Rhode Island Abortion Statute

Section 1:

Every person who shall be convicted of wilfully administering to any pregnant woman, or to any woman supposed by such person to be pregnant, or of advising or prescribing for such woman or causing to be taken by her, anything whatever, or shall employ any means whatever, with intent thereby to procure the miscarriage of such woman, or of aiding and assisting therein, or by counselling and procuring the same, unless the same is necessary to preserve her life, shall, if the woman die in consequence thereof, be imprisoned not exceeding twenty years nor less than five years; and if she do not die in consequence thereof, shall be imprisoned not exceeding seven years nor less than one year: Provided, that the woman whose miscarriage shall have been caused or attempted, shall not be liable to the penalties prescribed by this section.

Section 2:

Any person who shall be indicted for the murder of any infant child, or of any pregnant woman, or of any woman supposed by such person to be or to have been pregnant, may also be charged in the same indictment with any or all of the offences mentioned in the preceding section, and if upon the trial the jury shall acquit such person on the charge of murder, and find him guilty of the other offences or either of them, judgment and sentence may be awarded against him accordingly.

Section 3:

Whoever knowingly advertises, prints, publishes, distributes or circulates, or knowingly causes to be advertised, printed, published, distributed or circulated, any pamphlet, printed paper, book, newspaper, notice, advertisement, or reference, containing words or language giving or conveying any notice, hint or reference to any person, or to the name of any person, real or fictitious, from whom, or to any place, house, shop, or office, where anything whatever, or any instrument or means whatever, or any advice, direction, information or knowledge may be obtained for the purpose of causing or procuring the miscarriage of any pregnant woman, shall be imprisoned not exceeding three years.

Source: Chapter 689, *Acts and Resolves of the General Assembly of the State of Rhode Island and Providence Plantation* (Providence: Providence Press Company, 1867), 148.

Notes

Chapter 1. A Brief Overview of American Reproductive History

1. For more on sexual regulation see Joffe, *The Regulation of Sexuality*; D'Emilio and Freedman, *Intimate Matters*.

2. Paul Lombardo, "Eugenic Sterilization Laws," Eugenics Archive, <www.eugenics archive.org/html/eugenics/essay8text.html>, accessed 24 October 2006.

3. For a study of doctors, clergy, and feminists in Massachusetts during the 1960s and 1970s see Cline, *Creating Choice*.

4. Gordon, *Woman's Body*; Gordon, "Voluntary Motherhood," 5–22; Gordon, "The Long Struggle," 75–88; Gordon, "Who Is Frightened," 23–26. See also Reed, *From Private Vice*. On birth control technology during the nineteenth century see Bullough, "A Brief Note," 104–11. On feminist propaganda see Gordon, "Social Purity," 32–56.

5. *Mitchell v. Commissioner*, 78 Ky. 204, 210 (1879) upheld the common-law interpretation of abortion: "It never was a punishable offense at common law to produce, with the consent of the mother, an abortion prior to the time when the mother became quick with child. It was not even murder at common law to take the life of the child at any period of gestation, even in the very act of delivery." Kentucky did not outlaw abortion until 1910 (*Kentucky Acts*, chap. 58, sec. 1, 2, 3, 4, at 189).

6. Jefferson quoted in Takaki, *Iron Cages*, 47, 49, 50.

7. Bobsein, Margaret Sanger's friend, used birth control in place of voluntary motherhood. Sanger used the term in the inaugural issue of the *Woman Rebel* (Tone, *Devices and Desires*, 118).

8. For doctors' roles see Cirillo, "Edward Foote's 'Medical Common Sense,'" 341–45; Cirillo, "Edward Bliss Foote: Pioneer," 471–79; Yates, "Birth Control Literature," 42–54; Reed, "Doctors"; Swierenga, "Physicians and Abortion Reform," 51–59; Butler and Walbert, *Abortion, Medicine, and the Law*, pt. 2; Morantz-Sanchez, *Sympathy and Science*; Morantz-Sanchez, *Conduct Unbecoming a Woman*.

9. Ray and Gosling, "American Physicians," 399–411; Reed, *From Private Vice*; Reed, "Doctors"; Tone, *Devices and Desires*.

10. Watkins, *On the Pill*, 12–13, 35. For development of the pill and other devices see Hutchinson, *Fair Sex*; Johnson, "Feminism," 63–78; Davis, "Story of the Pill," 80–91.

11. Critchlow, *Intended Consequences*, 5, 9, 118, 120, 131–32.

12. Ginsburg, *Contested Lives*, 14, 23, 29.

13. Barker-Benfield, *Horrors of the Half-Known Life*; Wertz and Wertz, *Lying-In*; Luker, *Abortion and the Politics of Motherhood*; Mohr, *Abortion*; Margolis and Neary, "Pressure Politics Revisited," 698–716; Smith-Rosenberg, "The Abortion Movement"; McCormack, *Abortion*; Sauer, "Attitudes," 53–68. For abortion's impact on role change for women see Gelb and Palley, *Women and Public Policies*, esp. 129, 134, 160–61;

D'Emilio and Freedman, *Intimate Matters*; Rothman, *Woman's Proper Place*; Harper, "Be Fruitful and Multiply."

14. Beisel, *Imperiled Innocents*, 3, 9, 11–12.

15. Ginsburg, *Contested Lives*, 30.

16. Reagan, *When Abortion Was a Crime*, 2–5.

17. Dienes, *Law, Politics, and Birth Control*; Bumpass and Presser, "Increasing Acceptance"; Reed, *From Private Vice*; Rubin, *Abortion*.

18. Doctors and social workers in 1900 estimated that between 20 and 25 percent of all pregnancies ended in abortion, the same for the 1980s. See Kennard, "Criminal Abortion," 7–16; Wynne, "Abortion," 21–30; Taussig, *Abortion, Spontaneous and Induced*, 388; Wiehl, "A Summary of Data," 80–87; Brinner and Newton, "Abortions," 80–91; Rosen et al., *Abortion Problem*; Calderone, *Abortion in the United States*; Bates and Zawadski, *Criminal Abortions*; Schur, *Crimes without Victims*; Packer, *The Limits of the Criminal Sanction*; Schur, *Law and Society*.

19. Reagan, *When Abortion Was a Crime*, 193–94, 211.

20. Reagan, *When Abortion Was a Crime*, 216, 218–20; Butler and Walbert, *Abortion, Medicine, and the Law*, pt. 1.

21. Dienes, *Law, Politics, and Birth Control*; Bumpass and Presser, "Increasing Acceptance"; Reed, *From Private Vice*; Rubin, *Abortion*.

22. Butler and Walbert, *Abortion, Medicine, and the Law*, pt. 1.

23. Greenhouse, *Becoming Justice Blackmun*, Blackmun quoted on 88, 92.

24. *Loving v. Virginia*, 388 U.S. 1 (1967), declared unconstitutional a Virginia statute that prohibited interracial marriage.

25. Greenhouse, *Becoming Justice Blackmun*, 95, Blackmun quoted on 96.

26. Roberts, *Killing the Black Body*, 6; Nelson, *Women of Color*, 1–3.

27. Wilder, "The Rule of Law," 73–76, 87–88; Ginsburg, *Contested Lives*, 6–7, 18.

28. Scientists Morowitz and Trefil argued that this film represents a "pathetic fallacy" because of its claim that a twelve-week fetus has had brain waves for six weeks and is capable of emotions such as fear and pain as well as motion, including moving to avoid the abortionist's instrument. Science has proven that a twelve-week fetus has virtually no connections in its cerebral cortex and thus is incapable of feeling emotions. Because the fetus is incapable of independent movement, the notion that it recognizes the instrument and tries to escape from it is "ridiculous." Moreover, the implication that the fetus experiences pain during the abortion is "misleading at best and fraudulent at worst" because before the "wiring up of the cortex, the fetus is simply incapable of feeling anything, including pain" (Morowitz and Trefil, *The Facts of Life*, 125–27, 158).

Chapter 2. Abortion and Contraception in the Nineteenth Century

1. The most comprehensive nineteenth-century abortion analysis is Mohr, *Abortion*. Other works include Spengler, "Notes on Abortion," 43–53, 158–69, 288–300; Smith, "Family Limitation," 40–57; LaSorte, "Nineteenth Century Family Planning Practices," 163–83; Kantrow, "Philadelphia Gentry," 21–30; Harper, "Be Fruitful"; Tolnay and Guest, "Childlessness," 200–219; Logue, "The Case for Birth Control," 371–91; David and Sanderson, "The Emergence of a Two-Child Norm," 1–41; Reagan, *When Abortion Was a Crime*; Beisel, *Imperiled Innocents*.

2. Brodie criticizes demographers for undermining breastfeeding as contraception and argues that women's determination to prolong breastfeeding, even though it is not as reliable as withdrawal as a method of birth control, could have influenced their later decisions to employ more effective means of control over their reproduction (*Contraception*, 48–49).

3. Dr. Robert Barnes, "Relations between Menstruation, Conception and the Influence of Lactation in Causing Abortion," *CMJ&R* 8 (1853): 260. Issues of the *CMJ&R* are found in the SCMS Records.

4. Brodie, *Contraception*, 60, 62, 64, 66, 68, 70, 79, 81, 115, 206–9, 213, 220–22. Entrepreneurs emphasized the secrecy with which these devices could be used, allowing the final decision to fall to women. Brodie challenges Gordon's assertion that the "task of inserting a vaginal pessary may have been beyond the emotional capabilities of many nineteenth-century women" (*Woman's Body*, 24). Brodie argues that "there is considerable evidence that women . . . learned to insert and remove vaginal pessaries" and sponges; the "number of women unable" to do so due to modesty was "quite small."

5. Tone, *Devices and Desires*, 49, 59, 61–62.

6. Brodie, *Contraception*, 87–89. In chapter 4 Brodie analyzes various editions of Owen's *Moral Physiology* (1831) and Knowlton's *The Fruits of Philosophy* (1832).

7. Graham, *Lecture to Young Men*, 22; Wright, *Marriage*, 23–25; Graham, *Lecture to Young Men*, 14; *Reproductive Control*, 44–58. See also Hollick, *The Marriage Guide*; Mauriceau, *Married Woman's Private Medical Companion*; Warren, *A Confidential Letter*; Soule, *Science of Reproduction*; Edward Bliss Foote, *Medical Common Sense* (New York, 1860); West, *Lectures on the Diseases of Women*.

8. Wright, *Marriage*, 23–25; *Reproductive Control*, vii, 11–14, 16, 18–19, 26–28.

9. Brodie, *Contraception*, 87–88.

10. "Criminal Abortions," *Boston Medical and Surgical Journal*, 15 May 1844, 302–3; *New York Herald*, 6 March 1840, 1, 15 July 1841, 4, 26 August 1841, 3, 26 November 1841, 4, 3 December 1841, 4, 22 September 1843, 4, 25 January 1844, 4, 14 April 1844, 4, 2 August 1844, 4, 8 October 1844, 4, 21 November 1844, 4, 6 January 1845, 4, 11 January 1845, 4; *New York Sun*, 27 March 1839, 1, 21 October 1841, 4, 24 February 1842, 4, 6 August 1842, 1.

11. Slave women resorted to infanticide and abortion not to reject motherhood but to undermine slavery; giving birth perpetuated the very system that oppressed them. Slave midwives passed down abortion and contraceptive information through oral transmission. Few written records exist. See Ross, "African-American Women," 276–77; Roberts, *Killing the Black Body*, 24, 46, 50.

12. *CMJ&R* 5 (1850): 458; *CMJ&R* 6 (1851): 448; SCMS, *Medical Society Minutes*, 1 August 1860, 17, SCMS Records.

13. *CMJ&R* 5 (1850): 119–20, 380; *CMJ&R* 6 (1851): 431–32; *CMJ&R* 7 (1852): 126–28; *CMJ&R* 8 (1853): 129, 259, 275, 562–63; *CMJ&R* 9 (1854): 117, 451, 460–61; *CMJ&R* 10 (1855): 134, 571; *CMJ&R* 11 (1856): 118–19, 121–22, 233, 416; *CMJ&R* 12 (1857): 131; *CMJ&R* 15 (1860): 540.

14. Keown, *Abortion, Doctors and the Law*, 25. According to Keown, whether common law prohibited abortion is controversial. Keown rejects the 1971 assertion by legal historian Cyril C. Means that British and American women were "totally free from

all restraints" to abort at any time during gestation. Keown argues that the failure to convict was not because the procedure was legal but because of problems of procedure and proof. Keown found evidence that legal authorities as early as the thirteenth century considered the deliberate expulsion of the fetus murder. Keown concludes that the "common-law courts, although not denying abortion to be a secular offence, were content to allow the exceptional difficulties of proof that it posed to be resolved in an ecclesiastical forum," a forum that punished both infanticide and abortion. This situation changed with Lord Ellenborough's Act of 1803. This law was a result of three factors: Ellenborough's desire to elucidate abortion law, the recognition of abortion as a growing "social problem," and the denial by doctors of any qualitative distinction between life before and after quickening (Keown, *Abortion, Doctors and the Law*, 3–25).

15. Burns, *Observations on Abortion*, 5.

16. J. McF. Gaston, "Treatment of Menorhagia with Ergot," *CMJ&R* 12 (1857): 459–60.

17. Hodge, "Introductory Lecture," 15, 24, 32–33.

18. Dayton, "Taking the Trade," 6.

19. Hugh Smith, *Letters to Married Women on Nursing and the Management of Children* (Philadelphia: Mathew Carey, 1796), 35, Rhode Island Medical Society Collection, John Hay Library.

20. Joseph Brevitt, *The Female Medical Repository* (Baltimore: Hunter & Robinson, 1810), Rhode Island Medical Society Collection, John Hay Library.

21. Buchan was an Englishman whose book was reprinted in the United States close to thirty times between 1770 and 1850. This quote is from the 1813 edition, quoted in Dayton, "'Taking the Trade,'" 23.

22. *CMJ&R* 5 (1850): 119–20, 380, 458; *CMJ&R* 6 (1851): 431–32, 448–49; *CMJ&R* 7 (1852): 126–28; *CMJ&R* 8 (1853): 129, 259, 275, 562–63; *CMJ&R* 9 (1854): 117, 451, 460–61; *CMJ&R* 10 (1855): 134, 571; *CMJ&R* 11 (1856): 118–19, 121–22, 233, 416; *CMJ&R* 12 (1857): 131; *CMJ&R* 14 (1859): 83–84; *CMJ&R* 15 (1860): 540.

23. John B. Beck, *An Inaugural Dissertation on Infanticide* (1817), in Sauer, "Attitudes," 53; Morse Steward, "Criminal Abortion," *Detroit Review of Medicine and Pharmacy* 2 (January 1867): 7–8.

24. Coale and Zelnik, *New Estimates of Fertility*, table 2, 36; Smith, "Family Limitation," 48.

25. Edward D. Mansfield, *Legal Rights, Liabilities and Duties of Women* (Salem, 1845), 136; Hugh L. Hodge, *On Criminal Abortion* (Philadelphia, 1854), 210; Wright, *Marriage*, 111; John Todd, *Serpents in the Dove's Nest* (Boston, 1867), 238; Nathan Allan, "Changes in Population," *Harper Magazine* 38 (February 1869): 389; Whitehead, *On the Causes*, 221–22; Thomas W. Blatchford, Troy, New York, to Horatio R. Storer, 25 March 1859, Storer Papers; Nebinger, *Criminal Abortion*, 55; James C. Burn, *Three Years among the Working Classes in the United States during the War* (London, 1865), 112, Rhode Island Medical Society Collection, John Hay Library; George Rose, *Great Country* (London, 1868), 97; William H. Dixon, *New America* (London, 1867), 240; Alfred Falk, *Trans-Pacific Sketches* (Melbourne, 1877), 117.

26. D'Emilio and Freedman, *Intimate Matters*, 58; Brodie, *Contraception*, xii; Gordon, *Woman's Body*, 11; Petchesky, *Abortion*, 39, 74. Limits exist to Petchesky's argu-

ment regarding changing notions of motherhood and its relationship to fertility decline. This framework does not apply to blacks, immigrants, the rural population who depended on child labor, and women who worked outside the home out of economic necessity. These women limited their fertility not to dote on their children but to free their time for paid labor (Petchesky, *Abortion*, 75).

27. D'Emilio and Freedman, *Intimate Matters*, 47–48, 58, 72; Smith, "Family Limitation," 40–57; Degler, *At Odds*, 246; Brodie, *Contraception*, xii; Petchesky, *Abortion*, 74–75; Smith-Rosenberg, "The Abortion Movement," 224–25.

28. Although primarily antiforeign and anti-Catholic, the Know-Nothing Party was sometimes a populist reformist organization. See, for example, Formisano, *Birth of Mass Political Parties*; Handlin, *Boston's Immigrants*; Holt, "The Antimasonic," 596, 600; Billington, *The Protestant Crusade*, 388–91.

29. "Criminal Abortions," *Boston Medical and Surgical Journal*, 15 May 1844, 302–3; Mohr, *Abortion*, 93, 167; Holbrook, *Parturition without Pain*, 16; Allan, "Changes," 390.

30. Gardner, *Conjugal Sins*; Crawford, "Criminal Abortion," 77–78; Mulheron, "Foeticide," 386–87; Trader, "Criminal Abortion," 587; Kellogg, *Plain Facts*; Johnson, "Abortion and Its Effects," 91; Scott, *The Sexual Instinct*, 293–94.

31. Mohr, *Abortion*, 160–64.

32. Burns, *Observations on Abortion*, 75–76; Hodge, "Introductory Lecture," 15, 24, 32–33; Whitehead, *Causes and Treatment*, 184; Storer, *Criminal Abortion*, 28, 14; J. R. McFadden, *An Inaugural Dissertation on Abortion* (1859), 2, SCMS Records; Barnes, "Relations between Menstruation," 259; *Satan in Society*, Starred Collection.

33. Whorton, *Nature Cures*, 3–24; Smith-Rosenberg, "The Abortion Movement," 232–33. For similar arguments see Mohr, *Abortion*; Margolis and Neary, "Pressure Politics Revisited," 698–716.

34. Sauer, "Attitudes," 57; Mohr, *Abortion*, chap. 2; Storer, *Criminal Abortion*, 14, 53; McFadden, *An Inaugural Dissertation on Abortion*, 19. Other nineteenth-century writings also attest to the dangers of many abortions. Cases of botched abortions reported in the *New York Times* often ended in the woman's death. See, for example, *New York Times*, 12 January 1863, 5, 21 January 1863, 3, 28 September 1865, 5, 5 May 1867, 6, 28 May 1867, 5, 19 March 1869, 8, 26 January 1871, 3, 30 August 1871, 8, 30 August 1871, 8, 12 February 1879, 5, 7 January 1880, 2, 19 May 1880, 1, 12 July 1880, 1, 25 March 1881, 1, 30 April 1881, 8, 22 February 1883, 1, 8 July 1886, 2, 22 January 1887, 2, 28 July 1892, 2. In many cases reported, police discovered the crime because the woman fell seriously ill. Undoubtedly, many abortions did not cause serious harm and did not make headline news.

35. *CMJ&R* 5 (1850): 119–20, 380; *CMJ&R* 6 (1851): 431–32; *CMJ&R* 7 (1852): 126–28; *CMJ&R* 8 (1853): 129, 259, 275, 562–63; *CMJ&R* 9 (1854): 117, 451, 460–61; *CMJ&R* 10 (1855): 134, 571; *CMJ&R* 11 (1856): 118–19, 121–22, 233, 416; *CMJ&R* 12 (1857): 131; *CMJ&R* 15 (1860): 540.

36. Rothman, *Woman's Proper Place*; Margolis, *Policies Studies Journal*; Mohr, *Abortion*; see also Harper, "Be Fruitful and Multiply."

37. Beisel, *Imperiled Innocents*, 9, 36–37, 84.

38. Ibid., 126–27.

39. "Proceedings of the American Medical Association," *CMJ&R* 12 (1857): 565. Special investigative committees were not new. Special committees on epidemics, new surgical techniques, suturing, fractures, obstetrics, fetal growth, chloroform in labor, etc., were common throughout the 1850s. See *CMJ&R* 9 (1854): 566–75; *CMJ&R* 10 (1855): 590–91.

40. The two cases were *Commonwealth v. Isaiah Bangs* (1812) and *Commonwealth v. Luceba Parker* 50 Mass. 263 (1845). The Shaw quote is from the latter case. Tone, *Controlling Reproduction*, 27–29.

41. Storer, *Why Not?* 6–8, 62–63, 84–85.

42. Storer, *Criminal Abortion in America*, 55; Storer, *Criminal Abortion*, 53.

43. Storer, *Criminal Abortion*, 9, 17, 18, 14.

44. "Proceedings of the American Medical Association," *CMJ&R* 14 (1859): 550–51, 563; Miller, *Principles and Practice*.

45. "Review of Transactions of the American Medical Association," *CMJ&R* 12 (1858): 215–16; "Review of Transactions of the American Medical Association," *CMJ&R* 15 (1860): 358–59; McFadden, *An Inaugural Dissertation on Abortion*, 13; "On the Death of Charlotte Brontë," *CMJ&R* 12 (1857): 826.

46. E. M. Pendleton, "On the Comparative Fecundity of the Caucasian and African Races," *CMJ&R* 6 (1851): 351–56; E. M. Pendleton, "Editorial," *CMJ&R* 7 (1852): 455.

47. *CMJ&R* 6 (1851): 448–49; SCMS, *Medical Society Minutes*, 1 August 1860, 17.

48. Storer, *Criminal Abortion*, 17–19, 7–8; Henry Miller, "Letter to the President and Councilors of the State Medical Society," 1860, and Henry Miller, "Memorial to the Governor and Legislature of the State of Rhode Island," 1860, Rhode Island Medical Society Library. Asking state medical societies for help in legislative campaigns was not unique to abortion. The AMA made similar requests to reform the coroner's office, to require state agencies to keep accurate and comprehensive records on births, marriages and deaths, and to carry "into effect the standard of preliminary education adopted by this Association" in 1847 ("Proceedings of the American Medical Association," *CMJ&R* 14 [1859]: 560).

49. Quay, "Justifiable Abortion." Quay printed most abortion statutes in this article. Individual codes need to be rechecked, as this article contains some mistakes. Quay printed the statutory materials on abortion in Rhode Island from the *General Laws of Rhode Island* in 1896, assuming it was the first, when a bill passed in 1861 and 1867.

50. Quay, "Justifiable Abortion."

51. SCMS, *Medical Society Minutes*, 1 February 1859, 3, 1 March 1859, 4, 1 April 1859, 5, 1 August 1859, 8, 1 August 1860, 17, 1 March 1861, 27.

52. Myddleton Michel, "Poisoning by Ergot in Attempting Criminal Abortion," *CMJ&R* 5 (1850): 39, 566–600; *CMJ&R* 11 (1856): 232–33.

53. "Dr. Storer's Address on Medical Jurisprudence," *CMJ&R* 6 (1851): 869.

54. Storer, *Criminal Abortion in America*, 94.

55. Ibid., 26, 54, 90–99.

56. AMA essay prizes began in 1852. See *CMJ&R* 11 (1856): 548.

57. Storer, *Criminal Abortion in America*, 26. There is no reaction from the SCMS to Storer's prize essay; the *CMJ&R* ceased publication from 1861 to 1873 due to the Civil War and Reconstruction.

58. Storer, *Why Not?* 6–8, 62–63, 84–85.

59. See F. W. Walker quoted in Takaki, *Iron Cages*, 183–84; Walker quoted in Spengler, "Notes on Abortion," 451; *New York Times*, 23 August 1871, 6, 21 June 1883, 1.

60. See Sauer, "Attitudes," 55; Storer, *Criminal Abortion*, 64–65; Allan, "Changes," 390; Nebinger, *Criminal Abortion*, 12.

61. *Reproductive Control.*

62. Storer, *Criminal Abortion in America*, 38.

63. Blanchard, *The Anti-Abortion Movement*, 11–12.

64. Storer, *Criminal Abortion in America*, 40–41; Mohr, *Abortion*, 186. Perhaps Storer printed this letter because Fitzpatrick, similar to most bishops, represented upper-class Catholics. Much anti-Catholic sentiment was directed at poor, immigrant Catholics.

65. Storer, *Criminal Abortion in America*, 40–41; Todd quoted in Takaki, *Iron Cages*, 216.

66. Rev. E. Frank Howe, *Sermon on Ante-Natal Infanticide*, 28 March 1869, in Rosenberg and Smith-Rosenberg, *Sex, Marriage and Society*, 1–6.

67. This author also commented on the difficulty preachers would face from the pulpit because "the very audience before whom the preacher fulminates against the 'great crime of the nineteenth century,' is so far sprinkled with the criminals that he feels the powerlessness of his words" ("A Physician," *Satan in Society*, 122, 128).

68. *Proceedings of the Old School Presbyterian Assembly*, New York, 22 May 1869, printed in *Satan in Society*, 129. For the doctor's quote see *Satan in Society*, 118–19.

69. Mohr, *Abortion*, 186–92; Blanchard, *The Anti-Abortion Movement*, 11.

70. Quay, "Justifiable"; Srebnick, *The Mysterious Death*, 29, 32.

71. Quay, "Justifiable."

72. Ibid.

73. SCMS, *Medical Society Minutes*. While the SCMS did not petition the legislature to ban abortion, it did petition for stronger city ordinances to promote public safety and health issues and for powers to deal with epidemics (SCMS, *Medical Society Minutes*, 25 May 1878, 314, 30 August 1878, 319). Why the SCMS did not take up abortion is puzzling. Perhaps members believed abortion was a northern problem; respectable southern white women would not resort to such practices.

74. Quay, "Justifiable."

75. Quay, "Justifiable."

76. *Laws and Resolutions of the State of North Carolina* (1881), 584–85. The passage of the North Carolina law drew little attention across the state. A perusal of the *Anson Times, Elizabeth City Weekly Economist, Carolina Watchman, Goldsboro Messenger, Greensboro Weekly, North State Weekly, Oxford Torchlight, People's Press, Weekly Economist*, and *Wilson Advance* found no mention of the new abortion law, even though these papers did summarize actions taken by the general assembly, such as prohibition and the incorporation of Durham.

77. Quay, "Justifiable."

78. Degler, *Out of Our Past*, 246; Smith-Rosenberg, "The Abortion Movement," 243; Petchesky, *Abortion*, 45.

79. Wright, *The Unwelcomed Child*, 35, 59; Wright, *Marriage*, 23, 25, 110.

80. E. C. Stanton, "Infanticide and Prostitution," *Revolution*, 5 February 1868, 65; for similar arguments see *Revolution*, 12 March 1868, 146–47 and 7 May 1868, 279; Mathilda E. J. Gage, no title, *Revolution*, 9 April 1868, 215–16.

81. Mohr, *Abortion*, chap. 4; Sears, *The Sex Radicals*, 120; D'Emilio and Freedman, *Intimate Matters*, 165.

82. Gordon, *Woman's Body*, chaps. 5, 6, but esp. 93–113; Reagan, *When Abortion Was a Crime*, 12. The Neo-Malthusian movement based its support on "economic, moral, or eugenic justifications," arguing for "fewer and better" children. Unlike Voluntary Motherhood, the Neo-Malthusian movement showed no concern for women's health or self-determination. Adherents assumed that motherhood was woman's highest duty. See Petchesky, *Abortion*, 41.

83. Ross, "African-American Women," 277.

84. Reagan, "'About to Meet Her Maker,'" 1244–45; Brodie, *Contraception*, 255, 281–83, 287; Petchesky, *Abortion*, 73.

85. Locke, *Report of the Trial*, hereafter cited parenthetically in the text; Aristides, *Strictures on the Case of Ephraim K. Avery*, 1833, box 94, no. 12, 76, Rider Collection; Catherine R. A. Williams, *An Authentic Narrative* (Providence: Marshall, Brown & Co., 1833), 19–28.

86. Staples, *Correct Report*, 15.

87. Ibid., 23.

88. Avery's lawyers had misinformed him that he could not be extradited to another state without the governor of New Hampshire's approval (Locke, *Report of the Trial*, 11).

89. *The Correct, Full and Impartial Report of the Trial of Rev. Ephraim K. Avery* (Providence: Marshall and Brown, 1833), box 94, no. 15, Rider Collection.

90. Staples, *Correct Report*, 8. The 1830s and 1840s witnessed numerous ministers scrutinized for sexual misconduct. The Great Awakening expanded Protestant sects and thus a need for ministers; guidelines for ordination were not always followed. Cohen deals with ministers' sexual scandals in "Ministerial Misdeeds," 34–57.

91. Staples, *Correct Report*, 22.

92. When Avery tried Cornell, he convinced her to leave Lowell prior to the church hearing because of the sensitive nature of the charges (Locke, *Report of the Trial*, 23). Her absence gave him power to persuade the church council to expel her; she could not defend herself.

93. Srebnick, *The Mysterious Death*, xviii, xix, 29, 32; Cohen, *The Murder of Helen Jewett*, 355–56, 358.

94. *Report of a Committee of the New England Annual Conference of the Methodist Episcopal Church* (Boston: David H. Ela., 1833), box 94, no. 13, Rider Collection.

95. Smith-Rosenberg, "The Abortion Movement," 225–32.

96. Records of the Ladies' Moral Reform Association, 1835, Rhode Island Historical Society Library; Report of the Ladies' Moral Reform Association, 9, 11 (Providence: Weeden and Cory, 1835), box 75, no. 12, Rider Collection.

97. Srebnick, *The Mysterious Death*, 136, 157.

98. Packard, *History of Medicine*, 51.

99. Clark B. Franklin, ed., *Rhode Island Medical Reformer: A Family Journal for the*

Promotion of Health and Longevity, 14 January 1843; "By-Laws of the Providence Medical Association," Miscellaneous Material of the Rhode Island Historical Society, vol. 2, document 3, May 1855; Records of the Davol Manufacturing Company.

100. *History of the State of Rhode Island: 1636–1878* (Philadelphia: Hoag, Wade & Co., 1878); Clarke, *Rhode Island*; Coleman, *Transformation of Rhode Island*, 109–10, 127, 137, 149, 229; Goldstein and Mauer, *The People of Rhode Island*, 5; Ray, "Anti-Catholicism," 28–29; Mayer, *Economic Development*, 41; McLoughlin, *Rhode Island*, 132.

101. *Emigration, Emigrants, and Know Nothings* (Philadelphia: Published for the Author, 1854); *The Satanic Plot, or Awful Crimes of Popery in High and Low Places* (Boston: N. B. Parsons, 1855); *The Sons of the Sires* (Philadelphia: Lippincott, Grambo & Co., 1855); *Startling Facts for Native Americans Called 'Know-Nothings'* (New York: 128 Nassau Street, 1855); *Providence Journal*, 1854–61. See also Raber, "Formation," 16–17.

102. Dr. Edwin Snow's copy of Storer's *Criminal Abortion in America*, Rhode Island Medical Society Library.

103. *Acts and Resolves* (1861), 133.

104. That important events in young men's lives could impact policy decisions later has been posited by historian Jane E. Schultz. She argues that Congress passed pensions for Civil War nurses in 1892 in part because many legislators had served in the war and benefited from nurses' aid ("Race, Gender," 45–69).

105. Vermont was the other state. That law, passed on 21 November 1867, was verbatim from the Rhode Island act of 14 March 1867 with only the words "in the State Prison" added to the Vermont law and the penalty if she did not die increased to three to ten years versus the one to seven in Rhode Island. For the Vermont law see Quay, "Justifiable Abortion," 516. New Jersey and Iowa exempted women through Court interpretation of existing law, not through the specific intention of legislators. See *Hatfield v. Gano*, 15 Iowa 177 (1863), and *State v. Murphy*, 27 N.J.L. 112 (Sup. Ct. 1858).

106. *Acts and Resolves* (1867), 148–49.

107. Smith-Rosenberg, "The Abortion Movement," 223, 235–39; McCormack, *Abortion*; D'Emilio and Freedman, *Intimate Matters*, 146–47; Petchesky, *Abortion*, 82.

108. In no way do I mean to challenge Smith-Rosenberg's conclusions. Her findings are valid for the larger picture. I do not believe that the woman-hating rhetoric so prevalent in the propaganda she analyzed was as important in Rhode Island as it was elsewhere.

109. *Acts and Resolves* (1867), 148–49. The state revised the abortion statute in 1872 and 1882, but the only changes made were commas and a few word changes such as "Every" to "Any" in 1872. See *The General Statutes of the State of Rhode Island and Providence Plantations* (Cambridge: Riverside Press, 1872), 541; *The Public Statutes of the State of Rhode Island and Providence Plantations* (Providence: E. L. Freeman & Co., 1882), 669.

110. Smith-Rosenberg, "The Abortion Movement," 238–42.

111. *CMJ&R* 7 (1852): 427; Michel, "Poisoning," 39; "On the Death of Charlotte Brontë," 825–26; *CMJ&R* 4 (1876–77): 140.

112. Smith-Rosenberg, "The Abortion Movement," 235, 243.

113. The text of the act reads: "Whoever imports, prints, publishes, sells, or dis-

tributes a book, pamphlet, ballad, printed paper or other thing containing obscene, indecent or impure language, or manifestly tending to the corruption of the morals of youth, or an obscene, indecent, or impure print, picture, figure or description, manifestly tending to the corruption of the morals of youth, or introduces into a family, school, or place of education, or buys, procures, receives or has in his possession any such book, pamphlet, ballad, printed paper, print, picture, figure or other thing, either for the purpose of sale, exhibition, loan or circulation, or with intent to introduce the same into a family, school, or place of education, shall be punished by imprisonment not exceeding two years, or by fine not exceeding one thousand nor less than one hundred dollars." This act encouraged citizens to turn in those distributing obscene materials because half the fine went to "the person who informed." *Acts and Resolves* (1897), 30.

114. My thanks to Esther Katz for pointing out divisions among ethnically diverse Catholics as a possible explanation for the church's inability to influence legislation.

115. Narragansett Bay is one of the two best natural harbors in North America. Halifax is the other.

116. See John Hay, *Life and Society in America*, 2nd ed. (London, 1880), 242; Nathan Allan,"The New England Family," *New Englander* March 1882: 137–60; F. Gaillardet, *L'aristocratie en Amérique* (Paris, 1883), 243; "Alleged Decay of the Family," *Methodist Review* LXIX (1887): 858–82; Samuel W. Dike, *Perils to the Family* (Washington, D.C., 1887), 112; J. S. Billings, "Diminishing Birth-rate in the United States," *Forum* (1893): 467–77; H. S. Pomeroy, *Is Man Too Prolific? The So-called Malthusian Idea* (1891), 55–56, in Rosenberg and Smith-Rosenberg, *Sex, Marriage and Society*.

117. Petchesky, *Abortion*, 53.

118. No record number, Clara E. Patterson, March 1876, box 17989; no record number, Josephine Hinton, October 1881, box 17989; no record number, Jannis D. Niven, August 1882, box 17989; no record number, Bertha Tost, December 1884, box 17994; record 168, Sarah Hood, June 1895, box 18000; record 318, Eugenia Reynolds, February 1896, box 17944; record 22, Alice Bodel, September 1897, box 17990; record 58, Lena Clarke, January 1900, box 17990; record 320, Annie Richardson, April 1901, box 17994; record 424, Nancy Pearson, December 1904, box 17995; record 456, Agnes Harrison, August 1906, box 17995; record 519, Rose Badger, December 1908, box 19997; record 560, Mary Meiggs, August 1910, box 17998; record 555, Maud Brautano, May 1910, box 17998; record 566, Helen Miller, October 1910, box 17998; record 607, Bertha Richards, May 1912, box 17999; record 625, Jane Cunningham, November 1912, box 17999; record 755, Ellen Fogarty, August 1918, box 18067; record 792, Eva Knight, January 1920, box 18068, all in Coroners' Records.

119. Blanchard, *The Anti-Abortion Movement*, 11–12; Reagan, *When Abortion Was a Crime*, 7.

120. Lewis, "Sociological Considerations," 85–96; Mapes, "Infanticide," 741–47; Atkinson, "Sociological Status," 182–86; "Infants' Rights," *Living Age*, 8 January 1916, 115–17.

121. *New York Times*, 5 May 1867, 6, 28 May 1867, 5, 25 August 1867, 8, 26 August 1867, 8, 24 November 1867, 5, 19 March 1869, 8, 30 August 1871, 8, 30 August 1871, 8, 6 September 1871, 8, 12 February 1879, 5, 13 February 1879, 8; *National Police Gazette*, 6

December 1879, 7; *New York Times,* 7 January 1880, 2, 14 March 1880, 12, 19 May 1880, 1, 12 July 1880, 1, 25 March 1881, 1, 6 April 1881, 1, 30 April 1881, 8, 22 February 1883, 1, 5 January 1884, 2, 8 July 1886, 2, 22 January 1887, 2, 28 July 1892, 2. See also lectures by Thomas, *Abortion and Its Treatment,* 43–44. Thomas claimed that although women from "the upper walks of life" still practiced abortion, they did so less than women "in the lower class." For scholars, see Mohr, *Abortion;* Smith-Rosenberg, "The Abortion Movement"; Rubin, *Abortion,* chap. 1.

122. *House Patients, Twin City Hospital,* 1896–1914, Twin City Hospital Records.

123. SCMS, *Medical Society Minutes,* 1 July 1872, 189, 9 December 1872, 195, 2 March 1874, 206, 1 April 1880, 354.

124. Whitehead, *On the Causes,* 192–93; Storer, *Criminal Abortion,* 51–52; George J. Engleman, "Education Not the Cause of Race Decline," *Popular Science Monthly* 63 (June 1903); Iseman, *Race Suicide,* 137; Jacoby, "First Conviction for Abortion," 59.

Chapter 3. Race Suicide, Eugenics, and Contraception, 1900–1930

1. Calhoun, *Social History,* 236; Faulkner, *The Quest for Social Justice,* 19; Schlesinger, *The Rise of the City,* 125–26.

2. Somerville, "Scientific Racism," 249.

3. Samuel W. Dike, "Perils to the Family," in *National Perils and Opportunities,* ed. Evangelical Alliance (Washington, D.C., 1887); William Potts, "Birth Rate," *Nation* 52 (1891): 440–41.

4. Francis A. Walker, "Immigration and Degradation," *Forum* 11 (August 1891): 637, 640–42.

5. Hunter, *Poverty,* 302–3, 312–13.

6. Ibid., 309–12.

7. Roosevelt, *Works,* 14:127, 135; Gordon, *Woman's Body,* 133.

8. Lewis, *Compilation,* 548; Theodore Roosevelt, "Race Decadence," *Outlook,* 13 September 1927, 764–67. For more on his race concepts see Dyer, *Theodore Roosevelt,* esp. chap. 7.

9. Commander, *American Idea,* 45–47, 16–17, 20–22.

10. Ripley, "Races in the United States," *Atlantic Monthly* 102 (December 1908): 745–59. See also *Reader Magazine* 7 (February 1906): 309–10; *Westminster Review* 165 (June 1906): 595–601; *World To-day* 10 (March 1906): 322–23; *Nation,* 16 August 1906, 134–35; *Popular Science Monthly* 69 (December 1906): 512–29; *Nineteenth Century and After* 60 (December 1906): 895–99; *North American Review,* 15 February 1907, 407–12; *Nation,* 7 March 1907, 215–16, 25 July 1907, 72–73; *American Magazine* 65 (March 1908): 545–46; *World's Work* 16 (September 1908): 10639–40; *Westminster Review* 172 (September 1909): 267–74.

11. J. W. Jenks and W. J. Lauck, *The Immigration Problem,* 6th ed. (New York, 1926) summarizes the forty-one-volume report of the Immigration Commission, Washington, D.C., 1911.

12. *Providence Journal,* 26 August 1912, 2.

13. Roosevelt, *Works,* 15:599, 14:164.

14. Pernick, *The Black Stork,* 23.

15. Rentoul, *Race Culture,* 106. Rentoul's arguments resemble those advanced by

Plato in *The Republic*. Commander quotes numerous others who held similar views (*American Idea*, 83, 43–44).

16. Commander, *American Idea*, 45, 22.

17. Commander, *American Idea*, 4–6, 8; Frank W. Nicolson, "Family Records of Graduates of Wellesley University," *Science*, 19 July 1912, 74–76; Emerick, "College Women," 269–83; A. L. Smith, "Higher Education of Women and Race Suicide," *Popular Science Monthly* 66 (March 1905): 466–73.

18. Charles F. Emerick, "Is the Diminishing Birth-rate Volitional?" *Popular Science Monthly* 28 (1911): 71–88; Hunsberger, no title, *Journal of the American Medical Association*, 10 August 1907, 538; Harrington quoted in Beale, *Racial Decay*, 271, 272.

19. Gordon, *Woman's Body*, 134, 145–46.

20. Rotundo, *American Manhood*.

21. Reilly, *Surgical Solution*, 3, 109; Larson, *Sex*, 18; Paul, *Controlling Human Heredity*, 3; Hasian, *The Rhetoric of Eugenics*, 27.

22. Hasian, *The Rhetoric of Eugenics*, 3, 13; Paul, *Controlling Human Heredity*, 18; Soloway, "The 'Perfect Contraceptive,'" 637–64.

23. Hasian, *The Rhetoric of Eugenics*, 22, 26, 30, 38–40, 43; Pernick, *The Black Stork*, 24, 41–42, 45; Ladd-Taylor, "Saving Babies," 139.

24. Paul, *The Politics of Heredity*, 63–64, 158; Dowbiggin, *Keeping America Sane*, 82.

25. Paul, *Controlling Human Heredity*, 42–44.

26. Reilly, *Surgical Solution*, 9–10; Larson, *Sex*, 19, 72.

27. Haller, *Eugenics*, 3–4, 160–63; Gordon, "The Politics," 66–67; Gordon, *Woman's Body*, 274–78; Reilly, *Surgical Solution*, 3, 109; Larson, *Sex*, 18.

28. Kline, *Gender, Sexuality, and Eugenics*, 2–3.

29. Gordon, *Woman's Body*, 270–71; Shapiro, *Population*, 34–35; Haller, *Eugenics*, 62; Kühl, *Nazi Connection*, 79; Dowbiggin, *Keeping America Sane*, 78–79.

30. Larson, *Sex*, 17, 30–31, 86, 89; Pernick, *The Black Stork*, 32.

31. Paul, *Controlling Human Heredity*, 56–57; Hasian, *The Rhetoric of Eugenics*, 52, 53, 73, 82–83, 86, 94, 101–2; Pernick, *The Black Stork*, 35, 54; Kline, *Gender, Sexuality, and Eugenics*, 5; Dowbiggin, *Keeping America Sane*, ix–xi, 99–100, 111; Grob, *The Mad among Us*.

32. Paul, *The Politics of Heredity*, 11, 13–16; Pernick, *The Black Stork*, 32.

33. Higham, *Strangers in the Land*, 72; Larson, *Sex*, 101.

34. Reilly, *Surgical Solution*, 25–26; Larson, *Sex*, 22–23.

35. Kühl, *Nazi Connection*, 13–15; Shapiro, *Population*, 35.

36. Reilly, *Surgical Solution*, 11; Larson, *Sex*, 23–25, 75, 79, 84; Paul, *Controlling Human Heredity*, 67–70; Paul, *The Politics of Heredity*, 117–21, 125.

37. Reilly, *Surgical Solution*, 29; Paul, *The Politics of Heredity*, 126–27; Kline, *Gender, Sexuality, and Eugenics*, 3.

38. Reilly, *Surgical Solution*, 30–31, 112; Larson, *Sex*, 27.

39. Chapple, *The Fertility of the Unfit*; Harry Sharp, *Eugenics Review* 4 (1912): 204–5; Reilly, *Surgical Solution*, 31–32.

40. Braslow, "In the Name of Therapeutics," 31, 38, 40, 42, 46, 48; Gugliotta, "Dr. Sharp with His Little Knife," 373.

41. Whitney, *The Case for Sterilization*, 126; Meyerson et al., *Eugenical Sterilization*, 4–5.

42. Pennsylvania passed bills in 1901 and 1905; the governor failed to sign them into law (Haller, *Eugenics*, 50).

43. Haller, *Eugenics*, 124; Reilly, *Surgical Solution*, 39; Larson, *Sex*, 31–32; Paul, *Controlling Human Heredity*, 82–83.

44. Dowbiggin, *Keeping America Sane*, 122–23.

45. Reilly, *Surgical Solution*, 40, 53, 55, 71–73, 89.

46. *Buck v. Bell*, 247 U.S. 200 (1927), my emphasis. A year after Carrie was sterilized the State Colony sterilized her sister Doris, who was told she was undergoing an appendectomy. Doris and her husband tried for years to have children and did not learn of this deception until 1980. Neither Carrie nor Doris was feebleminded but instead were daughters of an "anti-social prostitute" (Smith, *Eugenic Assault*, 4–6; see also Shapiro, *Population*, 3–4).

47. Laughlin, *Legal Status*, 65; Salmon to Davis, 28 May 1920, and Davis to Raymond B. Fosdick, 2 February 1921, file 177, series 3, box 8, BSH Records.

48. The new laws protected due process and the equal protection clause by mandating that eugenicists scan the whole populace, not just those institutionalized (Reilly, *Surgical Solution*, 84).

49. H 1050, 20 March 1925, *Failed Bills of 1925*, 1–7, State Archives.

50. Rhode Island did not keep records of hearings. Thus, historians cannot discern the vote or arguments used for or against proposed legislation. The bill received no attention in the newspapers.

51. Dennett, *Birth Control Laws*, 20–22, 63–65; I. N. Thurman, "Excerpts from Address of I. N. Thurman on the Legal Status of Birth Control," 1926, box 12, ABCL Papers.

52. Tone, *Devices and Desires*, xvii, 26, 30, 32, 40, 48, 65.

53. Parmelee, *Poverty and Social Progress*, 184–86, 309.

54. See Ellis, *Problem of Race-Regeneration*; Saleeby, *Methods of Race Regeneration*; *Popular Science Monthly* 78 (January 1911): 81–83; *Scientific American*, 2 September 1911, 206; *Westminster Review* 177 (March 1912): 348–52; *Current Literature* 52 (April 1912): 436–39; *Westminster Review* 177 (May 1912): 579–81; *Survey*, 23 November 1912, 244–46; *World's Work* 25 (December 1912): 238–34; *National Education Association, Proceedings and Addresses* (1913): 772–83; *Scientific American*, 10 May 1912, 426; *Literary Digest*, 18 October 1913, 676; *Technical World Magazine* 20 (November 1913): 328–29; *Outlook*, 15 November 1913, 585–88; *Living Age*, 29 November 1913, 566–69; *Independent*, 28 September 1914, 430–31; *Nineteenth Century and After* 75 (February 1915): 434–45; *Survey*, 1 January 1916, 407–8; *Literary Digest*, 3 February 1917, 244–45. This list is a selection of articles dealing with the "problem" of population.

55. Roosevelt, *Works*, 4:77–79, 152–53, 14:172.

56. Gordon, *Woman's Body*, 236–37; Petchesky, *Abortion*, 95.

57. Paul, *Conversations with Alice Paul*, 494.

58. For radical elements of the birth control movement see Gordon, *Woman's Body*; Gordon, "The Long Struggle," 75–88; Schofield, "Rebel Girls and Union Maids," 335–58.

59. Goldman, "Love and Marriage," 3.

60. Grant Sanger, interview with Ellen Chesler, August 1976, 20, Family Planning Oral History Project.

61. For more on Sanger see Kennedy, *Birth Control in America*; Douglas, *Margaret Sanger*; Gordon, *Woman's Body*; Reed, *From Private Vice*; and Chesler, *Woman of Valor*. Manuscript collections include ABCL Papers and Margaret Sanger Papers.

62. See Reed, *From Private Vice*, 135, 403 n. 18.

63. Grant Sanger interview, 18.

64. Chesler, *Woman of Valor*, 216; Gordon, *Woman's Body*, 275.

65. Franks, *Margaret Sanger's Eugenic Legacy*, 1.

66. The only device at the clinic was the Mizpah Pessary, also available at pharmacies for women with a prolapsed uterus; it also served as a contraceptive device. Chesler, *Woman of Valor*, 151.

67. Chesler, *Woman of Valor*, 151–52; Reed, *From Private Vice*, 106–14; Gaulard, "Woman Rebel." Approximately twenty activists were arrested on federal charges and more on state charges (Gordon, *Woman's Body*, 228).

68. Anne Kennedy, "Report of the American Birth Control League Activities," 1923, box 11, ABCL Papers.

69. D'Emilio and Freedman, *Intimate Matters*, 233; Peiss, "Charity Girls," 78–80; Meyer, *Any Friend of the Movement*, 50.

70. Gordon, *Woman's Body*, 186–203.

71. Tone, *Devices and Desires*, 106–10; Meyer, *Any Friend of the Movement*, 56.

72. Gordon, *Woman's Body*, 240–41; Haag, "In Search of 'The Real Thing,'" 163–64.

73. This shift in tactic has parallels in the suffrage movement, which split in 1869 into the National Woman Suffrage Association and the American Woman Suffrage Association. The former maintained its relatively radical stance, continuing to fight for the vote but also labor, marriage and divorce reform, and free love, and it closed its ranks to men. The American Woman Suffrage Association fought only for the vote and chose male leaders to gain legitimacy.

74. U.S. Congress, Senate, Committee on the Judiciary, *Hearings*, 31.

75. Chesler, *Woman of Valor*, 225–26.

76. Kennedy, "Report of the ABCL Activities"; "Some Material for Publicity Season 1922–1923," 1922, box 2, file 2, ABCL Papers; "American Birth Control League," n.d., file 4, series 3, box 1, BSH Records.

77. "America's Need for a Federal Birth Control Commission," n.d., box 10, ABCL Papers.

78. The Immigration Act of 1917 excluded "all idiots, imbeciles, feeble-minded persons, epileptics, insane persons; . . . persons of constitutional psychopathic inferiority," as well as alcoholics, beggars, vagrants, paupers, those with contagious diseases, criminals, polygamists, prostitutes, and "persons likely to become a public charge" (U.S. Congress, House, Committee on Ways and Means, *Report*, 14).

79. The 1921 and 1924 acts set quotas favoring northwestern over southeastern Europeans and virtually eliminated immigration from Asia ("America's Need").

80. For nativist reactions see Higham, *Strangers in the Land*.

81. Dublin, "The Fallacious Propaganda," 186–87; Rossiter, *Increase of Population*, 28, 101.

82. William Louis Poteat, "The Social Significance of Hereditary," Presidential Address to the Southern Baptist Education Association, 21 February 1923, file 1078, box 9, WFRG 0091, Poteat Collection.

83. Slosson, *The Great Crusade*, 146; E. W. MacBride to Margaret Sanger, 10 October 1923, box 10, ABCL Papers; Lynd and Lynd, *Middletown*, 123–25; *Nation*, 2 November 1921, 495; *American Mercury* 2 (June 1924): 231–36; *Literary Digest*, 22 November 1924, 36; *Survey*, 15 May 1925, 25; *North American Review* 224 (December 1927): 622–29.

84. Brandt, *No Magic Bullet*; Gordon, *Woman's Body*; Gelb and Palley, *Women and Public Policies*, 5–6, 129, 134, 160–61.

85. Bellingham and Mathis, "Race, Citizenship," 157.

86. The Bureau of Social Hygiene was established in 1911 by John D. Rockefeller, Jr., for the "study, amelioration, and prevention of those social conditions, crimes and diseases which, adversely, affect the wellbeing of society." The BSH was independent of the Rockefeller Foundation but supported by Rockefeller, Jr. It initially concentrated on prostitution but shifted to the study of sex, "the fundamental on which the life of the race depends." Dr. Katherine B. Davis served as general secretary from 1918 to 1928. "A Report for the Year 1929," file 2, series 3, box 1; Katherine B. Davis to John D. Rockefeller, Jr., 27 April 1927, file 44, series 3, box 7; "Attitude of Maternity Center Association to Birth Control," 22 April 1931, file 166, series 3, box 7, all in BSH Records.

87. See Campbell, "Birth Control," 131–47; Sulloway, *Birth Control*; Curran, *Issues in Sexual and Medical Ethics*.

88. Cardinal Gibbons quoted in Commander, *American Idea*, 84–86; Blanchard, *The Anti-Abortion Movement*, 11–12.

89. Kennedy, "Report of an Interview with Fr. Ward of the National Welfare Conference," 1926, box 11, ABCL Papers.

90. Hardin, *Population*, 242.

91. "Committee on Maternal Health Revised Statement," 9 March 1923, file 172, series 3, box 7, BSH Records; Louise Gilman Hutchins, M.D., interview with James W. Reed, January 1975, 7, Family Planning Oral History Project; "Interview with Boughton," 17 April 1931, file 162, series 3, box 7, BSH Records; "CMH Statement," 7 December 1928, file 173, series 3, box 7, BSH Records.

92. Brandt, *No Magic Bullet*, 8–9; Reed, *From Private Vice*, chap. 3; Reed, "Doctors," 111–12.

93. Tone, *Devices and Desires*, 66.

94. John Fulton to Mary Ware Dennett, 30 April 1918, and Fulton to Dennett, 9 May 1918, box 12, ABCL Papers; Robinson, *Seventy Birth Control Clinics*, 105, 260–61. See also Dublin, "The Fallacious Propaganda," 190–92; Blacker, *Birth Control*, 9, 13.

95. For a discussion of this controversial decision see Ray and Gosling, "American Physicians," 399–411; Gordon, "The Long Struggle."

96. "Some Material for Publicity Season 1922–1923," 1922, file 2, box 2, and Kennedy to the Secretary of the Winnipeg Medical Society, 4 May 1923, file 1, box 2, ABCL Papers.

97. "Noted Obstetrician Will Lecture Here on Birth Regulation," *Ann Arbor Michigan Daily*, 24 November 1926, box 11; James Cooper, "Report on Meeting, Reading, Pennsylvania," 29 May 1925, box 11; James Cooper, "Dr. Cooper's Report," 7–13 October, no year, all in ABCL Papers.

98. U.S. Congress, Senate, Committee on the Judiciary, *Hearings*, 12, 38. The American Gynecological Society in 1925 called for the mail to transmit medical and scientific journals and other pamphlets containing birth control information, but it recanted this resolution for "political reasons." U.S. Congress, Senate, Committee on the Judiciary, *Extract*, 40.

99. Gordon, *Woman's Body*, 249–50, 270.

100. Smith, *Eugenic Assault*, 13–25; Dorr, "Arm and Arm," 142–44. For more on the alliance between this club and Garvey see Smith, *Eugenic Assault*, chap. 2.

101. "The New Family and Race Improvement," *Virginia Health Bulletin* 17 (November 1925): 3–30.

102. "People's Foundation," 11 April 1932, file 178, series 3, box 8, BSH Records; Shapiro, *Population*, 45–47; Gordon, *Woman's Body*, 274.

103. Irving Fisher to Katharine Davis, 24 November 1924, and Davis to Fisher, 26 November 1924, file 181, series 3, box 8; Lawrence B. Dunham to Miss Topping, 27 September 1932, file 178, series 3, box 8, both in BSH Records.

104. "Committee on Maternal Health Revised Statement," 9 March 1923, file 172, series 3, box 7; "A Report to the Trustees Covering the Years 1928, 1929, 1930," 15 December 1930, file 1, series 3, box 1, 72–73, both in BSH Records.

105. Robert Latou Dickinson, "Birth Control: Some Definitions and Comments," n.d., file 173, series 3, box 7, BSH Records.

106. "A Report to the Trustees Covering the Years 1928, 1929, 1930," 69.

107. "CMH Statement." Despite similarities, the CMH did not cooperate with the ABCL because of the lay- versus medical-directed nature of the ABCL.

108. "American Birth Control League," n.d., file 4, series 3, box 1; "A Report of the Trustees Covering the Years 1928, 1929, 1930," 15 December 1930, 76–80, file 1, series 3, box 1; "Birth Control Clinical Research Bureau," n.d., file 12, series 3, box 1; "A Report for the Year 1929," n.d., file 2, series 3, box 1; and "Annual Report to the Trustees," 1931, 71, file 4, Series 3, box 1, all in BSH Records.

109. Harry H. Laughlin to Sanger, 24 March 1923, file 3, box 2, ABCL Papers.

110. By the 1920s the ABCL had open racists and eugenicists on its board such as Lothrop Stoddard, author of *The Rising Tide of Color against White World-Supremacy*, and C. C. Little. The *Birth Control Review* also reflected eugenic and racist attitudes. See Gordon, *Woman's Body*, 278.

111. "Some Material for Publicity Season 1922–1923," file 2, box 2, ABCL Papers. For examples of speeches see "Notes on Meeting at Colony Club," 4 February 1923, box 11; Anne Kennedy to Mrs. Park Matthewson, 27 June 1923, file 2, box 2; Kennedy to Mrs. George Forbes, 24 April 1923, file 1, box 2, all in ABCL Papers.

112. Margaret Sanger to Dr. William Thomas Belfield, 5 July 1923, file 4, box 2, ABCL Papers; Robinson, *Seventy Birth Control Clinics*, 104.

113. Margaret Sanger to Harry H. Laughlin, 7 September 1923, file 3, box 2; Sanger to Dr. Madison Grant, 24 September 1923, file 3, box 2; Professor William McDougall

to Sanger, 24 September 1923, file 4, box 2; Pauline Carvel Daniel to Miss Emeth Tuttle, 6 September 1923, file 3, box 2; Sanger to Horatio M. Pollack, 31 August 1923, file 3, box 2; "Statistics Compiled from Reports of the Department of Correction and Department of Public Welfare, New York State," 1921, box 11, all in ABCL Papers.

114. Anne Kennedy to Professor William Herbert Hobbs, 7 July 1923, file 4, box 2, ABCL Papers.

115. Sanger to Eliot, 15 November 1923, file 6, box 2; Julia Kirkwood to Sanger, 7 November 1923, file 5, box 2; James Cooper, "Dr. Cooper's Reports," 7–13 October, no year, box 11; "Intelligent Motherhood Is Birth Control Gospel," *Aberdeen Morning American*, 18 September 1926, box 11, all in ABCL Papers.

116. Sanger, "Address of Welcome, Sixth International Neo-Malthusian and Birth Control Conference," 25 March 1925, box 10, ABCL Papers.

117. Again, parallels between birth control and suffrage movements can be seen. Many suffragists adopted racial arguments to justify women's suffrage following the Civil War, contending that white educated women's vote could offset the vote of ignorant black men enfranchised through the Fifteenth Amendment.

118. Owen R. Lovejoy, "Birth Control and Child Labor," 27 March 1925, box 10; message from Hendrick W. van Loon to Sixth International Neo-Malthusian Conference (hereafter referred to as SINC), March 1925, box 10; message from Upton Sinclair to SINC, March 1925, box 10, all in ABCL Papers. Numerous additional speeches and letters argued the same point: "Professor Pearl Calls for a Militant Crusade," 26 March 1925, box 10; message from Henry W. Nevinson to SINC, March 1925, box 10; Norman Thomas, "Some Objections to Birth Control Considered," March 1925, paper delivered at SINC, box 10; see also "The Race Suicide Bogie," for release 26 March 1925, box 10; Dr. Aletta Jacobs, "A Generation of Birth Control in Holland," paper delivered at SINC, box 10, all in ABCL Papers.

119. Message from Oswald Garrison Villard to SINC, March 1925, box 10; message from Hudson Maxim to SINC, March 1925, box 10; message from Major Haldane Mac-Fall to SINC, March 1925, box 10; message from M. P. Willcocks to SINC, March 1925, box 10; message from Charles E. S. Wood to SINC, March 1925, box 10, all in ABCL Papers.

120. "Summary of Proceedings at Sixth International Neo-Malthusian and Birth Control Conference," n.d., box 10; "Eugenics," 28 March 1925, box 10, both in ABCL Papers.

121. See Reed, *From Private Vice*, 135, 403 n. 18. His source for this conclusion is a 1946 letter from Clarence Gamble to the PPFA and a 1946 letter from Sanger to Gamble, yet he locates her rejection of eugenics in the 1920s. By the 1940s eugenics had been discredited by its association with Hitler. She probably disavowed her eugenic leanings in hindsight. See Sanger, "Why Not Birth Control," 10–11; Sanger, *Woman and the New Race*, 34; Sanger, *The Pivot of Civilization*, 177–78.

122. The VPL was established by Dennett in 1919. See Dennett, *Birth Control Laws*; Mary Ware Dennett, "The Birth Control Conference," *Nation*, 8 November 1922, 500–501.

123. Sanger, *Margaret Sanger*, 414; Anne Kennedy to Mrs. Mary Ware Dennett, 6 June 1923, file 3, box 2, ABCL Papers.

124. H 665, 6 February 1923, *Failed Bills of 1923*, 23, State Archives.

125. Sanger, *Margaret Sanger*, 415.

126. Ida H. Timme, "Report to the Congressional Committee of the American Birth Control League," 1 March 1926, box 11, ABCL Papers; Sanger, *Margaret Sanger*, 415. Although the BSH refused to fund the ABCL's propaganda work, it did financially support the ABCL's push for a doctors-only bill because the BSH believed the "responsibility for this problem" should rest squarely "on the shoulders of the medical profession." "American Birth Control League, Inc.," n.d., file 12, series 3, box 1, BSH Records.

127. Grant Sanger interview, 47–50.

128. H 807, 26 February 1926, *Failed Bills of 1926*, 26, State Archives; Kennedy, congressional report (hereafter referred to as CR) nos. 33, 36, 1 January–1 May 1926, box 11, ABCL Papers.

129. Kennedy, CR nos. 33, 36, 12, 11, and 2, 1 January–1 May 1926, box 11, ABCL Papers.

130. Kennedy, CR no. 12, 11 February 1926, box 11, ABCL Papers.

131. Kennedy, CR nos. 26, 25, and 14, 24 February–1 April 1926, box 11; and Kennedy and M. Huse, "Interview with the Officials of the Ku Klux Klan," n.d., box 11, all in ABCL Papers.

132. For statements regarding immorality see Senator Kenneth McKellar (D-TN) and Senator George W. Pepper (R-PA) in CR nos. 37 and 5, box 11; for statements regarding the public/private split see CR nos. 34 and 14, box 11, all in ABCL Papers.

133. Kennedy, CR nos. 27, 38, 21, and 3, 1 January–1 May 1926, box 11; and for additional statements against the medical profession see CR nos. 35, 33, and 27, 1 January–1 May 1926, box 11, all in ABCL Papers.

134. Sanger's mother was Catholic; Sanger was raised Catholic but raised her children Episcopalian. According to Grant, Sanger "just couldn't stand the Irish Catholics.... They were ignorant, and they were the Irish types that she abominated" (Grant Sanger interview, 53–55).

135. Sanger, *Margaret Sanger*, 416.

136. *Woman Rebel* 1, no. 1 (March 1914): 1–3, 8.

137. Chesler, *Woman of Valor*, 271–72, 300.

138. James F. Cooper, "Report on Dallas Texas A.M.A. Meeting," 20–23 April 1926, box 11, ABCL Papers; Sanger, *Margaret Sanger*, 417.

139. The religious affiliation of Congress was Senate, 90 Protestants, 4 Catholics, and 2 Mormons; House of Representatives, 393 Protestants, 34 Catholics, 1 Mormon, and 7 Jews.

140. Kennedy, CR nos. 23 and 40, 1 January–1 May 1926, box 11, ABCL Papers.

141. Kennedy, "Short Synopsis of Interviews with Senators," 1 May 1926, box 11; Kennedy, CR nos. 33, 30, 22, and 19, 1 January–1 May 1926, box 11, all in ABCL Papers.

142. Kennedy, "Short Synopsis," 1 May 1926, box 11; and Kennedy, CR no. 38, 19 April 1926, box 11, both in ABCL Papers. Kennedy did not explain her interviewing so few members; perhaps the ABCL lacked adequate staff to question each House member.

143. "A Report to the Trustees Covering the Years 1928, 1929, 1930," 76–80. Chesler argues that Sanger left the ABCL not only to head the BCCRB but also because she

was not prepared to follow new regulations passed in her absence (she spent eighteen months in Europe). Sanger also disagreed with the board's views. Last, she was "testy" toward the second generation of reformers who "thought they knew better than she did" (Chesler, *Woman of Valor*, 238).

144. "Interview with Dr. Alice C. Boughton," 17 April 1931, file 162, series 3, box 7, BSH Records.

145. Piotrow, *World Population Crisis*, 8.

146. "Katharine Bement Davis to Mr. Raymond B. Fosdick," 9 December 1927, file 173, series 3, box 7, BSH Records; and "CMH Statement."

147. Mrs. Alan F. Guttmacher, interview with James W. Reed, November 1974, 4–5, Family Planning Oral History Project; and U.S. Congress, Senate, Committee on the Judiciary, *Hearings*, 4.

148. Sarah Marcus, M.D., interview with Ellen Chesler, April and September 1976, ii–iv, 16–25; and Emily Hartshorne Mudd, interview with James W. Reed, May–August 1974, 26–31, Family Planning Oral History Project.

149. Twin City Hospital was a segregated facility.

150. *House Patients, Twin City Hospital.*

151. *House Patients, Twin City Hospital.*

152. Mohr, *Abortion in America*, 240–42.

153. Salem College is one of the oldest American female colleges.

154. *State v. Walter L. Johnson*, 41 R.I. 253 (1918).

155. Reagan, *When Abortion Was a Crime*, 37, 70.

156. *Providence Evening Bulletin*, 5 August 1921, 1.

157. *Providence Evening Bulletin*, 24 November 1924, 2; *Providence Journal*, 22 March 1926, 4.

158. *Providence Evening Bulletin*, 8 September 1921, 4, 25 January 1923, 4, 11 April 1923, 3, 27 August 1923, 4, 20 February 1924, 2, 20 May 1924, 4, 3 June 1924, 4, 29 June 1926, 3, 23 November 1926, 3, 22 July 1926, 1, 15 November 1927, 1.

159. "R. Topping to Mr. Dunham," 5 January 1932, file 162, series 3, box 7; "American Birth Control League," 5 and 9 January 1934, file 163, series 3, box 7; and "American Birth Control League," 1935, file 163, series 3, box 7, all in BSH Records.

Chapter 4. Population Control and the Great Depression, 1930–1939

1. S. J. Holmes, "Will Birth Control Lead to Extinction?" *Scientific Monthly* 34 (March 1932): 247, 250; "Approval Is Seen on Birth Control," *Evening Star* (Washington, D.C.), 5 June 1935. See Hofstadter, *Social Darwinism*; Haller, *Eugenics*.

2. Hutchins interview, 20; Loraine Leeson Campbell, interview with James W. Reed, December 1973–March 1974, 28, Family Planning Oral History Project; and Mudd interview, 27.

3. "A Report to the Trustees Covering the Years 1928, 1929, 1930," 76–80; "Birth Control for Jobless New Goal," *Providence Journal*, Social Section, bk. 2, and "Birth Control League to Open Sessions," *New York Herald Tribune*, Social Section, bk. 2, both in PPRI Records. When I examined the PPRI records in the summer of 1997, they were housed at the clinic. In the spring of 1998 they were moved to the Rhode Island Historical Society. My citations correspond to the PPRI filing system.

4. Sydenstricker and Perrott, "Sickness," 127, 129–30, 132–33.

5. Bromley, "Birth Control," 563–64; *Providence Journal*, 9 April 1935, 10 October 1935.

6. Mudd interview, 33; James Rorty, "What's Stopping Birth Control?" *New Republic*, 3 February 1932, 313–14; Bromley, "Birth Control," 563–64.

7. Pearl, "Preliminary Notes," 46, 53; Pearl, "Second Progress Report," 250, 258, 268–69; Pearl, "Third Progress Report," 258, 260, 266–67, 271–72, 279–81; Pearl, "Fertility," 505.

8. The 1930s introduction of latex condoms increased sales, with 1.5 million produced daily at about a dollar per dozen, most within disease prevention, dissociating the condom from sexual pleasure and reproduction and sidestepping prohibitions on contraceptives. See Gamson, "Rubber Wars," 265, 277.

9. Andrea Tone, "Political Economy," in Tone, *Controlling Reproduction*, 212; Tone, *Devices and Desires*, xvi, 152, 163, 165, 170.

10. Petchesky, *Abortion*, 10.

11. Clinics by state: Arizona, 1; California, 20; Colorado, 1; Delaware, 1; Florida, 1; Illinois, 9; Iowa, 1; Maryland, 1; Massachusetts, 1; Michigan, 6; Minnesota, 2; New Jersey, 3; New York, 23; Ohio, 4; Pennsylvania, 9; Rhode Island, 1; Virginia, 1; West Virginia, 1. See U.S. Congress, House, Committee on Ways and Means, *Report*, 22.

12. *Providence Journal*, 5 March 1931, 2.

13. About a thousand people at the conference called on FDR to distribute contraceptives through public health and social welfare programs; he refused to meet delegates. See Chesler, *Woman of Valor*, 344.

14. "Goldstein Asks U.S. Sanction Birth Control," *New York Herald Tribune*, 16 January 1934; "Says Birth Control Gains Public Favor," *Providence Journal*, 22 January 1932.

15. Gordon, *Woman's Body*, 309; Bromley, "Birth Control," 567–68. Some social workers may have been a legacy of middle-class Progressives. Their "moral superiority" may have influenced their decisions as to who should limit families. Gordon concluded that most social workers were "condescending": they believed they "knew what kind of help was good for the poor" and considered their clients "the problem," not as "having problems" (*Woman's Body*, 320). Yet other social workers were genuinely concerned with maternal and infant health and mortality. They sent women to clinics to help, not control, them.

16. *Providence Journal*, 14 October 1936; *Star Eagle* (Newark, N.J.), 16 February 1935, 4.

17. "Fraud of Sterilization," *Commonweal*, 21 February 1936, 451–52.

18. U.S. Congress, House, Committee on Ways and Means, *Report*, 18.

19. "American Birth Control League," n.d., file 4, series 3, box 1, BSH Records; U.S. Congress, Senate, Committee on the Judiciary, *Hearings*, 31; Grant Sanger interview, 25; Chesler, *Woman of Valor*, 326–27.

20. Sanger, *Margaret Sanger*, 417–20.

21. Ibid., 417–20.

22. U.S. Congress, House, Committee on Ways and Means, *Report*, 51. Charlotte Perkins Gilman also spoke of a woman's "right to decide," not whether or not to have

children but "how often" she would perform her "duty, in childbearing, to improve the human race." Gilman believed poor, "defective" women had no right to procreate, while rich, educated women had no right *not* to procreate (U.S. Congress, House, Committee on Ways and Means, *Report*, 55–57).

23. Sanger's advocacy of a doctors-only bill eliminated feminist demands for birth control. At the 1932 hearings Sanger argued that condoms were "generally unsafe" when bought "over the counter" and were reliable only with proper medical instructions (U.S. Congress, Senate, Committee on the Judiciary, *Hearings*, 14; Grant Sanger interview, 51). The Bureau of Social Hygiene also supported a doctors-only bill. See Dunham to Fosdick, 19 March 1931, file 166, series 3, box 7; "American Birth Control League," 19 April 1932, file 162, series 3, box 7, both in BSH Records.

24. U.S. Congress, Senate, Committee on the Judiciary, *Hearings*, 2, 31, 36, 10, 11, 5, 32–35, 48, 55. Similar arguments were made before the House Committee on HR 11082. See U.S. Congress, House, Committee on Ways and Means, *Report*, 138, 7, 58, 43, 44, 50.

25. U.S. Congress, Senate, Committee on the Judiciary, *Hearings*, 2; U.S. Congress, House, Committee on Ways and Means, *Report*, 57; Sanger, *Margaret Sanger*, 422–23; Robert S. Allan, "Congress and Birth Control," *Nation*, 27 January 1932, 104–5.

26. The Population Reference Bureau, established in 1930, distributed data concerning "population problems" and published research in the *Population Bulletin*, a quarterly bulletin with Guy Irving Burch, a student of Fairchild, as general editor. Ruth Topp to Mr. Lawrence Dunham, 1 May 1931, file 190, series 3, box 9, BSH Records; U.S. Congress, Senate, Committee on the Judiciary, *Hearings*, 8, 11–12, 36, 60; U.S. Congress, House, Committee on Ways and Means, *Report*, 6, 8, 14, 26, 33, 34, 55, 57.

27. U.S. Congress, Senate, Committee on the Judiciary, *Hearings*, 8, 43, 55–57; U.S. Congress, House, Committee on Ways and Means, *Report*, 30, 8, 140, 47, 59, 28, 33.

28. The House committee voted nineteen to four against the bill because it was "too controversial" to take up congressional time during this period of "economic unrest and discontent" (U.S. Congress, House, Committee on Ways and Means, *Report*, 2).

29. U.S. Congress, Senate, Committee on the Judiciary, *Hearings*, 23.

30. U.S. Congress, House, Committee on Ways and Means, *Report*, 1, 78–80; Allan, "Congress," 104–5; "Mrs. Sanger Asks Congress to Act," Political Section, bk. 2, PPRI Records. Ryan opposed contraception based on Catholic doctrine but chose politically expedient terms to voice his objections and remained silent on the church's official stance. For more on the church and birth control see Sulloway, *Birth Control*; Campbell, "Birth Control"; Noonan, *Contraception*; Egner, *Contraception*.

31. U.S. Congress, Senate, Committee on the Judiciary, *Hearings*, 64, 75, 79, 80–81, 65–66, 68–69, 77; U.S. Congress, House, Committee on Ways and Means, *Report*, 93, 72, 73, 55–56, 115, 75, 89, 112, 91.

32. Chesler, *Woman of Valor*, 339.

33. As with mainland tactics, no effort was made to reform abortion, which remained a felony. U.S. Congress, Senate, Committee on Interoceanic Canals, *Hearings*, 13, 84–85.

34. Sanger, *Margaret Sanger*, 429–30; U.S. Congress, House, Committee on Ways and Means, *Report*, 31–33, 41, 58.

35. U.S. Congress, Senate, Committee on the Judiciary, *Extract*; U.S. Congress, House, Committee on the Judiciary, *Extract*; Sanger, *Margaret Sanger*, 424–25; "Congress Will Get Birth Control Bills," *Providence Journal*, 16 January 1934; "Birth Control: Capitol Has Bill to Repeal Comstock Law," *Newsweek*, 27 January 1934, 28.

36. "Document 10: Proposal to Amend the Comstock Act to Allow Doctors to Prescribe Contraceptives. Testimony Opposing the Amendment by Father Charles E. Coughlin, 1934," in Rubin, *The Abortion Controversy*, 30; "Birth Control: Capitol Has Bill to Repeal Comstock Law," *Newsweek*, 27 January 1934, 28; "Birth Control Act Hearing Crowded," *Providence Journal*, 19 January 1934; Emma Bugbee, "'Commercial' Hint Stirs Ire of Mrs. Sanger," *New York Herald Tribune*, 20 January 1934.

37. U.S. Congress, House, Committee on the Judiciary, *Extract*, 5–8, 63, 96–97; "Birth Control Act Hearing Crowded."

38. "Birth Control Move Gaining," *Washington Post*, 29 May 1935.

39. Chester T. Crowell, "Babies Just Babies," *New Republic*, 29 May 1935, 71.

40. *Farm and Fireside* and *Churchman* surveys quoted in Wecter, *Age of the Great Depression*, 179; *Fortune*, 14 July 1936, 158; Gallup, *Gallup Poll Public Opinion, 1935–1971*, 41.

41. May, *Homeward Bound*, 40, 93.

42. Blanchard, *The Anti-Abortion Movement*, 12.

43. Grant Sanger interview, 26.

44. Sanger, *Margaret Sanger*, 427; Dienes, *Law, Politics, and Birth Control*, 109.

45. *United States v. One Package*, 13 F. Supp. 334 (E.D. N.Y. 1936), aff'd F. 2d 737 (2d Cir. 1936); Sanger, *Margaret Sanger*, 427.

46. *United States v. Dennet*, 39, F. 2d 564 (2d Cir. 1930); *United States v. One Obscene Book Entitled "Marriage Love,"* 48 F. 22d 821 (S.D.N.Y. 1931); *United States v. One Book Entitled "Contraception,"* 51 F. 2d 525 (S.D.N.Y. 1931); *Young's Rubber Co. v. C. T. Lee and Co.*, 45 F. 2d 103 (2d Cir. 1930).

47. Chesler, *Woman of Valor*, 331; Gamson, "Rubber Wars," 269–70; Gordon, *Woman's Body*, 319; Tone, *Devices and Desires*, 149, 151–54.

48. Tone, *Devices and Desires*, 115, 134–35, 138; Meyer, *Any Friend of the Movement*, 15, 44; Piotrow, *World Population Crisis*, 8.

49. Chesler, *Woman of Valor*, 376–77; Reed, *From Private Vice*, 266; Grey, *New Deal Medicine*, 98, 9, 10, 16, 172; Schoen, *Choice & Coercion*, 55–56.

50. Mary Steichen Calderone, M.D., interview with James W. Reed, August 1974, 11–12, Family Planning Oral History Project.

51. Much of North Carolina's public health expansion was funded by out-of-state sources, namely, the Rockefeller Foundation, the United States Public Health Service, and the Children's Bureau. See Reed, *From Private Vice*, 253.

52. Historian James Reed cites reasons for this low percentage: no significant campaigns to reach clients occurred, some doctors believed patients had no use for services, and some health officers argued that large families continued to be an asset in many rural areas (*From Private Vice*, 253–55). See also Schoen, *Choice & Coercion*, 60.

53. Reed, *From Private Vice*, 252–57.

54. "Birth Control: South Carolina Uses It for Public Health," *Life*, 6 May 1940, 64–68; U.S. Congress, Senate, Committee on Government Operations, *Hearings* (1965); Schoen, "Fighting for Child Health," 90–113.

55. Briggs, *Reproducing Empire*, 74–76.

56. Hartman, *Reproductive Rights*, 231–32.

57. Cadbury, "Outlook," 319–20; Thimmesch, "Puerto Rico," 252–62; Curt, "Puerto Rico," 229–30; Piotrow, *World Population Crisis*, 31–32.

58. Shapiro, *Population*, 53; Cadbury, "Outlook," 320; Reed, *From Private Vice*, 259–60; Gordon, *Woman's Body*, 332; Briggs, *Reproducing Empire*, 149.

59. Tone, *Devices and Desires*, 86; Roberts, *Killing the Black Body*, 78, 82–83.

60. Kelly Miller, "Eugenics of the Negro Race," *Scientific Monthly* 5 (July 1917): 57–59; Rodrique, "The Black Community," 336.

61. Cobb, "The Negro as a Biological Element," 345–46.

62. W.E.B. DuBois, "Black Folk and Birth Control," *Birth Control Review* (June 1932): 166–67; George Schuyler, "Quantity or Quality," *Birth Control Review* (June 1932): 165–66; Charles H. Garvin, "The Negro Doctor's Task," *Birth Control Review* (November 1932): 269–70.

63. Hill, *The Marcus Garvey*, 7:603–5.

64. Rodrique, "The Black Community," 339–40.

65. DuBois, "The Damnation of Women"; DuBois, "Birth"; Garvin, "The Negro Doctor's Task"; Chandler Owen, "Women and Children of the South," *Birth Control Review* 3 (September 1919): 9, 20; Rodrique, "The Black Community," 336.

66. Mary Burrill, "They That Sit in Darkness," *Birth Control Review* 3 (September 1919): 5–8; Grimké, *Rachel*.

67. Ross, "African-American Women," 168.

68. Ross, "African-American Women," 169, 171.

69. Newell L. Sims, "Hostages to the White Man," *Birth Control Review* 16 (July–August 1932): 214–15; Rodrique, "The Black Community," 337; Smith, *Sick and Tired*, 92–93; Roberts, *Killing the Black Body*, 86.

70. The Birth Control Federation of America was the name given to the reorganized ABCL in 1939.

71. "American Birth Control League," 3 December 1932, file 162, series 3, box 7, BSH Records; Rodrique, "The Black Community," 339; Ross, "African-American Women," 168; Roberts, *Killing the Black Body*, 101.

72. Ross, "African-American Women," 277–78; Ross, "African-American Women," 170–71; Rodrique, "The Black Community," 341.

73. Schoen, *Choice & Coercion*, 44.

74. This group was established in 1927 following the First World Population Conference in Geneva. See "Population Problems," 4 July 1931, file 191, series 3, box 9, BSH Records.

75. "A Report to the Trustees Covering the Years 1928, 1929, 1930," 79; *Historical Statistics*, 51; Ross, "African-American Women," 277–78; Rodrique, "The Black Community," 339; McCann, *Birth Control Politics*, 136–37, 146; McFalls and Masnick, "Birth Control," 89–106; McBride, "Medicine and the Health Crisis," 112–16; Ross, "African-

American Women," 161–207; Rodrique, "The Black Community"; Tolnay, "The Decline of Black Marital Fertility," 211, 217; Tolnay, "Family Economy," 267–83; Masnick and McFalls, "A New Perspective," 217–44; Engerman, "Black Fertility," 117–38.

76. Executive Secretary's Report, February 1947, file 1947, PPRI Records.

77. Annual Report, 7 May 1931, file 1931; *Manual for Board of Directors 1948–1949*, 28 April 1948, 7–13, file 1948; Mrs. Lomas Memo, n.d., file 1935; Report Given by Mrs. Henry Salomon, 21 January 1932, file 1932; Annual Report of the President, 2 November 1933, file 1933; and Minutes of the Board of Directors, 12 June 1940, all in PPRI Records.

78. Minutes of Committee on Contraceptive Advice of the RIBCL, 12 June 1931, file 1931, PPRI Records; *Providence Journal*, 29 July 1931, 1.

79. *Providence Journal*, 7 August 1931, 1, 4 September 1931, 1; Minutes of Regular Monthly Meeting, 5 November 1931, file 1931, PPRI Records; H 736, *Failed Bills of 1935*, 12 March 1935, 35, State Archives; Report of the Executive Secretary—Five Months, November 1939–April 1940, file 1940, PPRI Records; "25th Anniversary," 11 April 1956, file 1956, PPRI Records.

80. Report of the Social Worker, February 1932, file 1932; Report of Chairman of Advisory Board Birth Control League of R.I., 3 November 1932, file 1932; Social Worker's Report, file 1933; Annual Report of the Social Worker, 1 November 1938–1 November 1939, file 1939; and Report of the President of the RIBCL, 20 January 1939, file 1939, all in PPRI Records.

81. Report of the Social Worker for September 1931, file 1931; Social Worker's Report, February 1932, file 1932; Notes for Talks on Birth Control, n.d., file 1933; Annual Report of Social Worker, 1 November 1934–1 November 1935, file 1935; Annual Report of Social Worker, 1 November 1935–1 November 1936, file 1936; Annual Report of Social Worker, 1 November 1936–1 November 1937, file 1937; Annual Report of Social Worker, 1 November 1937–1 November 1938, file 1938; and Annual Report of Social Worker, 1 November 1938–1 November 1939, file 1939, all in PPRI Records.

82. Tone, *Devices and Desires*, 136.

83. Kopp studied medicine for 3.5 years but discontinued for family reasons. She later completed her doctorate in philosophy, not medicine, at the University of Ferrara. Marie E. Kopp, Resume 1932, file 183, series 3, box 8, BSH Records.

84. Marcus interview, 18–25; Kopp, *Birth Control in Practice*, 133; Himes, *Medical History of Contraception*, 336–37.

85. Monthly Reports of Social Worker, file 1932; Monthly Reports of Social Worker, file 1933; Monthly Reports of Social Worker, file 1935; Annual Report of the Social Worker, 1 November 1935–1 November 1936, file 1936; Annual Report of the Social Worker, 1 November 1937–1 November 1938, file 1938; Annual Statistical Report of the Social Workers, April 1940–April 1941, file 1941; Annual Statistical Report of the Social Workers, April 1941–April 1942, file 1942; and Supplementary Annual Report of Social Worker, March 1943, file 1943, all in PPRI Records.

86. Report of the Social Worker, February 1932, file 1932; Report of Chairman of Advisory Board Birth Control League of R.I., 3 November 1932, file 1932; Social Worker's Report, file 1933; Annual Report of the Social Worker, 1 November 1938–1 November

1939, file 1939; and Report of the President of the RIBCL, 20 January 1939, file 1939, all in PPRI Records.

87. The "other" category included referrals from the Birth Control Research Bureau, husbands, employers, and midwives.

88. Reports of the Physician in Charge, 1931, file 1931; Social Worker's Reports, 1932, file 1932; Statistics for June, July, August 1932, file 1932; Reports of the Social Worker, 1933, file 1933; Annual Report of the Social Worker, file 1935; Annual Report of the Social Worker, file 1936; Annual Report of the Social Worker, file 1937; Annual Report of the Social Worker, file 1938; and Annual Report of the Social Worker, file 1939, all in PPRI Records.

89. Annual Report of the Social Worker, 1 November 1938–1 November 1939, file 1939, PPRI Records. For national trends see Tone, *Devices and Desires*, 135; Meyer, *Any Friend of the Movement*, 31.

90. Annual Report of the Social Worker, 1 November 1938–1 November 1939, file 1939, PPRI Records.

91. Report of Social Worker, September 1932, file 1932; Report of the Social Worker, March 1933, and Social Worker Reports, file 1933; and Supplementary Report for November 1940, file 1940, all in PPRI Records.

92. Six Months' Review, 1 November 1934–1 May 1935, file 1935; Annual Report of Social Worker, file 1935; Annual Report of Social Worker, file 1936; Annual Report of Social Worker, file 1937; Annual Report of Social Worker, file 1938; Annual Report of Social Worker, file 1939; and Supplementary Annual Report of Social Workers, file 1941, all in PPRI Records.

93. Report of the Social Worker, August 1931, file 1931; and Social Worker's Monthly Report, January 1942, file 1942, both in PPRI Records.

94. Annual Report of the Social Worker, November 1932, file 1932; Annual Report of Social Worker, 1 November 1935–1 November 1936, file 1936; and Annual Report of Social Worker, 1 November 1938–1 November 1939, file 1939, all in PPRI Records.

95. *Providence Journal*, 3 November 1933, 8; Address by Mrs. F. Robertson Jones Delivered at the Annual Meeting of the RIBCL, 2 November 1933, file 1933, PPRI Records.

96. RIBCL to Richard S. Aldrich, 6 May 1932, Legislative Action 1934 file; and RIBCL to Senator Felix Hebert, 8 May 1934, Legislative Action 1934 file, both in PPRI Records.

97. Notes for B.C. Talks—M. S. Foster, n.d., file 1933, PPRI Records.

98. Meyer, *Any Friend of the Movement*, xv, xx–xi, 26, 32, 85, 109.

99. Reagan, *When Abortion Was a Crime*, 133, 149–53, 155.

100. Reports of the Physician in Charge for August 1931, October 1931, and November 1931, file 1931; Annual Report of the Social Worker, 1 November 1934–1 November 1935, file 1935; Notes for Talks on Birth Control, file 1933; and Annual Reports of the Social Workers, files 1936, 1937, 1938, 1939, all in PPRI Records.

101. *Providence Evening Bulletin*, 10 March 1931, 4; *Providence Journal*, 13 November 1932, 11; *Providence Evening Bulletin*, 9 May 1933, 21; *State v. Concetta Guaraneri*, 59 R.I. 173; 194 A. 589, 1937.

102. Rongy, *Abortion: Legal or Illegal?* 36–37, 40–41, 56, 73, 112.

103. Ibid., 112, 115–16, 96–97.

104. Ibid., 108–9, 140–47, 21.

105. Rongy estimated that abortion fees ranged from $50 to $250 during the 1920s and 1930s (*Abortion: Legal or Illegal?* 137).

106. Rongy, *Abortion: Legal or Illegal?* 103, 133–34, 136, 143.

107. Ibid., 200–209.

108. Reagan, *When Abortion Was a Crime*, 143.

109. Ladd-Taylor, "Saving Babies," 138; Reilly, *Surgical Solution*, 93, 101; Larson, *Sex*, 119; Paul, *Controlling Human Heredity*, 84.

110. Haller, *Eugenics*, 160–63; Petchesky, *Abortion*, 87.

111. HBF, *Human Sterilization*, n.d., file 545, box 5, Poteat Collection.

112. HBF, "Effects of Eugenical Sterilization as Practiced in California," n.d., file 178, series 3, box 8, BSH Records; HBF, *Human Sterilization*.

113. "Mrs. Sanger Hits New Deal Attitude on Birth Control," *Providence Journal*, 9 April 1935.

114. Laughlin quoted in Kühl, *Nazi Connection*, 48.

115. Laughlin, *Eugenical Sterilization*, 338–39; "Sterilization Laws," *Science*, 4 December 1936, supp. 9–10; "Sterilization Operation Performed in the United States," *Science*, 11 December 1936, supp. 7; J. H. Landman, "Sterilization—A Pointedly Frank Discussion of a Grave Social Problem," *Current History* 44 (August 1936): 91.

116. HBF, "Human Sterilization," n.d., file 190, series 3, box 9, BSH Records; HBF, "Effects of Eugenical Sterilization"; HBF, *Human Sterilization*.

117. Landman, *Current History*, 93–94; "CMH Statement."

118. U.S. Congress, House, Committee to Investigate the Interstate Migration of Destitute Citizens, *Interstate Migration*, 305.

119. Popenoe and Gosney, *Twenty-Eight Years of Sterilization in California*, ii–6, 14; HBF, "A Report to All Our Correspondents," 1933, file 178, series 3, box 8, BSH Records.

120. Reilly, *Surgical Solution*, 94–98; Braslow, "In the Name of Therapeutics," 45; Carey, "Gender and Compulsory Sterilization," 74–105; Ladd-Taylor, "Saving Babies," 136–53.

121. Smith, *Eugenic Assault*, 6; Kühl, *Nazi Connection*, 23–39; Whitney and Kopp quoted in Kühl, *Nazi Connection*, 36, 56. Unlike American eugenicists, those in Great Britain were "relatively critical" of Nazi Germany.

122. Campbell quoted in Kühl, *Nazi Connection*, 34–35.

123. Myerson et al., *Eugenical Sterilization*, 2–5, 24; "Sterilization Flayed," *Time*, 16 November 1936, 80; Myerson, "Sterilization," *Atlantic Monthly* 186 (November 1950): 52; "Racial Superiority and Sterilization," *Science*, 15 November 1935, supp. 7; "People's Foundation," 11 April 1932, file 178, series 3, box 8, BSH Records.

124. Kühl, *Nazi Connection*, 77–78; Paul, *Controlling Human Heredity*, 120; "Eugenics Research Association," 27 April 1932, file 178, series 3, box 8, BSH Records; Reilly, *Surgical Solution*, 122–23; Dowbiggin, *Keeping America Sane*, 98–99, 114.

125. "Methodist Conference Approves Sterilization," *Commonweal*, 26 April 1940, 2–3; Myerson, "Sterilization," 52.

126. S 203, 7 March 1940, *Failed Bills of 1940*, 40–44, State Archives.

127. Report of Clinic Committee for November 1935, file 1935, PPRI Records.

128. Russell Owen, "Hawaii Experimenting with Birth Control, Sterilization," *Providence Journal*, 1932, Social Section, bk. 2, PPRI Records.

129. "Hawaii Debates a Sterilization Law," *America*, 11 April 1953, 34.

130. Ross, "African-American Women," 278; *Pittsburgh Courier*, 30 March 1935, 10. See also Rodrique, "The Black Community," 337–38.

131. Robert A. Cook, "Population Policy and the Japanese Peace Treaty," *Population Bulletin* 7 (August 1951): 12–15; see also Landman, *Current History*, 91; Abraham Myerson, *Speaking of Man* (New York: Knopf, 1950).

132. Quoted in Kühl, *Nazi Connection*, 60.

133. Kühl, *Nazi Connection*, 59–63.

134. Kühl, *Nazi Connection*, 79–80, 105; Dowbiggin, *Keeping America Sane*, 79; Braslow, "In the Name of Therapeutics," 49; Paul, *The Politics of Heredity*, 103–4, 129.

135. Kline, *Gender, Sexuality, and Eugenics*, 4, 6; Briggs, *Reproducing Empire*, 126.

Chapter 5. World War II, the Baby Boom, and the Population Explosion, 1939–1963

1. "Parran Assails National Health" and "Draft Rejections Pass 40 Percent," Health of Draftees 1941 file, box 15, Rhode Island Medical Society Collection, Rhode Island Historical Society Library (hereafter cited as RIMS, RIHS Library); Farley quoted in Burch, "America's Manpower," 5; Burch, "Is American Intelligence Declining?" 19.

2. Truman quoted in Burch, "Is American Intelligence Declining?" 14.

3. "Doctor Discusses Draftee's Health," "Our Unfit Youth; Fact or Fancy," and *Government Service* 26, no. 2, all in Health of Draftees 1941 file, box 15, RIMS, RIHS Library. Similar conclusions can be found in "Health of Young Men under Selective Service," *Journal of the American Medical Association*, 4 January 1941, and National Headquarters, Selective Service System, Washington, D.C., Release no. 195, 22 April 1941, both in Health of Draftees 1941 file, RIMS, RIHS Library; "Analysis of Reports of Physical Examination," *Medical Statistics Bulletin*, 10 November 1941, and "Cause of Rejection and Incidence of Defects," *Medical Statistics Bulletin*, 1 August 1943, both in Analysis of Draftee Examination Data file, 1941, 1943, box 15, RIMS, RIHS Library.

4. Thomas Parran, "Why Don't We Stamp Out Syphilis?" *Reader's Digest* (July 1936): 65–73; Brandt, *No Magic Bullet*, 138–46, 156–59.

5. Cosmas and Cowdry, *Medical Department*, 22, 142–47; Lee, *The Employment of Negro Troops*, 240, 277, 280–89. Concern for the health and fitness of black soldiers did not extend to all black men. While the military paid attention to VD among black troops, the Public Health Service participated in the Tuskegee Syphilis Study in Alabama with four hundred black sharecroppers. Initiated in 1932, it attempted to discover the course of syphilis without medical intervention. For over forty years the Public Health Service informed these men that government doctors were treating the disease when in reality they received no medication. One quarter succumbed to tertiary syphilis. Brandt, *No Magic Bullet*, 157–58.

6. Cosmas and Cowdry, *Medical Department*, 144–45; Meyer, "Creating G.I. Jane," 582–87; May, *Homeward Bound*, 69–71.

7. Fairchild, "Family Limitation," 85; Mildred Gilman, "Babies: Quantity or Quality?" *American Mercury* 56 (April 1943): 450–55. Gilman pointed to an institute for the feebleminded in Mansfield, Connecticut, that had room for 1,000 patients with another 1,000 on a wait list. In one year, wait-listed women gave birth to 650 babies; Gilman would have prevented this "breeding" with contraceptives and, if necessary, sterilization.

8. Gordon, *Woman's Body*, 344–52.

9. Fairchild, "Family Limitation," 81; Chesler, *Woman of Valor*, 390; Gordon, *Woman's Body*, 347; Paul, *Controlling Human Heredity*, 121; Kolbert and Miller, "Legal Strategies," 77.

10. Fairchild, "Family Limitation," 81; "Doctors on Contraception," *Newsweek*, 24 February 1947, 58.

11. "From Birth Control to Fertility," *Time*, 27 October 1941, 74.

12. "The Fortune Survey," *Fortune* 28 (August 1943): 24, 30.

13. Fairchild, "Family Limitation," 82; Chesler, *Woman of Valor*, 387–90.

14. May, *Homeward Bound*, 149; Gordon, *Woman's Body*, 336–53; Chesler, *Woman of Valor*, 393–95.

15. Minutes of the Annual Meeting, 14 November 1939, Minutes of the Meeting of the Clinic Committee, 26 January 1939, file 1939; Report of the Executive Secretary—Five Months, November 1939–April 1940, Minutes of the Board of Directors, 12 June 1940, 13 November 1940, file 1940; Report of the President, 8 April 1942, file 1942; Social Service Department Report, 18 April 1951, file 1951; Five Year Plan, 1946–51, file 1946; Supplementary Annual Report of Social Worker, April 1940–April 1941, file 1941, all in PPRI Records.

16. Annual Report of Executive Secretary, 14 November 1939, file 1939; Minutes of the May Meeting of the Board of Directors, 8 May 1940; Report of Executive Secretary on Birth Control Federation Board Meeting Held in New York City, 15 May 1940, file 1940, all in PPRI Records.

17. Annual Report of the President of RIBCL, 7 November 1938, file 1937 [*sic*]; Minutes of the May Meeting of the Board of Directors, 8 May 1940, Supplementary Report for November 1940, file 1940; Workers Manual for Tenth Annual Campaign of the RIMHA, March 1941, file 1941; Supplementary Annual Report of the Social Worker, April 1942, Report of the President, 8 April 1942, file 1942, all in PPRI Records.

18. Workers' Manual for Tenth Annual Campaign of RIMHA, March 1941, Supplementary Report for 1 October 1941, file 1941; Minutes of the Board of Directors, 12 April 1944, and D. Kenneth Rose to Elizabeth G. Lisle, 22 May 1944, Summary of Discussion by Members of the Board on State Financial Participation, October 1944, file 1944, in PPRI Records.

19. Supplementary Annual Report of Social Worker, August 1940–April 1941, Minutes of the Board of Directors, 12 February 1941, 14 May 1941, file 1941; Annual Report of the President, April 1944, Report of the Meeting in New York, 19 October 1944, file 1944; Annual Report, 1945, file 1945; Minutes of Executive Committee Meeting, 18 June 1946, file 1946, all in PPRI Records.

20. Minutes of the Board of Directors, 13 November 1940, file 1940; Workers' Man-

ual for Tenth Annual Campaign of the RIMHA, March 1941, Minutes of the Board of Directors, 12 November 1941 and 10 December 1941, file 1941; Report of the President, 14 April 1943, Supplementary Annual Report of Social Worker, March 1943, file 1943, all in PPRI Records.

21. Monthly Reports of Social Worker, file 1932; Monthly Reports of Social Worker, file 1933; Monthly Reports of Social Worker, file 1935; Annual Report of the Social Worker, 1 November 1935–1 November 1936, file 1936; Annual Report of the Social Worker, 1 November 1937–1 November 1938, file 1938; Annual Statistical Report of the Social Workers, April 1940–April 1941, file 1941; Annual Statistical Report of the Social Workers, April 1941–April 1942, file 1942; Supplementary Annual Report of Social Worker, March 1943, file 1943, all in PPRI Records; U.S. Bureau of the Census, *Fifteenth Census*, 755, 771; U.S. Bureau of the Census, *Sixteenth Census*, 290, 320.

22. Meyer, *Any Friend of the Movement*, 88.

23. "Major Relationships of Urban League of Rhode Island," n.d., no. 2, box 10, file 398; and "National Leaders Agree—Planned Parenthood Means Better Families," no. 7, box 2, folder 60, both in Urban League of Rhode Island Papers.

24. Annual Meeting of the RIMHA, April 1943, Report of the President, 14 April 1943, Minutes of Board Meeting, 13 October 1943, file 1943; Minutes of Board Meeting, January 1944, 8 March 1944, Executive Secretary's Annual Report, 27 April 1944, file 1944, all in PPRI Records; "Major Relationships of Urban League of Rhode Island."

25. Supplementary Annual Report of the Social Worker, April 1942, Minutes of October Board Meeting, 1942, Social Worker's Report, September 1942, file 1942; Supplementary Social Worker's Annual Report for 1943, file 1943; Executive Secretary's Annual Report, 27 April 1944, Untitled Report, January 1944, file 1944; President's Annual Report, April 1946, file 1946, all in PPRI Records.

26. In 1940 the RIMHA served one hundred clients from Massachusetts and ten from Connecticut. Report of the President, 24 January 1941, file 1941, PPRI Records.

27. Annual Report of the Social Worker, 1 November 1939, file 1939; Report for the Providence Maternal Health Center, 1 April 1940, Supplementary Report, September 1940, Minutes of the Clinic Meeting, May 1940, file 1940; Social Worker's Supplementary Summer Report, 1941, Supplementary Annual Report of Social Worker, April 1941, file 1941; Annual Statistical Report of the Social Workers, April 1942, Minutes of Board Meeting, November 1942, file 1942; Clinic Total Sheet, April 1943, Annual Meeting of the RIMHA, April 1943, Supplementary Annual Report of Social Worker, March 1943, file 1943; Untitled Report, January 1944, Annual Meeting of the RIMHA, April 1944, file 1944; Annual Meeting of the RIMHA, April 1945, and Annual Report 1945, file 1945; Social Worker's Report, April 1946, file 1946, all in PPRI Records.

28. President's Report, April 1945, Annual Report, 1945, file 1945; Outline of Activities, 1946, Executive Secretary's Annual Report, April 1946, President's Annual Report, April 1946, file 1946; Executive Secretary's Annual Report, April 1947, Social Worker's Report, April 1947, file 1947; Social Worker's Annual Report, April 1948, file 1947 [*sic*], all in PPRI Records.

29. Reilly, *Surgical Solution*, 95, 125.

30. "Protestant Babies," *Time,* 4 February 1946, 46.

31. Burch, "Is American Intelligence Declining?" 17–18; Burch, "A Revolution," 20; comments by Dr. H. J. Muller, 1946 Nobel Prize winner, and J. B. D. Haldane, British biologist, in Burch, "Is American Intelligence Declining?" 16–17; P. K. Whelpton and Clyde V. Kiser, *Milbank Memorial Fund Quarterly* (July 1943). See also Burch, "America's Manpower"; Burch, "Needed—Higher Birth Rate," 7.

32. Census data quoted in Burch, "Differences in Birth Rate," 25–26; Burch, "Birth Rates and Education," 3; Edgar Schmiedeler, OSB, "Are American Women Shirkers?" *Catholic World* 153 (July 1941): 426–29.

33. "Are You Too Educated to Be a Mother?" *Ladies Home Journal* 63 (June 1946): 6; "Fewer Babies and Why," *Collier's,* 2 December 1944, 86.

34. See May, *Homeward Bound.*

35. Bouvier, "America's Baby Boom," figure 1.

36. Bouvier, "America's Baby Boom," figure 3; Francis X. Murphy, CSSR, "Catholic Perspectives on Population Issues II," *Population Bulletin* 35 (February 1981): figure 3.

37. Easterlin, *American Baby Boom*; Friedan, *The Feminine Mystique*; Easterlin, *Population, Labor Force,* 18; DeJong and See, "Changes in Childlessness," 129–42; Bouvier, "America's Baby Boom," 8–9; Cherlin, "Explaining," 57–63; Nugent, *Structures,* 128; Hayden, *Redesigning the American Dream*; Minutes of Board Meeting, January 1944, file 1944, PPRI Records.

38. "Books versus Babies," *Newsweek,* 14 January 1946, 79.

39. "Are You Too Educated to Be a Mother?" 6.

40. Hartmann, *The Home Front and Beyond,* 70.

41. Elizabeth Cohen Arnold, interview with James Reed, November 1974, 42, 55–57, Family Planning Oral History Project. Sanger opposed the fertility clinic at the MSRB because she believed this service should remain in the hands of private physicians, not clinical workers. See Arnold interview, 42.

42. Calderone interview, 1–7, 25–26; Beatrice Blair, interview with Ellen Chesler, April 1976, 25–26, Family Planning Oral History Project; Marcus interview, 28–29.

43. Blair interview, 25–26; Calderone interview, 25; Marcus interview, 23–29; Campbell interview, 73.

44. Piotrow, *World Population Crisis,* 13–15. See also Shapiro, *Population,* chap. 3; Critchlow, *Intended Consequences,* 14, 27.

45. Campbell interview, 79–82.

46. Piotrow, *World Population Crisis,* 16.

47. Chesler, *Woman of Valor,* 438–39; Piotrow, *World Population Crisis,* 18–19; Reed, *From Private Vice,* 282–83.

48. Draper Report quoted in Piotrow, *World Population Crisis,* 36–41.

49. Eisenhower quoted in D. S. Greenberg, "Population Planning: 1963 Marked by Reduction of Controversy and Shift in Government Attitude," *Science,* 20 December 1963, 1554–55.

50. Piotrow, *World Population Crisis,* 42–46.

51. John F. Kennedy quoted in U.S. Congress, Senate, Committee on Government Operations, *Hearings* (1965), 1347; *New York Times,* 20 September 1961, 23.

52. Piotrow, *World Population Crisis,* 59–63.

53. United Nations document X/C. 2/L.657, in Gardner, *Population Growth*, 13.

54. The narrow defeat of this resolution, according to Gardner, was "the price that had to be paid for achieving a broad consensus among the membership" (*Population Growth*, 8–9). See also Gardner, "Toward a World Population Program," 350; Gardner, "The Politics of Population," 19. American public opinion seemed influenced by the emphasis on the population explosion. A Gallup poll in December 1959 found that only 54 percent favored contraceptive distribution to other nations versus 72 percent of Americans who agreed it should be available at home. By 1963 65 percent favored distribution to other nations; in 1965 77 percent approved. See Gallup, *Gallup Poll Public Opinion*, 1654, 1822; Erskine, "The Polls," 311.

55. National Academy of Sciences, Committee on Science and Public Policy, *The Growth of World Population*, 1–9; John F. Kennedy quoted in U.S. Congress, Senate, Committee on Government Operations, *Hearings* (1965), 1347; "Congress May Approve First Birth Control Bill in 1966," *Congressional Quarterly*, 10 June 1966, 1235–38.

56. Foreign Assistance Act of 1963, 88th Cong., 1st sess., Report no. 588, HR 7855, 19; U.S. Congress, Senate, Committee on Foreign Relations, *Legislation*, 19.

57. Eisenhower quoted in U.S. Congress, Senate, Committee on Government Operations, *Hearings* (1965), 1790. He made a similar statement in his article, "Let's Be Honest with Ourselves," *Saturday Evening Post*, 26 October 1963, 27.

58. "All about Birth Control," *Newsweek*, 7 January 1963, 36–37.

59. Watkins, *On the Pill*, 19–21, 28–29.

60. Briggs, *Reproducing Empire*, 130, quote on 140, 110.

61. The International Planned Parenthood Federation was formed in 1948 at an international conference held at Cheltenham.

62. Hartman, *Reproductive Rights*, 232; Mass, "Puerto Rico," 73; Cadbury, "Outlook," 321.

63. Briggs, *Reproducing Empire*, 148–49, 152–57.

64. Ramirez de Arellano and Seipp, *Colonialism*, 93–95; Minutes of Board of Directors Meeting, 10 May 1955, file 1955, PPRI Records.

65. Gamble quoted in Ramirez de Arellano and Seipp, *Colonialism*, 99, 107.

66. Hartman, *Reproductive Rights*, 177; McCormick quoted in Ramirez de Arellano and Seipp, *Colonialism*, 99, 107; Finch and Green, *Contraception through the Ages*, 115–16; Briggs, *Reproducing Empire*, chap. 3.

67. Watkins, *On the Pill*, 30–31; Tone, *Devices and Desires*, 220–22.

68. Mastroianni, Faden, and Federman, *Women and Health Research*, 118–19; Macklin, "Justice in International Research," 134–35; Tone, *Devices and Desires*, 222.

69. Chesler, *Woman of Valor*, 434–44; Reed, *From Private Vice*, 359–62; Ramirez de Arellano and Seipp, *Colonialism*, 116; Tone, *Devices and Desires*, 226.

70. Gordon, *Woman's Body*, 421, 177; Hardin, *Birth Control*, 82–83; Ramirez de Arellano and Seipp, *Colonialism*, 116–17.

71. Calderone interview, 21.

72. Minutes of Clinic Functions Committee, 30 October 1952, file 1952; Minutes of Board of Directors Meeting, 13 January 1953, and Annual Meeting, "Talk Given by Mrs. C. Tracy Barnes," 14 April 1953, file 1953; Minutes of Executive Committee Meeting,

24 September 1954, file 1954; Report of President, Annual Meeting 1955, Minutes of Joint Clinic Functions and Medical Advisory Committees, 23 May 1955, and Minutes of Board of Directors Meeting, 10 May 1955, file 1955, all in PPRI Records.

73. With FDA approval of the pill Searle sent fifteen thousand "detailmen" to convince physicians to prescribe it. See Watkins, *On the Pill*, 36–37.

74. *Providence Journal*, 9 April 1957, 4; RIMHA Minutes, 13 May 1958, file 1958; Board of Directors Meeting, 11 October 1960, and RIMHA Executive Committee Meeting, n.d., file 1960, all in PPRI Records; "Birth Control Pill under Probe Sold in R.I. since 1957," *Providence Journal*, 6 August 1962, 21.

75. Watkins, *On the Pill*, 32; Ramirez de Arellano and Seipp, *Colonialism*, 188; WHO task force member quoted in Hartman, *Reproductive Rights*, 177.

76. Cadbury, "Outlook," 321; Kantner and Stycos, "Non-Clinical Approach," 573–81; Vazquez, "Fertility and Decline," 864–65; Thimmesch, "Puerto Rico," 252–62.

77. Kantner and Stycos, "Non-Clinical Approach," 578; Thimmesch, "Puerto Rico," 252–62.

78. Schoen, *Choice & Coercion*, 210–11, 213.

79. Reagan, *When Abortion Was a Crime*, 15, 161–64; Ross, "African-American Women," 173.

80. Potter, Informal Talk Given to Brown-Pembroke Students, 13 April 1948, file 1948; Social Worker's Annual Report, April 1948, file 1947 [*sic*], both in PPRI Records; *State v. Peter Lorenzo*, 72 R.I. 175 (1946); *State v. Angelo*, 72 R.I. 412, 52 A. 2d 513 (1947); *General Laws of Rhode Island 1956*, 7–9; *Providence Journal*, 17 October 1959, 17; Mary Steichen Calderone, "E x A = BR," 29 November 1956, in PPRI Records.

81. Potter, Informal Talk; Social Worker's Annual Report, April 1948, file 1947 [*sic*], PPRI Records.

82. Kopp, *Birth Control in Practice*; Rubin, *The Abortion Controversy*, 36–37; Calderone, "E x A = BR"; Gebhard et al., *Pregnancy, Birth, and Abortion*, 162; Calderone, *Abortion in the United States*, 180; Schur, *Crimes without Victims*, 25; Tietze, "Induced Abortion and Sterilization," 1161–71; Kinsey, "Illegal Abortions," 196–97.

83. Solinger, "'A Complete Disaster,'" 243–44. Solinger challenges Kristin Luker's assertion that between 1920 and 1960 the therapeutic abortion rates compared to delivery rates did not change. See Luker, *Abortion and the Politics of Motherhood*, 46.

84. Reagan, *When Abortion Was a Crime*, 174, 176, 193; Solinger, "'A Complete Disaster,'" 242–48, 258, 263. Solinger also found changes with respect to single pregnant women. Prior to World War II the belief in the genetically flawed illegitimate mother and child prevailed, and society pressured these mothers to keep their children. The postwar era witnessed a decline in the genetic deficiency argument; thus, white babies became a valuable commodity, and mothers faced pressure to surrender their infants to white middle-class couples. See Solinger, *Wake up Little Susie*, 9–17.

85. Maternal Health Committee Report, Appendix B, 19 May 1970, Abortion Reports file, box 39, RIMS, RIHS Library.

86. Solinger, "'A Complete Disaster,'" 259–60; Reagan, *When Abortion Was a Crime*, 174, 176, 193, 194, 196–97, 198–99, 211.

87. Joffe, "'Physicians of Conscience,'" 47–52.

88. Joffe, "'Physicians of Conscience,'" 46–50; Arnold interview, 57; "Healthier Mothers," 1809; Ross, "African-American Women," 279–80.

89. Calderone, "Illegal Abortion," 948–53; Calderone interview, 15.

90. Campbell interview, 31–41; Grant Sanger interview, 55.

91. Meyer, *Any Friend of the Movement*, 58.

92. Minutes of Executive Committee Meeting, 22 April 1946, file 1946; Mrs. Richard B. Knight, President, 28 September 1951, Knight to Mrs. Philip W. Pillsbury, 24 September 1951, file 1951; Minutes of Board of Directors Meeting, 9 June 1948, file 1948; Minutes of Board of Directors Meeting, 11 October 1949, all in PPRI Records.

93. PPFA, *Planned Parenthood Worker's Handbook*, 1948, RIMHA, "Suppose You Were?"; RIMHA, *Manual for Board of Directors 1948–1949*, 28 April 1948, file 1948; Clinic Committee Report, 28 March 1950, file 1950; Annual Meeting Report, 18 April 1951, file 1951, all in PPRI Records.

94. Social Service Department Report, 18 April 1951, file 1951; Minutes of Board of Directors Meeting, 12 December 1950, file 1950; Minutes of Annual Meeting, 8 April 1952, file 1952; Minutes of Joint Meeting of the Clinic Functions and Medical Advisory Committees, 19 February 1953, file 1953, and 17 June 1954, file 1954; Minutes of Medical and Clinic Functions Committee Meeting, 16 June 1953, Annual Meeting, 14 April 1953, file 1953; Report of President, Annual Meeting 1955, file 1955, all in PPRI Records.

95. Annual Report—Social Service Department, 1948, file 1948; Annual Report of Social Service Department, 1949, file 1949; Medical Advisory and Clinic Meeting, 22 January 1951, file 1951; Minutes of Annual Meeting, 8 April 1952, file 1952; Annual Meeting, 14 April 1953, file 1953; Minutes of Annual Meeting, 27 April 1954, file 1954; Report to the Board of Directors, 12 January 1960, file 1960, all in PPRI Records.

96. President's Report and RIMHA Minutes, 14 January 1958, 13 May 1958, 25 November 1958, 9 December 1958, file 1958; RIMHA Minutes, 13 January 1959, an Invitation and a Report from the RIMHA, Inc., 1959, RIMHA Minutes, 10 February 1959, Meeting of the Board, 10 February 1959, Social Worker's Report, 14 April 1959, Minutes of the Medical Advisory Committee, 2 February 1959, file 1959, all in PPRI Records.

97. President's Report, "25th Anniversary Annual Report," 11 April 1956, file 1956; President's Annual Meeting Report, 8 April 1957, file 1957; RIMHA Minutes, 14 October 1958, file 1958; Excerpts from Minutes of Meeting of Medical Advisory Committee, 2 February 1959, Board of Directors Meeting, 10 February 1959, file 1959; Board of Directors Meeting, 14 November 1961, file 1961, all in PPRI Records.

98. Social Worker's Report, April 1947, file 1946 [*sic*]; *Manual for Board Members, 1948–1949*, 28 April 1948, file 1948; Campaign Report for 1950, file 1950; Report on Campaign and Education, May 1953, file 1953; Minutes of Board of Directors Meeting, 9 March 1954; 19 May 1954, file 1954; Report to the Board of Directors, 12 January 1960, file 1960; Outline of Activities, 1946, file 1946; Social Worker's Annual Report, April 1948, file 1947 [*sic*]; Annual Report—Social Service Department, 1948, file 1948; Annual Report of Social Service Department, 1949, file 1949; Social Service Department Report, 18 April 1951, file 1951; Report of Annual Meeting, 8 April 1952, file 1952; Annual Meeting, 1954 Report, file 1954; Report of President, Annual Meeting

1955, Minutes of Board of Directors Meeting 10 May 1955, file 1955; President's Report, "25th Anniversary Annual Report," 11 April 1956, file 1956; President's Report, Annual Meeting, 1958, RIMHA Minutes, 9 December 1958, file 1958; Social Worker's Report, Annual Meeting 1959, file 1959, all in PPRI Records.

99. The RIMHA discussed services for unmarried women in 1958, but the presence of the Catholic Church led them to maintain the married-only policy. Women's ages: 62 percent between twenty-one and thirty; 23 percent between thirty-one and forty; 12 percent under twenty; 3 percent over forty. Board of Directors' Minutes, 25 November 1958, file 1958; Social Worker's Report, April 1947, file 1946 [sic]; Social Worker's Annual Report, April 1948, file 1947 [sic]; Annual Report—Social Service Department, 1948, file 1948; Annual Report of Social Service Department, 1949, file 1949; Social Service Department Report, 18 April 1951, file 1951; Minutes of Annual Meeting, 8 April 1952, Report of Annual Meeting, 8 April 1952, file 1952; Annual Meeting, Report of 1954, file 1954; Executive Director's Report, Annual Meeting 1959, Social Worker's Report, Annual Meeting 1959, file 1959; Report to the Board of Directors, 12 January 1960, file 1960, all in PPRI Records.

100. McBride, "Medicine and the Health Crisis," 113–14.

101. Five Year Plan, 1946–51, Executive Secretary's Report, November 1946, file 1946; Executive Secretary's Report, January 1947, Annual Luncheon, 22 April 1947, file 1947; Executive Director's Report, 29 September 1948, President's Annual Report, April 1948, file 1948; Report of Executive Director Board Meeting, 9 March 1949, Report of Executive Director for June–September, 1949, file 1949, all in PPRI Records; Betty Lisle to Mrs. Hunt, 24 January 1947, no. 6, box 1, file 39, Urban League of Rhode Island Papers.

102. Minutes of Executive Board Meeting, 18 April 1955, Minutes of Board of Directors Meeting, 10 May 1955, file 1955; President's Report, "25th Anniversary Annual Report," 11 April 1956, file 1956, all in PPRI Records; U.S. Bureau of the Census, *Census of Population: 1950*, 39; U.S. Bureau of the Census, *Census: 1960*, 17.

103. Minutes of Executive Board Meeting, 18 April 1955, Minutes of Board of Directors Meeting, 10 May 1955, file 1955; President's Report, "25th Anniversary Annual Report," 11 April 1956, file 1956, both in PPRI Records.

104. Mrs. Federico F. Mauck to Chairman of the Regional Long Range Planning Committees, 29 April 1949, Long Range Planning Report, 1949, Report of the Long Range Planning Committee, 27 October 1949, file 1949, PPRI Records.

105. Report on New York Conference, 1944, file 1944; Minutes of Board of Directors Meeting, 11 December 1951, file 1951; Dr. Brock Chisholm, "The World's Most Pressing Problem," delivered to PPFA annual luncheon, 3 May 1956, Calderone, "E x A = BR"; President's Report, "25th Anniversary Annual Meeting," 11 April 1956, file 1956, all in PPRI Records.

106. *Manual for Board of Directors 1948–1949*, 28 April 1948, 5–14, file 1948; *Manual for Board of Directors, 1950–1951*, 28 April 1950, file 1950; Annual Meeting of RIMHA, 18 April 1951, file 1951; Minutes of Annual Meeting, 8 April 1952, file 1952; Minutes of Annual Meeting, 14 April 1953, file 1953; Minutes of Annual Meeting, 27 April 1954, file 1954; Report of President, Annual Meeting 1955, file 1955; Attendance—Board Meeting, December 1957, file 1957; Attendance—Board Meeting, 6

June 1958, file 1958; Report to the Board of Directors, 13 October 1959, Minutes of the Annual Meeting, 1959, file 1959, all in PPRI Records.

107. RIMHA Minutes, 6 June 1958, file 1958; Meeting of the Board, 10 February 1959, Board of Directors Meeting, 8 December 1959, President's Report on Annual Meeting, 1959, file 1959; Executive Director's Report, 11 October 1960, file 1960, box 2; Mrs. John L. Clark to Board of Directors, 14 March 1961, file 1961, box 2, all in PPRI Records.

108. RIMHA Minutes, 11 February 1958, file 1958; Report to the Board of Directors, 12 January 1960, file 1960, box 2; Board of Directors' Attendance Sheet, 13 February 1962, Board of Directors Meeting, 8 May 1962 and 20 November 1962, file 1962, box 2, all in PPRI Records.

Chapter 6. Who Pays? Contraceptive Services and the Welfare State, 1963–1975

1. Lader, *Breeding Ourselves to Death*.

2. D'Emilio and Freedman, *Intimate Matters*, 250–51; Patricia Maginnis, interview with Jeannette Bailey Cheek, November 1975, 78, Family Planning Oral History Project; Calderone quoted in U.S. Congress, Senate, Committee on Government Operations, *Hearings* (1965), 1382.

3. Board of Directors Meeting, 9 May 1961, Minutes of the Clinical Staff Meeting, 26 September 1961, Minutes of the Clinical Staff Meeting, 15 November 1961, Board of Directors Meeting, 12 December 1961, file 1961, box 2; Medical Director's Report to Board of Director, 26 May 1964, file 1964, box 2, all in PPRI Records.

4. Methods of birth control at RIMHA October 1961: diaphragm, 1,954; pill, 47; jelly or cream, 25; Emko (foam), 7; rhythm, 2. Board of Directors Meeting, 10 October 1961, file 1961, box 2, PPRI Records. RIMHA home visitors used Emko because it could be given without a doctor's exam.

5. Board of Directors Meeting, 13 February 1962, 9 October 1962, file 1962, box 2; Board of Directors Meeting, 12 March 1963, 1 October 1963, file 1963, box 2; Annual Report for 1963, Medical Director, 17 April 1964, Medical Director's Report to Board of Directors, 26 May 1964, file 1964, box 2, all in PPRI Records.

6. Board of Director Meeting, 19 November 1963, file 1963, box 2; Annual Report of Medical Director for 1963, 17 April 1964, Executive Committee Meeting Minutes, 20 April 1964, Medical Director's Report to Board of Directors, 26 May 1964, file 1964, box 2, all in PPRI Records.

7. Marshall A. Taylor to Executive Committee, 8 June 1964, file 1964, box 2, PPRI Records.

8. Mrs. John L. Clark, President, to Board of Directors, 14 March 1961, file 1961, box 2; Medical Director's Report to Board of Directors, 26 May 1964, file 1964, box 2, both in PPRI Records.

9. Board of Directors Meeting, 14 November 1961, Summary of Dr. Guttmacher's Speech, 30th Annual Meeting, 11 April 1961, file 1961, box 2; Board of Directors Meeting, 20 November 1962, file 1962, box 2, in PPRI Records; Arnold interview, 46.

10. Minutes of Board Meeting, 20 May 1965 and 30 September 1965, Executive Committee Minutes, 13 April 1965, file 1965, box 2; Report of the Medical Director 1966, January 1967, file 1967, box 2, in PPRI Records.

11. Watkins, *On the Pill*, 6–7, 43, 48, 50, 52, 53; Tone, *Devices and Desires*, xv, 82, quote on 203, 239–40.

12. Watkins, *On the Pill*, 3–4, 86–88, 89, 90, 96, 99, 109, 115, 120.

13. Alan Guttmacher to Charles Potter, 3 October 1968, file 1968, box 2; Medical Director's Report 1969, file 1969, box 2; Board Meeting Minutes, 22 June 1970, Staff Meeting Minutes, 23 September 1970, file 1970, box 2; Executive Committee Minutes, 15 January 1973, Staff Meeting Minutes, 31 January 1973, and 25 April 1973, file 1973, box 2, all in PPRI Records.

14. U.S. Congress, Senate, Committee on Government Operations, *Hearings* (1965), 1068; "Fact Sheet on Birth Control," *Congressional Quarterly*, 10 June 1966, 1235–38.

15. *New York Times*, 9 February 1964; Patterson, *America's Struggle*, 142–54.

16. Piotrow, *World Population Crisis*, 91; Critchlow, *Intended Consequences*, 68–69.

17. State of the Union Address, 4 January 1965; 20th Anniversary of the United Nations in San Francisco, 25 June 1965; the swearing-in ceremony of John W. Gardner as secretary of the Department of Health, Education and Welfare, 18 August 1965; and letter to the secretary general of the United Nations, second United Nations World Population Conference, Belgrade, Yugoslavia, 30 August 1965. Quoted in U.S. Congress, Senate, Committee on Government Operations, *Hearings* (1965).

18. National Academy of Sciences, *The Growth of U.S. Population*, 23; Piotrow, *World Population Crisis*, 90–93.

19. Critchlow, *Intended Consequences*, 52.

20. U.S. Congress, House, Committee on Education and Labor, *Hearings*; U.S. Congress, Senate, Committee on Labor and Public Welfare, *Hearing* (1966), 130.

21. U.S. Congress, *Congressional Record* 3 (21 July 1965): S 17729.

22. Greene, "Federal Birth Control," 35–36.

23. U.S. Congress, Senate, Committee on Government Operations, *Hearings* (1965), 1465–70; U.S. Congress, Senate, Committee on Government Operations, *Hearings* (1967), 34; Elinor Langer, "Birth Control: Academy Report Stresses Burdens of High Birth Rate among the Impoverished Here," *Science*, 28 May 1965, 1206.

24. Estelle Griswold, interview with Jeannette Bailey Cheek, March 1976, 30–46, Family Planning Oral History Project.

25. Erskine, "The Polls," 306–7; U.S. Congress, Senate, Committee on Labor and Public Welfare, *Hearing* (1966), 61–74; John Finney, "Poll Finds Catholics Back Birth Curb Aid," *New York Times*, 17 February 1966; "Ahead of Washington," *Time*, 25 February 1966, 25; D'Antonio, "Birth Control," 249.

26. HR 8440 and HR 8451, 89th Cong., 1st sess., U.S. Congress, *Congressional Record*, 111 (25 May 1965), 89th Cong., 2nd sess. (1965), 19; Public Law 91-662, 8 January 1971, *United States Statutes at Large* 84 Stat. 1973; "Congressional Quarterly Fact Sheet on Birth Control," *Congressional Quarterly*, 10 June 1966, 1235–38.

27. U.S. Congress, Senate, Committee on Government Operations, *Hearings* (1965), 1455, 1470, 1663.

28. U.S. Congress, Senate, Committee on Government Operations, *Hearings* (1965), 1465–10, 1314–16.

29. U.S. Congress, Senate, Committee on Labor and Public Welfare, *Hearing* (1966),

111–13; U.S. Congress, Senate, Committee on Government Operations, *Hearings* (1965), 1056–60, 1064–70, 1074–75, 1133, 1781, 1788.

30. U.S. Congress, Senate, Committee on Government Operations, *Hearings* (1965), 1064–70, 1074–75, 1781.

31. "Family-Planning Campaign—The Louisiana Story," *U.S. News and World Report*, 28 July 1969, 55–57.

32. U.S. Congress, Senate, Committee on Government Operations, *Hearings* (1967), 34; "Congressional Quarterly Fact Sheet on Birth Control," *Congressional Quarterly*, 10 June 1966, 1235–38; Arthur J. Lesser, "Equalizing Opportunity," *PTA Magazine* 61 (April 1967): 21–22.

33. "Birth Control 'Cost-Effectiveness,'" *Science*, 12 May 1967, 766.

34. U.S. Congress, Senate, Committee on Labor and Public Welfare, *Hearing* (1966), 2–8, 81, 113–29.

35. U.S. Congress, Senate, Committee on Labor and Public Welfare, *Hearing* (1966), 9, 35; U.S. Congress, Senate, Committee on Government Operations, *Hearings* (1967), 99.

36. U.S. Congress, Senate, Committee on Government Operations, *Hearings* (1967), 14, 18.

37. U.S. Congress, Senate, Committee on Government Operations, *Hearings* (1967), 20–22.

38. U.S. Congress, Senate, Committee on Government Operations, *Hearings* (1967), 3–9, 12–13, 17, 28–29, 36, 137; U.S. Congress, House, Committee on Education and Labor, *Hearings*, 2159–60.

39. *Pittsburgh Courier*, 30 September 1967, 1; *Pittsburgh Peace and Freedom News* 2, no. 2 (September–October 1967): 6.

40. *Social Security Amendments of 1967*, Public Law 90-248, 90th Cong., 1st sess. (1967), 58, 102–6.

41. *New York Times*, 11 January 1967, 11 May 1967, 16 May 1967; Piotrow, *World Population Crisis*, 133–45.

42. PPFA survey in U.S. Congress, House, Committee on Education and Labor, *Hearings*, 2179; *Washington Post*, 9 April 1967, A2.

43. U.S. Office of Economic Opportunity, *Need for Subsidized Family Planning Services*.

44. "$500 for Not Having a Baby," *America*, 16 March 1968, 336; Ann Ludwigsen Goodstadt, "How Many Children Are We Entitled to Have?" *Redbook* 136 (March 1971): 12.

45. "Congress Votes Monies for Family Planning," *Christian Century*, 4 December 1968, 1530.

46. U.S. Congress, House, Committee on Education and Labor, *Hearings*, 2162; David, "Unwanted Pregnancies," 449–50.

47. Menken, "Teenage Childbearing," 334–35; Zelnik and Kantner, "Sexuality," 358, 372–73. See also Wendy H. Baldwin, "Adolescent Pregnancy and Childbearing—Growing Concerns for Americans," *Population Bulletin* 31 (September 1976).

48. U.S. National Center for Health Statistics, *Vital Statistics*; Cutright, "Illegitimacy," 408–9.

49. Roberts, *Killing the Black Body*, 119.

50. Sadja Goldsmith, M.D., interview with Jeannette Bailey Cheek, November 1975, v, Family Planning Oral History Project; Mudd interview, 247–48.

51. U.S. National Center for Health Statistics, *Vital Statistics*; Cutright, "Illegitimacy," 408–9; Dryfos et al., "Eighteen Months Later," 29–44; National Academy of Sciences, *Resources and Man*, 2.

52. *Federal Register* 34 (28 January 1969): 1356; Nixon, "Special Message," 521–30.

53. *New York Times*, 3 February 1970, 23.

54. *New York Times* 15 July 1970, 1 December 1970, 27 December 1970, 1.

55. Critchlow, *Intended Consequences*, 173.

56. President's Report, *Annual Report 1970*, 7–8, Executive Committee Minutes, 16 February 1970, Board of Directors Meeting, 19 October 1970, file 1970, box 2, PPRI Records.

57. Calderone interview, 12; U.S. Congress, Senate, Committee on Labor and Public Welfare, *Hearing* (1966); Greene, "Federal Birth Control," 36.

58. Laura Bergquist, "Kentucky Doctor: One Man's War Against Poverty," *Look*, 16 November 1965, 77.

59. Jack Shepherd, "Birth Control and the Poor: A Solution," *Look*, 7 April 1964, 63–64; Schoen, *Choice & Coercion*, 65.

60. Lonny Myers, M.D., interview with Ellen Chesler, September 1976, iii, 23–29, Family Planning Oral History Project.

61. U.S. Congress, Senate, Committee on Government Operations, *Hearings* (1965), 1754–58; Bruno, "Birth Control," 32–34; "Unmanaged News," *America*, 18 May 1963, 701.

62. Myers interview, 26; Littlewood, *The Politics of Population Control*, 34; Bruno, "Birth Control," 33–34.

63. Myers interview, 24; U.S. Congress, Senate, Committee on Government Operations, *Hearings* (1965), 1754–58.

64. "Birth Control and Welfare," *Commonweal*, 7 February 1964, 560–61.

65. The states were Alabama, Arizona, Arkansas, California, Colorado, Florida, Georgia, Illinois, Indiana, Kansas, Kentucky, Maine, Maryland, Michigan, Mississippi, Nevada, New Jersey, New Mexico, New York, North Carolina, North Dakota, Oklahoma, South Carolina, Tennessee, Texas, Virginia, Washington, West Virginia, Wisconsin. See U.S. Congress, Senate, Committee on Government Operations, *Hearings* (1965), 1183.

66. U.S. Congress, Senate, Committee on Labor and Public Welfare, *Hearing* (1966), 10, 88–89, 93.

67. U.S. Congress, Senate, Committee on Government Operations, *Hearings* (1965), 1779.

68. U.S. Congress, House, Committee on Education and Labor, *Hearings*, 56; Donald Harting et al., "Family Planning Policies and Activities of State Health and Welfare Departments," *Public Health Reports* 84 (February 1969): 127–28.

69. Critchlow, *Intended Consequences*, chap. 4.

70. "Silence Is Broken," *America*, 11 September 1965, 256; Davis, "Of Many Things," 511.

71. Bishops' statement quoted in D'Antonio, "Birth Control," 247.

72. "Birth-Control Plea Denied in Maryland," *New York Times,* 26 March 1964; "Welfare Birth Control," *America,* 1 February 1964, 157; James O'Gara, "Birth Control and Public Policy," *Commonweal,* 23 August 1963, 504.

73. D'Antonio, "Birth Control," 247.

74. Watkins, *On the Pill,* 47.

75. During the 1940s this debate received publicity in the *Negro Digest.* Dr. Julian Lewis, pathologist and former professor at the University of Chicago, argued that the black race was dependent on a high birthrate and that birth control was a white plot to weaken blacks. E. Franklin Frazier, distinguished sociologist, disagreed, asserting that "more and more babies born indiscriminately, without thought of the parent's health or ability to rear them, [was] not the answer." The survival of the race depended upon strong healthy babies. See Lewis, "Can the Negro Afford Birth Control," *Negro Digest* 3 (May 1945): 19–22; Frazier, "Birth Control for More Negro Babies," *Negro Digest* 3 (July 1945): 41–44.

76. Ross, "African-American Women," 280; Greene, "Federal Birth Control," 37; Davis, "Of Many Things," 511.

77. Baraka, *African Congress,* 419; Weisbord, *Genocide?* 94.

78. *Muhammad Speaks,* 24 January 1969, 4 July 1969, 11 July 1969, 29 August 1969; Malcolm X, "The Black Revolution," 45–46; Barbara A. Sizemore, "Sexism and the Black Male," *Black Scholar* (March–April 1973): 6.

79. PPCP *Newsletter* 1, no. 1 (1966), and 1, no. 3 (1967), PPCP Papers.

80. PPCP *Newsletter* 1, no. 3 (1967), PPCP Papers.

81. I contacted Greenlee in 1992 to interview him, but he refused to discuss the genocide controversy.

82. *Pittsburgh Press,* 21 August 1968; Hallow, "The Blacks Cry Genocide," 535–37; Smith, "Birth Control," 29.

83. "Family Planning and Maternal Health," 10 May 1967, Homewood-Brushton City Renewal Council, FF 202.M, box 11B, Rice Papers. Pittsburgh was one of five OEO programs funded in 1966. David Epperson, interview with the author at his office at the University of Pittsburgh, 16 October 1992.

84. PPCP Letter of Introduction for Home Visitors, 1 August 1966, Planned Parenthood file, FF 371, box 18B, Rice Papers.

85. *Pittsburgh Post Gazette,* 30 July 1974, Haden file, FF 193, box 11A, Rice Papers.

86. "Report on the By-laws Committee Meeting," n.d., Homewood-Brushton Alliance file, 1967–68, FF 200, box 11A, Rice Papers.

87. Radio Sunday, 20 November 1966, WWSW, Radio Broadcasts, 1966, 4th quarter, FF 759, box 29, Rice Papers; *Pittsburgh Press,* 21 August 1968, 18.

88. "Mullen's Maneuver," *Pittsburgh Catholic,* 1966, FF 856, box 32, Rice Papers.

89. Rice to Editor of *Village Voice,* 1 March 1968, Correspondence, 1968, FF 637, box 26, Rice Papers.

90. "Population Planners Miss Point," *Pittsburgh Catholic,* 27 December 1968, 1968 file, FF 857, box 32, Rice Papers; *Pittsburgh Press,* 21 August 1968, 18; NAACP, "The Statement by Planned Parenthood That They Do Not Solicit Clientele in the Black

Neighborhoods Is an Out & Out Lie," 28 December 1967, Planned Parenthood file, FF 371, box 18B, Rice Papers; Epperson interview.

91. CAP's goal was to "attack poverty through a comprehensive plan focused on means of removing the causes of social disorder and bringing people out of poverty and into the mainstream of life in the community." The eight targeted neighborhoods included North Side, Homewood-Brushton, Hill District, South Oakland, Southwest Pittsburgh, Hazelwood-Glenwood, Lawrenceville, and East Liberty–Garfield. CAP's structure encompassed a board of directors responsible for policy and chaired by the mayor, Joseph M. Barr in this case. The mayor appointed two-thirds of the board (sixteen), and the neighborhoods elected one delegate from each of the eight targeted neighborhoods. See "Community Action Program for the City of Pittsburgh" and "CAP Interim Report," both in Community Action Pittsburgh file, Rice Papers.

92. *Pittsburgh Press*, 5 February 1969, 1; *Pittsburgh Courier*, 9 November 1968, 1; *Pittsburgh Courier*, 30 December 1967, 2.

93. "OEO Neighborhood Proposals, Fiscal Year 1 July 1967 to 30 June 1968," FF 202. G, box 11B, Rice Papers.

94. PPCP *Newsletter* 3, no. 5 (1969), PPCP Papers.

95. "United Movement for Progress," 8 July 1967, Homewood-Brushton Alliance, 1967–68, FF 200, box 11A, Rice Papers.

96. This grant came out of the Fund for Aid of Neighbors in Need, established by Bishop John Wright of Pittsburgh, to fund programs in disadvantaged areas. *Pittsburgh Courier*, 13 July 1968, 1.

97. *Pittsburgh Courier*, 13 July 1968, 1; "Anonymous Letter to Rice," 11 October 1968, Correspondence 1968, FF 637, box 26, Rice Papers. More hate mail and abusive phone calls are in Correspondence 1968, FF 637, box 26, Rice Papers.

98. Epperson interview; Sarah Bradford Campbell, interview with author conducted at Campbell's home, 15 October 1992.

99. This threat was serious. In 1969 Rice discovered two hundred sticks of dynamite near Holy Rosemary and called the police as well as Haden. After the police left Haden laughed as he told Rice that he had hidden the explosives, planning to blow up clinics, but had forgotten about the dynamite. See McGeever, *Reverend Charles Owen Rice*, 178.

100. Homewood-Brushton file, 1967–68, FF 200, box 11A; "Birth Control Unit Warned by Haden," 1 August 1968, no newspaper title, clipping sent anonymously to Rice, Haden file, FF 193, box 11A; "Haden Denies Negroes' Rights," Haden file, FF 193, box 11A, all in Rice Papers; *Pittsburgh Press*, 15 August 1968, 41.

101. *New York Times*, 11 August 1968, 44; *Pittsburgh Press*, 15 August 1968, 41.

102. Ibid.

103. Ibid.

104. Epperson interview.

105. *Pittsburgh Press*, 5 February 1969, 1. For comments by Rice see *Pittsburgh Catholic*, 1968 file, FF 857, box 32, Rice Papers, especially a December 1968 article entitled "Population Planners Miss Point," in which he stated that "black militants could use some allies these days in their almost hopeless fight against policies that they justly condemn as genocidal."

106. *Pittsburgh Press*, 24 February 1969, 2.

107. *Pittsburgh Press*, 5 March 1969, 1.

108. Sarah Bradford Campbell interview; Epperson interview. PPCP had 2,215 clients from the areas under question who made a total of 8,368 visits during 1968. These figures suggest that clients returned, apparently without coercion, for follow-up visits. See Planned Parenthood file, PPCP Papers.

109. Epperson interview; "M.D. Column," *Pittsburgh Courier*, 31 August 1968, 7; "Brief Summaries of Programs and Budgets for Fiscal 1970," in CAP file, Rice Papers.

110. Smith, "Birth Control," 28.

111. Smith, "Birth Control," 29; *Pittsburgh Courier*, 27 July 1968, 3.

112. "Analysis of the Pill," *Thrust*, 19 July 1968, 1.

113. "Birth Control: Losing Support of Negroes?" *U.S. News and World Report*, 7 August 1967, 11; Task Force, "Ethics," 24–25; Hallow, "The Blacks Cry Genocide," 535; *New York Times*, 15 November 1968.

114. Turner and Darity, "Fears of Genocide," 1029–34.

115. Frances M. Beal, "Double Jeopardy: To Be Black and Female," in Morgan, *Sisterhood Is Powerful*, 343–44; Davis, *Angela Davis*, 161; LaRue, "Black Liberation," 61. See also Giddings, *Where and When I Enter*, 314–19.

116. LaRue, "Black Liberation," 62; Toni Cade, "The Pill: Genocide or Liberation?" in Cade, *The Black Woman*, 163–64.

117. Black Women's Liberation Group, "Statement on Birth Control," Mt. Vernon, New York, in Morgan, *Sisterhood Is Powerful*, 360–61; Dara Abubakari, "The Black Woman Is Liberated in Her Own Mind," in Lerner, *Black Women*, 587.

118. Bogue, "Family Planning in the Negro Ghettos of Chicago," *Milbank Memorial Fund Quarterly*, no. 2 (April 1970): pt. 2: 283–99; Lipson and Wolman, "Polling Americans," 39–42; Weisbord, *Genocide?* 182.

119. "Planned Parenthood Honors Founder's Son," *Pittsburgh Courier*, 21 October 1967, 10; King quoted in Smith, "Birth Control," 37; "Chivers Warns Parents," *Pittsburgh Courier*, 29 June 1968, 16; U.S. Congress, Senate, Committee on Government Operations, *Hearings* (1966), 1549; U.S. Congress, Senate, Committee on Labor and Public Welfare, *Hearings*, 2255.

120. Langston Hughes, "Population Explosion," *New York Post*, 10 December 1965; Joseph H. Fichter, "ZPG: A Bourgeois Conspiracy?" *America*, 19 August 1972, 89; Hannah Lees, "The Negro Response to Birth Control," *Reporter*, 19 May 1966, 46.

121. Blair interview, 21; Myers interview, 30–32.

122. Board of Directors Meeting, 8 March 1960, file 1960, box 2; Board of Directors Meeting, 10 October 1961, Minutes of the Clinical Staff Meeting, 26 September 1961, file 1961, box 2; President's Report, 10 April 1962, Board of Directors Meeting, 13 February 1962 and 13 March 1962, file 1962, box 2; Fact Sheet, n.d., Social Worker's Annual Report, 1963, Medical Director's Annual Report, 1963, file 1963, box 2; Minutes of Board Meeting, 20 May 1965, file 1965, box 2, all in PPRI Records.

123. Report to the Board of Directors, 12 January 1960, file 1960, box 2; Clark to Board of Directors, 14 March 1961, file 1961, box 2; Board of Directors Meeting, 13 March 1962 and 9 October 1962, file 1962, box 2; Board of Directors Meeting, 12 February 1963, 21 May 1963, Medical Director's Annual Report 1963, file 1963, box 2; Execu-

tive Committee Meeting, 14 July 1964, Executive Director's Report, 26 May 1964, file 1964, box 2; Campaign Committee Report, 2 March 1965, file 1965, box 2; Executive Director's Annual Report 1969, file 1969, box 2, all in PPRI Records.

124. President's Report, 10 April 1962, file 1962, box 2; Fact Sheet, n.d., file 1963, box 2; Mrs. Henry Wise to Mr. Augustine W. Riccio, Director, 1963, file 1964 [*sic*], box 2; Annual Report, April 1965, file 1964 [*sic*], box 2; Executive Director's Annual Report 1969, file 1969, box 2, all in PPRI Records.

125. 1966 Annual Report of Social Worker, January 1967, file 1967, box 2, PPRI Records.

126. Women continued to hold the presidency and were the majority of vice presidencies, all secretaries, executive directors, and medical directors until the late 1960s. Women also continued to dominate the board of directors.

127. RIMHA, Inc., Report on Audit, 31 December 1962, file 1962, box 2; 1964 Campaign Report, n.d., United Fund to PPRI, 23 July 1964, President's Report, 14 May 1964, file 1964, box 2; Campaign Report, 1965, file 1965, box 2; Statement of Accounts, file 1966, box 2, all in PPRI Records.

128. Annual Report of President, January 1967, file 1967, box 2; Executive Director's Annual Report 1967, 29 January 1968, Medical Director's Report to the Board of Directors: February 1968, 31 January 1968, Executive Director's Report, 19 November 1968, Executive Committee Minutes, 23 October 1968, file 1968, box 2; Executive Committee Minutes, 31 July 1969, Executive Director's Report, 11 December 1969, file 1969, box 2, all in PPRI Records.

129. Executive Committee Minutes, 9 February 1966, Minutes of Board Meeting, 25 October 1966, file 1966, box 2; Midsummer Memo, 5 August 1967, Executive Director's Report, 24 October 1967, file 1967, box 2; Executive Committee Minutes, 17 December 1968, file 1968, box 2, all in PPRI Records.

130. Board Meeting Minutes, 15 February 1966, file 1966, box 2; Executive Director's Annual Report 1966, 17 January 1967, Board Meeting Minutes, 16 May 1967, Statement of Accounts, file 1967, box 2; Executive Director's Annual Report 1969, file 1969, box 2; Treasurer's Report, 31 December 1959, file 1960 [*sic*], box 2, all in PPRI Records.

131. Anne Wise, March 1964, file 1964, box 2; Executive Director's Report, January 1965, file 1964 [*sic*], box 2; Executive Director's Annual Report 1966, 17 January 1967, file 1967, box 2; Executive Director's Annual Report 1967, 29 January 1968, Executive Committee Minutes, 18 June 1968, file 1968, box 2; Executive Committee Minutes, 9 January 1969, 11 June 1969, and 31 July 1969, file 1969, box 2, all in PPRI Records.

132. Social Worker's Annual Report 1968, Executive Director's Report, 24 September 1968, file 1968, box 2; Social Worker's Annual Report 1969, Annual Report of President, 22 January 1969, file 1969, box 2, all in PPRI Records.

133. Medical Director's Report to the Board of Directors: February 1968, 31 January 1968, file 1968, box 2, PPRI Records.

134. Watkins, *On the Pill*, 115.

135. Medical Director's Report to the Board of Directors: February 1968, 31 January 1968, file 1968, box 2; Medical Director's Report, *Annual Reports 1970*, 4, file 1970, box 2, both in PPRI Records.

136. Executive Director's Annual Report, 1968, Board Meeting Minutes, 24 September 1968, file 1968, box 2, PPRI Records.

137. Medical Director's Report 1966, January 1967, file 1967, box 2; Executive Director's Annual Report 1967, 29 January 1968, file 1968, box 2; Executive Director's Annual Report 1969, file 1969, box 2; Director of Education, 13 March 1970, file 1970, box 2; *Annual Reports 1973*, 9–11, file 1973, box 2, all in PPRI Records; Committee on Medicine and Religion Report, n.d., Maternal Health 1966–69 file, box 39, RIMS, RIHS Library.

138. Meyer also speaks of this embarrassment in *Any Friend of the Movement*, 147–48.

139. Annual Report of the President, 25 February 1970, file 1969, box 2; Executive Committee Minutes, 2 April 1970, file 1970, box 2; Staff Meeting, 25 April 1973, file 1973, box 2, all in PPRI Records.

140. PPFA *Annual Report 1973*, Staff Meeting, 31 January 1973, file 1973, box 2, PPRI Records.

141. Executive Committee Minutes, 11 May 1966, file 1966, and 15 November 1966, file 1965 [*sic*], box 2; Executive Director's Report, 24 October 1967, file 1967, box 2; Executive Director's Report, 30 April 1968, Executive Committee Minutes, 13 March 1968, file 1968, box 2, all in PPRI Records; *Providence Journal*, 2 May 1968, 1, 12 May 1968, N40, 14 May 1968, 1.

142. *Providence Journal*, 16 May 1968, 29; Executive Committee Minutes, 22 May 1968, 18 June 1968, Executive Director's Annual Report 1968, 22 January 1969, file 1968, box 2, all in PPRI Records.

143. Lionel J. Jenkins to James N. Williams, Monthly Report for June 1966, no. 2, box 28, file 1800, Urban League of Rhode Island Papers.

144. Report on South Providence, n.d., file 1965, box 2; Board Meeting Minutes, 15 February 1966, Executive Committee Minutes, 11 May 1966, file 1966, box 2; Annual Report of the President, January 1967, file 1967, box 2; Board of Directors Meeting, 20 April 1970, Situation Testing, n.d., file 1970, box 2, all in PPRI Records.

145. The slate of officers was 1968, female president, male first vice president, two female and two male vice presidents, male secretary, male treasurer, and male assistant treasurer; 1969, male president, female first vice president, three male vice presidents, female secretary, male treasurer, and female assistant treasurer; 1970, same exact slate as 1969; 1971, female president, three male vice presidents, male treasurer, female assistant treasurer, and female secretary; 1972, female president, male first vice president, two male vice presidents, female secretary, female treasurer, and male assistant treasurer; 1973, female president, male first vice president, two male vice presidents, female secretary, female treasurer, and male assistant treasurer.

146. Executive Director's Report, 19 April 1966, file 1966, box 2; Board Meeting Minutes, 25 September 1969, Social Worker's Annual Report 1969, file 1969, box 2; Executive Director's Report, 22 June 1970, 19 October 1970, Report of Discussion Group II, 23 June 1970, file 1970, box 2; Board of Directors Meeting, 20 December 1971, file 1971, box 2; Executive Director's Report, 26 June 1972, file 1972, box 2, all in PPRI Records.

147. Executive Director's Report, 18 January 1971, 22 March 1971, file 1971, box 2; *Annual Reports, 1972*, 3, 11, file 1972, box 2, both in PPRI Records.

148. Executive Director's Report, *Annual Reports 1970*, 2, 17, Executive Committee Minutes, 16 February 1970, file 1970, box 2; Minutes of Staff Meeting, 8 May 1971, file 1971, box 2; Minutes of Staff Meeting, 26 January 1972, file 1972, box 2; Report of the Planning Committee of Planned Parenthood of Rhode Island, 22 May 1974, 2, file 1974, box 2; PPRI Statement for Period Ending December, 31 December 1976, file 1976, box 2, all in PPRI Records.

149. Family Planning Training Curriculum Syllabi, September 1970, file 1970, box 2, PPRI Records.

150. Watkins, *On the Pill*, 64.

151. Medical Director's Report, *Annual Reports 1970*, 5, Board of Directors Meeting, 20 April 1970, 19 October 1970, Executive Committee Minutes, 20 July 1970, 21 September 1970, file 1970, box 2; Board Minutes, 13 March 1972, *Annual Reports 1970*, 2, 4, 11, file 1972, box 2; *Annual Reports 1973*, 15, file 1973, box 2; *1974 Annual Report*, file 1974, box 2; "Referral Guidelines," file 1975, box 2; Viola Landes, no title, February 1976, file 1976, box 2, all in PPRI Records.

152. U.S. Congress, Senate, Committee on Labor and Public Welfare, *Hearing* (1966), 7; U.S. Congress, Senate, Committee on Government Operations, *Hearings* (1967), 52; and U.S. Congress, Senate, Committee on the Federal Role in Health, *Report*, 485.

153. Cutright and Jaffe, *Impact of Family Planning*.

Chapter 7. Who Pays for What? Abortion and Sterilization, 1960–1975

1. Abernathy, Greenberg, and Horvitz, "Estimates of Induced Abortion," 19.

2. "More Abortions: The Reasons Why," *Time*, 17 September 1965, 82; "Abortions on the Increase," *America*, 25 September 1965, 311; Hern, "Family Planning," 17–19.

3. *Providence Journal*, 24 August 1962, 15, 9 October 1962, 35.

4. Helen B. Taussig, M.D., interview with Charles A. Janeway, M.D., August 1975, v, 41–46, Family Planning Oral History Project.

5. Finkbine, "Sherri Finkbine's Story," in Rubin, *The Abortion Controversy*, 69–70.

6. Sarah Weddington, interview with Jeannette Cheek, March 1976, 54, Family Planning Oral History Project; Gallup, *Gallup Poll Public Opinion*, 19 September 1962, 1784.

7. U.S. Congress, *Congressional Record* 13 (3 May 1971): 157; Schoen, *Choice & Coercion*, 179.

8. Schoen, *Choice & Coercion*, 176–77.

9. Maginnis interview, 105–6.

10. Schoen, *Choice & Coercion*, 185.

11. Arlene Carmen, interview with Ellen Chesler, January 1976, 2–6, 9–10, 35–36, Family Planning Oral History Project.

12. Goldsmith interview, 22–23; Weddington interview, 43; Carmen interview, iii, 21.

13. Hern, "Family Planning," 17–18; *Christian Century*, 11 January 1961, 37; *America*, 21 May 1966, 738–42; *Newsweek*, 14 November 1966, 92; *Parents Magazine* 45 (Oc-

tober 1970): 58–61; *Redbook* 125 (October 1965): 70–71, 147–50; *New Republic*, 25 October 1969, 12.

14. Cutright, "Illegitimacy," 382; Teitelbaum, "Some Genetic Implications," 495.

15. Gallup, *Gallup Poll Public Opinion*, 19 September 1962, 1784, and 21 January 1966, 1985.

16. Jones and Westoff, "Attitudes toward Abortion," 570–71.

17. Greene, "Federal Birth Control," 35–36; U.S. National Center for Health Statistics, *Vital Statistics*; Cutright, "Illegitimacy," 408–9.

18. U.S. Congress, *Congressional Record* 117 (3 May 1971): 13161.

19. Task Force Report on Family Law and Policy, "Personal Rights Relating to Pregnancy," in Rubin, *The Abortion Controversy*, 57–63.

20. Nelson, *Women of Color*, 5–6.

21. NOW, "Bill of Rights," in Morgan, *Sisterhood Is Powerful*, 512–14; Wandersee, *On the Move*, 18–19.

22. Hole and Levine, *Rebirth of Feminism*, 298; Cisler, "Unfinished Business," 246, 276–78.

23. ACOG, College Statement and Minority Report on Therapeutic Abortion, May 1969, Abortion Reports file, box 39; "280 Psychiatrists Urge End of Abortion Laws," *Boston Globe*, 5 November 1969, Maternal Health 1966–69 file, box 39, both in RIMS, RIHS Library.

24. David, "Unwanted Pregnancies," 455–56; J. de Moerloose, "Abortion Legislation throughout the World," *WHO Features*, no. 3 (March 1971); Francome, *Abortion Freedom*; Sachdev, *International Handbook on Abortion*.

25. The Society for Humane Abortion, originally named the Citizen's Committee for Humane Abortion Laws, changed permanently to the Society for Humane Abortion in 1964 and existed until 1975. Maginnis interview, 79–97; Lana Clarke Phelan, interview with Jeannette Baily Cheek, November 1975, iv–v, 34, Family Planning Oral History Project.

26. Maginnis interview, 99–102, 149; Goldsmith interview, 14.

27. Phelan interview, 17–18; Maginnis interview, 100–101, 150–52.

28. Myers interview, 36–48.

29. Jain and Sinding, *North Carolina Abortion Law 1967*, 15–16, 48–51.

30. Myers interview, 36–39; Maginnis interview, 152–54. Estimates for legal abortions in 1970 range from 197,000 to 236,000. See David, "Unwanted Pregnancies," 456; Tietze, "The Potential Impact," in 581.

31. Constance Cook, interview with Ellen Chesler, January 1976, 27–28, 34–38, 42–45, 48–49, 52, 54, 56–64, 72–73, 79, Family Planning Oral History Project; Guttmacher quoted in President's Report, *Annual Reports 1970*, 6–7, file 1970, box 2, PPRI Records.

32. David, "Unwanted Pregnancies," 456; *New York Times*, 7 February 1971, 70, 6 April 1971, 78, 21 August 1971, 26, 15 October 1971, 38.

33. Pakter and Nelson, "Abortion," 1–15. See also Djerassi, "Fertility Control," 9–14, 41–45.

34. Chisholm, *Unbought*, 120.

35. Pakter and Nelson, "Abortion," 1–15; *New York Times*, 13 October 1971, 15; Carmen interview, 59–60, 73, 80, 82–83. Church reaction was swift: twenty Catholic bishops in New York warned in a pastoral letter that "the church disowns by immediate excommunication any Catholic who deliberately procures an abortion or helps someone else to do so" (*New York Times*, 7 April 1971, 43).

36. Pakter and Nelson, "Abortion," 1–15; Pakter et al., "Two Years Experience," 524–35.

37. Carmen interview, 45.

38. Frances M. Beal, "Double Jeopardy: To Be Black and Female," in Morgan, *Sisterhood Is Powerful*, 349–50; Ross, "African-American Women," 161; Renee Ferguson, "Women's Liberation Has a Different Meaning for Blacks," in Lerner, *Black Women*, 587–92.

39. Chisholm, *Unbought*, 114–16, 122; Carmen interview, 45. See also Carolyn Jones, "Abortion and Black Women," *Black America* 5 (September 1970): 49; Marsha Coleman, "Are Abortions for Black Women Racist?" *Militant*, 21 January 1972, 19; Treadwell, "Is Abortion Black Genocide?" 4–5.

40. *New York Times*, 20 July 1971, 30, 21 November 1971, 95.

41. "A.M.A. Eases Abortion Rules," *New York Times*, 26 June 1970, 1.

42. The case was *United States v. Vuitch*, 402 U.S. Reports 62 (1971). See *New York Times*, 4 May 1971, 38, 15 August 1971, 56.

43. *New York Times*, 20 December 1970, 42, 28 October 1971, 1.

44. "ABA Convention Approves Abortion 'On Demand,'" in *News Dictionary 1972* (New York: Facts on File, Inc., 1973), 1; "Worldwide Use Widespread," in *News Dictionary 1972*, 2; "Liberalized Laws Urged, Rejected," in *News Dictionary 1971* (New York: Facts on File, Inc., 1972), 2. This report was read into the record during the introduction of the Abortion Rights Act of 1972. See U.S. Congress, *Congressional Record* 118 (2 May 1972): 15331.

45. Nixon-Agnew Campaign Committee, *Nixon on the Issues*, 124.

46. "Speech by Senator Bob Packwood," in Rubin, *The Abortion Controversy*, 72–74.

47. U.S. Congress, *Congressional Record* 116 (15 June 1970): S 20079–80; U.S. Congress, *Congressional Record* 116 (25 August 1970): S 30000; U.S. Congress, *Congressional Record* 116 (12 March 1970): H 5619.

48. U.S. Congress, *Congressional Record* 116 (12 March 1970): H 7415–16; U.S. Congress, *Congressional Record* 116 (12 June 1970): S 19600.

49. U.S. Congress, *Congressional Record* 116 (3 March 1970): S 5616–17.

50. U.S. Congress, *Congressional Record* 116 (3 March 1970): S 5617–18, 116 (15 June 1970): 20079, 116 (25 August 1970): 30001–2, 116 (23 March 1970): H 9450, 116 (12 March 1970): H 7415.

51. U.S. Congress, *Congressional Record* 117 (3 March 1971) 4950; *New York Times*, 21 January 1971, 37. To put the statistic in context, WHMC had 1,953 births between 1 October 1969 and 30 September 1970. See *Selected Statistical Summary for Administrator at Wilford Hall Medical Center*, 1990, in History files at Wilford Hall Medical Center, provided to me by WHMC historian George Kelling, 11 August 1999.

52. U.S. Congress, *Congressional Record* 116 (9 October 1970):35994. In February

1971 Schmitz introduced HR 4257, concerning abortion in the military, but no action was taken. See U.S. Congress, *Congressional Record* 117 (10 February 1971), 2394.

53. *New York Times*, 17 January 1971, 43.

54. U.S. Congress, *Congressional Record* 117 (1 March 1971), 4496; *New York Times*, 21 January 1971, 37.

55. *New York Times*, 7 April 1971, 43.

56. *New York Times*, 4 October 1971, 27.

57. Nixon, "Statement about Policy," 500.

58. U.S. Congress, *Congressional Record* 117 (20 April 1971): H 11016.

59. Ibid.

60. American Friends Service Committee, *Who Shall Live?*

61. U.S. Congress, *Congressional Record* 117 (5 October 1971): 35140, 117 (7 December 1971): 45244.

62. In March 1968 Lt. William Calley led American soldiers into the village of My Lai, where his men murdered more than two hundred civilians, most of them young children, women, and elderly. Three years later a military court convicted him of murder and sentenced him to life in prison. Nixon reduced the sentence to twenty years and then granted him parole in 1974 after serving only three. See Herring, *America's Longest War*, 212, 236.

63. *New York Times*, 13 April 1971, 38.

64. *New York Times*, 5 April 1971, 32.

65. *New York Times*, 22 April 1971, 30.

66. *New York Times*, 13 April 1971, 38, 7 April 1971, 54, 16 April 1971, 73.

67. *New York Times*, 5 April 1971, 32.

68. U.S. Congress, *Congressional Record* 117 (3 May 1971): 13155–61.

69. U.S. Congress, *Congressional Record* 117 (31 July 1971): 28608.

70. U.S. Congress, *Congressional Record* 118 (2 May 1972): 15327–28.

71. Walter quoted in U.S. Congress, *Congressional Record* 118 (2 May 1972): 15331.

72. Nixon, "Statement about the Report," 576.

73. Haldeman, *Haldeman Diaries*, 370.

74. Quoted in Wandersee, *On the Move*, 29.

75. Weddington interview, 7–11; Weddington, *Question of Choice*, 44–70.

76. Weddington, *Question of Choice*, 102–6; Weddington interview, 12–15, 24–28, 60; Greenhouse, *Becoming Justice Blackmun*, 127.

77. *Roe v. Wade*, 166; Greenhouse, *Becoming Justice Blackmun*, 98–99.

78. Carmen interview, 71–72; Goldsmith interview, 16.

79. Shapiro, *Population*, 23; Petchesky, *Abortion*, 117.

80. Kolbert and Miller, "Legal Strategies," 99; "Healthier Mothers," 1809.

81. Executive Committee Minutes, 17 December 1968, file 1968, box 2; Executive Committee Minutes, 11 June 1969, 11 September 1969, and 26 November 1969, Board Minutes, 8 May 1969, Executive Director's Report, "Abortion and the Law," 8 May 1969, file 1969, box 2, all in PPRI Records.

82. Maternal Health Committee Report, Appendix A, 24 January 1968, Abortion Reports file, box 39, RIMS, RIHS Library; H 1659, H 1660, H 1661 all introduced 12 March 1968, *Failed Bills of 1968*, State Archives; *Providence Journal*, 18 March 1968, 23;

H 1400, H 1401, H 1402 all introduced 14 February 1969 and H 1776, 28 March 1969, *Failed Bills of 1969*, State Archives.

83. H 1653, 30 March 1966, *Failed Bills of 1966*, State Archives; *Providence Journal*, 31 March 1966, 1, 2 April 1966, 17, 12 January 1967, 7; H 1069, 11 January 1967, H 1716, 21 March 1967, H 1806, 31 March 1967, *Failed Bills of 1967*, State Archives.

84. Executive Committee Minutes, 16 February 1970, 20 July 1970, and 16 November 1970, Board of Directors Meeting, 20 April 1970, 19 October 1970, file 1970, box 2; Board of Directors Meeting, 18 January 1971, 18 October 1971, file 1971, box 2; Board Minutes, 26 June 1972, Staff Meeting, 29 November 1972, file 1972, box 2, all in PPRI Records.

85. Executive Committee Minutes, 16 February 1970, 20 July 1970, and 16 November 1970, Board of Directors Meeting, 20 April 1970, 19 October 1970, file 1970, box 2; Board of Directors Meeting, 18 January 1971, 18 October 1971, file 1971, box 2; Board Minutes, 26 June 1972, Staff Meeting, 29 November 1972, file 1972, box 2, all in PPRI Records.

86. Executive Committee, 1 February 1973, 16 July 1973, Wise to Executive Committee, 28 February 1973, Wise to Board Members, 20 June 1973, file 1973, box 2, PPRI Records.

87. Wise to Board Members, 20 June 1973, Staff Meeting, 25 April 1973, file 1973, box 2, PPRI Records.

88. Board Meeting Minutes, 25 June 1973, 24 September 1973, file 1973, box 2; Staff Meeting, 4 October 1973, file 1972 [*sic*], box 2, all in PPRI Records.

89. Staff Meeting, 4 October 1973, file 1972 [*sic*], box 2, PPRI Records.

90. *Annual Reports 1973*, 12, file 1973, box 2, PPRI Records.

91. Staff Meeting, 4 October 1973, Cost/Profit Projections of Full Operation in Abortion Services, December 1973, file 1973, box 2, PPRI Records.

92. *Annual Report 1975*, Executive Committee, 14 April 1975, 12 May 1975, Board of Directors Meeting, 27 June 1975, 21 July 1975, file 1975, box 2, PPRI Records.

93. Stein to Viola C. Crolius, Executive Director of PPRI, 12 September 1975, Mimi Frank to Viola C. Crolius, 17 December 1975, file 1975, box 2, PPRI Records.

94. Director of Social Service's Report, *Annual Reports 1973*, 13, file 1973, box 2; Some Thoughts on the Planning Process of PPRI, 1 May 1974, file 1974, box 2; Stein to Crolius, 11 September 1975, file 1975, box 2; Handwritten Sheet and "Planned Parenthood Delivers," *Providence Journal*, February 1976, file 1976, box 2, all in PPRI Records.

95. "Sterilization: New Argument," *U.S. News and World Report*, 24 September 1962, 55.

96. James Ridgeway, "Birth Control by Surgery," *New Republic*, 11 November 1964, 11.

97. "Cruel and Unjust?" *Newsweek*, 13 June 1966, 46; "Jail or Sterilization?" *Time*, 3 June 1966, 46.

98. "Cruel and Unjust?" 46; "Jail or Sterilization?" 46; William F. Buckley, "Sterilize That Woman!" *National Review*, 12 July 1966, 666.

99. "Sterilization Sentiment Focuses on the Poor," *Science News*, 14 May 1966, 371; Slater, "Sterilization," 152.

100. Slater, "Sterilization," 154.

101. Reilly, *Surgical Solution*, 117.

102. "Sterilization Sentiment," 371; Slater, "Sterilization," 152.

103. "Sterilization: New Argument," 55.

104. *New York Times*, 12 September 1962, 13 September 1962; "Sterilize Them!" *America*, 22 September 1962, 764.

105. "Sterilization: New Argument," 55; "A Sterile Issue?" *Newsweek*, 24 September 1962, 88; "Sterilize Them!" 764; "Sterilization in Virginia," *Commonweal*, 28 September 1962, 3.

106. Beal, "Double Jeopardy," in Morgan, *Sisterhood Is Powerful*, 347–49.

107. Hutchins interview, 16; U.S. Congress, Senate, Committee on Government Operations, *Hearings* (1965), 1768; Ridgeway, "Birth Control by Surgery," 9–10; "Voluntary Sterilization," *Time*, 15 January 1965, 43–44. Hartman gave $25,000 for a similar program in several poor Florida counties.

108. The Association for Voluntary Sterilization encouraged sterilization throughout the twentieth century, changing its name several times before it settled in 2001 on EngenderHealth to increase funding opportunities. See <http://www.engenderhealth.org/pubs/ehnews/sp01/sp01_2.html>, accessed 18 September 2006.

109. Gallup, *Gallup Poll Public Opinion*, 2000; Association for Voluntary Sterilization quoted in Shapiro, *Population*, 57–58, 73; "Voluntary Sterilization Approved by Majority," *Science News*, 8 October 1966, 277.

110. Gallup, *Gallup Poll Public Opinion*, 2262; Presser, "Demographic and Social Aspects," 529–33; "One Man's Answer to Over Population," *Life*, 6 March 1970, 42–47; Lawrence Lader, "Laws to Limit Family Size," *Parents Magazine* 45 (October 1970): 58–61; and Walter Goodman, "Abortion and Sterilization: The Search for Answers," *Redbook* 125 (October 1965): 148.

111. U.S. Congress, Senate, Committee on the Federal Role in Health, *Hearings*; Commission on Population Growth and the American Future, *Population and the American Future*, 171.

112. D'Emilio and Freedman, *Intimate Matters*, 255.

113. *Pittsburgh Courier*, 9 November 1968, 1, 24 May 1968, FF 857, box 32, Rice Papers.

114. Slater, "Sterilization," 152; Caress, "Sterilization," 4.

115. Measham, Hatcher, and Arnold, "Physicians and Contraception," 499.

116. National Abortion Action Committee, press release, 12 July 1973, National Abortion Action Committee Files; *New York Times*, 23 April 1971.

117. Measham, Hatcher, and Arnold, "Physicians and Contraception," 499; Shapiro, *Population*, 6–7, 97–98, 116; Petchesky, *Abortion*, 178–82; Roberts, *Killing the Black Body*, 90–91; Schoen, *Choice & Coercion*, 108.

118. U.S. Congress, Senate, Committee on the Federal Role in Health, *Hearings*, 1562–62; Richard R. Babcock, Jr., "Sterilization: Coercing Consent," *Nation*, 12 January 1974, 51; Judith Coburn, "Sterilization Regulations: Debate Not Quelled by HEW Document," *Science*, 8 March 1974, 935–39; Slater, "Sterilization," 150.

119. *Chicago Daily Defender*, 25 July 1973; *Black Panther*, 7 July 1973; *Muhammad Speaks*, 13 July 1973; *New York Daily Challenger*, 17 July 1973; *Pittsburgh Courier*, 21

July 1973; *Afro-American,* 28 July 1973. The Jordan column was also printed in the *Pittsburgh Courier,* 28 July 1973.

120. Babcock, "Sterilization," 51; Coburn, "Sterilization Regulations," 150; Caress, "Sterilization," 1–13.

121. *Pittsburgh Courier,* 21 July 1973, 3; Babcock, "Sterilization," 51; Coburn, "Sterilization Regulations," 150; Caress, "Sterilization," 1–13.

122. *Black Panther,* 11 August 1973; *Afro-American,* 28 July 1973; *Pittsburgh Courier,* 28 July 1973.

123. U.S. Congress, Senate, Committee on the Federal Role in Health, *Hearings,* 1562–63; *Muhammad Speaks,* 31 May 1969, 26 December 1969; *Pittsburgh Courier,* 21 July 1973, 16.

124. Slater, "Sterilization," 152.

125. Dreifus, *Sterilizing the Poor,* 105–7; Judith Herman, "Forced Sterilization," *Sister Courage* (January 1976): 8; Shapiro, *Population,* 90–91; Velez-Ibanez, "Se Me Acabó," 71–91.

126. Rosenfeld, Wolfe, and McGarrah, *Health Research*; Dreifus, *Sterilizing the Poor,* 105–7; Herman, "Forced Sterilization," 8.

127. Torpy, "Native American Women," 8.

128. Shapiro, *Population,* 6–7, 54, 91–92.

129. Shapiro, *Population,* 111, 117–21.

130. Coburn, "Sterilization Regulations," 936; Caress, "Sterilization," 4; Vaughan and Sparer, "Ethnic Group," 224–29.

131. "Sterilization Guidelines: 22 Months on the Shelf," *Medical World News,* 9 November 1973; "White House Named," *Pittsburgh Courier,* 21 July 1973, 1.

132. "White House Named."

133. *Pittsburgh Courier,* 21 July 1973, 1; *Relf et al. v. Weinberger et al.,* 372 F. Supp. 1196 (D.D.C. 1974); *National Welfare Rights Organization v. Weinberger,* Civil Action no. 74-243, 1973. These two cases were consolidated into the Relf case.

134. *Relf et al.*; Babcock, "Sterilization," 51; Coburn, "Sterilization Regulations," 935–39; Slater, "Sterilization," 150; "A Well-Meaning Act," *Newsweek,* 16 July 1973, 26.

135. Coburn, "Sterilization Regulations," 935–39; Babcock, "Sterilization," 52–53.

136. Ibid.

137. Gordon, *Woman's Body,* 433–34; Shapiro, *Population,* 92–93, 107.

138. Hutchins interview, 34–35.

139. Roberts, *Killing the Black Body,* 91.

140. Shapiro, *Population,* 124.

141. Nelson, *Women of Color,* 5–6.

142. Shapiro, *Population,* 142, 148; Gordon, *Woman's Body,* 435.

143. Williams, "Blacks Reject Sterilization," 26; Mudd interview, 254.

144. Annual Report of Medical Director for 1963, 17 April 1964, file 1964, box 2; Medical Director's Report to the Board of Directors, 31 January 1968, file 1968, box 2; *Annual Reports 1970,* 2, file 1970, box 2, all in PPRI Records.

145. *Annual Reports 1970,* Board of Directors Meeting, 19 October 1970, Executive Committee Minutes, 16 November 1970, file 1970, box 2, PPRI Records.

146. Board of Directors Meeting, 18 January 1971, Executive Director's Report, 18

October 1971, file 1971, box 2; Board Minutes, 13 March 1972, and 16 October 1972, file 1972, box 2; Annual Report 1974, file 1974, box 2; *Annual Report 1975*, file 1975, box 2, all in PPRI Records.

147. *Providence Journal*, 20 September 1970, W1.

148. Ibid.

149. Ibid.

150. Restrictions in abortion funding and through parental consent led to increasing illegitimate pregnancies among indigent teens. See *Providence Journal*, 13 June 1989, 3. This report found teen pregnancy highly correlated with poverty: birthrates were ten times higher among poor than among high-income teens. Moreover, more poor teens carried their pregnancies to term than wealthy teens (31 percent of indigent versus 71 percent of wealthy teens aborted).

Chapter 8. Backlash, 1973–2000

1. U.S. Congress, House, Committee on Interior and Insular Affairs, *Oversight Hearing*, 21–24, 38, 42, 156–57, 162, 204.

2. U.S. Congress, House, Committee on Interior and Insular Affairs, *Oversight Hearing,*, 122, 130, 145, 211.

3. U.S. Congress, House, Committee on Interior and Insular Affairs, *Oversight Hearing,*, 1–3, 6, 33, 63, 106, 118, 123, 156–57.

4. U.S. Congress, House, Committee on Interior and Insular Affairs, *Oversight Hearing,*, 30, 134, 140–41, 144, 146, 157, 162.

5. U.S. Congress, House, Committee on Interior and Insular Affairs, *Oversight Hearing,*, 157, 162, 194, 198, 205.

6. U.S. Congress, House, Committee on Interior and Insular Affairs, *Oversight Hearing,*, 50, 168, 170, 199, 205.

7. Samuels and Smith, *Norplant and Poor Women*, ix; Jacqueline Darroch Forrest, "Norplant and Poor Women," in Samuels and Smith, *Norplant and Poor Women*, 21–27; Julia Scott, "Norplant and Women of Color," in Samuels and Smith, *Norplant and Poor Women*, 47.

8. Irving Sivin, "Norplant Clinical Trials," in Samuels and Smith, *Norplant and Poor Women*, 9; Scott, "Norplant and Women of Color," 41; Gehlert and Lickey, "Social and Health Policy Concerns," 333–35; "Hopkins Q&A: Implants, Shots, Effectively Prevent Pregnancy," *Johns Hopkins University/PointCast Network*, 8 July 1999.

9. Samuels and Smith, *Norplant and Poor Women*, x–xi; Gehlert and Lickey, "Social and Health Policy Concerns," 329.

10. "Native American Women Uncover Norplant Abuses," *Ms.* 4 (September–October 1993): 69; Gehlert and Lickey, "Social and Health Policy Concerns," 335; Young, "Reproductive Technologies," 278.

11. Scott, " Norplant and Women of Color," 39, 41–45; "The Norplant Debate," *Newsweek*, 15 February 1993, 40.

12. Beilenson et al., "Politics and Practice," 309–11; "Ending Child Labor," *Economist*, 30 January 1993, 27.

13. Barbara Feringa et al., "Norplant: Potential for Coercion," in Samuels and Smith, *Norplant and Poor Women*, 59–60; Young, "Reproductive Technologies," 264–65.

14. Feringa et al., "Norplant: Potential for Coercion," 59–60; Gehlert and Lickey, "Social and Health Policy Concerns," 328; Young, "Reproductive Technologies," 268; Roberts, *Killing the Black Body*, 108.

15. Scott, "Norplant and Women of Color," 44; Gehlert and Lickey, "Social and Health Policy Concerns," 328.

16. Scott, "Norplant and Women of Color," 44; Young, "Reproductive Technologies," 272, 276, 279; Gehlert and Lickey, "Social and Health Policy Concerns," 328–29; "Shot in the Arm," *New Republic*, 9 December 1991, 16.

17. Gehlert and Lickey, "Social and Health Policy Concerns," 329; Young, "Reproductive Technologies," 276; Alexander Cockburn, "Norplant and the Social Cleansers," *Nation*, 25 July 1994, 116–17; Roberts, *Killing the Black Body*, 112.

18. Nelson and Nelson, "Feminism," S30–32.

19. Feringa et al., "Norplant: Potential for Coercion," 58–60; Young, "Reproductive Technologies," 270, 275.

20. Scott, "Norplant and Women of Color," 45; Young, "Reproductive Technologies," 275–76.

21. Scott, "Norplant and Women of Color," 46; Roberts, "Punishing Drug Addicts," 127, 134; Gehlert and Lickey, "Social and Health Policy Concerns," 330, 332.

22. Feringa et al., "Norplant: Potential for Coercion," 56; Robertson, "Norplant and Irresponsible Reproduction," S23.

23. Young, "Reproductive Technologies," 272–73.

24. "Ein Volk," *Economist*, 1 June 1991, 21.

25. Donald Kaul, "Solution: To Reform Welfare, Consider the Sterilization Bounty," *Winston-Salem Journal*, 12 August 1995, A14.

26. "Controversial Birth-Control Program Gaining Momentum Nationwide," *Associated Press/PointCast Network*, 24 July 1999.

27. Petchesky, *Abortion*, 180; Shapiro, *Population*, 134.

28. Oudshoorn, *The Male Pill*; INFO Project, "Male Hormonal Contraception," April 2005, <http://www.infoforhealth.org/pr/m19/m19chap11.shtml>, accessed 26 December 2005.

29. Oudshoorn, *The Male Pill*, 6, 21–23, 25, 40, 189–90, 224; Tone, *Devices and Desires*, 246, 254, 286, 288.

30. Petchesky, *Abortion*, 173; Oudshoorn, *The Male Pill*, 109–10.

31. "Seeking Viagra Equity," *Associated Press/Pointcast Network*, 30 June 1999; Rick Hepp, "Codey Gets Coverage on Birth Control," *Star Ledger*, 13 December 2005, <http://www.nj.com/statehouse/ledger/index.ssf?/base/news-0/1134454921143580.xml&coll=1>, accessed 31 December 2005.

32. "Hopkins Q&A: 'Morning After' Emergency Contraception," *Associated Press/Pointcast Network*, 23 July 1999.

33. Tamar Lewin, "Abortion Rate," *New York Times*, 5 December 1997; "A Look at the Pill and Other Contraceptive Methods," *Associated Press/Pointcast Network*, 8 July 1999.

34. "The Little White Bombshell," *New York Times Magazine*, 25 July 1999.

35. Goggin, "Understanding," 11–12; Guth et al., "Sources of Antiabortion Attitudes," 75; Petchesky, *Abortion*, 241.

36. Petchesky, *Abortion*, 242–54.

37. Ginsburg, "Rescuing the Nation," 229.

38. Ginsburg, "Rescuing the Nation," 234, 238; Ginsburg, *Contested Lives*, xi–xii.

39. *New York Times*, 18 June 1995, A1.

40. <http://www.usdoj.gov/crt/split/facestat.htm>. The Supreme Court upheld the act as constitutional on 16 April 2001. See <http://usgovinfo.about.com/library/weekly/aa041601a.htm>, accessed 18 October 2001.

41. Ginsburg, *Contested Lives*, xii–xiv, xvi, xxviii–xxix.

42. Ibid., 11, 83–84, 109, 193, 201.

43. Ibid., 78, 170.

44. Wilder, "The Rule of Law," 73–76.

45. Black Americans for Life, *Newsletter* 1, no. 1, n.d., ms. 76.1, HH 984, box 1B, Hall-Hoag Collection.

46. Black Americans for Life, *Newsletter*.

47. Black Americans for Life, *Uniting the Black Community for Life*, 1986, ms. 76.1, HH 984, box 1B, Hall-Hoag Collection.

48. Black Americans for Life, "ABORTION and SLAVERY: arguments parallel," n.d., ms. 76.1, HH 984, box 1B, Hall-Hoag Collection.

49. Black Americans for Life, no title, n.d., pamphlet, ms. 76.1, HH 984, box 1B; MBL, no title, 1989, ms. 76.1, HH 1462, box 1B; MBL, booklet, 1990, ms. 76.1, HH 1462, box 1B, all in Hall-Hoag Collection.

50. MBL, no title, n.d., ms. 76.1, HH 1462, box 1B, Hall-Hoag Collection.

51. Fried, "Abortion in the United States," 212; Ross, "African-American Women," 185, 192–93, 199; Bass, "Toward Coalition," 251–52; Roberts, *Killing the Black Body*, 231, 233.

52. U.S. Congress, *Congressional Record* 119 (31 May 1973): 17538–47; U.S. Congress, Senate, Committee on the Judiciary, Subcommittee on Constitutional Amendments, *Hearings*, 1; U.S. Commission on Civil Rights, *The Constitutional Aspects*.

53. Maginnis interview, 152; Blair interview, 78–81.

54. Greenhouse, *Becoming Justice Blackmun*, 134.

55. Appendix to Opinion of the Court: *Planned Parenthood of Central Missouri v. Danforth*, 428 U.S. Reports 85 (1976); Mudd interview, 265.

56. Rubin, *The Abortion Controversy*, 229; Blair interview, 75.

57. *Weekly Compilation of Presidential Documents* 12, no. 15 (2 April 1976): 552; Carter, *First Lady*, 164; *Weekly Compilations of Presidential Documents* 13, no. 29 (12 July 1977): 990–91.

58. Gelb and Palley, *Women and Public Policies*, chap. 6. In October 1989 Congress altered the Hyde Amendment to conform to the 1977 version. Bush vetoed it, and Congress failed to override it.

59. Call for Action, 6 August 1976, file 1976, box 2, PPRI Records

60. Nicholson and Stewart, "Supreme Court," 159–78. Nicholson and Stewart followed through in "Abortion Policy," 161–68.

61. By the 1980s American Catholics supported abortion and birth control at the same rates as Protestants. Meier and McFarlane, "The Politics of Funding Abortion," 92; Berkman and O'Connor, "Do Women Legislators Matter?" 106–10.

62. Barnartt and Harris, "Recent Changes," 320–34; Cormack, "Women and Social Change," 10–14; Swan, "Gender, the Judiciary," 323–41; Skerry, "Class Conflict," 69–84; Tedrow and Mahoney, "Trends," 181–89; Baker et al., "Matters of Life and Death," 89–102; Legge, "Determinants," 479–90; Benin, "Determinants of Opposition to Abortion," 199–216.

63. Robbins, "Religious Involvement," 365–74; McFalls and Masnick, "Birth Control," 89–106; Combs and Welch, "Blacks, Whites," 510–20; Ezzard et al., "Race-Specific Patterns," 809–14; Hall and Ferree, "Race Differences," 193–207; Moore, Simms, and Betsy, *Choice and Circumstance.*

64. *CQ Almanac* (1980), 63-B, 97-B.

65. Weddington, *Question of Choice*, 203–8; Roberts, *Killing the Black Body*, 118.

66. The House gained twenty-five prochoice votes, and no senators targeted by antichoice forces lost an election. Weddington, *Question of Choice*, 207–8.

67. Senate Joint Resolution 3, 98th Cong., 1st sess., 1983; Weddington, *Question of Choice*, 202–3.

68. Blackmun quoted in Greenhouse, *Becoming Justice Blackmun*, 143.

69. *Akron v. Akron Center for Reproductive Health, Inc.*, 462 U.S. 416; *Planned Parenthood Association of Kansas City v. Ashcroft*, 462 U.S. 476; Weddington, *Question of Choice*, 201–2; Petchesky, *Abortion*, 314. The Court upheld in *Ashcroft* the requirement of a pathology report for abortion, that a second physician be present during abortions performed after viability, and that a minor secure parental consent or consent from the juvenile court for an abortion.

70. *New York Times*, 19 July 1984, 21, 18 August 1984, 8, 22 August 1984, 18; *CQ Almanac* (1985), 55-B, 93-B.

71. U.S. Congress, House, Committee on the Judiciary, *Oversight Hearings*, 6 March, 12 March, and 3 April 1985 and 17 December 1986, 1–2, 39–41, 60–65; Gordon, *Woman's Body*, 412–13.

72. *Thornburgh v. American College of Obstetricians and Gynecologists*, 476 U.S. 747 (1986); Petchesky, *Abortion*, 315; Weddington, *Question of Choice*, 208–9.

73. Rubin, *The Abortion Controversy*, 277; U.S. Congress, House, Committee on Government Operations, Human Resources and Intergovernmental Relations Subcommittee, *Medical and Psychological Impact of Abortion*, 193–96; "Abortion Experience Does Not Appear to Reduce Women's Self-Esteem," *Family Planning Perspectives* 24 (November 1992): 282–83; Lunneborg, *Abortion*, chap. 4.

74. U.S. Congress, House, Committee on Small Business, Subcommittee on Regulation, Business Opportunities and Energy, *Hearings*, 1–3.

75. *Boston Globe*, 10 April 1989, 1.

76. *Boston Globe*, 7 April 1989, 3. Sixty percent of those surveyed in March 1989 did not believe *Roe* should be overturned.

77. *Boston Globe*, 27 April 1989, 1.

78. Eighty-eight percent died in committee, 7 percent died on the floor, 1 percent were vetoed, and 4 percent passed. Berkman and O'Connor, "Do Women Legislators Matter?" 112. One prochoice example is Washington State, which adopted a new amendment to the state constitution that upheld *Roe*.

79. Dellinger quoted in "The Family vs. the State," *Newsweek*, 9 July 1990, 23.

80. Fried, "Abortion in the United States," 215.

81. *Washington Post*, 24 May 1991, A1.

82. *Washington Post*, 24 May 1991, A1; David A. Kaplan, "Abortion: Just Say No Advice," *Newsweek*, 3 June 1991, 18.

83. *Washington Post*, 26 June 1991, A1, 27 June 1991, A8; Tatalovich and Schier, "Persistence of Ideological Cleavage," 135. Bush vetoes occurred on 21 October 1989, 27 October 1989, 20 November 1989, 17 August 1991, and 19 November 1991. George Bush, "President Bush on the Right to Life," 14 April 1992, in Bush Campaign Speeches.

84. Women Exploited by Abortion, *Healing in His Wings*, ms. 76.1, HH 1471, box 2C, Hall-Hoag Collection.

85. *Sisterlife* 10, no. 4 (1990): 2–3, ms. 76.1, HH 1239, box 1B, Hall-Hoag Collection.

86. George Bush, "President Bush on the Right to Life," 22 January 1992, and "Abortion," 3 March 1993, both in Bush Campaign Speeches.

87. "Women on the Run," *Newsweek*, 4 May 1992, 24–25.

88. William J. Clinton, Remarks on Signing Memorandums on Medical Research and Reproductive Health, 22 January 1993, <www.presidency.ucsb.edu/ws/index.php?pid=426198st=Memorandum&st1=Health>, accessed 18 June 2007; Rubin, *The Abortion Controversy*, 285–86.

89. Ginsburg quoted in Greenhouse, *Becoming Justice Blackmun*, 225.

90. Rubin, *The Abortion Controversy*, 287; *New York Times*, 25 January 1994, A1.

91. *New York Times*, 16 June 1995, A19.

92. *Winston-Salem Journal*, 3 August 1995, A7.

93. Black illegitimacy was 22 percent in 1960, 70.4 percent in 1994, 68.4 percent in 2001, and 68 percent in 2002. White illegitimacy increased from 1.9 percent in 1956 to 16.9 percent in 1990 to 22.5 percent in 2001 to 22.9 percent in 2002. Steve Sailer, "Black Illegitimacy Rate Declines," 27 June 2003, <http://www.isteve.com/2003_Black_Illegitimacy_Rate_Declines.htm>, accessed 28 July 2005; Hernstein and Murray, *The Bell Curve*; Kline, *Gender, Sexuality, and Eugenics*, 159.

94. "A Listening Law," *Newsweek*, 6 September 1999, 10; *Los Angeles Times*, 17 September 1999.

95. James Vicini, "Supreme Court Invalidates Anti-Abortion Laws," 28 June 2000, <http://content.entrypoint.com>; Linda Greenhouse, "Court Rules That Governments Can't Outlaw Type of Abortion," 29 June 2000, <http://content.entrypoint.com>, both accessed 7 July 2000.

96. Dayton, "'Taking the Trade,'" 5.

Chapter 9. Conclusion

1. *Winston-Salem Journal*, 5 November 2005, B7.

2. "Welfare Reform," <http://www.libertynet.org/edcivic/welfref.html>, accessed 15 November 2005; <http://thomas.loc.gov/cgi-bin/bdquery/z?d104:h.r.03734/>, accessed 15 November 2005.

3. "Senate Approves Cuts, but Not Drilling," *Washington Post*, 22 December 2005, <http://www.washingtonpost.com/wp-dyn/content/article/2005/12/21/AR2005122100748.html>, accessed 22 December 2005.

4. Roberts, *Killing the Black Body*, 4, 10, 248, 254–55; Feldstein, *Motherhood in Black and White*.

5. "A Mouse That Roars Turns 25: An Interview with CFFC President Frances Kissling," May 1998, <http://www.cath4choice.org/lowbandwidth/aboutus.htm>, accessed 1 December 2005.

6. Gretchen Cook, "The Battle over Birth Control," 27 April 2005, <http://www.salon.com/news/feature/2005/04/27/birth_control/print.html>, accessed 31 December 2005.

7. Nancy McVicar, "Morning-after Pill Becomes Flashpoint in Abortion Debate," *Kansas City Star*, 28 December 2005, <http://www.kansascity.com/mld/kansascity/news/nation/13500155.htm>, accessed 31 December 2005.

Bibliography

Archival Sources

American Birth Control League (ABCL) Papers. Houghton Library, Harvard University, Cambridge, Massachusetts.

Bureau of Social Hygiene (BSH) Records. Rockefeller Archives Center, North Tarrytown, New York.

Bush, George. Campaign Speeches. Sunsite Archives, University of North Carolina, Chapel Hill.

Coroners' Records, Supreme Court. Judicial Records Center, 1 Hill Street, Pawtucket, Rhode Island.

Family Planning Oral History Project, Records 1909–84, MC 223. Schlesinger Library, Radcliffe Institute, Harvard University, Cambridge, Massachusetts.

Hall-Hoag Collection. John Hay Library, Brown University, Providence, Rhode Island.

Lownes Science Collection. John Hay Library, Brown University, Providence, Rhode Island.

National Abortion Action Committee Files. Schlesinger Library, Radcliffe College, Cambridge, Massachusetts.

Planned Parenthood Center of Pittsburgh (PPCP) Papers. University of Pittsburgh, Pittsburgh, Pennsylvania.

Planned Parenthood League of Massachusetts. Smith College, Northampton, Massachusetts.

Poteat, William Louis. Collection. Baptist Collection. Z. Smith Reynolds Library, Wake Forest University, Winston-Salem, North Carolina.

Records of the Davol Manufacturing Company; Records of the Ladies Moral Reform Association; Providence Female Domestic Missionary Society Records; Providence Physiological Society Records; Miscellaneous Material of the Rhode Island Historical Society; Rhode Island Medical Society (RIMS) Collection; Planned Parenthood of Rhode Island (PPRI) Records. Rhode Island Historical Society Library (RIHS), Providence, Rhode Island.

Records of the Rhode Island Medical Society. Rhode Island Medical Society Library, Providence, Rhode Island.

Rhode Island Collection. Providence Public Library, Providence, Rhode Island.

Rhode Island Medical Society Collection. John Hay Library, Brown University, Providence, Rhode Island.

Rice, Charles Owen. Papers. Hillman Library, University of Pittsburgh, Pittsburgh, Pennsylvania.

Sanger, Margaret. Papers. Sophia Smith Collection. Smith College, Northampton, Massachusetts.

Sidney S. Rider Collection. John Hay Library, Brown University, Providence, Rhode Island.

South Carolina Medical Society (SCMS) Records. Waring Historical Library, Charleston, South Carolina.

Starred Book Collection, HQ31 C77 1872. John Hay Library, Brown University, Providence, Rhode Island.

State Archives. Providence, Rhode Island.

Storer, Horatio R. Papers. Rare Book Room, Countway Medical Library, Harvard Medical Library.

Twin City Hospital Records. Dorothy Carpenter Medical Archives, Wake Forest University School of Medicine, Winston-Salem, North Carolina.

Urban League of Rhode Island Papers. Phillips Memorial Library, Providence College, Providence, Rhode Island.

Books and Articles

Abernathy, James R., Bernard G. Greenberg, and Daniel G. Horvitz. "Estimates of Induced Abortion in Urban North Carolina." *Demography* 7 (February 1970): 19.

Abramovitz, Mimi. *Regulating the Lives of Women: Social Welfare Policy from Colonial Times to the Present.* Boston: South End Press, 1991.

Acts and Resolves of the General Assembly. Providence: Knowles, Anthony and Company, 1861.

Acts and Resolves of the General Assembly of the State of Rhode Island and Providence Plantation. Providence: A. Crawford Greene, 1861.

Acts and Resolves of the General Assembly of the State of Rhode Island and Providence Plantation. Providence: Providence Press Company, 1867.

Acts and Resolves Passed by the General Assembly. Providence: E. L. Freeman and Sons, 1897.

American Friends Service Committee. *Who Shall Live? Man's Control over Birth and Death.* New York: Hill and Wang, 1970.

Atkinson, Thomas G. "Sociological Status of the Fetus in Utero." *Medical Standard* April 1906: 182–86.

Babcock, Richard R., Jr. "Sterilization: Coercing Consent." *Nation,* 12 January 1974, 51.

Baehr, Ninia. *Abortion without Apology: Radical History for the 1990s.* Boston: South End Press, 1991.

Baker, Ross K., et al. "Matters of Life and Death: Social, Political, and Religious Correlates of Attitudes on Abortion." *American Political Quarterly* 9 (1981): 89–102.

Baraka, Imamu Amiri, ed. *African Congress—A Documentary of the First Modern Pan-African Congress.* New York: William Morrow, 1972.

Barker-Benfield, G. J. *The Horrors of the Half-Known Life: Male Attitudes toward Women and Sexuality in Nineteenth Century America.* New York: Harper and Row, 1976.

Barnartt, Sharon N., and Richard J. Harris. "Recent Changes in Predictors of Abortion Attitudes." *Sociology and Social Research* 66 (1982): 320–34.

Bartholomew, Berta C. "A Follow-up Study of 376 Patients from the Maternal Health Center of Syracuse, New York." *Human Fertility* 5 (1940): 89–111.

Bass, Marie. "Toward Coalition." In Solinger, *Abortion Wars*, 251–68.

Bates, Jerome E., Edward S. and Zawadski. *Criminal Abortions*. Springfield, Ill.: Charles C. Thomas, 1964.

Bates, Marston. *The Prevalence of People*. New York: Charles Scribner's Sons, 1955.

Beale, Octavius Charles. *Racial Decay*. London: Angus and Robertson, 1911.

Beebe, Gilbert Wheeler. *Contraception and Fertility in the Southern Appalachians*. Baltimore: Williams and Wilkins Company, 1942.

Beilenson, Peter L., et al. "Politics and Practice: Introducing Norplant into a School-Based Health Center in Baltimore." *American Journal of Public Health* 85 (March 1995): 309–11.

Beisel, Nicola. *Imperiled Innocents: Anthony Comstock and Family Reproduction in Victoria America*. Princeton: Princeton University Press, 1997.

Bellingham, Bruce, and Mary Pugh Mathis. "Race, Citizenship, and the Bio-politics of the Maternalist Welfare State: 'Traditional' Midwifery in the American South under the Sheppard-Towner Act, 1921–1929." *Social Politics* 1 (Summer 1994): 157–89.

Benin, Mary Holland. "Determinants of Opposition to Abortion: An Analysis of the Hard and Soft Scales." *Sociological Perspectives* 28 (1985): 199–216.

Berkman, Michael B., and Robert E. O'Connor. "Do Women Legislators Matter? Female Legislators and State Abortion Policy." *American Politics Quarterly* 21 (January 1993): 102–24.

Billington, Ray Allen. *The Protestant Crusade, 1800–1860*. New York: Macmillan, 1938.

Blacker, C. P. *Birth Control and the State*. New York: E. P. Dutton and Company, 1926.

Blanchard, Dallas A. *The Anti-Abortion Movement and the Rise of the Religious Right: From Polite to Fiery Protest*. New York: Twayne Publishers, 1994.

Blank, Robert H. "Judicial Decision Making and Biological Fact: *Roe v. Wade* and the Unresolved Question of Fetal Viability." *Western Political Quarterly* 37 (1984): 584–602.

Bogue, Donald J. *The Population of the United States*. Oxford, Ohio: Scripps Foundation, 1959.

Boles, Janet K. "Abortion Policymaking a Decade after *Roe*." *Policy Studies Review* 2 (1982): 133–35.

Bouvier, Leon F. "America's Baby Boom Generation: The Fateful Bulge." *Population Bulletin* 35 (April 1980): 8–9.

Branca, Patricia. *Silent Sisterhood: Middle Class Women in the Victorian House*. London, 1975.

Brandt, Allan M. *No Magic Bullet: A Social History of Venereal Disease in the United States since 1880*. New York: Oxford University Press, 1985.

Braslow, Joel T. "In the Name of Therapeutics: The Practice of Sterilization in a California State Hospital." *Journal of the History of Medicine and Allied Sciences* 51 (January 1996): 29–51.

Bravmann, Scott. "(Almost) Nothing Queer Here: Comment on Joshua Gamson's 'Rubber Wars.'" *Journal of the History of Sexuality* 2 (July 1991): 98–102.

Briggs, Laura. *Reproducing Empire: Race, Sex, Science, and U.S. Imperialism in Puerto Rico*. Berkeley: University of California Press, 2002.

Brinner, Endre K., and Louis Newton. "Abortions in Relation to Births in 10,609 Pregnancies." *American Journal of Obstetrics and Gynecology* 38 (1939): 80–91.

Brodie, Janet Farrell. *Contraception and Abortion in 19th-Century America*. Ithaca: Cornell University Press, 1994.

Bromley, Dorothy Dunbar. "Birth Control and the Depression." *Harper's Monthly Magazine* 169 (October 1934): 563–74.

Brooks, Carol Flora. "The Early History of the Anti-Contraceptive Laws in Massachusetts and Connecticut." *American Quarterly* 18 (Spring 1966): 3–23.

Brown, H. Rap. *Die Nigger Die*. New York: Dial Press, 1969.

Bruno, Hal. "Birth Control, Welfare Funds, and the Politics of Illinois." *Reporter*, 20 June 1963, 32–34.

Bullough, Vern L. "A Brief Note on Rubber Technology and Contraception: The Diaphragm and the Condom." *Technology and Culture* 22 (1981): 104–11.

———. "Women: Birth Control, Prostitution, and the Pox." *Transactions of the Conference Group for Social and Administrative History* 6 (1976): 20–28.

Bumpass, Larry L., and Harriet B. Presser. "Contraceptive Sterilization in the United States: 1965 and 1970." *Demography* 9 (November 1972): 531–46.

———. "The Increasing Acceptance of Sterilization and Abortion." In *Toward the End of Growth*, edited by Charles Westoff. 33–46. Englewood Cliffs, N.J.: Prentice-Hall, 1973.

———. "The Risk of an Unwanted Birth: The Changing Context of Contraceptive Sterilization in the United States." *Population Studies* 41 (1987): 347–63.

Burch, Guy Irving. "America's Manpower in the Postwar World." *Population Bulletin* 1 (September 1945): 1–7.

———. "Birth Rates and Education." *Population Bulletin* 2 (January–February): 1–11.

———. "Differences in Birth Rate." *Population Bulletin* 1 (December 1945): 25–31.

———. "Is American Intelligence Declining?" *Population Bulletin* 3 (June 1947): 9–18.

———. "Needed—Higher Birth Rate among Scientists." *Population Bulletin* 1 (October 1945): 9–15.

———. "A Revolution in Birth Rates." *Population Bulletin* 5 (July 1949): 17–23.

Burns, John. *Observations on Abortion*. Troy, NY: Wright, Goodenow, and Stockwell, 1808. Rhode Island Medical Society Collection, John Hay Library.

Bush, Lester E., Jr. "Birth Control among the Mormons: Introduction to an Insistent Question." *Dialogue* 10 (1976): 12–44.

Butler, J. Douglas, and David F. Walbert, eds. *Abortion, Medicine, and the Law*. 3rd ed. New York: Facts on File Publications, 1986.

Cadbury, George W. "Outlook for Government Action in Family Planning in the West Indies." In *Research in Family Planning*, edited by Clyde Kiser. 317–33. Princeton, N.J.: Princeton University Press, 1962.

Cade, Toni, ed. *The Black Woman: An Anthology*. New York: New American Library, 1970.

Calderone, Mary Steichen, ed. *Abortion in the United States*. New York: Hoeber, 1958.

———. "Illegal Abortion as a Public Health Problem." *American Journal of Public Health* 50 (July 1960): 948–54.

Calhoun, Arthur W. *A Social History of the American Family*. Vol. 3. New York: Barnes and Noble, 1917. Reprint, 1945.

Calverton, V. F. *The Bankruptcy of Marriage*. New York: Macauley, 1928.

Campbell, Flann. "Birth Control and the Christian Churches." *Population Studies* 14 (1960): 131–47.

Caress, Barbara. "Sterilization: Women Fit to Be Tied." *Health/PAC Bulletin*, no. 62 (January–February 1975): 1–13.

Carey, Allison C. "Gender and Compulsory Sterilization Programs in America: 1907–1950." *Journal of Historical Sociology* 11 (1998): 74–105.

Carpenter, Niles. *Immigrants and Their Children 1920*. Washington, D.C.: Government Printing Office, 1927.

Carter, Rosalynn. *First Lady from Plains*. Boston: Houghton Mifflin, 1984.

Chapple, W. A. *The Fertility of the Unfit*. London: Whitcombe and Tombs, 1905.

Cherlin, Andrew J. "Explaining the Postwar Baby Boom." *Social Science Research Council Items* 34 (1981): 57–63.

Chesler, Ellen. *Woman of Valor: Margaret Sanger and the Birth Control Movement in America*. New York: Simon and Schuster, 1992.

Chisholm, Shirley. *Unbought and Unbossed*. Boston: Houghton Mifflin, 1970.

Cirillo, Vincent J. "Edward Bliss Foote: Pioneer American Advocate of Birth Control." *Bulletin of the History of Medicine* 47 (1973): 471–79.

———. "Edward Foote's 'Medical Common Sense': An Early American Comment on Birth Control." *Journal of the History of Medicine and Allied Science* 25 (1970): 341–45.

Clarke, Prescott O. *Rhode Island and Providence Plantations*. Providence: E. A. Johnson, Printers, 1885.

Cline, David P. *Creating Choice: A Community Responds to the Need for Abortion and Birth Control, 1961–1973*. New York: Palgrave Macmillan, 2006.

Coale, Ansley J., and Melvin Zelnik. *New Estimates of Fertility and Population in the United States*. Princeton: Princeton University Press, 1963.

Cobb, W. Montague. "The Negro as a Biological Element in the American Population." *Journal of Negro Education* 8 (July 1939): 341–52.

Coburn, Judith. "Sterilization Regulations: Debate Not Quelled by HEW Document." *Science*, 8 March 1974, 935–39.

Cohen, A. S. "No Legal Impediment: Access to Abortion in the United States." *Journal of American Studies* 20 (1986): 189–205.

Cohen, Patricia Cline. "Ministerial Misdeeds: The Onderdonk Trial and Sexual Harassment in the 1840s." *Journal of Women's History* 7 (Fall 1995): 34–57.

———. *The Murder of Helen Jewett: The Life and Death of a Prostitute in Nineteenth-Century New York*. New York: Alfred A. Knopf, 1998.

Colaianni, James. *The Catholic Left*. Philadelphia: Chilton Book Company, 1968.

Coleman, Peter J. *The Transformation of Rhode Island, 1790–1860*. Providence: Brown University Press, 1963.

Colker, Ruth. *Abortion and Dialogue*. Bloomington: Indiana University Press, 1992.

Combs, Michael W., and Susan Welch. "Blacks, Whites, and Attitudes toward Abortion." *Public Opinion Quarterly* 46 (1982): 510–20.

Commander, Lydia Kingsmill. *The American Idea*. New York: A. S. Barnes and Company, 1907.

Commission on Population Growth and the American Future. *Population and the American Future*. New York: Signet, 1972.

Cook, Elizabeth Adell, Ted G. Jelen, and Clyde Wilcox. *Between Two Absolutes: Public Opinion and the Politics of Abortion*. Boulder: Westview Press, 1992.

———. "Generational Differences in Attitudes toward Abortion." *American Politics Quarterly* 21 (January 1993): 31–53.

Cook, Robert A. "Population Changes in the United States." *Population Bulletin* 9 (December 1953): 89–99.

Cormack, Margaret. "Women and Social Change." *Pacific History* 26 (1982): 10–14.

Cosmas, Graham S., and Albert E. Cowdry. *The Medical Department: Medical Service in the European Theatre of Operations*. Washington, D.C.: Center of Military History United States Army, 1992.

Cox, Earnest S. *White America*. Richmond, Va.: White America Society, 1923. Rev. ed. 1937 <www.churchoftrueisrael.com/cox>.

CQ Almanac. Washington, D.C.: Congressional Quarterly, Inc., 1980.

CQ Almanac. Washington, D.C.: Congressional Quarterly, Inc., 1985.

Crawford, S. K. "Criminal Abortion." Illinois State Medical Society, *Transactions* (1872): 77–78.

Critchlow, Donald T. *Intended Consequences: Birth Control, Abortion, and the Federal Government in Modern America*. New York: Oxford University Press, 1999.

Crum, Gary, and Thelma McCormack. *Abortion: Pro-Choice or Pro-Life?* Washington, D.C.: American University Press, 1992.

Curran, Charles E. *Issues in Sexual and Medical Ethics*. Notre Dame: University of Notre Dame, 1978.

Cutright, Phillips. "Illegitimacy in the United States: 1920–1968." In Westoff and Parke, *Demographic and Social Aspects of Population Growth*, 375–438.

Cutright, Phillips, and Frederick S. Jaffe. "Family Planning Program Effects on the Fertility of Low-Income U.S. Women." *Family Planning Perspectives* 8 (May–June 1976): 100–120.

———. *Impact of Family Planning Programs on Fertility: The U.S. Experience*. New York: Praeger, 1977.

Cvornyek, Robert L., and Dorothy L. Cvornyek. "'I Know Something Awful Is Going to Happen': Abortion in the Early Twentieth Century." *Southern Studies* 24 (1985): 229–32.

D'Antonio, W. V. "Birth Control and Coercion." *Commonweal*, 2 December 1966, 249.

David, Henry P. "Unwanted Pregnancies: Costs and Alternatives." In Westoff and Parke, *Demographic and Social Aspects of Population Growth*, 449–50.

David, Paul A., and Warren C. Sanderson. "The Emergence of a Two-Child Norm among American Birth Controllers." *Population and Development Review* 13 (March 1987): 1–41.

Davis, Angela. *Angela Davis: An Autobiography*. New York: Random House, 1974.

———. *Women, Race and Class*. New York: Random House, 1981.

Davis, Kenneth S. "The Story of the Pill." *American Heritage* 29 (1978): 80–91.

Davis, Nanette J. *From Crime to Choice: The Transformation of Abortion in America.* Westport, Conn.: Greenwood Press, 1985.

Davis, Sue. *Women under Attack: Victories, Backlash, and the Fight for Reproductive Freedom.* Boston: South End Press, 1991.

Davis, Thurston N. "Of Many Things." *America,* 6 November 1965, 511.

Dawson, Deborah A., Denise J. Meny, and Jeanne Clare Ridley. "Fertility Control in the United States before the Contraceptive Revolution." *Family Planning Perspectives* 12 (1980): 76–86.

Day, Lincoln H., and Alice Taylor Day. *Too Many Americans.* Boston: Houghton Mifflin, 1964.

Daynes, Byron W., and Raymond Tatalovich. "Religious Influence and Congressional Voting on Abortion." *Journal for the Scientific Study of Religion* 23 (1984): 197–200.

Dayton, Cornelia Hughes. "'Taking the Trade': Abortion and Gender Relations in an Eighteenth-Century New England Village." In *Controlling Reproduction: An American History,* edited by Andrea Tone, 3–19. Wilmington, Del.: Scholarly Resources, Inc., 1997.

Degler, Carl N. *At Odds: Women and the Family in America from the Revolution to the Present.* New York: Oxford University Press, 1980.

———. *Out of Our Past.* New York: Harper and Brothers, 1959.

DeJong, G. F., and R. R. See. "Changes in Childlessness in the United States: A Demographic Path Analysis." *Population Studies* 31 (1977): 129–42.

D'Emilio, John, and Estelle B. Freedman. *Intimate Matters: A History of Sexuality in America.* New York: Harper and Row, 1988.

Dennett, Mary Ware. *Birth Control Laws: Shall We Keep Them, Change Them, or Abolish Them.* New York: Grafton Press, 1926.

Dennison, George M. *The Dorr War: Republicanism on Trial, 1831–1861.* Seattle: University of Washington Press, 1976.

Desmond, Annabelle. "U.S.A. Population Growth: Projections to 1980." *Population Bulletin* 15 (May 1959): 37–59.

Dienes, C. Thomas. *Law, Politics, and Birth Control.* Urbana: University of Illinois Press, 1972.

Djerassi, Carl. "Fertility Control through Abortion: An Assessment of the Period 1950–1980." *Science and Public Affairs* 28 (1972): 9–14, 41–45.

———. *The Politics of Contraception.* New York: W. W. Norton, 1979.

Dorr, Lisa Lindquist. "Arm and Arm: Gender, Eugenics, and Virginia's Racial Integrity Acts of the 1920s." *Journal of Women's History* 11 (Spring 1999): 143–66.

Douglas, Emily Taft. *Margaret Sanger: Pioneer of the Future.* New York: Holt, Rinehart and Winston, 1970.

Dowbiggin, Ian Robert. *Keeping America Sane: Psychiatry and Eugenics in the United States and Canada, 1880–1940.* Ithaca: Cornell University Press, 1997.

Dreifus, Claudia. *Sterilizing the Poor.* Madison: Progressives, Inc., 1975.

Dressel, Paula. "Patriarchy and Social Welfare Work." *Social Problems* 34 (June 1987): 294–309.

Driver, Edwin D., ed. *Essays on Population Policy*. Lexington, Mass.: D. C. Heath and Company, 1972.

Dryfos, J. G., et al. "Eighteen Months Later: Family Planning Services in the United States, 1969." *Family Planning Perspectives* 3 (1971): 29–44.

Dublin, Louis I. *The Excesses of Birth Control*. New York: 1925.

———. "The Fallacious Propaganda for Birth Control." *Atlantic Monthly* 137 (February 1926): 186–94.

DuBois, W.E.B. "Birth." *Crisis* 24 (October 1922): 248–50.

———. "Black Folk and Birth Control." *Birth Control Review* June 1932: 166–67.

———. "The Damnation of Women." In *Darkwater: Voices from within the Veil*, edited by Herbert Aptheker. 163–86. New York, 1921. Reprint, Millwood, N.Y., 1975.

Durand, John D. "Married Women in the Labor Force." *American Journal of Sociology* 52 (November 1946): 217–23.

Dyer, Thomas G. *Theodore Roosevelt and the Idea of Race*. Baton Rouge: Louisiana State University Press, 1980.

Easterlin, Richard A. *The American Baby Boom in Historical Perspective*. New York: National Bureau of Economic Research, 1962.

———. "Factors in the Decline of Farm Fertility in the United States: Some Preliminary Research Results." *Journal of American History* 63 (December 1976): 600–614.

———. *Population, Labor Force and Long Swings in Economic Growth*. New York: National Bureau of Economic Research, 1968.

Egner, G. *Contraception vs. Tradition: A Catholic Critique*. New York: Herder and Herder, 1967.

Ehrenreich, Barbara, and Deirdre English. *For Her Own Good: 150 Years of the Experts' Advice to Women*. New York: Anchor Press/Doubleday, 1978.

———. *Witches, Midwives, and Nurses: A History of Women Healers*. Oster Bay, N.Y.: Glass Mountain Pamphlets, 1973.

Ellis, Havelock. *The Problem of Race-Regeneration*. New York: Cassell and Company, 1911.

Emerick, Charles F. "College Women and Race Suicide." *Political Science Quarterly* 24 (June 1909): 269–83.

Emigration, Emigrants, and Know Nothings. Philadelphia: Published for the Author, 1854.

Erskine, Hazel. "The Polls: More on the Population Explosion and Birth Control." *Public Opinion Quarterly* Summer 1967: 303–13.

Ezzard, Nancy V., Willard Cates, Jr., Dorine G. Kramer, and Christopher Tietze. "Race-Specific Patterns of Abortion Use by American Teenagers." *American Journal of Public Health* 72 (August 1982): 809–14.

Fairchild, Henry Pratt. "Family Limitation and the War." *Annals of the American Academy* 229 (September 1943): 79–86.

Falik, Marilyn. *Ideology and Abortion Policy Politics*. New York: Praeger Publishers, 1983.

Faulkner, Harold Underwood. *The Quest for Social Justice 1898–1914*. Vol. 11 of *A History of American Life*. Edited by Arthur M. Schlesinger and Dixon Ryan Fox. 12 vols. New York: Macmillan, 1927–44.

Fauset, Jessie Redmon. *The Chinaberry Tree: A Novel of American Life*. New York: Negro Universities Press, 1931.

Feldstein, Ruth. *Motherhood in Black and White: Race and Sex in American Liberalism, 1930–1965*. Ithaca: Cornell University Press, 2000.

Field, Marilyn Jane. *The Comparative Politics of Birth Control: Determinants of Policy Variation and Change in the Developed Nations*. New York: Praeger, 1983.

Finch, B. E., and Hugh Green. *Contraception through the Ages*. Springfield, Ill.: Charles C. Thomas, Publishers, 1963.

Finkle, Jason L., and Barbara B. Crane. "Ideology and Politics at Mexico City: The United States at the 1984 International Conference on Population." *Population and Development Review* 11 (1985): 1–28.

Fiscus, Ronald Jerry. "Before the Velvet Curtain: The Connecticut Contraceptive Cases as a Study in Constitutional Law and Supreme Court Behavior." Ph.D. dissertation, University of Wisconsin, Madison, 1983.

Fish, Carl Russell. *The Rise of the Common Man, 1830–1850*. Vol. 6 of *A History of American Life*. Edited by Arthur M. Schlesinger and Dixon Ryan Fox. 12 vols. New York: Macmillan, 1927–44.

Formisano, Ronald P. *The Birth of Mass Political Parties: Michigan 1827–1861*. Princeton: Princeton University Press, 1971.

Forrest, J. D., E. Sullivan, and C. Tietze. "Abortion in the United States, 1977 and 1978." *Family Planning Perspectives* 11 (November–December 1978): 330–41.

Forrest, Jacqueline Darroch. "Norplant and Poor Women." In *Norplant and Poor Women*, edited by Samuels and Smith. 19–38.

Foster, Colin, and G. S. L. Tucker. *Economic Opportunity and White American Fertility Ratios, 1800–1860*. New Haven: Yale University Press, 1972.

Francome, Colin. *Abortion Freedom: A Worldwide Movement*. London: George Allen and Unwin, 1984.

Franks, Angela. *Margaret Sanger's Eugenic Legacy: The Control of Fertility*. Jefferson, N.C.: McFarland and Company, 2005.

Franz, Margaret-Mary, and Motoko Chibak. "Abortion, Contraception, and Motherhood in Post-war Japan and the United States." *International Journal of Women's Studies* 3 (1980): 66–75.

Fried, Marlene Gerber. "Abortion in the United States—Legal but Inaccessible." In Solinger, *Abortion Wars*, 208–26.

———, ed. *From Abortion to Reproductive Freedom: Transforming a Movement*. Boston: South End Press, 1990.

Friedan, Betty. *The Feminine Mystique*. New York: Dell Publishing Company, 1963.

Frieze, Jacob. *Concise History of the Efforts to Obtain an Extension of Suffrage in Rhode Island; from the Years 1811–1842*. Providence: Benjamin F. Moore, Printer, 1842.

Frohock, Fred M. *Abortion: A Case Study in Law and Morals*. Westport, Conn.: Greenwood Press, 1983.

Furstenberg, F., et al. "Birth Control Knowledge and Attitudes among Unmarried Pregnant Adolescents: A Preliminary Report." *Journal of Marriage and the Family* 31 (1969): 34–42.

Gallup, George Horace. *The Gallup Poll: Public Opinion, 1935–1971.* New York: Random House, 1972.

Gamson, Joshua. "Rubber Wars: Struggles over the Condom in the United States." *Journal of the History of Sexuality* 1 (October 1990): 262–82.

Gardner, Augustus K. *Conjugal Sins against the Laws of Life and Health and Their Effect upon the Father, Mother, and Child.* New York, 1870.

Gardner, Richard N. "The Politics of Population: A Blueprint for International Cooperation." *Department of State Bulletin,* 10 June 1963, 19.

———. *Population Growth: A World Problem, Statement of U.S. Policy.* Washington, D.C.: U.S. Department of State, 1963.

———. "Toward a World Population Program." *International Organization* 22 (1968): 350.

Garfinkel, Irwin, and Sara S. McLanahan. *Single Mothers and Their Children.* Washington, D.C.: Urban Institute Press, 1986.

Gaulard, Joan M. "Woman Rebel: A Rhetorical Analysis of Margaret Sanger and the Birth Control Movement in America, 1912–1938." Ph.D. dissertation (Indiana University, 1978).

Gebhard, Paul, et al. *Pregnancy, Birth and Abortion.* New York, 1958.

Gehlert, Sarah, and Sarah Lickey. "Social and Health Policy Concerns Raised by the Introduction of the Contraceptive Norplant." *Social Service Review* 69 (June 1995): 323–37.

Gelb, Joyce, and Marian Lief Palley. *Women and Public Policies.* Princeton: Princeton University Press, 1982.

General Laws of Rhode Island 1956. Indianapolis: Bobbs-Merrill Company, 1956.

General Laws of the State of Rhode Island and Providence Plantations of the United States and of the State. Providence: E. L. Freeman and Sons, 1896.

Giddings, Paula. *Where and When I Enter: The Impact of Black Women on Race and Sex in America.* New York: Bantam Books, 1984.

Ginsburg, Faye D. *Contested Lives: The Abortion Debate in an American Community.* Berkeley: University of California Press, 1989. Rev. ed., 1998.

———. "Rescuing the Nation." In Solinger, Abortion Wars, 227–50.

Gittins, Diana. *Fair Sex: Family Size and Structure, 1900–1939.* London: Hutchinson, 1982.

Glen, Kristin Booth. "Abortion in the Courts: A Laywoman's Historical Guide to the New Disaster Area." *Feminist Studies* 4 (1978): 1–26.

Goddard, William G. *An Address to the People of Rhode Island.* Providence: Knowles and Vose, Printers, 1843.

Goggin, Malcolm L. "Understanding the New Politics of Abortion: A Framework and Agenda for Research." *American Politics Quarterly* 21 (January 1993): 4–30.

Goldman, Emma. "Love and Marriage." In *Woman Rebel,* edited by Alex Baskin. 3. New York: Archives of Social History, 1976.

Goldstein, Leslie F. *The Constitutional Rights of Women.* New York: Longman, 1979.

Goldstein, Michael S. "Creating and Controlling a Medical Market: Abortion in Los Angeles after Liberalization." *Social Problems* 31 (1984): 514–29.

Goldstein, Sidney, and Kurt B. Mayer. *The People of Rhode Island, 1960*. Providence: Rhode Island Development Council, 1963.

Gordon, Linda. "The Long Struggle for Reproductive Rights." *Radical America* Spring 1981: 75–88.

———. "The Politics of Population: Birth Control and the Eugenics Movement." *Radical America* 8 (1974): 61–98.

———. "Social Purity and Birth Control: The Use of Eugenics Ideas by Feminists in the 1890s." *Transactions of the Conference Group for Social and Administrative History* 6 (1976): 32–56.

———. "Voluntary Motherhood: The Beginnings of Feminist Birth Control Ideas in the United States." *Feminist Studies* 1 (1973): 5–22.

———. "Who Is Frightened of Reproductive Freedom for Women and Why? Some Historical Answers." *Frontiers* 9 (1986): 23–26.

———. *Woman's Body, Woman's Right: A Social History of Birth Control in America*. Rev. ed. New York: Penguin Books, 1990.

Gould, Ketayun H. "Family Planning and Abortion Policy in the United States." *Social Service Review* 53 (1979): 452–63.

Graham, Sylvester. *Lecture to Young Men*. Providence: Weeden and Cory, 1834. John Hay Library at Brown University.

Granberg, Donald. "The Abortion Activists." *Family Planning Perspectives* 13 (July–August 1981): 45–56.

———. "An Anomaly in Political Perception." *Public Opinion Quarterly* 49 (1985): 504–16.

———. "Pro-Life or Reflection of Conservative Ideology? An Analysis of Opposition to Legalized Abortion." *Sociology and Social Research* 62 (1978): 414–29.

Granberg, Donald, and Donald Denney. "The Coathanger and the Rose." *Society* 19 (1982): 39–46.

Granberg, Donald, and Beth Wellman Granberg. "Pro-Life Versus Pro-Choice: Another Look at the Abortion Controversy in the U.S." *Sociology and Social Research* 65 (July 1981): 424–34.

Greene, Wade. "Federal Birth Control: Progress without Policy." *Reporter,* 18 November 1965, 36.

Greenhouse, Linda. *Becoming Justice Blackmun: Harry Blackmun's Supreme Court Journey*. New York: Henry Holt and Company, 2005.

Greer, Germaine. *Sex and Destiny: The Politics of Human Fertility*. New York: Harper and Row, 1984.

Grey, Michael R. *New Deal Medicine: The Rural Health Programs of the Farm Security Administration*. Baltimore: Johns Hopkins University Press, 1999.

Grimké, Angelina W. *Rachel*. In *Black Theatre U.S.A.: Forty-Five Plays by Black Americans, 1847– 1974*, edited by James Hatch, 149–72. New York: Macmillan, 1974.

Grob, Gerald N. *The Mad among Us: A History of the Care of America's Mentally Ill*. Cambridge, Mass.: Harvard University Press, 1994.

Gugliotta, Angela. "'Dr. Sharp with His Little Knife': Therapeutic and Punitive Origins of Eugenic Vasectomy—Indiana, 1892–1921." *Journal of the History of Medicine and Allied Sciences* 53 (October 1998): 371–406.

Gustaveson, Patricia B. *Implementation of Family Planning Policy by Public Welfare.* Chapel Hill: Carolina Population Center, 1970.

Guth, James L., Corwin E. Smidt, Lyman A. Kellstedt, and John C. Green. "The Sources of Antiabortion Attitudes: The Case of Religious Political Activists." *American Politics Quarterly* 21 (January 1993): 65–80.

Guttmacher, Alan F. "Conception Control and the Medical Profession." *Human Fertility* 12 (1947): 1–10.

Haag, Pamela S. "In Search of 'The Real Thing': Ideologies of Love, Modern Romance, and Women's Sexual Subjectivity in the United States, 1920–1940." In *American Sexual Politics*, edited by John C. Fout and Maura Shaw Tantillo, 161–92. Chicago: University of Chicago Press, 1993.

Haldeman, H. R. *Haldeman Diaries: Inside the Nixon White House.* New York: G. P. Putnam's Sons, 1994.

Hall, Elaine J., and Myra Marx Ferree. "Race Differences in Abortion Attitudes." *Public Opinion Quarterly* 50 (1986): 193–207.

Haller, Mark H. *Eugenics: Hereditarian Attitudes in American Thought.* New Brunswick: Rutgers University Press, 1963.

Hallow, Ralph Z. "The Blacks Cry Genocide." *Nation*, 28 April 1969, 535–37.

Hamilton, Alice. *Exploring the Dangerous Trades: The Autobiography of Alice Hamilton, M.D.* Boston: Little, Brown and Company, 1943.

Handlin, Oscar. *The Americans.* Boston: Little, Brown and Company, 1963.

———. *Boston's Immigrants.* Cambridge, Mass.: Harvard University Press, 1941.

Hansen, Susan B. "State Implementation of Supreme Court Decisions: Abortion Rates since *Roe v. Wade*." *Journal of Politics* 42 (1980): 372–95.

———. "The Supreme Court, the States, and Social Change: The Case of Abortion." *Peace and Change* 6 (1980): 20–32.

Hardin, Garrett. *Birth Control.* New York: Pegasus, 1970.

———, ed. *Population, Evolution, and Birth Control.* San Francisco: W. H. Freeman and Company, 1965.

Harper, John Paul. "'Be Fruitful and Multiply': Origins of Legal Restrictions on Planned Parenthood in Nineteenth-Century America." In *Women of America: A History*, edited by Carol Ruth Berkin and Mary Beth Norton, 245–69. Boston: Houghton Mifflin, 1979.

Harris, Richard J., and Edgar W. Mills. "Religion, Values and Attitudes toward Abortion." *Journal for the Scientific Study of Religion* 24 (1985): 137–54.

Hartmann, Betty. *Reproductive Rights and Wrongs: The Global Politics of Population Control and Contraceptive Choice.* New York: Harper and Row, 1987.

Hartmann, Susan. *The Home Front and Beyond: American Women in the 1940s.* Boston: Twayne Publishers, 1982.

Hasian, Marouf Arif, Jr. *The Rhetoric of Eugenics in Anglo-American Thought.* Athens: University of Georgia Press, 1996.

Hayden, Dolores. *Redesigning the American Dream.* New York: Norton, 1984.

Hayler, Barbara. "Abortion." *Signs* 5 (1979): 307–23.

"Healthier Mothers and Babies—1900–1999." *Journal of the American Medical Association*, 17 November 1999, 1809.

Herman, Judith. "Forced Sterilization." *Sister Courage* (January 1976): 8.

Hern, Warren M. "Family Planning and the Poor." *New Republic*, 14 November 1970, 17–19.

Hernstein, Richard J., and Charles Murray. *The Bell Curve: Intelligence and Class Structure in American Life*. New York: Free Press, 1994.

Herring, George C. *America's Longest War: The United States and Vietnam, 1950–1975*. New York: John Wiley and Sons, 1979.

Higham, John. *Strangers in the Land*. 2nd ed. New York: Athenaeum, 1963.

Hilgers, Thomas W., and Dennis J. Horan, eds. *Abortion and Social Justice*. New York: Sheed and Ward, 1972.

Hill, Robert A., ed. *The Marcus Garvey and Universal Negro Improvement Association Papers. Vol. 7: November 1927–August 1940*. Berkeley: University of California Press, 1990.

Himes, Norman E. *Medical History of Contraception*. Baltimore: Williams and Wilkins Company, 1936.

Hine, Darlen Clark. "Rape and Inner Lives of Black Women: Preliminary Thoughts on the Culture of Dissemblance." *Signs* 14 (Summer 1989): 912–20.

Historical Statistics of the United States, Colonial Times to 1970. Pt. 1. Washington, D.C.: U.S. Government Printing Office, 1975.

History of the State of Rhode Island: 1636–1878. Philadelphia: Hoag, Wade and Company, 1878.

Hodge, Hugh L. *Foeticide or Criminal Abortion*. Philadelphia: Livingston and Blake, 1872.

———. "Introductory Lecture, 1839." In *Sex, Marriage and Society*, edited by Charles Rosenberg and Carroll Smith-Rosenberg, 15–33. New York: Arno Press, 1974.

Hofstadter, Richard. *Social Darwinism in American Thought*. Boston: Beacon Press, 1955.

Holbrook, Martin Luther. *Parturition without Pain: A Code of Directions for Escaping from the Primal Curse*. New York: Wood and Holbrook, 1871.

Hole, Judith, and Ellen Levine. *Rebirth of Feminism*. New York: Quadrangle, 1971.

Holt, Michael F. "The Antimasonic and Know Nothing Parties." In *History of U.S. Political Parties*, edited by Arthur M. Schlesinger, Jr., 575–620. New York: Chelsea House Publishers, 1973.

Howell, Susan E., and Robert T. Sims. "Abortion Attitudes and the Louisiana Governor's Election." *American Politics Quarterly* 21 (January 1993): 54–64.

Hunter, Robert. *Poverty*. New York: Macmillan, 1905.

Imber, Jonathan B. *Abortion and the Private Practice of Medicine*. New Haven: Yale University Press, 1986.

"Infants' Rights." *Living Age*, 8 January 1916, 115–17.

Iseman, M. S. *Race Suicide*. New York: Cosmopolitan Press, 1912.

Jacoby, Douglas. "First Conviction for Abortion in the State of Rhode Island." *Providence Medical Journal* 4 (1903): 57–59.

Jaffe, Frederick S., Barbara L. Lindheim, and Philip R. Lee. *Abortion Politics: Private Morality and Public Policy*. New York: McGraw-Hill Book Company, 1981.

Jain, Sagar C., and Steven W. Sinding. *North Carolina Abortion Law 1967: A Study in*

Legislative Process. Monograph 2, Carolina Population Center. Chapel Hill: University of North Carolina, 1968.

Jefferis, Benjamin Grant, and J. L. Nichols. *Light on Dark Corners: A Complete Sexual and Science Guide to Purity.* New York, 1894.

Jenks, J. W., and W. J. Lauck. *The Immigration Problem.* 6th ed. New York, 1926.

Joffe, Carole. "Portraits of Three 'Physicians of Conscience': Abortion before Legalization in the United States." *Journal of the History of Sexuality* 2 (July 1991): 46–67.

———. *The Regulation of Sexuality: Experiences of Family Planning Workers.* Philadelphia: Temple University Press, 1986.

Johnson, Charles A., and Jon R. Bond. "Policy Implementation and Community Linkages: Hospital Abortion Services after *Roe v. Wade.*" *Western Political Quarterly* 35 (1982): 385–405.

Johnson, Joseph Taber. "Abortion and Its Effects." *American Journal of Obstetrics* 33 (1896): 91.

Johnson, R. Christian. "Feminism, Philanthropy and Science in the Development of the Oral Contraceptive Pill." *Pharmacy in History* 19 (1977): 63–78.

Jones, Carolyn. "Abortion and Black Women." *Black America* (September 1970): 49.

Jones, Elise F., and Charles F. Westoff. "Attitudes toward Abortion in the United States in 1970 and the Trend since 1965." In Westoff and Parke, *Demographic and Social Aspects of Population Growth,* 569–78.

Kaestle, Carl F., and Maris A. Vinovskis. *Education and Social Change in Nineteenth Century Massachusetts.* Cambridge: Cambridge University Press, 1980.

Kahn, Jeffrey P., Anna C. Mastroianni, and Jeremy Sugarman. *Beyond Consent: Seeking Justice in Research.* New York: Oxford University Press, 1998.

Kantner, John F., and J. Mayone Stycos. "A Non-Clinical Approach to Contraception: Preliminary Report on the Program of the Family Planning Association of Puerto Rico." In *Research and Family Planning,* edited by Clyde V. Kiser, 573–81. Princeton: Princeton University Press, 1962.

Kantrow, Louise. "Philadelphia Gentry: Fertility and Family Limitation among an American Aristocracy." *Population Studies* 34 (1980): 21–30.

Keller, Allan. *Scandalous Lady: The Life and Times of Madame Restell, New York's Most Notorious Abortionist.* New York: Athenaeum, 1981.

Kelley, William R., and Phillips Cutright. "Economic and Other Determinants of Annual Change in U.S. Fertility, 1917–1976." *Social Science Research* 13 (1984): 250–67.

Kellogg, John Harvey. *Plain Facts for Old and Young.* Burlington, Iowa, 1881.

Kennard, K. Sellars. "Criminal Abortion." *Medico-Legal Journal* 39 (1922): 21–30.

Kennedy, David. *Birth Control in America.* New Haven: Yale University Press, 1970.

Kennedy, Eugene. *Tomorrow's Catholics Yesterday's Church.* New York: Harper and Row, 1988.

Keown, John. *Abortion, Doctors and the Law: Some Aspects of the Legal Regulation of Abortion in England from 1803 to 1982.* Cambridge: Cambridge University Press, 1988.

Kinsey, Alfred. "Illegal Abortions in the United States." In *The Unwed Mother,* edited by Robert W. Roberts, 194–199. New York: Greenwood Publishers, 1966.

Kiser, Clyde V., ed. *Research in Family Planning*. Princeton: Princeton University Press, 1962.

Kline, Wendy. *Gender, Sexuality, and Eugenics from the Turn of the Century to the Baby Boom*. Berkeley: University of California Press, 2001.

Kolbert, Kathryn, and Andrea Miller. "Legal Strategies for Abortion Rights in the Twenty-First Century." In Solinger, *Abortion Wars*, 95–110.

Kopp, Marie. *Birth Control in Practice*. New York: Robert McBride, 1933.

Kühl, Stefan. *The Nazi Connection: Eugenics, American Racism, and German National Socialism*. New York: Oxford University Press, 1994.

Ladd-Taylor, Molly. *Raising a Baby the Government Way: Mothers' Letters to the Children's Bureau, 1915–1932*. New Brunswick: Rutgers University Press, 1986.

———. "Saving Babies and Sterilizing Mothers: Eugenics and Welfare Politics in the Interwar United States." *Social Politics* 4 (1997): 136–53.

Lader, Lawrence. *Abortion II: Making the Revolution*. Boston: Beacon Press, 1974.

———. *Breeding Ourselves to Death*. New York: Ballantine Books, 1971.

Landman, J. H. "Sterilization—A Pointedly Frank Discussion of a Grave Social Problem." *Current History* 44 (August 1936): 91.

Larsen, Nella. *Quicksand*. 1928. New Brunswick: Rutgers University Press, 1986.

Larson, Edward J. *Sex, Race, and Science: Eugenics in the Deep South*. Baltimore: Johns Hopkins University Press, 1995.

LaRue, Linda J. M. "Black Liberation and Women's Lib." *Transaction* November–December 1970: 61.

LaSorte, Michael A. "Nineteenth Century Family Planning Practices." *Journal of Psychohistory* 4 (1976): 163–83.

Laughlin, Harry H. *Eugenical Sterilization in the United States*. Long Island, N.Y., 1922.

———. *The Legal Status of Eugenical Sterilization*. Washington, D.C.: Eugenics Record Office, 1930.

Lee, Ronald Demos, ed. *Population Patterns in the Past*. New York: Academic Press, 1977.

Lee, Ulysses. *The Employment of Negro Troops*. Washington, D.C.: Office of the Chief of Military History United States Army, 1966.

Legge, Jerome S., Jr. "The Determinants of Attitudes toward Abortion in the American Electorate." *Western Political Quarterly* 36 (1983): 479–90.

Leon, Joseph J., and Patricia G. Steinhoff. "Catholics' Use of Abortion." *Sociological Analysis* 36 (1975): 125–36.

Lerner, Gerda, ed. *Black Women in White America: A Documentary History*. New York: Pantheon Books, 1972.

———. *The Female Experience*. Indianapolis: Bobbs-Merrill Educational Publishing, 1977.

———. "Motherhood in Historical Perspective." *Journal of Family History* 3 (1978): 297–301.

Lewis, Alfred Henry, ed. *A Compilation of the Messages and Speeches of Theodore Roosevelt 1901–1905, Supplement to Messages and Papers of the Presidents*. Washington, D.C.: Bureau of National Literature and Art, 1906.

Lewis, Denslow. "Sociological Considerations Relative to Criminal Abortion, Infanticide, and Illegitimate Pregnancy." *Chicago Clinical Review* 5 (1895–96): 85–96.

Lincoln, Richard, Brigitte Doring-Bradley, Barbara L. Lindheim, and Maureen A. Cotterill. "The Court, the Congress, and the President: Turning Back the Clock on the Pregnant Poor." *Family Planning Perspectives* 9 (September–October 1977): 207–14.

Lipson, Gerald, and Dianne Wolman. "Polling Americans on Birth Control and Population." *Family Planning Perspectives* 4 (January 1972): 39–42.

Littlewood, Thomas B. *The Politics of Population Control.* Notre Dame: University of Notre Dame Press, 1977.

Locke, Richard Adams. *Report of the Trial of the Rev. Ephraim K. Avery, Methodist Minister for the Murder of Sarah Maria Cornell.* New York: William Stodart, 1832. Box 325, no. 14, Rider Collection.

Logue, Barbara J. "The Case for Birth Control before 1850: Nantucket Reexamined." *Journal of Interdisciplinary History* 15 (1985): 371–91.

Lovenduski, Joni, and Joyce Outshoorn, eds. *The New Politics of Abortion.* New York: Sage Publications, 1986.

Luker, Kristin. *Abortion and the Politics of Motherhood.* Berkeley: University of California Press, 1984.

———. *Taking Chances: Abortion and the Decision Not to Contracept.* Berkeley: University of California Press, 1975.

Lunneborg, Patricia. *Abortion: A Positive Choice.* New York: Bergin and Garvey, 1992.

Lynd, Helen, and Robert Lynd. *Middletown.* New York: Harcourt, Brace, 1929.

MacKinnon, Catharine. "The Male Ideology of Privacy: A Feminist Perspective on the Right of Abortion." *Radical America* 17 (1983): 23–35.

Macklin, Ruth. "Justice in International Research." In *Beyond Consent: Seeking Justice in Research,* edited by Jeffrey P. Kahn, Anna C. Mastroianni, and Jeremy Sugarman, 131–46. New York: Oxford University Press, 1998.

MacLeod, Charlotte M. "Community Reaction to the Establishment of an Abortion Clinic in Duluth, Minnesota." *North Dakota Quarterly* 52 (1984): 34–47.

Malcolm X. "The Black Revolution." In *Malcolm X Speaks,* edited by George Breitman, 45–57. New York: Grove Weidenfeld, 1965.

Manier, Edward, William Liu, and David Solomon, eds. *Abortion: New Directions for Policy Studies.* Notre Dame: University of Notre Dame Press, 1977.

Mapes, C. C. "Infanticide." *Medical Age: A Semi Monthly Journal of Medicine and Surgery* 15 (1897): 741–47.

Margolis, Michael, and Kevin Neary. "Pressure Politics Revisited: The Anti-Abortion Campaign." *Policy Studies Journal* 8 (1980): 698–716.

Masel-Walters, Lynne. "For the 'Poor Mute Mothers'? Margaret Sanger and *The Woman Rebel.*" *Journalism History* 1 (1984): 3–10, 37.

Masnick, George S., and Joseph A. McFalls. "A New Perspective on the Twentieth Century American Fertility Swing." *Journal of Family History* 1 (1976): 216–43.

Mass, Bonnie. "Puerto Rico: A Case Study of Population Control." *Latin American Perspectives* 4 (Fall 1977): 66–81.

Mastroianni, Anna C., Ruth Faden, and Daniel Federman, eds. *Women and Health Re-*

search: Ethical and Legal Issues of Including Women in Clinics Studies. Washington, D.C.: National Academy Press, 1994.

Mauriceau, A. M. *Married Woman's Private Medical Companion*. New York, 1851.

May, Elaine Tyler. *Great Expectations: Marriage & Divorce in Post-Victorian America*. Chicago: University of Chicago Press, 1980.

———. *Homeward Bound: American Families in the Cold War Era*. New York: Basic Books, 1988.

Mayer, Kurt B. *Economic Development and Population Growth in Rhode Island*. Providence: Brown University Press, 1953.

McBride, David. "Medicine and the Health Crisis of the Urban Black American Family, 1910–1945." In *The American Family: Historical Perspectives*, edited by Jean E. Hunter and Paul T. Mason, 112–24. Pittsburgh: Duquesne University Press, 1988.

McCann, Carole R. *Birth Control Politics in the United States, 1916–1945*. Ithaca: Cornell University Press, 1994.

McCormack, Thelma. *Abortion: Pro-Choice or Pro-Life?* Washington, D.C.: American University Press, 1992.

McCormick, E. Patricia. *Attitudes toward Abortion: Experiences of Selected Black and White Women*. Lexington, Mass.: Lexington Books, 1975.

McDonnell, Kathleen. *Not an Easy Choice: A Feminist Re-examines Abortion*. Boston: South End Press, 1991.

McFalls, Joseph A., Jr., and George S. Masnick. "Birth Control and the Fertility of the U.S. Black Population, 1880–1980." *Journal of Family History* 6 (1981): 89–106.

McGeever, Patrick. *Reverend Charles Owen Rice: Apostle of Contradiction*. Pittsburgh: Duquesne University Press, 1989.

McIntosh, William Alex, and Jon P. Alston. "Acceptance of Abortion among White Catholics and Protestants, 1962 and 1975." *Journal for the Scientific Study of Religion* 16 (1977): 295–304.

McLoughlin, William Gerald. *Rhode Island: A Bicentennial History*. New York: W. W. Norton, 1978.

Mears, Judith M. "The Doctor as Abortion Ally." *Civil Liberties Review* 1 (1974): 134–36.

Measham, Anthony R., A. A. Hatcher, and C. B. Arnold. "Physicians and Contraception: A Study of Perceptions and Practices in an Urban Southeastern U.S. Community." *Southern Medical Journal* 64 (1971): 499.

Meier, Kenneth J., and Deborah R. McFarlane. "The Politics of Funding Abortion: State Responses to the Political Environment." *American Politics Quarterly* 21 (January 1993): 81–101.

Menken, Jane A. "Teenage Childbearing: Its Medical Aspects and Implications for the United States Population." In Westoff and Parke, *Demographic and Social Aspects of Population Growth*, 334–35.

Merton, Andrew H. *Enemies of Choice: The Right-to-Life Movement and Its Threat to Abortion*. Boston: Beacon Press, 1981.

Messer, Ellen, and Kathryn May. *Back Room: Voices from the Illegal Abortion Era*. New York: St. Martin's Press, 1988.

Meyer, Jimmy Elaine Wilkinson. *Any Friend of the Movement: Networking for Birth Control, 1920–1940.* Columbus: Ohio State University Press, 2004.

Meyer, Leisa D. "Creating G.I. Jane: The Regulation of Sexuality and Sexual Behavior in the Women's Army Corps during World War II." *Feminist Studies* 18 (Fall 1992): 581–601.

Meyerson, Abraham, et al. *Eugenical Sterilization: A Reorientation of the Problem.* New York: Macmillan, 1936.

Miller, Henry. *The Principles and Practice of Obstetrics; Including the Treatment of Chronic Inflammation of the Uterus, Considered as a Frequent Cause of Abortion.* Philadelphia: Blanchard and Lea, 1858.

Miller, Lawrence G. "Pain, Parturition, and the Profession: Twilight Sleep in America." In *Health Care in America: Essays in Social History*, edited by Susan Reverby and David Rosner, 19–43. Philadelphia: Temple University Press, 1979.

Mohr, James C. *Abortion in America: The Origins and Evolution of National Policy, 1800–1900.* New York: Oxford University Press, 1978.

Moore, Kristin A. "Teenage Childbirth and Welfare Dependency." *Family Planning Perspectives* 10 (July–August 1978): 233–35.

Moore, Kristin A., and Steven B. Caldwell. "The Effect of Government Policies on Out-of-Wedlock Sex and Pregnancy." *Family Planning Perspectives* 9 (July–August 1977): 164–69.

Moore, Kristin, Margaret C. Simms, and Charles L. Betsy. *Choice and Circumstance: Racial Differences in Adolescent Sexuality and Fertility.* New Brunswick: Transaction Books, 1986.

Mora, Magdalena, and Adelaide R. DelCastillo, eds. *Mexican Women in the United States: Struggles Past and Present.* Los Angeles: University of California Chicano Studies Research Center, 1980.

Morantz-Sanchez, Regina Markell. *Conduct Unbecoming a Woman: Medicine on Trial in Turn-of-the-Century Brooklyn.* New York: Oxford University Press, 1999.

———. *Sympathy and Science: Women Physicians in American Medicine.* New York: Oxford University Press, 1985.

Morantz, Regina, and Sue Zsoche. "Professionalism, Feminism, and Gender Roles: A Comparative Study of Nineteenth Century Medical Therapeutics." *Journal of American History* 67 (December 1980): 568–88.

Morgan, Robin, ed. *Sisterhood Is Powerful: An Anthology of Writings from the Women's Liberation Movement.* New York: Vintage Books, 1970.

Morowitz, Harold J., and James S. Trefil. *The Facts of Life: Science and the Abortion Controversy.* New York: Oxford University Press, 1992.

Morrison, Joseph L. "Illegitimacy, Sterilization, and Racism: A North Carolina Case History." *Social Science Review* (March 1965): 1–10.

Morton, Marian J. "Seduced and Abandoned in an American City: Cleveland and Its Fallen Women, 1869–1936." *Journal of Urban History* 11 (August 1985): 443–69.

Mosher, William D. *Trends in Contraceptive Practice: United States, 1965–1976.* Hyattsville, Md.: National Center for Health Statistics, 1982.

Mulheron, J. J. "Foeticide." *Peninsular Journal of Medicine* 10 (September 1874): 386–87.

Myer, Jimmy Elaine Wilkinson. *Any Friend of the Movement: Networking for Birth Control, 1920–1940.* Columbus: Ohio State University Press, 2004.

Myerson, Abraham, James B. Ayer, Tracy J. Putnam, Clyde E. Keeler, and Leo Alexander. *Eugenical Sterilization: A Reorientation of the Problem.* New York: Macmillan 1936.

Nathanson, Bernard. *Aborting America.* New York: Doubleday, 1979.

National Academy of Sciences. *The Growth of U.S. Population.* Washington, D.C., May 1965.

———. *Resources and Man.* San Francisco: Freeman, 1969.

National Academy of Sciences, Committee on Science and Public Policy. *The Growth of World Population.* Washington, D.C., 1963.

Nebinger, Andrew. *Criminal Abortion: Its Extent and Prevention.* Philadelphia: Collins Printer, 1870.

Nelson, Hilde Lindemann, and James Lindemann Nelson. "Feminism, Social Policy, and Long-Acting Contraception." *Hastings Center Report* 25 (January 1995): S30–32.

Nelson, Jennifer. *Women of Color and the Reproductive Rights Movement.* New York: New York University Press, 2003.

Neubeck, Kenneth J., and Jack L. Roach. "Racism and Poverty Policies." In *Impacts of Racism on White Americans,* edited by Benjamin P. Bowser and Raymond G. Hunt, 153–64. Beverly Hills: Sage Publications, 1981.

Newman, Lucile. *Women's Medicine: A Cross-Cultural Study of Indigenous Fertility Regulation.* New Brunswick: Rutgers University Press, 1986.

Nicholson, Jeanne Bell, and Debra W. Stewart. "Abortion Policy in 1978: A Follow-up Analysis." *Publius* 9 (Winter 1979): 161–67.

———. "The Supreme Court, Abortion Policy, and State Response: A Preliminary Analysis." *Publius* 8 (Winter 1978): 59–78.

Nixon-Agnew Campaign Committee. *Nixon on the Issues.* New York: Nixon-Agnew Campaign Committee, 1968.

Nixon, Richard. "Special Message to Congress on Problems of Population." 18 July 1969. In *Public Papers of the Presidents of the United States: Richard Nixon.* Washington, D.C.: Government Printing Office, 1969.

———. "Statement about Policy on Abortion at Military Base Hospitals in the United States." 3 April 1971. In *Public Papers of the Presidents of the United States: Richard Nixon.* Washington, D.C.: Government Printing Office, 1972.

———. "Statement about the Report of the Commission on Population Growth and the American Future." 5 May 1972. In *Public Papers of the Presidents of the United States: Richard Nixon.* Washington, D.C.: Government Printing Office, 1972.

Noonan, John T., Jr., ed. *Contraception: A History of Its Treatment by the Catholic Theologians and Canonists.* Cambridge, Mass.: Harvard University Press, 1965.

———. *The Morality of Abortion: Legal and Historical Perspectives.* Cambridge, Mass.: Harvard University Press, 1970.

———. *A Private Choice.* New York: Free Press, 1979.

Nugent, Walter. *Structures of American Social History.* Bloomington: Indiana University Press, 1983.

O'Connell, Martin, and Maurice J. Moore. "The Legitimacy Status of First Births to U.S.

Women Aged 15–24, 1939–1978." *Family Planning Perspectives* 12 (January–February 1980): 16–24.

O'Connor, John. *The People versus Rome*. New York: Random House, 1969.

Olasky, Marvin N. *The Press and Abortion, 1838–1988*. Hillsdale, N.J.: Lawrence Erlbaum Associates, Publishers, 1988.

Ostheimer, John M. "Abortion and American Population Politics." *Policy Studies Journal* 6 (1977): 216–22.

Oudshoorn, Nelly. *The Male Pill: A Biography of a Technology in the Making*. Durham, N.C.: Duke University Press, 2003.

Owen, Robert Dale. *Moral Physiology; or, a Brief and Plain Treatise on the Population Question*. New York, 1831.

Packard, Francis R. *History of Medicine in the United States*. New York: Hafner Publishing Company, 1963.

Packer, H. L. *The Limits of the Criminal Sanction*. Stanford, Calif.: Stanford University Press, 1968.

Pakter, Jean, and Frieda Nelson. "Abortion in New York City: The First Nine Months." *Family Planning Perspectives* 3 (July 1971): 1–15.

Pakter, Jean, Donna O'Hare, Frieda Nelson, and Martin Svigar. "Two Years Experience in New York City with the Liberalized Abortion Law—Problems and Progress." *American Journal of Public Health* 63 (June 1973): 524–35.

Palley, Howard A. "Abortion Policy: Ideology, Political Cleavage and the Policy Process." *Policy Studies Journal* 7 (1978): 224–33.

Parke, Robert, Jr., and Charles F. Westoff. *Aspects of Population Growth Policy*. Washington, D.C.: Government Printing Office, 1972.

Parmelee, Maurice. *Poverty and Social Progress*. New York: Macmillan, 1916.

Patterson, James T. *America's Struggle against Poverty, 1900–1980*. Cambridge, Mass.: Harvard University Press, 1981.

Paul, Alice. *Conversations with Alice Paul: Women Suffrage and the Equal Rights Amendment*. Berkeley: Berkeley Regional Oral History Office, 1976. Microfilm version at University of North Carolina–Greensboro.

Paul, Diane B. *Controlling Human Heredity: 1865 to the Present*. Atlantic Highlands, N.J.: Humanities Press, 1995.

———. *The Politics of Heredity: Essays on Eugenics, Biomedicine, and the Nature-Nurture Debate*. Albany: State University of New York Press, 1998.

Pearl, Raymond. "Fertility and Contraception in Urban Whites and Negroes." *Science*, 22 May 1936, 503–6.

———. "Preliminary Notes on a Cooperative Investigation of Family Limitation." *Milbank Memorial Fund Quarterly Bulletin* 11 (January 1933): 36–60.

———. "Second Progress Report on a Study of Family Limitation." *Milbank Memorial Fund Quarterly Bulletin* 11 (July 1934): 248–69.

———. "Third Progress Report on a Study of Family Limitation." *Milbank Memorial Fund Quarterly Bulletin* 14 (July 1936): 258–84.

Peiss, Kathy. "'Charity Girls' and City Pleasures: Historical Notes on Working-Class Sexuality, 1880–1920." In *Powers of Desire: The Politics of Sexuality*, edited by Ann

Snitow, Christine Stansell, and Sharon Thompson, 74–87. New York: Monthly Review Press, 1983.

Perales, Cesar A., and Lauren S. Young, eds. *Women, Health, and Poverty*. New York: Haworth Press, 1987.

Pernick, Martin S. *The Black Stork: Eugenics and the Death of 'Defective' Babies in American Medicine and Motion Pictures since 1915*. New York: Oxford University Press, 1996.

Petchesky, Rosalind Pollack. *Abortion and Woman's Choice: The State, Sexuality, and Reproductive Freedom*. Boston: Northeastern University Press, 1990.

———. "AntiAbortion, AntiFeminism, and the Rise of the New Right." *Feminist Studies* 7 (1981): 206–46.

———. "'Woman's Body, Woman's Right' and the Current Reproductive Movement." *Radical America* 16 (1982): 155–61.

Piotrow, Phyllis Tilson. *World Population Crisis: The United States Response*. New York: Praeger Publishers, 1973.

Pivar, David. *Purity Crusade: Sexual Morality and Social Control, 1868–1900*. Westport, Conn.: Greenwood Press, 1973.

Polgar, Steven. "Sociocultural Research in Family Planning in the United States: Review and Prospects." *Human Organization* 25 (1966): 321–29.

Pomeroy, H. S. *The Ethics of Marriage*. New York: Funk and Wagnall's, 1888.

Popenoe, Paul, and E. S. Gosney. *Twenty-Eight Years of Sterilization in California*. Pasadena: Human Betterment Foundation, 1938.

Popenoe, Paul, and Roswell H. Johnson. *Applied Eugenics*. New York: The MacMillan Co., 1918.

Presser, Harriet B. "Demographic and Social Aspects of Contraceptive Sterilization in the United States: 1965–1970." In Westoff and Parke, *Demographic and Social Aspects of Population Growth*, 529–33.

Quay, Eugene. "Justifiable Abortion—Medical and Legal Foundations." *Georgetown Law Journal* 49 (Spring 1961): 395–538.

Railsback, Celeste Condit. "The Contemporary American Abortion Controversy: Stages in the Argument." *Quarterly Journal of Speech* 70 (1984): 410–24.

Rainwater, Lee. *And the Poor Get Children*. Chicago: Quadrangle Books, 1960.

Ramirez de Arellano, Annette B., and Conrad Seipp. *Colonialism, Catholicism and Contraception: A History of Birth Control in Puerto Rico*. Chapel Hill: University of North Carolina Press, 1983.

Rand, Larry Anthony. "The Know Nothing Party in Rhode Island: Religious Bigotry and Political Success." *Rhode Island History* 23 (1964): 102–16.

Ravitch, Diane. *The Troubled Crusade: American Education, 1945–1980*. New York: Basic Books, 1983.

Ray, John Michael. "Anti-Catholicism and Know Nothingism in Rhode Island." *Ecclesiastical Review* 148 (1963): 27–36.

Ray, J. M., and F. G. Gosling. "American Physicians and Birth Control, 1936–1947." *Journal of Social History* 18 (1985): 399–411.

Reagan, Leslie J. "'About to Meet Her Maker': Women, Doctors, Dying Declarations, and the State's Investigation of Abortion, Chicago, 1867–1940." *Journal of American History* 77 (March 1991): 1240–64.

———. *When Abortion Was a Crime: Women, Medicine and Law in the United States 1867–1973*. Berkeley: University of California Press, 1997.

Reed, James. "Doctors, Birth Control, and Social Values: 1830–1970." In *The Therapeutic Revolution*, edited by Morris J. Vogel and Charles E. Rosenberg, 109–34. Philadelphia: University of Pennsylvania Press, 1979.

———. *From Private Vice to Public Virtue: The Birth Control Movement and American Society since 1830*. New York: Basic Books, 1978.

———. "Public Policy on Human Reproduction and the Historian." *Journal of Social History* 18 (1985): 383–98.

Reilly, Philip. *The Surgical Solution: A History of Involuntary Sterilization in the United States*. Baltimore: Johns Hopkins University Press, 1991.

Rentoul, Robert Reed. *Race Culture or Race Suicide?* New York: Walter Scott Publishing Company, 1906.

Report upon the Census of Rhode Island, 1865. Providence: Providence Press Company, State Printers, 1867.

Reproductive Control, or, a Rational Guide to Matrimonial Happiness. Cincinnati, 1855. Lownes Science Collection, John Hay Library.

Ridgeway, James. "Birth Control by Surgery." *New Republic*, 14 November 1964, 9–11.

Rindfuss, Ronald R., and James A. Sweet. *Postwar Fertility Trends and Differentials in the United States*. New York: Academic Press, 1977.

Robb, George. "The Way of All Flesh: Degeneration, Eugenics, and the Gospel of Free Love." *Journal of the History of Sexuality* 6 (1996): 589–603.

Robbins, James M. "Religious Involvement: Asceticism and Abortion among Low Income Black Women." *Sociology Analysis* 41 (1980): 365–74.

Roberts, Dorothy. *Killing the Black Body: Race, Reproduction, and the Meaning of Liberty*. New York: Pantheon Books, 1997.

Roberts, Dorothy E. "Punishing Drug Addicts." In Solinger, *Abortion Wars*. 124–56.

Robertson, John A. "Norplant and Irresponsible Reproduction." *Hastings Center Report* 25 (January 1995): S23.

Robinson, Caroline Hadley. *Seventy Birth Control Clinics*. Baltimore: Williams and Wilkins Company, 1930.

Rodrique, Jessie M. "The Black Community and the Birth Control Movement." In *Unequal Sisters: A Multicultural Reader in U.S. Women's History*, edited by Ellen Carol DuBois and Vicki L. Ruiz. 333–44. New York: Routledge, 1990.

Rongy, A. J. *Abortion: Legal or Illegal?* New York: Vanguard Press, 1933.

Roosevelt, Theodore. *The Works of Theodore Roosevelt, Memorial Edition*. 24 vols. New York: Charles Scribner's Sons, 1923–26.

Rosen, Harold, et al., eds. *Abortion Problem*. New York, 1944.

Rosenberg, Charles, and Carroll Smith-Rosenberg, eds. *Sex, Marriage and Society*. New York: Arno Press, 1974.

Rosenfeld, Bernard, Sidney Wolfe, and Robert McGarrah. *A Health Research Group Study of Surgical Sterilization: Present Abuses and Proposed Regulations*. Washington, D.C.: Public Citizen Health Research Group, 1973.

Rosenquist, Valerie. "NARAL's New Way: Women in Politics." *Southern Exposure* 12 (1984): 26–31.

Ross, Loretta J. "African-American Women and Abortion." In *Abortion Wars*, edited by Solinger. 161–207.

———. "African-American Women and Abortion: A Neglected History." *Journal of Health Care for the Poor and Underserved* 3 (Fall 1992): 274–84.

Rossi, Alice S. "Abortion and Social Change." *Dissent* 16 (1969): 338–46.

Rossiter, William S. *Increase of Population in the United States, 1910–1920.* Census Monographs 1, 1920. Washington, D.C.: Government Printing Office, 1922.

Rothman, Sheila M. "Sterilizing the Poor." *Society* 1977: 36–40.

———. *Woman's Proper Place: A History of Changing Ideals and Practices, 1870 to Present.* New York: Basic Books, 1978.

Rotundo, E. Anthony. *American Manhood: Transformations in Masculinity from the Revolution to the Modern Era.* New York: Basic Books, 1993.

Rubin, Eva R., ed. *The Abortion Controversy: A Documentary History.* Westport, Conn.: Greenwood Press, 1994.

———. *Abortion, Politics, and the Courts: "Roe v. Wade" and Its Aftermath.* Westport, Conn.: Greenwood Press, 1982.

Sachdev, Paul, ed. *International Handbook on Abortion.* Westport, Conn.: Greenwood Press, 1988.

Saleeby, C. W. *The Methods of Race Regeneration.* New York: Cassell and Company, 1911.

Sallume, Xarifa, and Frank W. Notestein. "Trends in the Size of Families Completed prior to 1910 in Various Social Classes." *American Journal of Sociology* 38 (November 1932): 398–408.

Samuels, Sarah E., and Mark D. Smith, eds. *Norplant and Poor Women.* California: Henry J. Kaiser Family Foundation, 1992.

Sanger, Margaret. *Margaret Sanger: An Autobiography.* New York: Dover Publications, 1938.

———. *The Pivot of Civilization.* New York: Brentano's Publishers, 1922.

———. "Why Not Birth Control in America?" *Birth Control Review* (May 1919): 10–11.

———. *Woman and the New Race.* New York: Brentano's Publishers, 1920.

Satanic Plot, or Awful Crimes of Popery in High and Low Places. Boston: N. B. Parsons, 1855.

Sauer, R. "Attitudes to Abortion in America, 1800–1973." *Population Studies* 28 (March 1974): 53–67.

Schlesinger, Arthur Meier. *The Rise of the City, 1878–1898.* Vol. 10 of *A History of American Life.* Edited by Arthur M. Schlesinger and Dixon Ryan Fox. 12 vols. New York: Macmillan, 1927–44.

Schneider, Carl E., and Maris A. Vinovskis, eds. *The Law and Politics of Abortion.* Lexington, Mass.: D. C. Heath and Company, 1980.

Schoen, Johanna. *Choice & Coercion: Birth Control, Sterilization, and Abortion in Public Health and Welfare.* Chapel Hill: University of North Carolina Press, 2005.

———. "Fighting for Child Health: Race, Birth Control, and the State in the Jim Crow South." *Social Politics* 4 (1997): 90–113.

Schofield, Ann. "Rebel Girls and Union Maids: The Woman Question in the Journals of the AFL and IWW, 1905–1920." *Feminist Studies* 9 (1983): 335–58.

Scholten, Catherine M. *Childbearing in American Society: 1650–1850*. New York: New York University Press, 1985.

Schultz, Jane E. "Race, Gender, and Bureaucracy: Civil War Army Nurses and the Pension Bureau." *Journal of Women's History* 6 (Summer 1994): 45–69.

Schur, Edwin M. *Crimes without Victims: Deviant Behavior and Public Policy*. Englewood Cliffs, N.J.: Prentice-Hall, 1965.

———. *Law and Society*. New York: Random House, 1968.

Scott, James Foster. *The Sexual Instinct: Its Use and Dangers as Affecting Heredity and Morals*. New York, 1899.

Scott, Julia. "Norplant and Women of Color." In *Norplant and Poor Women*, edited by Samuels and Smith. 39–52.

Scully, Diana. *Men Who Control Women's Health*. Boston: Houghton Mifflin, 1980.

Sears, Hal D. *The Sex Radicals: Free Love in High Victorian America*. Lawrence, Kans.: Regents Press, 1977.

Segal, Sheldon J. "Contraceptive Research: A Male Chauvinist Plot?" *Family Planning Perspectives* 4 (July 1972): 21–25.

Shapiro, Thomas M. *Population Control Politics: Women, Sterilization, and Reproductive Choice*. Philadelphia: Temple University Press, 1985.

Sheeran, Patrick J. *Women, Society, the State, and Abortion: A Structural Analysis*. Westport, Conn.: Praeger Publishers, 1987.

Sicherman, Barbara, ed. *Alice Hamilton: A Life in Letters*. Cambridge, Mass.: Harvard University Press, 1984.

Sivin, Irving. "Norplant Clinical Trials." In *Norplant and Poor Women*, edited by Samuels and Smith. 1–18.

Skerry, Peter. "The Class Conflict over Abortion." *Public Interest* 52 (1978): 69–84.

Slater, Jack. "Sterilization: Newest Threat to Poor." *Ebony* 28 (October 1973): 150–56.

Sloane, R. Bruce, and Diana F. Horvitz. *A Guide to Abortion*. Chicago: Nelson-Hall Publishers, 1974.

Slosson, Preston William. *The Great Crusade and After, 1914–1928*. Vol. 12 of *A History of American Life*, ed. Arthur Schlesinger and Dixon Ryan Fox. 12 vols. New York: Macmillan, 1927–44.

Smith, Daniel Scott. "Family Limitation, Sexual Control, and Domestic Feminism in Victorian America." *Feminist Studies* 1 (Spring 1973): 40–57.

Smith, J. David. *The Eugenic Assault on America: Scenes in Red, White and Black*. Fairfax, Va.: George Mason University Press, 1993.

Smith, Mary. "Birth Control and the Negro Woman." *Ebony* 23 (March 1968): 29–37.

Smith, Susan L. *Sick and Tired of Being Sick and Tired: Black Women's Health Activisim in America, 1890–1950*. Philadelphia: University of Pennsylvania Press, 1995.

Smith-Rosenberg, Carroll. "The Abortion Movement." In *Disorderly Conduct*, edited by Carroll Smith-Rosenberg. 217–44. New York: Oxford University Press, 1985.

Solinger, Rickie, ed. *Abortion Wars: A Half Century of Struggle, 1950–2000*. Berkeley: University of California Press, 1998.

——. "'A Complete Disaster': Abortion and the Politics of Hospital Committees, 1950–1970." *Feminist Studies* 19 (Summer 1993): 249–68.

——. *Wake up Little Susie: Single Pregnancy and Race before "Roe v. Wade."* New York: Routledge, 1992.

Soloway, Richard A. "The 'Perfect Contraceptive': Eugenics and Birth Control Research in Britain and America in the Interwar Years." *Journal of Contemporary History* 30 (1995): 637–64.

Somerville, Siobhan. "Scientific Racism and the Emergence of the Homosexual Body." *Journal of the History of Sexuality* 5 (October 1994): 243–66.

Sommers, Paul M., and Laura S. Thomas. "Restricting Federal Funds for Abortion: Another Look." *Social Science Quarterly* 64 (1983): 340–46.

Sons of the Sires; a History of the Rise, Progress, and Destiny of the American Party, and Its Probable Influence on the Next Presidential Election. Philadelphia: Lippincott, Grambo and Company, 1855.

Soule, James. *Science of Reproduction and Reproductive Control.* New York, 1856.

Spengler, Joseph J. "The Decline in the Birth Rate of the Foreign Born." *Scientific Monthly* 32 (January 1931): 54–59.

——. *The Fecundity of Native and Foreign-Born Women in New England.* Washington, D.C.: Brookings Institution Press, 1930.

——. "Notes on Abortion, Birth Control, and Medical and Sociological Interpretations of the Decline of the Birth Rate in Nineteenth Century America." *Marriage Hygiene* November 1935: 43–53, 158–69, 288–300.

Srebnick, Amy Gilman. *The Mysterious Death of Mary Rogers: Sex and Culture in Nineteenth-Century New York.* New York: Oxford University Press, 1995.

Stage, Sarah. *Female Complaints.* New York: W. W. Norton, 1979.

Stanworth, Michelle, ed. *Reproductive Technologies: Gender, Motherhood, and Medicine.* Minneapolis: University of Minnesota Press, 1987.

Staples, W. M. R., Esq. *Correct Report of the Examination of Rev. Ephraim K. Avery, Minister of the Methodist Church in Bristol, R.I. Who Was Charged with the Murder of Sarah M. Cornell.* Providence: Marshall and Brown, n.d. Box 291, no. 8, Rider Collection.

Startling Facts for Native Americans Called 'Know-Nothings,' or a Vivid Presentation of the Dangers to American Liberty, to Be Apprehended from Foreign Influence. 128 Nassau Street, New York, 1855.

Steiner, Gilbert Y., ed. *The Abortion Dispute and the American System.* Washington, D.C.: Brookings Institution Press, 1983.

Steinhoff, Patricia G., and Milton Diamond. *Abortion Politics: The Hawaii Experience.* Honolulu: University Press of Hawaii, 1977.

"Sterilization: New Argument." *U.S. News and World Report*, 24 September 1962, 55.

"Sterilization Sentiment Focuses on the Poor." *Science News*, 14 May 1966, 371.

"Sterilize Them!" *America*, 22 September 1962, 764.

Stewart, Debra W., and Jeanne Bell Nicholson. "Abortion Policy in 1978: A Follow-up Analysis." *Publius* 9 (1979): 161–68.

Stewart, Morse. "Criminal Abortion." *Detroit Review of Medicine and Pharmacy* 2 (January 1867): 7–8.

Stix, Regine K., and Frank W. Notestein. *Controlled Fertility: An Evaluation of Clinic Service*. Baltimore: Williams and Wilkins Company, 1940.

———. "Effectiveness of Birth Control: A Study of Contraceptive Practice in a Selected Group of New York Women." *Milbank Memorial Fund Quarterly* 12 (January 1934): 57–68.

Storer, Horatio R. *Criminal Abortion: Its Nature, Its Evidence, and Its Law*. Boston: Little, Brown and Company, 1868.

———. *Criminal Abortion in America*. Philadelphia: J. B. Lippincott and Company, 1860.

———. "Studies of Abortion." *Boston Medical and Surgical Journal* (February 1863).

———. *Why Not? A Book for Every Woman*. Boston: Lee and Shepard, 1866.

Sulloway, Alvah W. *Birth Control and Catholic Doctrine*. Boston: Beacon Press, 1959.

Swan, George S. "Gender, the Judiciary, and U.S. Public Opinion." *Journal of Social, Political and Economic Studies* 8 (1983): 323–41.

Swierenga, Robert P. "Physicians and Abortion Reform in the Nineteenth Century: Social Control as the New Orthodoxy." *Fides et History* 11 (1979): 51–59.

Sydenstricker, Edgar, and G. St. J. Perrott. "Sickness, Unemployment, and Differential Fertility." *Milbank Memorial Fund Quarterly* 12 (April 1934): 126–33.

Taeuber, Irene B. "Migration, Mobility, and the Assimilation of the Negro." *Population Bulletin* 15 (November 1958): 125–51.

Takaki, Ronald. *Iron Cages: Race and Culture in 19th-Century America*. New York: Oxford University Press, 1979.

Task Force on Ethics and Population. "Ethics, Population and the American Tradition." In *Aspects of Population Growth Policy*, edited by Parke Jr. and Westoff.

Tatalovich, Raymond, and Bryon W. Daynes. *The Politics of Abortion: A Study of Community Conflict in Public Policy Making*. New York: Praeger Publishers, 1981.

Tatalovich, Raymond, and David Schier. "The Persistence of Ideological Cleavage in Voting on Abortion Legislation in the House of Representatives, 1973–1988." *American Politics Quarterly* 21 (January 1993): 125–39.

Taussig, Frederick J. *Abortion: Spontaneous and Induced: Medical and Social Aspects*. St. Louis: C. V. Mosby Company, 1936.

Tedrow, Lucky M., and E. R. Mahoney. "Trends in Attitudes toward Abortion: 1972–1976." *Public Opinion Quarterly* 43 (1979): 181–89.

Teitelbaum, Michael S. "Some Genetic Implications of Population Policies." In Westoff and Parke, *Demographic and Social Aspects of Population Growth*,489–504.

Thimmesch, Nick. "Puerto Rico and Birth Control." *Journal of Marriage and the Family* 30, no. 2 (1968): 252–62.

Thomas, T. Gaillard. *Abortion and Its Treatment, from the Standpoint of Practical Experience*. New York: D. Appleton and Company, 1890.

Tietze, Christopher. "History of Contraceptive Methods." *Journal of Sex Research* 1 (July 1965): 69–85.

———. "Induced Abortion and Sterilization as Methods of Fertility Control." *Journal of Chronic Diseases* 18 (1965): 1161–71.

———. "The Potential Impact of Legal Abortion on Population Growth in the United States." In Westoff and Parke, *Demographic and Social Aspects of Population Growth.* 579–85.

Tolchin, Susan J. "The Impact of the Hyde Amendment on Congress: Effect of Single Issue Politics on Legislative Dysfunction: June 1977–June 1978." *Women and Politics* 5 (1985): 91–106.

Tolnay, Stewart E. "The Decline of Black Marital Fertility in the Rural South: 1910–1940." *American Sociological Review* 52 (1987): 211–17.

———. "Family Economy and the Black American Fertility Transition." *Journal of Family History* 11 (1986): 267–83.

Tolnay, Stewart E., and Avery M. Guest. "Childlessness in a Transitional Population: The United States at the Turn of the Century." *Journal of Family History* 7 (1982): 200–219.

Tone, Andrea, ed. *Controlling Reproduction: An American History.* Wilmington, Del.: Scholarly Resources, 1997.

———. *Devices and Desires: A History of Contraceptives in America.* New York: Hill and Wang, 2001.

Torpy, Sally J. "Native American Women and Coerced Sterilization: On the Trail of Tears in the 1970s." *American Indian Culture and Research Journal* 24 (2000): 1–22.

Trader, John W. "Criminal Abortion." *St. Louis Medical and Surgical Journal* 11 (November 1874): 587–89.

Treadwell, Mary. "Is Abortion Black Genocide?" *Family Planning Perspectives* 4 (January 1972): 4–5.

Trumbach, Randolph. "The Condom in Modern and Postmodern Culture." *Journal of the History of Sexuality* 2 (July 1991): 95–98.

Turner, Castellano, and William A. Darity. "Fears of Genocide among Black Americans as Related to Age, Sex, and Region." *American Journal of Public Health* 63 (December 1973): 1029–34.

U.S. Bureau of the Census. *Census of Population: 1950.* Vol. 22, pt. 39. Washington, D.C.: Government Printing Office, 1952.

———. *Eighteenth Census of the United States: 1960.* Vol. 1, pt. A. Washington, D.C. Government Printing Office, 1961.

———. *Fifteenth Census of the United States: 1930.* Vol. 3, pt. 2. Washington, D.C.: Government Printing Office, 1932.

———. *Sixteenth Census of the United States: 1940.* Vol. 2, pt. 6. Washington, D.C.: Government Printing Office, 1943.

U.S. Commission on Civil Rights. *The Constitutional Aspects of the Right to Limit Childbearing.* Washington, D.C.: Government Printing Office, 1975.

U.S. Congress. House. Committee on Education and Labor. *Hearings before the Committee on Education and Labor on H.R. 8311.* 90th Cong., 1st sess., 1967.

———. Committee on Government Operations, Human Resources and Intergovernmental Relations Subcommittee. *Medical and Psychological Impact of Abortion.* 101st Cong., 1st sess., 1989, 193–96.

———. Committee on Interior and Insular Affairs. *Oversight Hearing before the Subcommittee on General Oversight and Investigations.* 100th Cong., 1st sess., 1987.

————. Committee on Small Business, Subcommittee on Regulation, Business Opportunities and Energy. *Hearings*. 101st Cong., 2nd sess., 1990, 1–3.

————. Committee on the Judiciary. *Extract from Hearings before the Committee on the Judiciary on H.R. 5978.* 73rd Cong., 2nd sess., 1934.

————. Committee on the Judiciary. *Oversight Hearings*, 1st and 2nd sess., 6 March, 12 March, and 3 April 1985, 17 December 1986.

————. Committee on Ways and Means. *Report No. 1435 to Accompany H.R. 11082.* 72nd Cong., 1st sess., 1932.

————. Committee to Investigate the Interstate Migration of Destitute Citizens. *Interstate Migration* by John H. Tolan. 77th Cong., 1st sess., 1941.

————. Foreign Assistance Act of 1963. 88th Cong., 1st sess., Report no. 588, 1963.

U.S. Congress. Senate. Committee on Foreign Relations. *Legislation on Foreign Relations.* 90th Cong., 2nd sess. 1969.

————. Committee on Government Operations. *Hearings before a Subcommittee on Foreign Aid Expenditures of the Committee on Government Operations on S. 1676.* 89th Cong., 1st sess., 1965.

————. Committee on Government Operations. *Hearings before a Subcommittee on Foreign Aid Expenditures of the Committee on Government Operations on S. 1676.* 89th Cong., 2nd sess., 1966.

————. Committee on Government Operations. *Hearings before the Subcommittee on Foreign Aid Expenditures on S. 1676.* 90th Cong., 1st sess., 1967.

————. Committee on Interoceanic Canals. *Hearings before the Committee on Interoceanic Canals on S. 7519.* 72nd Cong., 2nd sess., 1933.

————. Committee on the Judiciary. *Extract from Hearings before a Subcommittee of the Committee on the Judiciary on S. 1842.* 73rd Cong., 2nd sess., 1934.

————. Committee on the Judiciary. *Hearings before a Subcommittee of the Committee on the Judiciary on S. 4436.* 72nd Cong., 1st sess., 1932.

————. Committee on the Judiciary, Subcommittee on Constitutional Amendments. *Hearings on Constitutional Amendments*, pt. 1. 93rd Cong., 1st sess., 4 March 1974.

————. Committee on Labor and Public Welfare. *Hearing before the Subcommittee on Employment, Manpower, and Poverty of the Committee on Labor and Public Welfare on S. 2993.* 89th Cong., 2nd sess., 1966.

————. Committee on Labor and Public Welfare. *Hearings before the Subcommittee on Employment, Manpower, and Poverty of the Committee on Labor and Public Welfare on S. 1545.* 90th Cong., 1st sess., 1967.

————. Committee on the Federal Role in Health. *Report of the Committee on Government Operations.* Report no. 91-809. 91st Cong., 2nd sess., 1969.

————. Committee on the Federal Role in Health. *Hearings before the Subcommittee on Quality of Health Care—Human Experimentation.* 93rd Cong., 1st sess., 1973.

U.S. National Center for Health Statistics. *Vital Statistics of the United States.* Washington, D.C.: Government Printing Office, 1968.

U.S. Office of Economic Opportunity. *Need for Subsidized Family Planning Services: United States, Each State and County, 1968.* Washington, D.C.: Government Printing Office, 1968.

Van der Tak, Jean. *Abortion, Fertility, and Changing Legislation: An International Review*. Lexington, Mass.: Heath, 1974.

Vaughan, Denton, and Gerald Sparer. "Ethnic Group and Welfare Status of Women Sterilized in Federally Funded Family Planning Programs, 1972." *Family Planning Perspectives* 6 (Fall 1974): 224–29.

Vazquez, José L. "Fertility and Decline in Puerto Rico: Extent and Causes." *Demography* 5, no. 2 (1968): 855–65.

Velez-Ibanez, Carlos G. "Se me acabó la canción: An Ethnography of Non-Consenting Sterilizations among Mexican Women in Los Angeles." In *Mexican Women in the United States: Struggles Past and Present*, edited by Magdalena Mora and Adelaida R. DelCastillo, 71–91. Los Angeles: University of California Chicano Studies Research Center, 1980.

Vinovskis, Maris A. "Abortion and the Presidential Election of 1976: A Multivariate Analysis of Voting Behavior." *Michigan Law Review* 77 (August 1979): 1750–71.

———. "Socioeconomic Determinants of Interstate Fertility Differentials in the United States." *Journal of Interdisciplinary History* 6 (Winter 1976): 375–96.

———, ed. *Studies in American Historical Demography*. New York: Academic Press, 1979.

Voegeli, William J., Jr. "A Critique of the Pro-Choice Argument." *Review of Politics* 43 (1981): 560–71.

Wandersee, Winifred D. *On the Move: American Women in the 1970s*. Boston: Twayne Publishers, 1988.

Ward, Martha C. *Poor Women, Powerful Men*. Boulder: Westview Press, 1986.

Warker, Ely Van de. *The Detection of Criminal Abortion and a Study of Foeticidal Drugs*. Boston, 1872.

Warren, G. W. *A Confidential Letter to the Married*. Cleveland, 1854.

Watkins, Elizabeth Siegel. *On the Pill: A Social History of Oral Contraceptives 1950–1970*. Baltimore: Johns Hopkins University Press, 1998.

Weddington, Sarah. *A Question of Choice*. New York: G. P. Putnam's Sons, 1992.

Weiner, Nella Fermi. "Of Feminism and Birth Control Propaganda." *International Journal of Women's Studies* 3 (1980): 411–30.

Weisbord, Robert G. *Genocide? Birth Control and the Black American*. Westport, Conn.: Greenwood Press, 1975.

Welch, Charles E., III. "The Regulation of American Fertility: Facts and Misconceptions." *International Journal of Women's Studies* 7 (1984): 273–81.

Welles, Robert V.
"Birth Control: Different Conceptions." *Journal of Interdisciplinary History* 10 (1979): 511–16.

———. "Demographic Change and the Life Cycle of American Families." *Journal of Interdisciplinary History* 2 (Autumn 1971): 280–96.

Wertz, Richard W., and Dorothy C. Wertz. *Lying-In: A History of Childbirth in America*. New York: Free Press, 1977.

West, Charles. *Lectures on the Diseases of Women*. Philadelphia, 1861.

Westoff, Charles F., and Robert Parke, Jr., eds. *Demographic and Social Aspects of Pop-*

ulation Growth. U.S. Commission on Population Growth and the American Future. Washington, D.C.: Government Printing Office, 1972.

Whitehead, James. *On the Causes and Treatment of Abortion and Sterility.* Philadelphia: Lea and Blanchard, 1848.

Whitney, Leon F. *The Case for Sterilization.* New York: Frederick A. Stockes Company, 1934.

Whorton, James C. *Nature Cures: The History of Alternative Medicine in America.* New York: Oxford University Press, 2002.

Wilder, Marcy J. "The Rule of Law, the Rise of Violence, and the Role of Morality." In Solinger, *Abortion Wars,* 73–88.

Williams, Barbara. "Blacks Reject Sterilization—Not Family Planning." *Psychology Today* 8 (July 1974): 26.

Williams, Doone, and Greer Williams. *Every Child a Wanted Child: Clarence James Gamble, M.D. and His Work in the Birth Control Movement.* Boston: Frances A. Countway Library of Medicine, 1978.

Williams, Lynora. "Violence against Women." *Black Scholar* 12 (1981): 18–24.

Wiltse, Charles M. *The Medical Department: Medical Service in the Mediterranean and Minor Theatres.* Washington, D.C.: Office of the Chief of Military History Department of the Army, 1965.

Witt, Stephanie L., and Gary Moncrief. "Religion and Roll Call Voting in Idaho." *American Politics Quarterly* 21 (January 1993): 140–49.

Woodside, Moya. *Sterilization in North Carolina.* Chapel Hill: University of North Carolina Press, 1950.

Wright, Henry C. *Marriage and Parenthood; or, The Reproductive Element in Man as a Means of His Elevation and Happiness.* Boston: Bela Marsh, 1858. Lownes Science Collection.

———. *The Unwelcomed Child; or, The Crime of an Undesigned and Undesired Maternity.* Boston, 1858.

Wynne, Frank. "Abortion." *Medico-Legal Journal* 39 (1922): 21–30.

Yasuba, Yasukichi. *Birth Rates of the White Population in the United States, 1800–1860: An Economic Study.* Baltimore: AMS Press, 1962.

Yates, Wilson. "Birth Control Literature and the Medical Profession in Nineteenth Century America." *Journal of the History of Medicine and Allied Science* 31 (1976): 42–54.

Young, Iris Marion. "Punishment, Treatment, Empowerment: Three Approaches to Policy for Pregnant Addicts." *Feminist Studies* 20 (Spring 1994): 33–57.

Young, Margot E. "Reproductive Technologies and the Law: Norplant and the Bad Mother." *Marriage and Family Review* 21 (1995): 259–81.

Zelnik, Melvin, and John F. Kantner. "Sexuality, Contraception and Pregnancy among Young Unwed Females in the United States." In Westoff and Parke, *Demographic and Social Aspects of Population Growth,* 358, 372–73.

Newspapers and Periodical Literature

Aberdeen Morning American
Afro-American
America, 1966–72
American Heritage, 1970–73
American Magazine, 1908
American Mercury, 1924, 1943
Amsterdam News
Ann Arbor Michigan Daily
Atlantic Monthly, 1908–50
Birth Control Review, 1922–39
Black America
Black Panther
Black Scholar
Boston Globe, 1920–89
Boston Herald, 1930–70
Boston Medical and Surgical Journal
Catholic World
Charleston Medical Journal and Review, 1845–1900.
Chicago Daily Defender
Christian Century
Churchman
Collier's, 1925
Commonweal, 1960–70
Congregationalist and Boston Recorder, 1867
Congressional Quarterly
Cosmopolitan, 1913
Current, 1968
Current History, 1930–36
Current Literature, 1912
Current Opinion, 1924–25
Detroit Review of Medicine and Pharmacy
Ebony, 1968–70
Economist
Eugenics Review
Evening Star
Family Planning Perspectives
Farm and Fireside
Federal Register
Fortune
Forum, 1891–1913
Genetics
Glamour
Good Housekeeping, 1912
Harper Magazine, 1869

Harper's Monthly Magazine, 1934
Health/PAC Bulletin
Independent, 1906–14
Journal of the American Medical Association
Kansas City Star
Ladies Home Journal, 1940–60
Life, 1938–70
Literary Digest, 1913–31
Living Age, 1895–1932
Look, 1964–65
Los Angeles Times
Medical Age: A Semi-Monthly Journal of Medicine and Surgery
Medical Society Minutes, 1860–84
Medical Statistics Bulletin
Medical World News
Milbank Memorial Fund Quarterly
Militant
Ms.
Muhammad Speaks
Nation, 1891–1974
National Education Association, Proceedings and Addresses
National Geographic Magazine, 1908
National Police Gazette
National Review
Negro Digest
New Republic, 1921–70
Newsweek, 1935–89
New York Daily Challenger
New York Herald
New York Post
New York Sun
New York Times, 1830–95
New York Tribune, 1840–60
Nineteenth Century and After, 1906–29
North American Review, 1896–1927
Outlook, 1913–28
Parents Magazine, 1970
Philadelphia Inquirer
Pittsburgh Catholic
Pittsburgh Courier
Pittsburgh Peace and Freedom News
Pittsburgh Post Gazette
Pittsburgh Press
Popular Science Monthly, 1896–1913
Population Bulletin

Providence Evening Bulletin, 1840–89

Providence Journal, 1840–89

Providence Visitor, 1930–91

Psychology Today, 1974

PTA Magazine, 1970

Public Health Reports

Reader Magazine, 1906

Redbook, 1965–71

Reporter, 1963–66

Review of Reviews, 1890–1924

Revolution

Rhode Island Medical Reformer: A Family Journal for the Promotion of Health and Longevity

San Francisco Spokesmen

Saturday Evening Post

Science, 1912–74

Science News

Scientific American, 1911–20

Scientific Monthly, 1924–32

Sister Courage, 1976

Sisterlife

Society, 1982

Star Eagle

Star Ledger

Sunday Star

Survey, 1910–25

Technical World Magazine, 1913

Time, 1960–89

Thrust

Transaction

U.S. News and World Report, 1969–70

Village Voice

Virginia Health Bulletin

Washington Post

Weekly Compilation of Presidential Documents

Westminster Review, 1899–1912

Winston-Salem Journal

Woman Rebel, 1914

World To-day, 1906

World's Work, 1908–12

Worldview, 1977

Index

ABCL, 61, 64–66, 67–74, 82–86, 89, 92, 93, 98–99, 105, 123, 130

Abortion, 2–3, 7–10, 40–43, 119, 231–32; African Americans, 23, 231–32; antiabortion campaign, 19–28; federal government, 198–202, 232, 236–39, 242; and feminists, 28–30; illegal, 75–79, 187–88; judicial review, 9–10, 202–4; military bases, 198–99; nineteenth-century, 15–17; opposition, 232–34, 235–36, 241–42, 246; postwar, 138–41; reform, 188–98; religion, 25–27; Rhode Island, 30–42, 106–7, 188, 204–6; state laws, 9, 23–24, 27–28, 30, 37–38, 237, 239, 244, 256; teenagers, 195, 221, 239, 244, 248–49; therapeutic, 76, 140–41, 194, 204

Abzug, Bella, 200–201

ACLU, 89, 191, 209, 214, 235

ACOG, 192, 196, 207, 223, 242

AFDC, 6, 117–18, 154, 156, 159, 161, 163–67, 175, 178, 187, 190, 194, 211, 252, 256

African Americans, 47, 52, 55, 65, 83–84, 88–90, 113, 128, 153; abortion, 23, 42, 188, 197, 234–36, 240; birth control, 95–99, 123, 156, 167–77, 218; Rhode Island, 125, 145; sterilization, 115, 209–12, 215, 218, 230. *See also* Genocide

ALI, 8–9, 189, 191, 194

AMA, 5, 9, 108, 194, 196, 272n48; antiabortion campaign, 14, 19–28, 36–38, 41, 43; birth control, 63–65, 71, 73, 77, 79–80, 87, 92, 93, 98, 99–100, 105–6, 108, 130, 165, 223

American Eugenics Society, 66, 112–13, 130

Anglo-Saxon Clubs of America, 65–66

Avery, Ephraim K., 30–35, 39

Baby Boom, 4, 119, 128–30, 139, 141, 147

BCCRB, 67, 74, 98, 101

BCFA, 97–98, 123

Beisel, Nicola, 7, 21

Bethune, Mary McLeod, 98, 123, 125

Birth control, 44, 57–70, 84, 149–53, 230–31;

black market, 5, 30, 58, 92, 106; courts, 60–61, 92–93; experiments, 133–38, 150, 224; federal involvement, 92, 131–33, 147, 153–60, 163–64; legislative campaigns, 71–74, 86–91; nineteenth-century, 14–15, 40, 57–58; public funding, 94, 148–49, 155, 160, 163–67, 180, 249, 253; teenagers, 11, 162, 179, 184–85, 226, 235, 239. *See also* Condoms; Depo Provera; IUD; Norplant; Rhythm method

Birth Control Review, 60, 61

Black Americans for Life, 235–36

Blackmun, Harry, 10, 12, 203, 238, 241, 244, 246

Black Muslims, 169

Black Panthers, 169, 212–13

Black Power, 173–75

Blair, Beatrice, 130, 176–77

Boughton, Alice, 64, 74

Bours v. United States, 4

Briggs, Laura, 116, 133–34

Bureau of Social Hygiene, 56, 63, 67, 97, 112, 281n86

Buck, Carrie, 1, 56, 212

Buck v. Bell, 1, 55–56, 80

Burch, Guy Irving, 90, 120, 127, 287n26

Bush, George H. W., 158, 160, 243–47, 319n58, 321n83

Bush, George W., 251, 253, 254

Calderone, Mary S., 129–30, 136, 139, 141, 146, 150

California, 9, 54, 93, 111, 189, 192–93, 207, 228–29, 230, 286n11

Campbell, Loraine L., 82, 130, 131, 141

Campbell, Sarah Bradford, 172–74

CAP, 171, 173–74, 306n91

Carter, James, 237–38, 240

Catholic Church, 6, 11, 26, 35, 41, 52, 57, 63, 73, 80, 91, 163, 300n99; abortion, 26–27, 40, 41, 108, 189, 193, 195, 202, 204, 237, 239; birth control, 80, 88–90, 94, 95, 121, 133–34, 138, 141, 165–68; sterilization, 110

Catholics, 3, 14, 18, 25, 37, 40, 44, 46, 76, 128; abortion, 187, 189, 191, 194, 196, 197, 198, 199, 201, 202, 232, 237, 239, 240, 242, 243, 255, 273n64; birth control, 63, 73, 75, 76, 84, 86, 88, 90, 91, 99, 100, 101, 113–14, 122, 129, 131–32, 133, 153, 155, 156, 160, 165, 166, 168; Pittsburgh, 170, 171, 172, 174; Rhode Island, 123–26, 137, 143–45, 147, 177–79, 181–82, 204–6; sterilization, 207, 215

Catholic Welfare Conference, 73, 88

Census data, 37, 45, 46, 62, 83, 95, 102, 127, 220

Children's Bureau, 122, 130, 154, 158

Chisholm, Shirley, 195, 196, 213

Clinics, 5, 11, 61, 63, 75, 78, 81, 84, 93, 98; African American, 97–98; in Rhode Island, 99–106; in Pittsburgh, 170–74; state-funded, 94–95

Clinton, William J., 234, 246, 253, 254

CMH, 64, 67, 74, 111

CM J & R, 16, 17, 20, 24, 40

Commander, Lydia Kingsmill, 46, 48

Commission on Population Growth, 187, 197, 210

Communism, 86, 88, 101, 126–28, 131

Comstock Law, 3, 4, 12, 21, 40, 57, 60, 61, 62, 70, 75, 86, 92, 154, 155

Condoms, 4, 15, 61, 92, 106, 119, 121, 147, 151, 180, 225, 226, 231, 256, 286n8, 287n23

Congress, 6, 57, 61, 62, 71–74, 86–91, 109, 121, 132–33, 153–60, 163–64, 198–99, 216–17, 222, 238–46, 253; investigations, 152, 212, 215, 222–23, 241, 243

Connecticut, 19, 36, 53, 117, 124, 142, 145–46, 178, 239, 294n7

Cook, Constance, 194–95

Cooper, James, 64–65, 69

CORE, 176, 178, 182

Cornell, Sarah, 30–35, 39

Cox, Nial, 212, 215, 255

Critchlow, Donald, 5, 154, 167, 180

Cummine-Vaile Bill, 70–71

Davenport, Charles, 49, 51, 53, 55, 66

Davis, Katherine, 56, 66, 74

Democratic Party, 199, 202, 237, 240

Dennett, Mary, 60, 70–71

Depo Provera, 211, 221–25, 230–31, 245, 249, 252, 256

DHEW, 154–59, 163, 179, 185, 215–18

Dickinson, Robert L., 64, 67, 74

Division of Negro Service, 97, 123

Doctors, 5, 7, 8, 12–14, 35; antiabortion campaign, 19–28; contraceptives, 58, 64, 65, 74–75, 92, 95, 100, 117, 151, 222–23; nineteenth-century abortion, 16–18, 33, 36–38, 40–43, 255; sterilization, 54–55, 114, 210, 211, 213–14, 216, 217; twentieth-century abortion, 76–78, 97, 106, 108–9, 122, 139–41, 189, 194, 196–97, 203, 233, 245, 248

Doe v. Bolton, 10, 202–3, 237, 238

Draper, William H., 131–32

DuBois, W.E.B., 96–98, 115, 123

Eisenhower, Dwight D., 131, 133

Eisenstadt v. Baird, 4, 10

Ellis, Havelock, 59–60

Enovid, 5, 136–37, 149–50. *See also* Pill

Epperson, David, 171–72, 174

Eugenicists, 6, 49–55, 57, 59, 65–68, 70, 77, 79, 82–83, 94, 110–13, 115–16, 255

Eugenics, 6, 49–54, 59, 65–71, 79, 110–13, 116, 117, 130, 216

Eugenics Record Office, 49, 51, 67, 111, 116

Family planning, 6, 98, 116, 136, 149, 167, 169, 190, 199, 203, 220–22, 227, 244–45, 246; African Americans, 173–77, 196, 225; Baby Boom, 129–30; federal government, 153–60, 163–64; Rhode Island, 145, 179–84, 206–7; sterilization, 210, 212–13, 215–17; World War II, 122–25

Farm Security Administration, 93

FDA, 93, 136, 137, 150, 152, 188, 198, 211, 222–24, 231, 243, 256, 298n73

Federal Council of Churches, 88, 89, 127

Feminism, 48, 61, 108, 195, 203, 232

Feminists, 2, 7, 9, 15–29, 52, 58, 59, 68, 69, 87, 95–99, 106, 109, 117, 123, 134, 138, 192, 193, 202, 203, 213, 214, 217, 218, 230, 231, 233, 234, 236, 242, 243, 246, 249; nineteenth-century, 28–30

Fetal rights, 39, 232, 235, 249, 251, 253

Ford, Gerald, 237

Free love, 29, 60, 88

Fulbright, William, 132, 160

Gamble, Clarence J., 94, 133, 134

Gardner, John, 156–59, 168

Garvey, Marcus, 65–66, 96
G. D. Searle, 137, 149–50, 298n73
Genocide, 134, 149, 168–76, 182–83, 187, 196, 207, 218, 226–27, 235–36
Gilman, Charlotte Perkins, 87, 286n22
Ginsburg, Faye, 7, 8, 11, 232–24
Goldman, Emma, 59
Goldsmith, Sadja, 162, 184, 189–90, 203
Greenlee, Charles, 169–73, 305n81
Griswold v. Connecticut, 4, 5, 9, 10, 154, 178, 243
Gruening, Ernest, 95, 133, 155–58
Guttmacher, Alan F., 122, 195

Haden, William, 170–74, 306n99
Hasian, Marouf A., 49, 50
Hispanics, 190, 214, 230, 255
Hodge, Hugh L., 17, 19
Holmes, Oliver Wendell, 1, 55–56
Homeward Brushton, 170–73, 182, 306n91
Human Betterment Foundation, 110–12
Hutchins, Louise Gilman, 82, 209, 217
Hyde Amendment, 12, 236, 238, 319n58

Illegitimacy, 109, 156–57, 159, 161–62, 164–66, 185, 188, 190, 192, 195, 220, 248
Illinois, 165–66, 193–94, 208, 239
Immigration, 1, 14, 21–22, 25, 28, 45–46, 62; in Rhode Island, 37
Indian Health Service, 214, 222, 225
IUD, 15, 58, 151, 179, 180, 215, 224, 230, 231

Jews, 41, 46, 126, 197, 202, 240, 284n139
Johnson, Lyndon B., 153–54, 158, 160, 167, 168
Jones, Eleanor, 82, 85, 105

Kennedy, Anne, 63, 64, 71, 73
Kennedy, John F., 131–33
Kline, Wendy, 51, 116–17
Know Nothing Party, 19, 28, 30, 37
Kopp, Marie, 101, 139
Ku Klux Klan, 62, 66, 72, 247

Laughlin, Harry, 56, 67–68
Louisiana, 19, 73, 156, 176, 210, 239
Loving v. Virginia, 10, 268n24

Maginnis, Patricia, 150, 189, 193
Marcus, Sarah, 75, 101, 130

Margaret Sanger Research Bureau, 129, 296n41
Maryland, 64, 72, 74, 166, 194, 208, 210, 225–27, 239
Massachusetts, 19, 21–22, 24, 36, 45, 117, 124, 133, 135, 141–42, 145, 146, 178, 204, 233, 236, 267n3
Massachusetts Blacks for Life, 236
McCormick, Katherine, 133, 135
Medicaid, 12, 144, 149, 203, 216, 217, 224, 227, 230, 237, 253
Midwives, 7, 8, 15, 17, 18, 41, 76–79, 139–41, 255
Milbank Memorial Foundation, 82–83
Miller, Henry, 22, 23, 36
Miller, Kelly, 95
Mississippi, 94, 207, 208, 211, 227
Mohr, James, 19
Mudd, Emily H., 75, 82, 83, 218

NAACP, 97, 168, 170, 171, 173, 176, 213, 234
NARAL, 11, 194, 200, 234, 240
National Academy of Sciences, 132, 153, 154, 163
National Birth Control League, 60, 67
National Women's Health Network, 223
National Women's Political Caucus, 202
Native Americans, 214, 217, 222, 223, 225
Nativism, 3, 14, 19, 25, 28, 37–38, 61–62, 251
NBWHP, 225, 236
NCFL, 86, 87, 90–91, 92
New York City, 34, 60, 61, 64, 67, 69, 101, 140, 156, 194–96, 203, 217
New York state, 9, 27, 36, 60, 61, 67, 68, 85, 92, 139, 160, 166, 189, 191, 194–97, 204, 286n11
NIH, 133, 198, 246
Nixon, Richard M., 163–64, 187, 197–203, 210, 215
Norplant, 221, 224–31, 245, 249, 252, 256
North Carolina, 42, 62, 66, 75–77, 87, 94, 156, 164, 188, 194, 208, 209, 211, 212, 215, 251
Norton, Mary T., 86, 88, 90
NOW, 192, 194, 201, 247
NUL, 97, 98, 168, 213, 234
NYCCSA, 189–90, 194

Office of Economic Opportunity, 153–54, 156–57, 159–60, 163, 170–72, 181–82, 190, 209–12, 215–16
Osborne, Frederick, 66

Packwood, Robert, 198, 201
Pap smears, 142, 143, 145, 177
Parran, Thomas, 120–21, 123
Paul, Diane, 49
Pearl, Raymond, 70, 83–84
Pill, 5, 119, 133–38, 149–52, 158, 164, 167,
    170–71, 174–75, 177–80, 185, 187, 199, 211,
    215, 219, 220, 222, 224, 226–27, 230–32,
    256
Pincus, Gregory, 133, 135–36
Popenoe, Paul, 55
Population control, 2, 3, 4, ,9, 12, 44; early
    twentieth-century, 51, 62, 63, 69, 75; 1930s,
    82, 88, 97–100, 109, 110, 117–19; 1940s–
    50s, 121–23, 127, 128, 130–34, 136–38,
    146–49; 1960s–70s, 150–51, 153–55,
    158, 160–63, 176, 178, 185, 187, 190, 192,
    198, 200, 203–7, 212–15, 217, 218, 221;
    1980s–90s, 223–26, 229, 234, 243, 249,
    251; twenty-first-century, 252, 254–56
Population Council, 130, 153, 155, 210, 224
Population Reference Bureau, 87, 90, 120, 130,
    132, 287n26
Potter, Charles, 139, 143, 219
PPCP, 169–74, 307n108
PPFA, 8, 13, 119, 123–24, 129–33, 136–37,
    139, 141–43; 145–46, 150–53, 158, 160,
    177–78, 182, 191, 194, 204–6, 223. See also
    ABCL
PPRI, 12, 149, 151, 164, 177–85, 187, 204–6,
    218–20, 219, 220, 238. See also RIBCL;
    RIMHA
Press, 15, 30, 83, 89, 121, 131–32, 149, 150,
    157, 207, 255–56; genocide, 169, 173, 212;
    individual publications, 20, 22, 42, 43, 85,
    90, 96, 97, 114, 115, 129, 153, 166, 167, 171,
    190, 200–201, 208, 209, 212, 220
Prochoice movement, 11–12, 205, 213,
    232–34, 236–37, 240, 243–44, 246–47,
    253, 320n66
Prolife (antichoice) movement, 11–12, 109,
    205–6, 221, 232, 236, 244, 246, 251, 253,
    255, 320n66
Protestants, 3, 19, 25, 27, 41, 44, 46, 51, 111,
    126, 128, 144, 155, 197, 240, 251, 255,
    284n139
Providence Lying-In, 99, 140, 179, 183
Psychiatrists, 8, 52, 113–14, 141, 189, 192–94
Public Health Service, 61, 83, 94, 122, 133,
    157, 238, 242

Public Opinion, 25, 46, 83, 91, 109, 122, 149,
    155, 160, 176, 190, 197, 206, 209, 218, 229,
    232, 240, 246, 256, 297n54
Puerto Rico, 53, 94–95, 114, 119, 133–40, 215

Quickening, 3, 7, 19, 28

Race suicide, 3, 42, 44–49, 51, 57, 58, 64, 66,
    69–70, 77, 79, 82, 90, 95, 96, 105, 124, 168,
    248
Randolph, A. Philip, 97, 125
Reagan, Leslie, 8, 41, 78, 106, 138, 139, 140,
    254
Reagan, Ronald, 9, 240–42, 247, 254
Relf family, 211–12, 215–17
Relief families, 82–86
Religion, 26–27, 31, 34–35. See also Catholics;
    Jews; Protestants
Rentoul, Robert R., 47
Republican Party, 11, 199, 202, 227, 240–43,
    246–47, 253–54
Restell, Madame (Ann Lohman), 16
Rhode Island, 12, 41, 47, 71, 81, 85, 135; clin-
    ics, 99–106; nineteenth-century abortion,
    30–42; postwar, 141–47; sterilization,
    56–57, 218–20; twentieth-century abor-
    tion, 77–79, 204–6, 139; World War II,
    123–26
Rhode Island Medical Society, 12, 36–38
Rhythm method, 6, 15, 35, 84, 126, 137, 167
RIBCL, 12, 99–106. See also PPRI; RIMHA
Rice, Charles Owen, 170–73, 306n99
Rice-Wray, Edris, 136
RIMHA, 123–26, 135–47, 150–51, 177; Medi-
    cal Advisory Committee, 137, 142, 146, 177
Roberts, Dorothy, 229, 254
Rock, John, 133, 135
Rockefeller, John D., III, 130–32, 156, 197
Roe v. Wade, 9–12, 188, 202–5, 215, 221, 232,
    234–38, 241–47, 251, 254
Rogers, Mary, 27
Roosevelt, Eleanor, 89, 122, 123
Roosevelt, Franklin D., 89, 122, 286n13
Roosevelt, Theodore, 46–48, 58, 66, 95
Ross, Loretta J., 97, 98, 236

Sanger, Grant, 60, 71, 91
Sanger, Margaret, 59–62, 64, 67–71, 73–74,
    79, 86–87, 89, 91, 92, 99, 110, 123, 129, 133,
    146, 151, 176

Schoen, Johanna, 84, 98, 115

Shriver, R. Sargent, 157, 168

Sixth International Neo-Malthusian Conference, 69–70

Slabey, Evelyne, 146, 179, 180

Smith-Rosenberg, Carroll, 36, 38, 40, 275n108

Social Purity, 7, 20–21, 40

Social Security Amendments, 154, 156, 158, 159, 164, 179, 217

Social workers, 13, 67, 68, 79, 85, 94, 103, 104, 106, 126, 143, 160, 166–67, 169, 176, 178–79, 180, 211, 216

South Carolina, 17, 22, 24, 39, 94, 98, 165, 194, 211, 213, 227, 228

South Carolina Medical Society, 16, 22–23, 24–25, 27–28, 39–40, 42

Sterilization, 2, 6, 12, 13, 152; early twentieth-century, 49–57, 69, 71–72; 1930s, 80–82, 95, 109–18; 1940s–50s, 127, 134–35, 138, 140, 148; 1960s–70s, 169, 184–87, 206–21; 1980s–90s, 223–26, 228–30, 232, 234, 239, 243, 245, 249; twenty-first-century, 251–56; state laws, 55–56; voluntary, 207–9, 315n108. *See also* Eugenics

Storer, Horatio, 14, 20–28, 36–39, 119, 122, 261

Supreme Court, 1, 4, 9–10, 55, 92–93, 116, 154–55, 197, 202–4, 234–35, 237–45, 247–248, 254. *See also individual cases*

Teenage births, 161–62, 187, 195, 212, 220, 225–26, 317n150

TFR, 14, 17–19, 29, 72, 99, 128

Thalidomide, 9, 188, 198

Tone, Andrea, 101, 151

Truman, Harry S., 120, 133

Tubal ligations, 112, 210, 211, 214, 219, 227

Tydings, Joseph, 157, 158

ULRI, 125, 145, 182

United States v. One Package, 4, 92, 95

United States v. Vuitch, 9

Vasectomy, 12, 54–55, 112, 187, 189, 211, 215, 218–20

Venereal disease, 4, 15, 33, 34, 41, 52, 61, 64, 93, 119–21, 169, 183, 293n5

Vietnam, 198–201

Virginia, 1, 10, 66, 94, 98, 194, 207, 208

Voluntary Parenthood League, 70–71

Watkins, Elizabeth Siegel, 5, 152, 184

Weddington, Sarah, 188, 202–3

Weinberger, Casper, 213, 216

Welfare, 2, 4, 6, 9, 11, 62, 85, 105, 111, 117–18, 125, 144, 188, 192, 194–95, 198–99, 201, 203, 205, 207–13, 216–18, 220, 222, 223, 226–31, 238, 243, 247, 248, 252–53, 256

WHO, 138, 199, 223

Wise, Anne, 177–78, 181–84, 204–5, 215

World War I, 52, 60–61, 62

World War II, 4, 6, 49, 93, 106, 117, 120–26, 128, 138

Wright, Henry C., 15, 28–29

Simone M. Caron is chair and associate professor of history at Wake Forest University. The author of articles dealing with birth control and genocide in the African American community and with abortion during the Nixon presidency, she is currently working on unwed mothers from the late nineteenth century to the post-*Roe* period. She lives in Winston-Salem, North Carolina, with her husband and two children.